Parkscapes

Parkscapes

Green Spaces
in Modern Japan

Thomas R. H. Havens

University of Hawai'i Press
Honolulu

Publication of this book has been assisted by a grant from the Kajiyama
Publications Fund for Japanese History, Culture, and Literature at the University of
Hawai'i at Mānoa.

16   15   14   13   12   11   6   5   4   3   2   1

Library of Congress Cataloging-in-Publication Data

Havens, Thomas R. H.
    Parkscapes : green spaces in modern Japan / Thomas R.H. Havens.
      p. cm.
    Includes bibliographical references and index.
    ISBN 978-0-8248-3477-7 (hardcover : alk. paper)
    1. Parks—Japan—History.   2. Parks—Government policy—
Japan.   3. National characteristics, Japanese.   I. Title.
    SB484.J3H385 2011
    333.78'30952—dc22

                                                        2010032654

Designed by Publishers' Design and Production Services, Inc.

Printed by Edwards Brothers, Inc.

To Karen,

for love, learning, and laughter
beyond measure or description

Contents

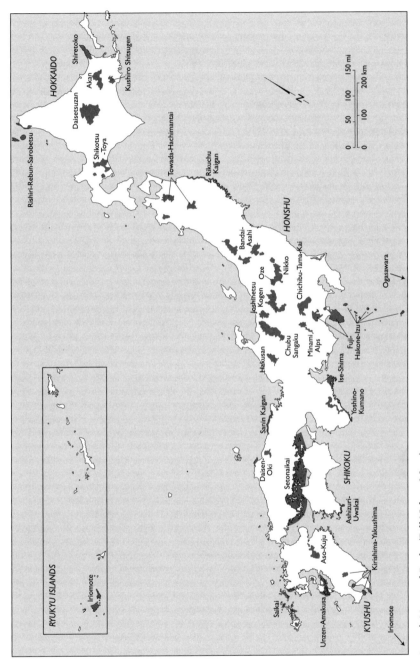

Japan's National Parks (Bill Nelson Maps)

RYUKYU ISLANDS

Iriomote

HOKKAIDO

Shiretoko
Akan
Daisetsuzan
Shikotsu-Toya
Kushiro Shitsugen
Rishiri-Rebun-Sarobetsu

Towada-Hachimantai
Rikuchu Kaigan

HONSHU

Bandai-Asahi
Oze
Nikko
Joshinetsu Kogen
Chichibu-Tama-Kai
Chubu Sangaku
Minami Alps
Fuji-Hakone-Izu
Hakusan
Ise-Shima
Sanin Kaigan
Yoshino-Kumano
Daisen-Oki
Setonaikai

Ogasawara

SHIKOKU

Ashizuri-Uwakai
Aso-Kuju
Saikai
Kirishima-Yakushima
Unzen-Amakusa

KYUSHU

Iriomote

0   50   100   150 mi
0   100   200 km

N

IX

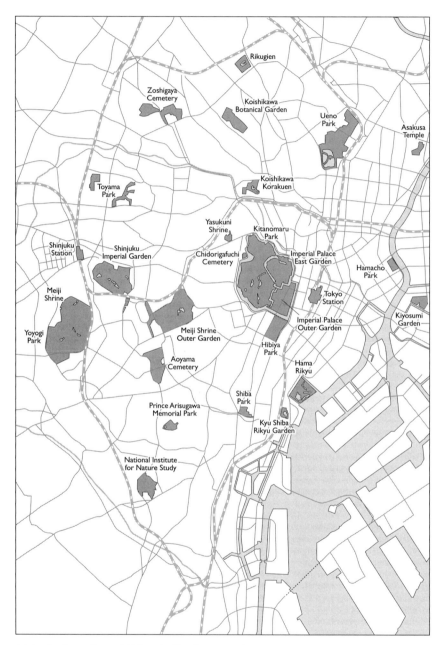

Major Parks in Central Tokyo (Bill Nelson Maps)

Preface

The inspiration to study the history of public parks and green spaces in Japan and its colonies arose from stimulating walks through Kinuta Family Park in southwestern Tokyo during a research year affiliated with the University of Tokyo in 2001–2002. My first encounter with Japanese parks occurred much earlier, when I lived in a student lodge across the street from Tokyo's Meiji Park and the Meiji Shrine Outer Garden during the turbulent summer of 1960; daily demonstrations and worker strikes persisted long after the national Diet (parliament) ratified revisions of the controversial Japan–United States Mutual Security Treaty in June of that year. Subsequent research trips included casual visits to parks large and small throughout the country, as well as some in Taiwan and South Korea guided by Karen L. Thornber. A great reward of studying this topic has been the chance, mainly between 2005 and 2009, to tour many of Japan's national and urban parks with a more practiced eye after researching their histories and design principles. *Parkscapes* explains the origins, development, and distinctive features of these public spaces, which were created by the national government for state purposes but later evolved into sites of negotiation between bureaucrats and the ordinary citizens who used them, a process that continues today.

The earth's biotic and abiotic ecosystems display every color of the spectrum, but this book uses "green" to describe nonhuman environments, reflecting the conventional Japanese terms *ryokuchi* and *midori*, both translated as "green space." Romanizations of Japanese terms follow the modified Hepburn system in *Kenkyusha's New Japanese-English Dictionary* (Tokyo: Kenkyūsha, 1974). Macrons are omitted over long vowels in the most widely known place names. Except for citations of Western-language publications, names of Japanese nationals are given in the customary Japanese manner, with the family name first. Unless otherwise indicated, photographs are my own. Metric square measures are used throughout:

1 square meter = 1.196 square yards = 10.764 square feet
1 hectare = 10,000 square meters = 2.471 acres
100 hectares = 1 square kilometer = 1 million square meters =
    247.1 acres = 0.3861 square miles
1 tsubo = 3.95 square yards = 3.31 square meters
1 chō = 2.45 acres = 0.992 hectares
1 square yard = 9 square feet = 0.836 square meters
1 acre = 0.4047 hectares
640 acres = 1 square mile = 259 hectares = 2.59 square kilometers

Funds from a Japan Foundation Short-Term Research Fellowship and from Northeastern University speeded my studies; I'm grateful to these sources for indispensable assistance. In preparing this account, I've benefited from the help of many individuals, libraries, and organizations. I'm especially thankful to Itō Taiichi for permission to reproduce his photographs of Japanese national parks and to Hashimoto Seiko and Hashimoto Minoru for gracious encouragement of my studies. I'm also grateful to many colleagues in conversation and correspondence, especially Ryūichi Abé, Robert A. Askins, Theodore C. Bestor, Victoria L. Bestor, Harold Bolitho, Beverly J. Bossler, Daniel V. Botsman, Mary C. Brinton, Edward I. Brodkin, Lawrence Buell, Cary Caracas, Albert M. Craig, Edwin A. Cranston, Deborah A. Deliyannides, Peter Duus, Laura L. Frader, Sheldon M. Garon, Timothy S. George, Christina K. Gilmartin, Carol Gluck, David G. Goodman, Andrew Gordon, Keven Halliday, Jeffrey E. Hanes, Valerie Hansen, Helen Hardacre, Laura E. Hein, Todd A. Henry, Howard Hibbett, David L. Howell, Akira Iriye, Wesley Jacobsen, William W. Kelly, Shigehisa Kuriyama, Yukio Lippit, Mark Metzler, Melissa McCormick, Clay McShane, Ian J. Miller, Robert C. Mitchell, Emer S. O'Dwyer, James J. Orr, Anthony N. Penna, Elizabeth J. Perry, Susan J. Pharr, Steve Ridgely, John M. Rosenfield, Jay Rubin, Kent C. Smith, Kerry D. Smith, Margaret

C. L. W. Smith, Alan Tansman, Julia A. Thomas, Tō Kimiharu, Conrad D. Totman, Jun Uchida, Ezra F. Vogel, Richard von Glahn, Wilhelm Vosse, Brett L. Walker, Dennis C. Washburn, Ikuko Watanabe Washburn, Watanabe Shun'ichi, Merry I. White, Gavin Whitelaw, Kären Wigen, Rod Wilson, Brian Woodall, Samuel H. Yamashita, Tomiko Yoda, and anonymous referees who read the manuscript. Bill Nelson provided expertise with the maps. I'm much indebted to Patricia Crosby, Ann Ludeman, Drew Bryan, Lucille Aono, Wendy Bolton, and the staff of the University of Hawai'i Press for expert editorial and production care.

I'm also grateful for the love and support of my family: my sister Anne Havens Fuller; my son Bill Havens and daughter-in-law Julie Hunt; my daughter Carolyn Havens Niemann, son-in-law Michael Niemann, and grandchildren Adam, Jacob, and Matthew Niemann; my daughter Kathy Havens Whitten and grandchildren Emily and Nate Whitten; and my in-laws Evan Preisser and the Thornbers: Carol, Juliette, Karvel, Katherine, Lois, and Nora. Above all, I'm thankful for the sage advice and staunch support of my spouse Karen L. Thornber, to whom this book is dedicated. Her extensive knowledge of East Asian cultural and environmental history and her expertise as a scholar of world literatures helped guide me around many snares. I'm deeply grateful to her for stimulating discussions, endless proofreading, and love, learning, and laughter beyond measure or description.

Introduction

Parklands and Japan

Writing in 1894 at the dawn of his country's Asian empire, the Japanese geographer Shiga Shigetaka (1863–1927) declared that his fellow citizens, "in order to continue improving Japanese culture in the future, must make every effort to protect Japan's natural landscape."[1] In this pithy call to action Shiga interwove the Japanese people and their surroundings into an unbroken fabric stretching from their past environmental inheritance to their future greatness as a distinct national culture. Exhortations by Shiga, Mori Ōgai (Rintarō, 1862–1922), Abe Isoo (1865–1949), and many other activists during the Meiji era (1868–1912) emboldened Japan's fledgling central government to convert sizable open spaces into parklands for the people. These advocates witnessed the Meiji state performing the power of display to instill Western cultural practices in the public, and they were gratified to see parks included with museums, exhibitions, zoological gardens, and other unifying institutions. A chief aim of this book is to explain how and why public parks—both national and urban—have served as key agents of state formation, signifiers of modern culture and national distinctiveness, instruments of military mobilization and disaster prevention, and sites of public assembly during Japan's experience of spatial and ecological modernity from 1868 to today.

Dissatisfied with conventional accounts extolling Japanese love or awe of their natural surroundings, I began this book by asking how public space in modern times has been constructed and consumed in a country where open land is scarce and the main islands have been populated since prehistoric times. Until now most writings on Japan's open spaces have focused

1

on urban land use or on agriculture. So far as I can tell, this is the first book in any language to examine urban and national parks together, in an effort to discover how Japan's experience of spatial modernity challenges current thinking about protection and use of the nonhuman environment globally. Although city and national parks might each merit separate treatment, in Japan they have many points in common: the creation of public spaces for state purposes, adaptation of Western prototypes, similar human interactions with the nonhuman, shared engagement with enterprise capitalism, roles in developing international tourism, and sites for promoting health, hygiene, and recreation. Although Japanese public parks resemble their Western forebears in some respects, they differ considerably in scale, design, and interactions between users and government administrators. Moreover, with a large population occupying a relatively narrow territory, Japan in the historical era has had diminished awareness of wilderness; the frontier as a modern concept existed only in Hokkaido in the late nineteenth century. As a result, the history of public space as a constructed environment forming a simulacrum of "nature" points to significant differences from how parks were produced in Europe and North America—even as Japan drew from Western models to create an alternative modernity partly symbolized by its new urban and national parklands.

Parkscapes: Green Spaces in Modern Japan shows how Meiji leaders appropriated previously private landholdings—both secular and religious— and canonized them as national spaces for managing a newly constituted public to be governed directly by an emperor-sanctioned state. Both urban and mountain spaces were turned into public parklands in emulation of state practices in Europe and America, models that continued to affect park development in Japan from the 1870s to the twenty-first century, but without necessarily embracing Western teleological rationales. Some early supporters of parks also touted quality-of-life benefits for individuals such as health, relaxation, clean air, appreciation of the outdoors, recreation, and self-uplift, but the prevailing goals were collective: mustering public adherence to the norms of the national state via socialization, public health, communal morality, and the economic stimuli of civic beautification and tourism in remote scenery.[2]

This book reveals how modern Japanese debates about preservation or exploitation of the nonhuman (natural) environment, in parks and private holdings alike, have taken place across a highly nuanced discursive spectrum with surprisingly little polarization. Nearly all parties have freely acknowledged that the day tourist or backpacker uses a forest tract very differently from a mining firm or timber company. Nonetheless the most common rhetorical outcome has been a doctrine of sustainable development of natural resources for national diplomatic, military, and economic advantage. Although the country's priorities shifted and introspections about national identity surfaced periodically after the mid-twentieth century, defining the best uses of public space remained a constant of civic consciousness and government policy throughout. Political parties weighed in on issues affecting parks, notably during the environmental crises of the late 1960s and early 1970s, the debates over the resort law of 1987, and criticisms of Construction Ministry priorities in the 1990s, but conflicts among administrative agencies, not politicians, sparked most of the discourse over park policies. The 1990s were marked by an increasing environmental consciousness and greater involvement of citizens in quality-of-life decisions, including the design and operation of parks, realms once considered the exclusive province of bureaucrats. Public-private partnerships increasingly became the norm for managing city parks and, to a lesser extent, natural parks (national, quasi-national, and prefectural nature reserves). Today the near-total urbanization of Japanese society, ubiquitous electronic simulations of natural reality, and budgetary belt-tightening all suggest that public concern for environmental protection may have plateaued vis-à-vis the claims of sustainable use.

Like many other domestic projects under official sponsorship, the countrywide effort to produce public parks began slowly, gathered momentum in the 1920s and 1930s, then sped forward during good economic times from the 1950s through the 1980s. Even today, amid deep ecological anxieties and economic uncertainties, Japan by some measures continues to guard its urban and mountain parks reasonably effectively from overuse by visitors and rank exploitation by developers.[3] Forests cover two thirds of the country's land area, a figure little changed since antiquity. As of 2009, a total of 394 natural parks of various sizes occupied one seventh of the country's land surface, a high proportion by international norms.[4] City parks, in contrast, were numerous (91,491 nationwide) but small (on average about 1 hectare or 2.47 acres each), providing just nine square meters of park area for each urban resident—half New York's per capita space and a third of London's.[5]

Sometimes maligned for its monotonous stretches of concrete apartment blocks and lack of large countryside parks in its central districts, Tokyo actually may be "the greenest of Japan's big cities,"[6] with its many trees, parks, gardens, plazas, cemeteries, schoolyards, and plantings around stores, offices, and individual residences of its 13 million citizens (2010 figure). Tokyo displays surprising biodiversity, reflecting in cameo the exceptional range of plant and animal species found throughout the country.[7] As bullet-speed elevators whisk sightseers to observation decks atop Tokyo's skyscrapers, visitors immediately realize how green the capital is, in every direction and every season: 37 percent of Tokyo's 2,200 square kilometers consist of natural parks, a higher proportion than any other prefecture.[8] Parklands and other green spaces help to explain why the London-based magazine *Monocle* in June 2008 rated the Tokyo region, with its 35 million residents, the world's third most-livable megalopolis after Copenhagen and Munich, each with a population of 1.2 million.[9]

The history of public spaces in Japan, like the story of the ecosystem writ large, is neither monolithic, static, nor entirely coherent. Instead it is vibrant, dynamic, complex—an imbricated cluster of multiple narratives in constant motion across time and space.[10] These narratives are best understood from the vantage of spatial history, as developed by the sociologists Henri Lefebvre and Saskia Sassen, geographer David Harvey, political scientist James Scott, literary critic Paul Carter, and various historians.[11] Spatial history, as distinct from environmental history, posits that space is politically and culturally constructed ("produced," in Lefebvre's terms) and that it is a product of history, not an inert backdrop for it. Space, like time, is constituted by social practices that differ from culture to culture. Tracing their intellectual origins to Émile Durkheim (1858–1917), modern constructions of space (e.g., the imperial, the global) often are thought to struggle against deeply rooted ideas of place (the local, the colonized), but actually the space/place dichotomy is a distinction without much difference. As one critic writes, "our notions of place are retroactive fantasy constructs determined precisely by the corrosive effects of modernity."[12]

When the Meiji leaders seized power in 1868, they established institutions to guarantee their own permanency; the new government resembled high-modernist states elsewhere in promoting progress, using new technology to exploit environmental resources, colonizing spaces for political ends, and ordering society according to rationalist principles. What Timothy Mitchell says of colonial Egypt applies to Japan as well: Meiji modernity meant "the spread of a political order that inscribes in the social world a new conception of space" and "new means of manufacturing the experience of the real."[13] The state used its power to measure and map social practices via institutions of law and administration, producing spaces that became "territories of control and surveillance,"[14] in Harvey's phrase. One element of the government's sociospatial engineering was the creation of public open areas in the form of urban parks, followed several decades later by national parks. As in other countries, parks became landscapes of power where human culture and the nonhuman environment interacted, but starting with the Hibiya demonstrations of 1905 some city parks also served as "spaces of representation," in Lefebvre's terms, where commoners aired views on public affairs and reconfigured parklands to create geographies of opposition to officialdom. Eventually certain parks and other public areas, such as Yoyogi Park today, transcended a power/resistance binary to become space shared by citizens and their rulers, land neither official nor popular yet both, a middle ground of collaboration, acquiescence, refusal, and renegotiation all at once.[15]

Nature and nation were close partners in building the Meiji regime, but nature in all its multiple meanings increasingly became subordinated to the patriotic demands of an expanding economy and empire. Because of the problematic meanings attributed to "nature"—sometimes including humans, sometimes excluding them, often privileging humans as dominant—it may be more accurate to refer to "the nonhuman" (biotic and abiotic) when everything in ecosystems except for people is meant. Japan's nonhuman and developed environments can be read as parallel, often intersecting texts to illuminate the state-building process, in that parks and the choice of flora and fauna featured in them were constructed through social practices and given meaning through cultural representations.[16] When Japan established its first national parks in 1934, they resembled their larger American counterparts, which were not untamed but instead were "produced environments in every conceivable sense. From the management of wildlife to the alteration of the landscape by human occupancy, the material environment bears the stamp of human labor . . . [they] are neatly packaged experiences of environment on which substantial profits are recorded each year."[17] Yet more recently—without overlooking the ability of bureaucrats, rangers, maps, and exhibits to script public space—ecologists and environmental historians since the 1970s have taken pains to reinsert humans into their natural surroundings, rather than regarding the environment as extrinsic and readily manipulable.[18] This approach has gradually won respect, even a degree of acceptance, among officials responsible for environmental policy in Japan.

Urban Green Spaces

When the Japanese began opening city parklands to the general public in the 1870s, they did so against a deep historical background of green spaces for human enjoyment throughout the world. The forerunners of modern public parks were private gardens and royal hunting grounds in antiquity, including a kind of Sumerian game park recorded in the *Epic of Gilgamesh* (1200 B.C.E.).[19] To writers as diverse as Aristotle, Virgil, Confucius, and the Japanese philosopher Ogyū Sorai (1666–1728), plants and animals comprised a symbolic landscape distinct from humanity, one where the power of leaders and the might of their soldiers were manifested through imposing the sophistication of culture over the putative peace and simplicity of the nonhuman, which they often labeled "nature."[20] In his studies of cultural modernity, the Japanese critic Maeda Ai (1931–1987) perceptively emphasized visuality, a core value of both the city and the country park.[21] Landscape as a painterly topic traces to the fourteenth-century Italian Renaissance and came into full flower four centuries later, nurtured by followers of the French artist Claude Lorrain (1600–1682).[22] By separating the viewer from the viewed, landscape art afforded the outsider visual control over picturesque aspects of the nonhuman, much as the camera today gives even the least ambitious tourist command of the Azusa River valley from the celebrated Kappa Bridge at Kamikōchi in the Japanese Alps. In the same way, English designers such as William Kent (1685–1748) and Capability Brown (1716–1783) created unkempt landscape gardens, less manicured but no less confected than their more formal Italian and French counterparts, to mimic the irregular arcadian qualities prized in the outdoors by their wealthy patrons.[23] In some respects the English landscape park resembled Japanese garden art of the same era; although more scissored and punctilious, gardens in Japan consciously rejected the formalism of continental Asia and contrived to reproduce in miniature a nonhuman of the imagination as much as of the senses. In both countries the waning of landed aristocracies in the nineteenth century imperiled the future of private landscaped grounds.

The public park, an artifact of the nineteenth century, offers the spatial historian an instrument for measuring technological progress, the dynamics of everyday living, the new state-society nexus, and an urban modernity expressed in taxonomies of spaces constituting the city. An early example was Regent's Park in London, planned in 1811 by John Nash (1752–1835) and partly opened to commoners in 1835.[24] Soon the world's first publicly funded park built for general use was established in 1843 at Birkenhead,[25] which the young American journalist and antislavery activist Frederick Law Olmsted (1822–1903) visited in 1850–1851. He absorbed its principles of intervention to convert private pasture into public parkland,[26] ideas adapted in his designs for New York's Central and Prospect Parks, Boston's Emerald Necklace, and many other public parks and college campuses throughout the United States. The British parks and their American cousins excited much interest among Japanese leaders when the first delegates from Edo began traveling to Europe and the United States in 1860 to investigate the secrets of capitalist modernity. Germany's Bismarckian open spaces also stirred much admiration among Japanese visitors, as did the efforts of Georges-Eugène Haussmann (1809–1891) to reconfigure the medieval city of Paris as an imperial capital of light, air, and broad boulevards.[27] Japanese designers eventually adapted these European models to include trees, shrubs, and waterways, as well as some local landscaping elements, without sacrificing regulation and order.

Throughout American city parks, Olmsted's vision of taking quiet pleasure in trees and lakes gave way by the end of the nineteenth century to new facilities for golf, tennis, cycling, skating, music, art, and observing exotic animals. Yet social control, an American term first used in 1901, became a key theme for the elite stewards of public spaces; the city park in Japan, as in North America, turned into something of "an outdoor reform school, with morality taught through the innovative medium of leisure."[28] Japanese park design, increasingly in the hands of municipal bureaucrats, became hard-surfaced and functionalist, with cookie-cutter layouts and standardized equipment, and remained so for much of the twentieth century.

Two developments during the 1960s redefined city parks globally: the open-space movement, which posited that "the city is an art form worth saving,"[29] and the construction of mini-parks (in New York, "vest-pocket" parks) to mitigate crime in thickly settled neighborhoods and to alleviate the sameness of corporate and commercial structures in city centers. In the open-space approach, public citizens partially reclaimed the parks from bureaucrats through negotiation, forcing municipalities to respond to the needs of the times.[30] The neighborhood mini-park, in contrast, brought snippets of greenery to vacant lots in densely populated housing blocks whose residents often lived far from a full-scale district park. The downtown mini-park faced fewer obstacles; many were built on donated land and maintained by subsidies from corporations eager to provide spots of relaxation for their employees and customers. At length the private model of management was extended to publicly owned spaces such as Bryant Park in Manhattan and to certain city parks in Tokyo; today private funds cover most of the costs of operating New York's Central Park,[31] effectively smudging the borders between public and private originally staked out by British designers in the 1840s. The same blurring of boundaries has slowly taken hold in a number of Japan's neighborhood parks and, more recently, even in the management of some of its national parklands.

Nations' Parks

The idea of the national public park, in mountains or seasides far from city populations, arose in the United States in the mid-nineteenth century and today has spread to most of the world's 204 countries.[32] It is a truism that ever since the agricultural revolution, most ancient peoples regarded wild lands as lacking inherent value, if not downright evil, something to be conquered and freely put to human use. It is also axiomatic that "civilization created wilderness," insofar as city people in the early nineteenth century, building on ideas from the European Enlightenment, romanticized and aestheticized the unruly state of nature that their forebears had sought to subdue.[33] They began to champion an idealized conception of the wilderness as something Other, endangered, in need of appreciation if not outright preservation—an antidote to growing urban ills. To urbanites, seemingly pristine landscapes such as the Yosemite Valley evoked the primeval, but actually Native Americans had lived there for centuries and many had to be resettled on reservations before parks could be built.[34] Likewise, the Amazon was never uninhabited primeval forest, despite the expectations of European explorers seeking an uncharted El Dorado.[35] In Tanzania's Arusha National Park, European settlers narrated their conquest of native peoples in terms of the nonhuman: "National parks, as representations of a harmonious, untouched space of nature, mask the colonial dislocations and obliterate the history of those dislocations, along with the history of the spaces that existed previously."[36] The American movement to create national parks took root in these reconfigurations of the pastoral into the primitive, ideas expressed a generation later in Japanese thinking about parks in Hokkaido. But the early twentieth-century founders of Japan's national parks confronted no removal of peoples because the Ainu in Hokkaido had already been sequestered in the early Meiji years.

Japanese philosophers since antiquity have pondered people's relationships with the natural,[37] but ideas of wilderness similar to those in Europe and the Americas arose mainly in the later twentieth century, particularly after the United States Congress enacted the Wilderness Act of 1964. Nonetheless, early advocates such as Shiga Shigetaka resembled the founders of Yellowstone (1872) and Yosemite (1890) National Parks in embracing a romantic nationalism about the grandness of nature. In Japan, as in the United States but not in Europe, enhancing national distinctiveness, rather than protecting the environment, was central to early ideas of the national park.[38] Even though many proposed parks lay in remote areas of limited economic value, the controlled development of timber, mining, and wildlife resources by private parties was another less widely recognized motive in both the United States and Japan, especially before preservationist discourses became prominent in the twentieth century.[39]

Conservation in the sense of sustainable use of material resources for human benefit underlay the drive to establish national parks and forest reserves in the United States from the beginning—and usually guided public policy in both the United States and Japan throughout the twentieth century.[40] Japan was predisposed by two centuries' experience to favor selective use of natural resources. The country's timber stock had periodically been ravaged for constructing impressive shrines, temples, and villas for successive governing regimes since at least the Nara period (710–784), eventually leading to a form of conservation through carefully managed silviculture during the Edo period (1600–1868). The Meiji government approved the country's first comprehensive forest law in 1897, based on principles of scientific conservation, and designated the first national forests two years later. As in Europe and North America, conservation laws favoring regulated use had the virtue of restraining loggers from overusing natural resources in protected forests and, after 1931, national parks.

Partly in reaction to the public's appetite for recreation in the parks, ecological concerns grew more evident in Japan during the 1960s, especially the desire to safeguard native plants, birds, fish, and terrestrial animals. Numerous reform environmentalists showed flexibility by joining in a biocentric approach to the outdoors, using science to address how humans relate to their surroundings—or, as many ecologists assumed, form a part of it.[41] Biocentrism did not stanch the flood of park visitors; officials were powerless to forestall the emergence of water-resistant, lightweight camping equipment, the proliferation of maps and guides to the outdoors, and the new phenomenon of ecotours that arose in Japan and many other countries from the revolution in youth culture that started in the late 1960s. The doctrine of pure preservation has enjoyed only narrow if articulate support in Japan, mainly among the educated and wellborn, embracing little alternative ecological vision other than protecting the pristine by leaving it alone—sometimes forgetting that the pristine is far from static and always in flux. In recent decades the world's dominant environmental discourses have drawn on the science of ecology to argue that human survival depends on the health of the earth's ecosystems, of which people are a part.[42] Japanese ecologists have protested the heavy use of national parks and forests ever since the noted botanist Numata Makoto (1917–2001) published the 1967 edition of his *Seitaigaku hōhōron* (Ecological methods).[43]

Dissatisfied with the compromises reached by reform environmentalists, a radical advocacy known as deep ecology emerged in the 1970s seeking not merely to preserve whatever remained untrammeled but also to restore the global ecosystem by minimizing the human bootprint on it. Deep ecologists in Japan and elsewhere regarded humans as merely one species, urging people to visit the outdoors but leave no trace behind, and they saw moral value in wilderness as a guide to reforming contemporary society. Parallel movements such as environmental justice and ecofeminism began to draw scattered support in Japan in the 1970s as well. Two decades later government officials, acknowledging that the concept of endangered species was now well established, began to recognize that ecologists could help the parks by assessing threats to indigenous flora and fauna from exotic ones, and that scientists could evaluate the natural dynamics of park resources with a view to protecting them more effectively.

Today in Japan, where sustainable use is taken for granted, nongovernmental organizations mobilize cash and volunteers to help verify that environmental laws are being obeyed. Park managers often welcome the volunteers while bewailing the lack of revenues to meet their obligations to the public, maintain the parklands, and protect the environment against unceasing pressures from developers.[44] Few groups seriously challenge sustainable development as the dominant narrative of Japan's national parks and forests, but still the clash of contending interests—bureaucratic, economic, ecological—is particularly sharp in that country's natural parks, despite a dip in attendance since its peak in the early 1990s.

A New Public, New Public Spaces

The idea of public spaces, especially green public spaces, at first must have perplexed city people in nineteenth-century Japan, because their country's numerous urban gardens, temple and shrine woodlots, and well-planted warrior residences were in the private hands of the elite and the wealthy before the Meiji Restoration of 1868. Amusement areas for commoners dotted the most populous city districts during the Edo period, but these tightly controlled, quasi-public spaces were given over to social pleasures with little connection to the nonhuman environment. Public and nonpublic were indistinct terms of discourse in nineteenth-century Japan. Like their counterparts in China and Korea, political thinkers in Japan had long pondered differences between the realm of public rule (*ōyake*) and the ambit of the people as the emperor's subjects (*tami*, the general public of the governed).

With industrial and political modernity came a sharpened awareness of the private (*shi, watakushi*), both in the sense of private property and as something personal or even selfish, in contrast with the great public power of the new Meiji state and the emerging self-awareness of both former samurai and ordinary people as a newly unified national citizenry, now that the finely graded social statuses of the Edo period had been dissolved by fiat in the 1870s. Unlike customary local privileges to use common lands or seek redress in premodern times, this new collective self-identity of citizen-subjects was nationwide in scope, most often expressed as *kōkyō,* "public society," "community," or "common weal."[45] The idea of public society was nurtured by government authorities (*okami*) as a tool of social mobilization; to a considerable degree, modern urban spatiality, including the creation of parklands to build nationhood and social consciousness, was part of the state system rather than a modality arising spontaneously from below. Nonetheless, by the late Meiji period open areas in the biggest cities sometimes became contested grounds for the production of space by public authorities on the one hand and the performance of space by an assertive public on the other.

Japan's earliest public parks, dating to 1873, were established in urban districts by bureaucratic decree as a part of the new regime.[46] Most city parks in the late nineteenth century were converted shrine or temple lands, deep inner spaces in what the contemporary architect Maki Fumihiko (1928–) describes as "multi-centered" Tokyo. Maki sees the essence of Japan's public architecture "in its space and territory . . . in spatial arrangements structured not by the idea of a center but by the idea of depth (*oku*),"[47] places not immediately evident or mentally mappable as is Western public space. At no point did the Meiji government or its successors express a clear theory of public space; even today, Maki notwithstanding, there is little agreement on what public space means, who produces it, for whose benefit it exists, or how it should be managed and used. Japan is far from unique: its leaders share uncertainty on this point with European thinkers such as Henri Lefebvre (1901–1991), Michel Foucault (1926–1984), Jean Baudrillard (1929–2007), and Jürgen Habermas (1929–), all of whom have struggled to conceptualize public space.[48] With or without theoretical underpinnings, high-modernist states everywhere in the late nineteenth century asserted their spatial sovereignty over society by officially designating public areas of various kinds including parks, symbolizing elite dominance while disciplining miscreants via police, courts, and prisons. Establishing such urban spaces was a part of legislative and cadastral standardization for governmentality—making society more "legible," as Scott puts it.[49]

At the same time the national park movement, which achieved its first formal success when Yellowstone Park was approved by the U.S. Congress in 1872, was driven partly by a need to assert the public interest against threats of monopolization by private developers in a new age of passenger railways. It is also true that, as in some European countries, privately owned holdings have long existed within America's national parks. Today just five of the country's fifty-eight official national parks consist of purely federal land, even though a third of the nation's territory is publicly owned.[50] Japan's national parks, first established in 1934, similarly blur public and private space: none of the country's twenty-nine national parks is entirely publicly owned, and commercial logging, agricultural, and tourist businesses have made deep inroads by commodifying many of the portions that remain in public hands. Yet it is also the case, especially in quasi-national and prefectural natural parks, that regional and local identities have emerged in the past two decades to define space very differently from the outlooks of central authorities and their commercial allies.[51]

In city or countryside, a public park in Japan since the late nineteenth century has usually meant a set-aside area reflecting the spatial aesthetics of Western middle-class society, juxtaposed but seldom mixed with time-honored principles of Japanese landscapes. Two late-Meiji examples were Hibiya Park, mainly designed along French and German lines, and Shinjuku Imperial Garden, which largely honored French principles; each contained a Japanese-style garden in one corner. As with the notion of public space, officials found little sustained ideology abroad or at home to undergird the park movement. Instead modern Japanese parks were constructed interfaces of human culture and the nonhuman environment, enclosed yet open, bucolic yet vigorous, sometimes tranquil, sometimes dangerous, their vegetation and fauna preserved yet controlled. In many respects they were tools of internal colonization of the general public by authorities bent on social management; in Taiwan, and to a degree in Korea, parklands were spatial levers of Japan's empire down to 1945. Unlike their Western counterparts, urban and national parks in Japan seldom were seen as agents of cultural diversity, equality of opportunity, or a utopian "exploration of hope" and optimism.[52]

The greatest public parks in Japan's cities trace their sources to five related wellsprings, according to the landscape architect Shinji Isoya: (1) modeling on Western public parks as a part of the Meiji effort to "civilize" the country (Hibiya Park); (2) gifts from on high, such as converted daimyo gardens and temple and shrine grounds, as well as lands granted by the imperial family (Ueno, Inokashira, Kyoto Imperial Palace Outer Garden Parks); (3) national prestige and defense, including flagpole parks, small parks nationwide in 1904–1905 with ponds in an "attack-Russia" design (*seiro*), air defense green spaces from 1940 to 1945 converted to postwar parklands, and Olympic parks; (4) commemorations and celebrations, such as expositions, reign anniversaries, and imperial memorials (Meiji Shrine Outer Garden, Shōwa Memorial Park); and (5) lands acquired from private owners, either as donations from industrial barons such as the Iwasakis (Rikugien, Kiyosumi Garden Parks) and Yasudas (Yasuda Garden Park) and from imperial relatives (Prince Arisugawa Memorial Park) or by land use statutes mandating green spaces.[53] Thousands of smaller playgrounds, neighborhood parks, sports fields, and district-wide public areas were added as municipal public works, starting with reconstruction after the Kanto earthquake and fires of September 1, 1923. Then as the country faced the crisis of World War Two, city parks took on new public roles: physical training, refuge from wartime air raids, food production, temporary graves, and emergency shelter after Japan's defeat in 1945. Postwar land reform and the constitutional separation of religion and politics removed many parklands from public use. Government investment in urban parks soared in the 1970s because of heightened environmental consciousness and demands for recreation as Japan grew more affluent. Yet nearly all Japanese city parks until the 1990s were designed and administered by city planning or construction officials with little regard for how they might be used.[54]

Nation-driven imperatives, not functionality for visitors, likewise prevailed for many decades in conceptualizing Japan's national parks. Both urban and national parks in Japan initially evolved to help establish a distinctive national culture, not primarily to fulfill environmental needs.[55] During the 1910s legislative supporters for establishing national parks first cited both Western precedents and pride in Japanese landscapes, then in the 1920s they also emphasized physical fitness and, in the 1930s, the need to earn foreign exchange by attracting foreign tourists during the world depression. Wartime spending from 1937 to 1945, followed by budgetary restraint during the early postwar recovery, left few surplus monies for the national parks. Gradually, new ones were added, especially when the Natural Parks Law of 1957 replaced the original National Parks Act of 1931. As with city parks, government financial support for natural parks (national, quasi-national, and prefectural) rose substantially during the 1970s and 1980s, then flattened thereafter.

The environmental writers Suzuki Satoshi and Sawada Seiichirō identify four main discourses on Japanese national parks, all with nationalist implications: (1) extensive parks on the Yellowstone model, such as Daisetsuzan (in Hokkaido), that conserve distinctive ecological features and provide recreation; (2) commemorative parks featuring national symbols, such as Mount Fuji; (3) historical sites, such as Nikkō north of Tokyo, where the first Tokugawa leader is enshrined; and (4) somewhat later, parks to encourage international tourism, at some cost to strict preservation. Nonetheless, small sections of a few remote national parks are carefully protected for scholarly investigation, much like national scientific parks in Russia, Scandinavia, and Switzerland.[56] Because natural parks in Japan include private and public lands, they usually mix forests, farming, hiking trails, and open country, as in many British parks.[57]

Long regarded as the responsibility of bureaucrats, the operation of public parks was taken over partly by private citizens in the 1990s through nongovernmental organizations engaged in civic reconstruction and rural reclamation.[58] Starting with the Basic Environmental Law of 1993 and Basic Environmental Plan of 1994, legal changes promoting local autonomy spawned uneasy coalitions of public officials and citizen volunteers who gradually began to manage many of Japan's city parks, as well as portions of some natural parks. The natural parks paid increasing heed to ecological factors, especially environmental protection and ecological education, despite their straightened revenues and ceaseless pressures from the tourist industry.

Whatever the changing definition and purpose of the public park, both urban and national park leaders consistently say the benefits to users are immeasurable—and thus subjective. So too with attendance: the figures are especially unreliable for Japan because few public parks of any type charge user fees or monitor comings and goings. Estimates tend to rise year after year, until it is clear that fewer visitors actually are appearing, whereupon the estimates ebb.[59] As attendance numbers crested in the early 1990s, the city planning specialist Shirahata Yōzaburō asked rhetorically whether urban parks were still needed at all. He observed that fewer adults used parks as sites of sociability, except to view spring blossoms and autumn leaves, because they preferred coffee shops, restaurants, bars, and hotel lobbies as meeting places.[60] It was clear even to their supporters in Japan and elsewhere that parks were not, as once claimed, the lungs of the city (trees absorbed relatively little carbon dioxide) or stabilizers of real estate values (some were, but shabby ones dragged prices down);[61] national parks invited more auto travel once car ownership became the norm for Japanese in the 1970s, leading to overdevelopment of tourist facilities, intolerable air pollution, and gargantuan holiday traffic jams on the country's web of expressways.

In the years since Shirahata's skeptical rhetoric of 1991, city parks have re-engineered themselves to prioritize recreation, fire defense, natural preservation, and urban scenery.[62] Governmental directives in the 1990s to create common social capital by encouraging a leisured and abundant lifestyle, especially for the elderly, gave renewed vigor, if little cash, to city parks that often had devolved into retreats for the socially weak—children, seniors, the homeless.[63] Today, as has been true for many decades, green spaces such as Kinuta Family Park in western Tokyo continue to draw hundreds if not thousands of daily walkers, runners, mothers with strollers, picnickers, and athletes of all ages. Solitary musicians practice brass instruments and woodwinds along the banks of Kyoto's Kamo River and in the woods of Tokyo's Inokashira Park. Other less expansive parks host cyclists, rollerbladers and skateboarders, gateball and chess players, pet walkers, footsore shoppers, teenage smokers, and nighttime romantics. In these ways parks of all types have gradually changed functions but continue to be vital zones of contact between people and their nonhuman surroundings.

Whether Japan's green consumerism of the 2000s benefited the environment in general or its public parks in particular is not yet clear. Perhaps the greater question is whether the nearly 80 percent of Japanese who live in cities, surrounded by a virtual world of electronic information, can still connect directly and meaningfully with their nonhuman environment. As the ornithologist Robert Askins puts it, "Japan is now so urbanized that two generations of people have grown up with almost no contact with nature. Will they devote themselves entirely to their urban world of artificial stimulation, or will they rebel against it? Probably a bit of each."[64]

This is a book about public space in modern Japan, the parks that were its most conspicuous and heavily used assets, and the changing historical environment in which green spaces were produced and reproduced through interactions between government officials and park users. A main task facing the historian of culture is to explain how and why the multiple meanings ascribed by human communities to parklands, their environments, and the ecosystem as a whole contended, comported, or conflicted with one another as these meanings altered across time. Japan, with its abundant ecological endowment, self-awareness as a distinct culture, and earnestness in exemplifying a new Asian modernity, is a rich source of insight into this process. The focus of this study is on parks, both urban and national, established by public authorities for the use of private citizens—the general public at large—to advance the central government's project of social unification. Because it is Japan's largest and greenest megalopolis with the greatest variety of public spaces, as well as a city constantly under reconstruction, Tokyo receives particular attention as the pacesetter for urban park development nationwide. Examining city parklands and natural parks (national, quasi-national, or prefectural) together provides a useful prism for refracting Japan's modern experience of public space and the environment writ large. Other fascinating realms of public space such as plazas, squares, arcades, malls, museums, shrines, zoos, theaters, and athletic arenas, each of considerable interest and import, are omitted because they are much better known.[65]

While respecting the individuality and diversity of park history, development, and use in modern Japan, this book emphasizes the dynamic, ever-shifting interactions of governments and citizens, humans and their nonhuman surroundings, and the nation with the outside world. Japan is the centerpiece, but comparative comments are offered when appropriate about transnational phenomena such as conservation, preservation, environmentalism, and ecology that swept the globe during the years examined here, even though it should not be expected that these phenomena meant precisely the same things from one culture to another. Chapter 1 discusses public parks in Japanese cities from the initial enabling act in 1873 through early forms of urban planning, ending with the City Planning Law of 1919. Chapter 2 takes up Japan's first efforts at designating forests, scenic monuments, and national parks as public reserves from the Meiji period to the late 1930s. Chapter 3 addresses visions of a new Tokyo from the earthquake and fires of September 1923 through the American occupation of 1945–1952, while chapter 4 treats urban and natural parks during the era of sustained economic growth from the 1950s through the 1980s. Chapter 5 examines new eco-regimes of volunteerism and ecological consciousness in both city and natural parks during the 1990s and early twenty-first century, followed by a brief afterword recapping the key themes of the book. Throughout, the focus is on the continual effort to reinvent modern Japan, a process at once thwarted by enterprise capitalism, with it demands for space and resources, but that also thwarts capitalist expansion via budgetary and environmental constraints. An important aim of this book is to encourage further research into how local ecosystems have been affected by human interventions, leading to a fuller cultural history of these spaces than is currently available.

Reconnoitering Japan's experience with public green space is complicated by uneven documentation, scanty scholarly attention, and the low priority given to public amenities like parks, libraries, and the arts for much of the period treated here. This account relies partly on statistics and histories from official sources, chronicles of individual parks prepared by longtime visitors, and the recollections of certain key figures in park management. For information and insight about public uses of green areas, I've been aided by the scholarship of the small coterie of Japanese academic specialists on the topic, supplemented by my own rambles around many of Japan's parks during research visits to that country. No single methodological approach or theoretical position can adequately interpret the multiple redefinitions of public space in modern Japan. Instead the reader can be reassured, as Victor Brombert writes, that "eschewing a dogmatic approach and stressing diversity and variation do not preclude a search for underlying patterns and common tendencies."[66] These patterns and tendencies form the matrix for the chapters that follow.

CHAPTER 1

From Private Lands to Public Spaces

Early City Parks

Five years after coming to power in 1868 the Meiji government began to define public spaces by seizing private properties abandoned by warrior elites and religious institutions, then converting them to city parks for the diversion, and the control, of citizen-subjects under the new imperial regime. During the previous Edo era relatively few places were available in city or country for ordinary people to experience the outdoors as a site of leisure, not labor. Beginning in 1873, dozens of city parks were created by fiat, bringing new opportunities to urban dwellers to interact with the natural environment, in spaces with clearly defined rules of conduct and practices of policing that advanced the state's objective of social integration. Ueno in northeastern Tokyo became not merely the premier city park of its age but also, through its close association with the imperial family and the central government, a veritable nation's park. Tokyo also undertook modern urban planning in the mid-1880s, including Japan's first Western-style park, opened at Hibiya in 1903 by a government determined to display the country's modernity at home and abroad. Together, Ueno and Hibiya Parks exemplified the official production of urban space and the unofficial consumption of it by the public.

Enjoying City Places in the Edo Period

Most people in preindustrial Japan worked in rural areas in daily contact with their natural surroundings of plants, animals, and geophysical terrain. The small proportion who lived in cities lacked such contact. In the early nineteenth century perhaps 10 percent lived in central places of 100,000 or more, of which the political center Edo (renamed Tokyo in 1868) numbered 1.4 million, the great commercial entrepôt Osaka nearly 500,000, and the imperial capital Kyoto 400,000. Merchants, artisans, and other commoners formed the majority of Edo's population but were confined to only 20 percent of its land area, mainly east of the shogun's castle. The samurai elite, including the shogun and attendant daimyos, took up 65 percent of the city; temple and shrine grounds (mainly the former) occupied another 15 percent. At its most crowded, the density of commoners was an astounding 67,000 per square kilometer, five times greater than in the twenty-three wards that make up the main city today.[1] To a population with little outdoor space for play, strolling, conversation, or impromptu performances, it was natural to turn to shrines, temples, riverbanks, and bridge plazas—all of them controlled by private elites—as de facto public spaces for relaxation. Edo's lack of open areas was doubtless idiosyncratic; reproductions of maps from the 1840s and 1850s suggest that Osaka, Kyoto, and other cities enjoyed considerably more green space.

The idea of recreation in the Edo period was sometimes expressed as "stretching the spirit" by visiting sites of beautiful vegetation not normally seen in daily city life, although the modern concept of outdoor recreation was not introduced until the Meiji era. Edo's thousand or more temples and shrines served as periodic agoras to attract local markets and entertainments, but these fell short of being true public spaces. Several dozen firebreaks established after the city's disastrous Meireki fire of 1657 and another fifty built in the early eighteenth century added something to the meager open space available to residents. The eighth shogun, Yoshimune (r. 1716–1745), encouraged popular pleasure unconnected with religious institutions by having peaches, willows, and cherries planted along the east bank of the Sumida River for Edo residents to enjoy under strict supervision.[2] Throughout Japan's great cities of the late Edo period, entertainment districts mixed secular pleasures and religious culture, most notably

Sensōji in the Asakusa district of Edo itself. As Max Horkheimer and Theodor W. Adorno observed about the culture industry elsewhere, these lively precincts were temporary escapes from the constraints of daily life, both mocking and reinforcing the norms of ordinary commoner society.[3]

The idea of the public park was premature for Japan in the Edo era, and most daimyo gardens were remote from commoners' lives, but a few forerunners of the modern urban park began to appear in regional cities in the early nineteenth century. In 1801 Matsudaira Sadanobu (1758–1829) aped his grandfather Yoshimune by planting cherries and building the Nanko Garden, which he opened to everyone living in Shirakawa, part of today's Fukushima Prefecture.[4] In Kanazawa the daimyo Maeda Narinaga (1782–1824) planned most of the Kenrokuen gardens from 1818 to 1822. Kenrokuen later became a public park under joint national and city auspices in 1875. Kairakuen, originally a twelve-hectare garden with upwards of three thousand plum trees, was built starting in 1841 expressly for the moral improvement of local people of all backgrounds in Mito. The garden's patron was the daimyo Tokugawa Nariaki (1800–1860), an outspoken advocate of learning about the West while maintaining Japan's long-standing policy of excluding Westerners.[5] At length the new Meiji government rejected Nariaki's exclusionist outlook, sent emissaries to visit Western capitals and their public spaces, and established modern city parks, of which Kairakuen was an ironic, if unintended, forerunner.

Japan's first official contacts in more than two hundred years with Westerners other than the Dutch took place under the dark cloud of military pressure from United States naval vessels led by Commodore Matthew C. Perry (1794–1858). The Kanagawa Treaty of Peace and Amity between Japan and the United States, negotiated by the shogun's representatives and Perry in 1854, opened ports to American shipping at Shimoda and Hakodate. The United States–Japan Treaty of Amity and Commerce, signed in 1858 by Consul General Townsend Harris (1804–1878) and high Edo officials, saddled Japan with unequal tariff and legal provisions for the next forty-one years. Britain, France, the Netherlands, and Russia soon demanded, and received, similar treaty arrangements. The Harris treaty added Niigata, Kobe, Nagasaki, and Kanagawa (Yokohama) as ports open to overseas commerce, and Japanese officials promised to make recreation areas available to the newcomers in these towns. Starting in 1862 foreigners began requesting tracks for horse racing and mounted military drill; these were quickly approved in Nagasaki, Kobe, and especially at the well-known Negishi racetrack in Yokohama, established in 1866.[6]

If Edo daimyo gardens were spaces of class exclusivity, the parks granted to the new international community were semicolonized zones of cultural and racial separation where not only foreign law but also foreign social customs, including views of gender, prevailed. Kobe's Higashi Park (Higashi Yūenchi or Tōyōen) was established in 1868 for the international community; as a recent official history dryly observes, "at that time it must have been quite a culture shock to see foreigners playing sports and games there."[7] Higashi Park became a public facility in 1875 when both Japanese and international residents were allowed to use it, and it reverted to full Japanese control in 1899 with the lapse of the unequal treaties. Even better known to Japanese and foreigners was Yamate Park in Yokohama, which in some ways was the most emulated public park in the country between

Founded in 1870 as a semicolonial club for foreign residents, Yamate Park today is home to the Yokohama International Tennis Community and a designated national scenic site and cultural property.

22

its founding in 1870 and the opening of Hibiya Park in Tokyo in 1903. Foreigners soon turned a rugged woodland with giant Himalayan cryptomeria (*sugi*), mistakenly called "cedars" but actually closely related to California's giant sequoias and coastal redwoods, into an attractive facility cultivated to Victorian tastes. In one respect Yamate Park was decidedly post-Victorian: women played tennis there at least as early as 1877. After the Kanto earthquake and fires of September 1923 the western half of the Yamate site was opened to the public as a city park. Today the tennis club is largely kept alive by its Japanese membership;[8] ironically, it is now so thoroughly indigenized that the Cultural Agency of the Education Ministry lists it as a scenic site and cultural property.

The Grand Council Parks

Japanese were forbidden to travel abroad during most of the Edo period, and those who managed to the leave the country illegally faced imprisonment or even death if they returned. Well before Perry brought American gunboat diplomacy to Uraga Bay in 1853, many politically aware Japanese feared for their country's independence, dreading a fate like China's semi-colonization by Britain through the Nanjing Treaty that settled the first Opium War of 1839–1842. The first Japanese travelers to the United States visited New York's Central Park on May 4, 1860, and recorded their surprise that areas were used for recreation and sports as well as the park's main function, enjoying restful scenery. Two years later another group toured the Bois de Boulogne in Paris, Regent's Park in London, and public spaces in other European countries, remarking especially on the handsome zoos they saw.[9] Most important of the early delegations was the embassy of 1871–1873 to the United States and Europe led by Iwakura Tomomi (1825–1883) to investigate industry, government, the military, education, and social practices in the major Western nations, a prelude to Japan's adapting many of the foreign ideas and institutions the visitors encountered. The historian Kume Kunitake (1839–1931), Iwakura's private secretary, noted that the delegates were much taken with the new city parks in the United States: Central Park, Boston Common and Public Garden, Saratoga Springs, and Philadelphia's Fairmount Park, which Kume described as "a magnificent park in terms of its landscape."[10] Early the following year they examined parks in England, the Englischer Garten in Munich, Prater Park in Vienna, and many others. Kume reported that they were impressed by how well groomed and landscaped these facilities were and what pivotal roles they played in the urban reform movements then in progress.[11] It is little wonder that many of these travelers sought to establish public parks for Japan's cities after they returned home in mid-1873. To their surprise, they discovered that the Grand Council of State had already taken steps to authorize urban parks in a decree issued on January 15 of that year.

One of the world's largest cities, at least since the shogun's census of 1721 counted 1.3 million persons, Tokyo (née Edo) suffered sudden massive depopulation three times in its modern history: with the Meiji restoration of 1868, after the earthquake and fires of September 1, 1923, and under sustained air attack by United States bombers in 1944 and 1945. When the office of shogun and the military government of the Tokugawa family were abolished at the end of 1867, daimyos, their warrior retinues, and many commoners whose livelihoods depended on serving the elites fled the capital for their respective domains. The city's population temporarily dropped from 1.4 million to half that number, leaving a great deal of abandoned land to be claimed by the new state, reallocated to private parties, taxed, and policed.[12] The authorities also transferred domain lands outside the capital to the new prefectures after 1871, a dramatic remapping of the political terrain. But the government kept large parcels for its own use, some of which it converted to a novel purpose in Japan: using state power to grant open spaces to the new public, via Directive No. 16 from the Grand Council of State on January 15, 1873.

By one reckoning, more than a thousand Tokyo properties were taken over by the Meiji authorities, some to be used for the imperial household, central government offices, military units, public works, or farm production. Many were sold at bargain prices to private businesspeople, who were subject to levy once the land-tax system adopted in 1873 created a clear separation between government and private ownership of property. Apart from religious structures and their immediate grounds, untaxed outlying temple and shrine lands were also claimed by the state—virtually without contest because so many institutions had atrophied after their samurai patrons vanished. The government also asserted control over riverbanks, roadways, reservoirs, bridges, and other tax-exempt infrastructure inherited from the old regime. The assumption was that any newly seized government lands not transferred to private hands or otherwise added to the tax rolls should be made available for common use by citizen-subjects of all social backgrounds.[13] In this respect, the January 1873 decree creating public parks was closely tied to the Land Tax Law enacted six months later as an integral part of governmental land management (producing space, to Lefebvre) and social control (legibility, in Scott's terms). Nonetheless, even if the modern city park was an expedient by-product of the state's real estate policy, the Grand Council's edict preserved open spaces to be converted, sooner or later, into public parklands.

Addressing the newly established prefectures, Directive No. 16 said:

> Beginning with the three *fu* [Tokyo, Kyoto, Osaka], you should select as [urban] parks places in each prefecture where people have long gathered for group enjoyment, such as sites of historic victories where people get together, customary tax-exempt lands, group-excursion locations (Kinryūzan Sensōji [Asakusa] and Tōeizan Kan'eiji [Ueno] in Tokyo, the precincts of the Yasaka Shrine, Kiyomizu Temple, and Arashiyama in Kyoto, and the publicly held lands that are tax-exempt in all temple and shrine grounds) and petition the Ministry of Finance, appending a detailed plan explaining the circumstances.[14]

The parks, the Grand Council declared, "are to become permanent pleasure grounds for all people," approved by the Finance Ministry but operated by the prefectures, which usually delegated their oversight to the temples and shrines—blurring the distinction between state and religions that the Meiji leaders were eager to uphold.[15] The government established rules for park users, imposing state discipline on concessions, open hours, cleaning, security, and fees. A follow-up decree in 1874 specified that only publicly owned lands could be nominated as parks. No construction or other improvements were authorized.[16] In effect, open areas long enjoyed by people for informal relaxation were now nationalized and renamed "public parks," strengthening the state's claims on vacant lands and providing a legal basis for evicting squatters, but with few immediate changes in how these spaces had been used by local residents before 1868. The ostensible motive for creating the earliest city parks was to provide open spaces under the government's aegis for public enjoyment, both scenic and recreational. Yet the government hardly masked the fact that land management and tax policy were its immediate agenda in issuing Directive No. 16.

The prefectures wasted little time before responding to the Grand Council's order to nominate spaces for approval as city parks. Of the eighty-two parks opened under the Grand Council's decree from 1873 to 1887, thirty-two were in temple or shrine precincts, thirty on former castle grounds taken over by the national government when daimyos surrendered their domain registers in 1871, and another thirteen at scenic sites picked by the prefectures; nearly two thirds are still in operation today. Separately, municipalities established thirty-four urban parks on their own during the same period, so that within the first two decades of Meiji rule Japan's cities could claim to operate 116 public parklands, a sound start by the international norms of the day in number if not amenities or financing.[17] Tokyo took the lead among the prefectures, nominating five Grand Council parks in 1873, all of them on temple or shrine lands: Asakusa, Shiba, Fukagawa, Asukayama, and Ueno, the largest at eighty-three hectares. Clearly the Grand Council parks were carryovers from the Edo period, not "investments in new social capital."[18] One new investment under separate development in Tokyo was unique, then and now: Yasukuni Shrine, built starting in 1869 as Kudan Shōkonsha, a shrine to welcome spirits of the dead. Yasukuni, which took its present name in 1879, later enshrined the spirits of those convicted in war crimes trials following World War Two and became a focus of international controversy.

Of Tokyo's parks opened in the late nineteenth century, Ueno rightfully is seen as the most public: the largest of its era, home to industrial exhibitions and exotic animals, host to foreign dignitaries, and site of imperial pomp and displays of state power. By the time the emperor presented the Meiji Constitution there on February 12, 1889, Ueno had become the nation's park, not just one for Tokyo residents, backed by central-government money via the Imperial Household Ministry starting in 1886. But Asakusa Park, scarcely remembered today because it was abolished when the American occupation enforced a separation of religion from the state after World War Two, was a fountain of yen for Tokyo's public parks from the Grand Council directive of 1873 until at least the earthquake a half-century later, and in many respects until 1945, regularly generating at least 80 percent of the funds required to operate the rest of the city's parklands.[19]

The commercial district in front of Sensōji Temple at Asakusa was the archetypal amusement area of the Edo period for commoners, with its ranks of shops, teahouses, theaters, and street entertainments thoroughly masking the boundaries between religious and secular culture. Even after it became a Grand Council park in 1873, the carefree, sybaritic character of the area changed only slowly, mostly in response to shifting consumer tastes rather than government decrees. From 1889 to 1898 Asakusa Park was the main profit center for Tokyo's parks, grossing ¥248,459 in revenues and spending only ¥61,214 on its own operations; the surplus went partly to running the other Tokyo parks and partly to funding an interest-bearing bank account that contributed more than ¥200,000 toward the design and construction of Hibiya Park, the country's first in the Western style, which opened in 1903.[20] As with Asakusa Park itself, the fiscal independence of Tokyo's city parks came to an end in 1945; thereafter the central government and municipalities became spigots, if not fountains, of yen to support the parks.[21]

Like modern regimes everywhere, the Meiji state quickly grew adept at requiring localities to take policy actions without providing resources from the center to implement them. Instructed in 1873 from on high to maintain parklands on government-owned parcels, prefectures and municipalities were obliged to operate urban parks on a pay-as-you-play basis. As a result, apart from Asakusa, the imperially supported facility at Ueno, and the European-style showpiece at Hibiya, the original Grand Council parks in Tokyo and the eighteen others built in the city in the next half-century only slowly shed their Edo-era flavor, getting by with a minimum of equipment, few if any structures, and scanty operating funds. Only Tokyo, Osaka, and the two prefectures of Nara and Fukuoka enjoyed enough revenues from their urban parks to make their operations self-sustaining.[22] But however frugal, these spaces differed considerably from their Edo-era forebears in that they were unmistakably public and modern in ownership, management, and clientele, creatures of the Meiji state yet ambiguous and chameleonic in the exercise of control, usually by bureaucrats but at times, such as at Hibiya, by users in negotiation with the authorities.

Imperial Ueno

Perhaps more than any other urban park in Japan, Ueno's evolution suggests a hybridity of premodern and modern, religious and secular, civil and military, as well as imperial and democratic characteristics. Like Asakusa, it has long been closely integrated with the surrounding shopping and transportation district. Its loam soil favorable for plant life, its ancient trees, and its commanding view of the city made Ueno Hill and its Kan'eiji Temple (est. 1622) favorite places to visit during the Edo period. More recently its zoo, art and science museums, concert halls, and spring cherry blossoms have attracted more than ten million visitors a year, making it the most popular city park in Japan.[23]

During the Boshin Civil War, Tokugawa troops were defeated at Ueno by restorationist forces led by Ōmura Masujirō (1824–1869),[24] whose monumental statue dominates the formal approach to the Yasukuni Shrine today. All of Ueno Hill except for the religious buildings became property of Tokyo in December 1868. A Dutch ophthalmologist, Anthonius F. Bauduin (1822–1885), visited Ueno, observed its many tall trees, and recommended that the government move a planned hospital elsewhere and turn the hilltop into a park. This happened when Ueno was designated one of Tokyo's first five Grand Council parks in 1873. Bauduin's role in these events, however modest, gave Ueno Park the cachet of European approval.[25]

Ueno Park eventually housed museums, a library, the Japan Academy (est. 1879), and the Tokyo Schools of Fine Arts (1889) and Music (1890), merged in 1949 as Tokyo University of Fine Arts and Music—showing that both national and city authorities wanted Ueno to perform modern statist functions by displaying national culture and enlightening the public as well as serving as open space for recreation. Reports from the Iwakura embassy had commented favorably on European museums, public parks, and the grand expositions periodically held there, recommending that they be considered for Japan. Machida Hisanari (1838–1891), a young bureaucrat who directed the Tokyo National Museum when its small collections were first assembled in 1871, petitioned the Grand Council two years later to establish public cultural facilities such as those he had visited in London and Paris from 1865 to 1867.[26] At length a two-story imperial museum designed by Josiah Conder (1852–1920) was built at Ueno and the collections

Saigō Takamori (1827–1877), in casual civilian dress accompanied by his dog, might be out for an evening stroll in Ueno Park in this realistic sculpture by Takamura Kōun (1852–1934). Another statue of Saigō in full military regalia stands in Kagoshima, capital of his home domain of Satsuma, where he led a fierce but doomed rebellion against imperial forces in 1877.

moved there in 1882, a start to the process of visually ordering Japan's past as its present nationalist government wished it to be viewed. Included was a deliberate effort to turn former privately held fine arts and Buddhist objects into the nation's art.[27]

The Meiji emperor officially opened Ueno Park on May 9, 1876, in an elaborate ceremony filled with both synchronic and diachronic implications. The ritual event was meant to lay imperial claim to this public space as a secular state gift to the people, as well as to impress foreign diplomats with Japan's modernity and to daunt lingering domestic opponents with the sovereignty of the new regime. The emperor's visit also linked the Meiji government to Ueno's past associations with state power through Kan'eiji, the guardian of Edo castle from the northeast. That same year a Western-style restaurant, the Seiyōken, opened in the park. The emperor returned in 1877, while the Satsuma Rebellion was raging in Kyushu, to open the first National Industrial Promotion Exposition at Ueno, a carefully choreographed piece of internal propaganda to solidify support for the new government while its survival was still in question. The ten-hectare site, modeled after the Vienna fair of 1873, ended up mixing the old and the new; the 453,000 visitors (nearly all Japanese) to the Western-style pavilion viewed indoor exhibits showing their country's progress in industry, learning, art, and civilization, while outdoor shops and stalls created a festival-like atmosphere reminiscent of the Edo amusement districts.[28]

If Ueno by the early 1880s was well en route to becoming an imperial park for the entire nation, it was also growing more publicly accessible with the rise of its nearby commercial district, now that the capital had recouped its sudden population loss when the Edo regime collapsed. A particular magnet was the Ueno Zoo, which the Imperial Household Ministry opened in 1882 for entertainment and as a mark of civilization, providing visual order to unfamiliar nonhuman fauna, much as the adjacent national museum arranged unfamiliar artifacts from Japan's past to assert control over the narrative of the country's progress. Scientific state management of animals from faraway lands became something of a metaphor for imperial domination of the territories Japan added to its empire after 1895.[29] Nearby Shinobazu Pond, in prehistoric times part of Tokyo Bay, was incorporated into the park in 1874 after authorities deflected calls to fill it in for rice paddies and chose instead to operate a small racetrack around its perimeter until 1894.

However strong the ties to its religious past, and whatever its appeal to the growing neighborhood population, Ueno Park by the mid-1880s was unmistakably a state space in function if not in finance. Its operating expenses greatly exceeded the modest rent paid by Seiyōken and other concessionaires, even after favorable revenues from the zoo were taken into account. Without subventions from the large surpluses recorded each year at Asakusa, Ueno Park faced insolvency because the Home Ministry held firm to its policy that urban parks should be self-sustaining in operations. The crisis was resolved in 1886 when the Imperial Household Ministry took over supervision of the park and turned it into a highly visible government enterprise openly serving the ritual needs of state formation.[30] Yet, unlike public spaces in countries at comparable points in their political development, such as Mexico,[31] Ueno Park was not converted into a stylish garden catering to elite tastes; instead refinements such as flower shows, art exhibits, and concerts took place side by side with diversions appealing to all social backgrounds and levels of taste.

The climax of Meiji state building arrived on February 11, 1889, when the emperor promulgated Asia's first constitution as a gift bestowed on his subjects. The following day the emperor and empress led a royal progress, reminiscent of daimyo processions in earlier generations, from the Europeanized central street of Ginza to Ueno Park for a tightly scripted ceremony formally announcing the constitution to an audience packed with dignitaries from near and far.[32] The public participated mainly by watching in silence along the parade route. The formalities reasserted Ueno's importance as a ritual space displaying the emperor's sovereignty as prescribed in the new constitution. The constitution also guaranteed freedom of religious belief and practice. Ueno Park spatially represented this distinction: the public areas were outer sites of secular political ceremony led by the emperor as chief ritualist; the Kan'eiji temple complex was deep inner space for religious purposes. More portentous for social mobilization was a sizable victory rally held at Ueno on December 9, 1894, to build public support for Japan's forces in the Sino-Japanese War, via speeches and exhibits of artifacts from the front, in a theatrical atmosphere unmatched by previous state events. This gathering was the first official ceremony attended by large numbers of the general public; a second was planned for "after the fall of Beijing," which never fell.[33] Similar hortatory gatherings were convened to stir popular enthusiasm for the much bloodier Russo-Japanese War of 1904–1905. From this point forward Ueno Park and the plaza in front of the Imperial Palace, completed in 1889 and renamed the Palace Outer Garden in 1945, became the chief public ceremonial spaces to link Japan's territorial ambitions on the Asian continent with the ideological and spiritual regulation of its citizens.

Ueno understandably came to be seen not mainly as a park for Tokyo residents but as imperial grounds for displaying a national agenda through periodic commemorations and its many cultural facilities, most of which continue to attract visitors and elicit pride in culture today. The Conder imperial museum was ruined in the great earthquake of 1923, then rebuilt from scratch next to the French neo-Baroque Hyōkeikan, an exhibition gallery conceived in commemoration of the future Taishō emperor's (r. 1912–1926) marriage and completed in 1908. Management of the park was turned over to the city of Tokyo in 1924. A prefectural art museum was ready in 1926 and a science museum five years later, adding to the cultural attractions without diminishing the ceremonial uses of the park, even though by now the space was no longer indispensable for mustering civic patriotism because of the greater sophistication of the government's internal propaganda techniques.

After World War Two a national museum of Western art (1960) and a striking building with concert halls mainly used for Western music (1961) began to give Ueno the flavor of European arts culture advocated many decades earlier by members of the Iwakura embassy. The prefectural art museum was thoroughly refurbished in 1975 and a museum of commoner culture added in 1980, continuing the Japanese government's lengthy history of using such facilities for what Pierre Bourdieu called the self-preservation of social regimes: "art and cultural consumption are predisposed, consciously and deliberately or not, to fulfill a social function of legitimating social differences" and thus contributing to social reproduction.[34] Although Ueno today is far more a people's park than the ceremonial space it often seemed to be before World War Two, even now when imperial family members visit its grounds, the homeless, who form a noticeable part of Ueno's public constituency, are politely but firmly asked to move out of sight—and they readily comply.

Images of the Imperial Capital

When the emperor used Ueno Park in 1889 to inform the world that Japan was now a constitutional monarchy, the capital of his empire was a fast-growing metropolis with big gaps in its physical infrastructure. Nearly four years earlier Nagayo Sensai (1838–1902), chief of the Hygiene Bureau in the Home Ministry, declared that city parks were needed "to nurture the spirits" of the Japanese people "in a healthy manner." If Japan failed to build modern public parks, "it will be increasingly shameful vis-à-vis foreign countries."[35] Nagayo, a medical doctor and member of the Iwakura delegation of 1871–1873, made his case for creating parks by appealing both to patriotism at home (lifting people's spirits) and nationalism abroad (avoiding shame and earning respect in the eyes of other countries), chords consistently sounded by the Meiji government.[36] Nagayo called for better public health as the key to hygienic modernity. He accepted the then-common European and American view that parks served as lungs of the city, and he believed that recreation in fresh air was good for all age groups. Providing more open spaces would not only offer relief from crowded housing but also promote national strength and social stability by helping to curb infectious diseases. The Home Ministry linked school grounds and parks to athletics, encouraging students to play sports; starting in the mid-1880s physical education became a regular part of the national school curriculum.[37] Other advocates pointed out that parks promoted hygiene, exercise, disaster relief as firebreaks and refuge spots, and civic culture—and the police saw advantages in controlling political dissenters by surveilling them in established public spaces.

The powerful Council of Elders, an advisory body to the new cabinet created in 1885, opposed Nagayo's view and instead prioritized armaments, but many other leaders sketched images of an imperial capital with public space appropriate to a modern nation. The economist Taguchi Ukichi (1855–1905) and the industrialist Shibusawa Eiichi (1840–1931) believed Tokyo should develop its harbor like London's to become a first-class commercial city. Instead Yokohama's port was chosen at a fraction of the cost, so planning for Tokyo refocused on its role as a political center, with support from Home Minister Yamagata Aritomo (1838–1922) and Finance Minister Matsukata Masayoshi (1835–1924), both future premiers. Yoshikawa Akimasa (1841–1920), governor of Tokyo and a prime mover of the Tokyo City Improvement Plan of 1888–1889, brokered a compromise that emphasized both politics and commerce, seeking to systematize public space of all sorts along the lines of Haussmann's Paris, as advocated by members of the Iwakura embassy. One result of Yoshikawa's efforts was Hibiya Park, opened in 1903, which differed from all previous public spaces in Japan—including the parks on extraterritorial land established for foreign residents—in being carefully planned by landscape architects familiar with European design principles, so as to advance the state project of spatial modernity befitting an emerging empire.

The cabinet formally established Tokyo City (Tokyoshi), corresponding to the central areas populated since the early Edo era, as fifteen wards within Tokyo Prefecture (Tokyofu) when it enforced a new local government system throughout the country from 1888 to 1890. Three counties in the Tama River district to the west were added to the prefecture in 1893, partly to assure safe water supplies in the wake of a cholera outbreak in 1886. The prefectural population of 1.4 million in the mid-1880s leaped to 2.6 million by the end of Meiji's reign in 1912. Rail lines from Ueno to the northeast starting in 1883 and from Naitō Shinjuku to Hachiōji in the west in 1889 expanded Tokyo's outward reach and swelled the daytime population of the capital with commuters and shoppers.[38] Providing clean water and adequate transit were just two of many problems facing the municipal authorities as they planned Tokyo's future: housing, utilities, schools, roads, shipping, warehousing, sanitation, medical care, and public safety all clamored for attention as the rise of commerce and industry drew rural workers to the urban economy. In light of these urgent needs, public parks might have seemed a low priority, yet they enjoyed a good measure of support in Japan's first stab at urban planning, the Tokyo City Improvement Plan of 1888–1889.

When Governor Yoshikawa sent the Home Ministry a preliminary proposal for improving Tokyo in 1884, he was chiefly concerned with upgrading land and water transport for industry as well as for residents. Although he made no mention of parks, by this point the Home Ministry was deeply committed to promoting parks for reasons of hygiene and social order. Tokyo fire officials regarded parks and schoolyards as key weapons in slowing the spread of structure fires. City police agreed about fire defense but otherwise held conflicting views on whether to encourage building more open spaces for them to patrol. Since 1878 police around the country had restricted outdoor political assemblies; in 1880 the government banned them outright via Regulation No. 9, trying to silence the clamor raised by the Freedom and Popular Rights Movement for broader power sharing by the Meiji government. The Police Bureau of the Home

Ministry added progressively harsher restrictions in 1885 and 1887. Under the 1885 regulations Tokyo police disbanded political gatherings in central substation districts such as Ogawamachi, Kyōbashi, and Atagochō, each of which the Tokyo City Improvement Commission had earmarked for a new public park. Such spaces meant potential trouble to the police because they drew crowds, but if there had to be parks, the police favored placing them near station houses for easy watching.[39] Parks would also give children safe places to play without fear of street accidents.

City planners played a big part in identifying public green space, starting with the first Tokyo City Improvement Commission meetings in 1885. The Japanese hardly lagged behind other countries; at this point city planning was embryonic in Europe and North America, and the term "city planning" itself was apparently first used in 1908 in the United States.[40] Based on investigations of conditions in London, Paris, Berlin, and Vienna, the commission reported in 1885 that "the first reason" for adding parks "relates to hygiene," especially bad air attributable to crowding and industrialization; without parks "it's the same as a house without a garden, a room without a window, a body without lungs."[41] The report also mentioned firebreaks and other practical considerations but paid scant heed to people's need for relaxation, let alone enjoyment. After languishing through several years of financial stringency, the commission—renamed committee—presented its final report to Home Minister Matsukata in 1889.[42] The report addressed the public infrastructure needs of the entire prefecture with special attention to railways, waterworks, sewers, rivers, bridges, and above all roads.[43] Still, acting on the principle that "the improvement of Tokyo is the country's business,"[44] the plan called for a modest 330 hectares of parklands in forty-nine locations, including the original Grand Council parks.

An enabling law in 1888 authorized special taxes for improvements in Tokyo, but the costs of buying land for the forty-two designated locations that were not already public parks were slight because the government already owned nearly 80 percent of the properties. Very few were proposed for temple or shrine precincts, presumably because the best outlying religious lands had by then been put to use for parks or other public purposes. The committee evidently counted on negotiated land purchases to acquire properties not already in government hands; the first instance of outright land expropriation by the government to build public parks did not occur until 1892, to construct Maruyama Park in Kyoto (the official explanation was that "the land is needed for the hygiene of the public").[45] The Tokyo City Improvement Committee projected that real estate and construction outlays to complete the forty-nine parks would total ¥1,670,000 (U.S. $835,000 in 1889 dollars), much of it to create a resplendent European-style park at Hibiya immediately adjacent to the imperial castle.[46]

A Broader Discourse on the Quality of Urban Life

Japan's top-down approach to producing and controlling public space in the Meiji period stirred little enthusiasm among advocates outside the government, mainly because they thought the state was not doing enough to provide parklands for city people who lived close to factories, railways, and other industrial sites. Socialists Abe Isoo and Katayama Sen (1859–1933), the Marxist economist Kawakami Hajime (1879–1946), and fiction writers Kōda Rohan (1867–1947) and Kunikida Doppo (1871–1908) all agitated in word and deed for more open spaces in working-class areas of Japanese cities. Even the novelist and government insider Mori Ōgai, who later became surgeon general of the imperial army, took great interest in urban planning, including public parks. Although partisans such as these had little effect on central or local government actions before the 1923 earthquake and fires, they broke the monopoly of discourse on public space by the Grand Council and Home Ministry and cleared the track for broader civic participation in deciding how city parklands should be used.

It was difficult and no doubt fruitless to argue against building a modern park for central Tokyo, nor did official or private critics outside the Home Ministry mount a serious assault against the Hibiya project despite reservations about the authoritarian high modernism it represented. Indeed, they often shared goals with Tokyo's city planners while wishing to see even more ambitious programs undertaken than those in the Tokyo City Improvement Plan. Yet before the 1890s there was a lack of discursive script about the meanings and purposes of public parks. Most pundits agreed with Nagayo Sensai that adding more public spaces would improve people's moral and spiritual lives as well as their physical well-being, and many shared his collectivist approach to urban problems. In 1897 Mori

Ōgai, who had studied public health in Germany from 1884 to 1888, advocated city planning for Japan to achieve better hygiene, clear slums, and open public parks "where residents can walk" and children can go "for play"[47] in their residential neighborhoods. His chief contribution was to introduce European theories of public health, but like Taguchi Ukichi he thought it vital for Tokyo to improve workers' housing and fire prevention.[48] Kunikida Doppo wrote the short story "Musashino" in 1898 extolling suburban beauty and autumn-leaf viewing as antidotes to ordinary urban life, at a time when railway companies were publishing guidebooks promoting day trips to the countryside and city dwellers were beginning to move to suburbs.[49] Kōda Rohan in 1899 parroted the notion widely accepted in the West that "parks are the lungs of the city" and stressed that "the city government must provide parks" with trees, grass, and bamboo to clean the air so people can avoid disease. "It's regrettable that Tokyo has only two large parks, Ueno and Shiba,"[50] he wrote before Hibiya was constructed; he suggested building a park in each of the city's fifteen wards as part of the solution to the capital's many social problems.[51]

Katayama Sen publicized the social functions of British and American city parks gleaned from his studies of urban reform during seven years abroad. "Parks are necessary for city life—not just for beautification but also for residents' health," he wrote in *Toshi shakaigaku* (Urban sociology, 1903). "Parks are places of entertainment for the urban poor and thus safety valves for the city. Whether there are parks has a direct bearing on citizens' public health" by providing clean air, as seen in New York City's public spaces.[52] He backed the Tokyo City Improvement Plan to provide small parks near schools, since few then had playgrounds, but called for far more of them than the improvement plan sought. Katayama also cited aesthetic and emulative reasons for building public parks: "The goal of city parks is to please the senses of urban dwellers. A civilized city [like London] not only has many parks but also provides facilities within them to satisfy citizens' five senses."[53]

Katayama's reformist inclinations focused on poverty and extended to improvements in housing, transportation, water supply and sewerage, utilities, education, finance, and markets—as broad a compass as any advocate of urban betterment in Meiji Japan. He criticized the rich for hogging their large gardens, believing that justice called for sharing such

Shiba Park in central Tokyo is one of the five original Grand Council parks established in 1873. Abutting the park is this outbuilding of the Zōjōji temple complex, to which the park was attached before state and religion were constitutionally separated in 1947.

spaces with the public, and later he wrote of both Hibiya Park and Shinobazu Pond at Ueno as "guestrooms for the poor," places for enjoyment and self-cultivation, including music.[54]

Abe Isoo, another socialist and Christian, studied from 1891 to 1895 in Hartford, London, and Berlin, where he learned about city problems firsthand. He returned to Japan and sought to help the urban poor by attacking land monopolization and high real estate prices. In *Ōyō shiseiron* (Practical city government, 1908) he also denounced air and water pollution resulting from industrialization and agreed with Katayama that widely distributed public parks, which "don't necessarily have to be all that large,"[55] were required to improve workers' health. This book was the first to introduce the American urban park system, such as Olmsted's Emerald Necklace in Boston, to Japanese city planners. Abe proposed selling portions of large public parks and using the proceeds to build more small ones, supplemented by special budget appropriations and taxes. Many of his ideas were ignored given the fiscal constraints ensuing from the recent war against Russia that he had vociferously opposed, but Waseda University further promoted his views by publishing Abe's *Toshi mondai* (Urban problems) in 1910.

"The three goals for city parks," according to *Toshi mondai*, "are hygiene, pleasure, and beautification"—none of which conflicted with the high modernist policies of the Home Ministry or Tokyo City authorities. What was different was that "as much as possible the city's finances should broaden and perfect these goals"[56] via taxes, land sales, and special appropriations. "With the great expansion of urban populations, open spaces have gradually shrunk, so we need to establish a number of public parks. Parks should not be provided simply to adorn the city; their first purpose should be public hygiene."[57] He ranked parks with clean water, adequate sewerage, hospitals, and disinfectants as good social investments to protect public health.[58] Even more than Katayama, Abe perceived a class bias in Tokyo's current policies on open space. Big parks, he noted, were fine for civic beautification, but "the people who most need small parks are not the upper social echelons but the lower-class poor."[59] Abe scorned the former daimyo gardens recently opened as public parks and saw far more utility in building children's playgrounds and playing fields for his favorite sport, baseball.

These voices from outside official policy chambers were heard, and sometimes heeded, by city planners in and out of government during the early twentieth century. But bureaucrats widely regarded parks as essential to social education and civic culture, desiderata of the Home Ministry's program of social management that were at great variance with Abe's and Katayama's class-based analyses of contemporary urban problems.[60] The production of public space during the Meiji period was mainly the province of the Home Ministry, but the national authorities by no means had exclusive control over the debate about where best to locate city parks, what goals they should meet, or how they should be used. If there was a uniform discourse about public parklands, it could be found in the planning and construction of Hibiya Park, yet conflicting meanings swirled around this facility once it opened in 1903.

Whose Hibiya?

Originally a fishing village fronting on tidal wetlands, Hibiya was home to major daimyo residences in the Edo period because it abutted the shogun's castle. In 1868 the new government seized the area and stationed troops there after 1871 to guard the emperor and organs of state. A park in the Western style was envisioned for Hibiya in the Tokyo City Improvement Plan of 1889. The army gave up the site in stages between 1892 and 1896 in favor of a parade ground and equestrian stables in Kita Aoyama, now a part of the Meiji Shrine Outer Garden. To the east across the street from the future Hibiya Park was Yamashitachō, where the two-story brick Rokumeikan, designed by Josiah Conder, opened in 1883 for official dance parties and other social events attended by elite Japanese and foreigners. Part of a "spatial practice in which the debates about Japanese modernity were elaborated in architecture,"[61] Rokumeikan (Deer Cry Pavilion) soon lost favor and became Kazoku Kaikan (Peers' Club) in 1890. Yet critics such as Isoda Kōichi have called Hibiya Park, which opened in 1903, a romanticized reimaging of the bygone Rokumeikan era two decades earlier, retroactively evoking a "Rokumeikan culture" perhaps more powerful, and more permanent, in nostalgia than the original.[62]

The models touted by members of the Iwakura embassy and other travelers abroad were the great urban parks of Europe and the United States, but the Hibiya grounds were less than one third the size of Ueno Park and barely 4 percent of New York's Central Park.[63] The challenge facing Hibiya's designers was to fulfill the government's civilizing intent by creating a park, not merely a garden, in the relatively confined space of sixteen hectares by observing up-to-date design principles for the larger Western-style portion while gracefully juxtaposing a smaller Japanese-style section. The eventual plan was prepared by Honda Seiroku (1866–1952), a professor of forestry and landscape gardening at Tokyo Imperial University who later became a powerful advocate of establishing national parks in Japan.[64]

Honda's grand design called for an outlay of ¥380,000; the final approved budget was barely ¥175,000, forcing him to scale mature trees down to small seedlings collected from the surplus at the university.[65] Including site preparation, overruns, and add-ons, the total cost of the park through 1905 approached ¥300,000.[66]

In conception the park was *bentō* box-lunch style, with one quadrant devoted to a Japanese garden and the other three to a mixture of French formalism and German naturalism, the latter aspect thick with native trees that gave the entire grounds a distinctly local feeling from the start. Also included were a Western-style restaurant and a pavilion for performing Western music. Paths for carriages and walkers, gas and electric lighting, benches, a running track, and playground equipment collectively resembled facilities in Hibiya's most modern counterparts abroad. The German-style open lawn gave immediate, if unintended, salience to the park as a

Hibiya Park today. The crane fountains in Unkei Pond lost their pedestals to scrap metal collection during World War Two. Most of the park, including this fenced lawn, reflects German design principles.

gathering spot for great crowds and soon signified Hibiya's indispensable role as a forum for popular protest—and periodic riots.[67]

Despite its aims to civilize and provide moral uplift for the public by requiring "virtuous conduct," the park drew criticism from fearful citizens even before it opened. Because it originally lacked gates for closing the park at night, some claimed that the Japanese pond might become the latest popular spot for suicide by drowning (it did not). Others worried that trees or flowers might be stolen.[68] Even though Hibiya from the start was one of Japan's most tightly regulated public spaces, couples soon discovered the more secluded parts of the park under the shroud of darkness, despite occasional crackdowns by the police. The authorities posted signs at the six entrances to the park encouraging conduct befitting a modern public facility in the West. Forbidden were freight trucks, empty jinrikishas and horse-drawn carriages, advertising signs, street performers, unlicensed merchants, inappropriate dress, and civil disturbances—virtually everything that characterized the lively commoner-oriented Asakusa Park across town.

Ostensibly managed by the city of Tokyo, Hibiya functioned as a state park on important occasions from its inception until the end of World War Two. It also proved immensely popular with the public, opening with a roar of approval in both the park and the press: The *Tokyo nichi nichi* reported that on June 1, 1903, "there were so many people waiting outside the gates that when the park actually opened there was no room to walk around."[69] Two years later the bandstand was inaugurated with a bravura program of operatic selections by Gounod and Wagner, a Strauss waltz, Rossini's *William Tell* overture, a Sousa march, and Japanese military music.[70] At first Hibiya attracted a good number of unruly locals, but soon the state's social controls took effect and the park became a highlight for visitors to the capital.[71] An anonymous silkscreen print from 1911 showed that the well-to-do dressed up to go to the park, as was once true at Central Park in New York. A springtime photograph of the north gate taken a few years later showed children in ordinary play clothes and women in kimonos holding parasols, all wearing clogs against the mud.[72]

A few socialist critics called for relaxing the rules of behavior to make Hibiya friendlier to ordinary citizens, so that it would be a truly public park rather than a government park. The June 18, 1903, issue of *Shakaishugi*

(Socialism) approved of the new facility because it was unconnected to a temple or shrine, but it complained that the entrance across from the Imperial Hotel, where foreign guests often stayed, symbolized Hibiya's orientation to business and state interests. Writing in *Shūkan heimin shinbun* (Weekly commoners' news) in July 1904, a socialist critic said "the iron fence around Hibiya Park creates the impression that it's private property." The presence of the hotel, Peers' Club, and courthouse nearby "does not create good feelings toward the park."[73] Socialists hoped that Hibiya would become a people's park open to all citizens and no longer a venue for official ceremonies, closed to unwanted visitors on such occasions for six hours at a time.[74] Their hopes were fully realized only after World War Two.

Clearly the government was well satisfied with its park, organizing or sanctioning twenty-two public events there in 1904 and 1905, many of which spilled over into the Imperial Palace plaza to the north. The largest state ceremony was a gathering of 100,000 persons on May 8, 1904, to support Japanese forces in the Russo-Japanese War, followed by rallies the next year to celebrate Japan's surprising victory. Ozaki Yukio (1859–1954), mayor of Tokyo, who later became a famous liberal parliamentarian and government critic, read proclamations congratulating the state and army.[75] These events were far more open to the general public than most earlier imperial ceremonies at Ueno, and they often were designed to muster popular backing for government policies in Japan's new age of parliamentary representation beginning in 1890.

With Hibiya, Japan's parks gave a new definition to the term "public," as citizen-subjects voluntarily mobilized en masse in support of state projects, paralleling the obligatory exposure of young men to the military draft, the Education Rescript of 1890 that established the duties of individuals to the nation, a shrine merger program from 1906 to 1912 to tighten government controls over localities, and new state-mandated ethics texts in the schools. The large turnouts in parks on official occasions also foreshadowed the guided participatory democracy for adult males associated with the Taishō emperor's reign, from 1912 to 1926. It is an irony of East Asian diplomatic history that Hibiya hosted a rally in May 1919 to celebrate the Versailles Treaty concluding World War One, whereas in Beijing and Shanghai patriotic Chinese demonstrated in huge numbers on May 4 of that year partly to protest the treaty's favorable treatment of Japan. Hibiya was also used for well-attended public funerals for the politician Inoue Kaoru (1836–1915), Prince Ōyama Iwao (1842–1916), and prime ministers Ōkuma Shigenobu and Yamagata Aritomo, both in 1922.[76]

But Hibiya Park soon provided a second new meaning of "public" arising from the politicization of public spaces. Shortly after noon on September 5, 1905, with temperatures reaching 35.5 degrees C (96 degrees F), protestors led by antigovernment lawyers, journalists, and politicians assembled in defiance of an official ban to denounce what they regarded as the humiliating terms of the Portsmouth Treaty, set to be signed later that day, ending the Russo-Japanese War. Thirty thousand demonstrators gathered there to demand that the imperial army continue the fight until Russia was crushed. Police eventually managed to clear the park, but individuals fanned out to burn streetcars, police boxes, government buildings, newspaper offices, and Christian churches throughout the city. More than a thousand persons suffered injuries, half of them police, fire, or military personnel, and seventeen demonstrators perished in the incident, which ended in heavy rain the following day.[77]

From that point forward parks throughout Japan became occasional venues for popular rallies, some of them antigovernment, often skirting the Police Peace Law of 1900 that regulated public conduct. During Japan's "era of popular violence" from the Hibiya riot of 1905 through the Rice Riot of 1918, six major and three minor demonstrations occurred in Tokyo, most of them originating at Hibiya Park. Andrew Gordon points out that the rioters "had a uniquely heterogeneous social base and voiced a distinctive ideology of populist nationalism."[78] Despite the government's earlier fears, socialists had little role in the tumult; instead chauvinistic nationalists opportunistically used the occasion to launch imperial democracy. Thus, even though Hibiya and some other parks continued to serve state interests between 1905 and the late 1920s by advancing national unity through official rites,[79] these public spaces also became regular sites of contestation and negotiation between state and nonstate actors—neither just safety valves for venting public passions nor mere locales for undisciplined mob actions aimed at wresting control of these spaces from the authorities. Elements of each were present in subsequent instances of representation for many decades thereafter; every demonstration or rally took on its own distinct colorations and conveyed multiple meanings that defied simple dichotomies.

People used parks in the Taishō period to speak out against the rise in train fares and rice prices, rally workers to join the labor movement, vent anti-Chinese sentiments during the early Republican period in that country, support universal male suffrage, and oppose behind-the-scenes politicking.[80] Popular movements in the early 1920s, particularly those seeking the vote for all adult males, used public spaces such as Hibiya to a degree unimagined by planners two decades earlier—Maeda Ai's "productions in space" to complement Lefebvre's production of space.[81] Naturally the more the police enforced the Police Peace Law of 1900 or its successor, the Peace Preservation Act of 1925, the more each demonstration drew media attention and took on an importance not fully anticipated by the authorities, and often by protestors themselves.

With the Palace Outer Garden closed to large gatherings once Japan regained autonomy in April 1952, Hibiya was chosen for even more rallies in the postoccupation period, at last free from the gaze of the Americans as well as that of the prewar Special Higher Police (Tokkō), a paramilitary force established in 1911 that enforced the Peace Preservation Act to squelch dissenters until 1945. New constitutional rights of assembly, speech, and labor organization made it easier to hold annual May Day gatherings, occasional protests against the Japan-U.S. Mutual Security Treaty, and fervent outcries against Japan's support for American military action in Southeast Asia from 1965 to 1973—the demonstrators now protected as well as inspected by the metropolitan police.[82] As a window on society, Hibiya shows that public concerns have shifted recently from foreign policy to how humans and the nonhuman shape each other; Tokyo Fantasia 2007, held there in late December, was part of an ecoproject to illuminate a forty-two-meter tree-shaped construction topped by a star, with lighting powered by biodiesel fuel that emitted no carbon dioxide and received a green-energy certificate.[83] Hibiya was rarely used for state ceremonies after World War Two—the Shōwa emperor's funeral was held instead at Shinjuku Imperial Garden during heavy rains in February 1989—and is now more than ever a people's park, with multiple horizons of meaning in Lefebvre's terms,[84] seldom in outright defiance of the state but usually in dynamic tension with it through negotiation and compromise.

Incremental Parkland Growth

As Tokyo prepared to inaugurate Hibiya Park in 1903, for budget reasons the city scaled back the number of urban parks projected in the 1888–1889 City Improvement Plan from forty-nine to twenty-two, of which fifteen were completed by 1907. Five years later city maps showed all twenty-two without indicating whether they were actually in use;[85] Tokyo could not afford more than slight increments because most of the required lands were in private hands. Land use data for 1915 show that 1.5 percent of the city was devoted to parks and other green spaces, 3.5 percent to residences for the imperial family, and 6 percent to cemeteries, temples, and shrines.[86] Temples and shrines had accounted for about 15 percent of the capital in the late Edo period, so the combined green areas as of World War One—just 11 percent of the modern city—had not kept pace with urban growth.

In other regions of Japan, city parks began with the Grand Council directive of 1873 and later stretched the understanding of "urban" to include certain landscapes that eventually were upgraded to national, quasi-national, or prefectural natural parks.[87] When members of the imperial family visited localities throughout the country, state-owned lands frequently were turned into small community parks to commemorate the occasion; wars likewise sometimes called for celebration when local leaders negotiated leases or gifts of government properties for memorial parks or stone monuments to honor the war dead. In these ways smaller cities benefited from new facilities whose character was closely identified with imperial power.[88]

The greatest commemorative project of the era took place in the heart of Tokyo in several stages between 1915 and 1926 with construction of the Meiji Shrine and nearby Outer Garden, a spatial division suggesting the inner and outer precincts at Ise, where the Shinto sun goddess Amaterasu is enshrined. A year after the emperor died in 1912, the Diet approved building a seventy-three-hectare shrine to Meiji's memory on public land directly west of today's Harajuku Station. At the same time, the Kita Aoyama military base two kilometers to the east, site of Meiji's state funeral, was renamed the Meiji Shrine Outer Garden and earmarked for public use as an outdoor recreation park on forty-eight hectares. To link the shrine and garden, a broad avenue, thirty-six meters wide and lined with cherries, was completed with pedestrian walkways and a bridle path in 1920.[89] Known as Omote Sandō, the street remains a constantly changing gallery of commercial architectural styles; its throngs and allure resemble those in the Nakamise shopping district outside Asakusa's Sensōji temple, but at loftier levels of taste and cachet.

One of Tokyo's must-see attractions ever since its sanctification in 1920, the Meiji Shrine grounds contain a garden once belonging to the villa

Tokyo's Meiji Shrine opened in 1920 with a great torii gateway of cypress from Japan's Taiwan colony.

of Katō Kiyomasa (1562–1611), a general in Hideyoshi's 1597 campaign in Korea. The garden was redesigned starting in 1917 by Honda Seiroku, Uehara Keiji (1889–1981), and others; it became famous for its beds of iris on display each June. The shrine and garden were soon surrounded by nearly 100,000 transplanted mature trees donated by communities all over the country to augment the existing trees, creating the illusion of a "natural" primeval forest.[90] Reflecting the imperial symbolism of this shrine, the two great torii gateways to the complex were erected using ancient cypress from Japan's colony in Taiwan. Today more than 160,000 trees of 365 different species populate the grounds, offering the atmosphere of a deep forest in the midst of the metropolis.[91] The mood is broken, however, each New Year's season when the shrine counts upwards of three million visitors.[92]

The Outer Garden is Tokyo's athletic venue par excellence, containing the National Stadium where the 1964 Olympics were based, a pool, Jingū Baseball Stadium, playing fields, a rugby ground, sumo ring, tennis courts, and ice rink. Next door in Meiji Park, a Tokyo-owned space, is

The Meiji Shrine Outer Garden, dating to 1926, features four rows of ginkgos leading to the Meiji Memorial Picture Gallery. This park is the city's premier athletic venue.

the Metropolitan Gymnasium. When the Outer Garden was completed in 1926, the main spatial focus of Honda Seiroku's design was the Meiji Memorial Picture Gallery, set nearly four hundred meters down a ginkgo-lined road from busy Aoyama Dōri (Route 246). The landscape architect Orishimo Yoshinobu (1881–1966) borrowed Western trompe l'oeil techniques, planting the trees in descending heights to make the gallery seem more distant than it was.[93] Despite its association with the imperial family and the high modernist approach of city planners in the 1920s, the Outer Garden today is a people's park for athletics, both active and spectator, and also the site of protests such as the October 2008 gathering of more than five thousand demonstrators calling for an end to poverty and unpaid overtime.[94]

The great expansion of Japan's industrial economy during World War One further increased the number of urban residents and made a shambles of Tokyo's city planning regulations from 1889. The first modern census in 1920 revealed that the city of Tokyo had swollen to 2,173,000 persons, with another 1,527,000 in the eighty-two towns and villages outside the city limits.[95] Infrastructure to support this great population became more and more inadequate. Other expanding metropolitan areas such as Osaka instituted planning rules of their own in 1917 and 1918. Seki Hajime (1873–1935), a professor at Hitotsubashi University in Tokyo, in 1913 became the first specialist in Japan to use the now-standard term *toshi keikaku* to mean "city planning."[96] The following year Seki became deputy mayor of Osaka and in 1923 was chosen as mayor. Seki steadfastly believed that city planning was a countrywide question and urged the Home Ministry to heed problems of population growth, housing, and infrastructure in Japan's major industrial centers. He took bold steps at the local level, often without fully consulting central government officials, to address the need for planning on Osaka's fringes. He was much concerned with social welfare and sought to rid the metropolis of slums by moving workers to garden suburbs, somewhat like those championed in Britain by Ebenezer Howard (1850–1928). But Seki criticized Howard's version of the garden city as too favorable to land developers,[97] and even Seki's variant was eventually thwarted by national officials and their real estate allies. The same was true in the capital. Starting in 1918 the Den'entoshi Company (later Tōkyū) built suburban housing southwest of Tokyo, joined after the 1923 earthquake and fire by the Tsutsumi family's Hakone-Kokudo-Seibu enterprises in the western and northwestern suburbs. Neither of these giant railway, retailing, and housing corporations produced Howard-like garden cities; in both Tokyo and Osaka, according to one city planning expert, the garden city was much discussed but little implemented, "used only as a slogan for land development by private developers."[98]

In order to update and systematize how the largest cities controlled their growth, the Diet passed the first national City Planning Law in 1919, legislation that largely remained in place for nearly half a century.[99] The City Planning Law in some respects proved to be a top-down exercise in spatial determinism by overly structuring and centralizing the approval process for urban improvements, starting with Tokyo, Yokohama, Nagoya, Kyoto, Osaka, and Kobe. The need to update urban areas was growing acute: in 1912 Japan counted about 15,000 factories; by 1922 the number had grown to 87,000.[100] The City Planning Law mandated that localities establish city planning districts and finance most of the improvements, but it also required them to obtain approvals for their major projects from municipal boards, the Home Ministry, and the cabinet.[101] These stifling conditions remained in effect with only minor changes until a new City Planning Law was enacted in 1968.[102]

In the hands of Home Ministry bureaucrats and their municipal counterparts, the City Planning Law became an auxiliary instrument of social management during the Red Scare and labor unrest that followed World War One. In a pamphlet published just months before the September 1923 earthquake and fires, the Tokyo Parks Department extolled the health, leisure, and aesthetic benefits of green spaces, as well as their educational advantages "for city children who live far from the natural world."[103] Tellingly, the document also called urban parks "places for public harmony" that provide training for social life: "they not only serve as a classroom for guiding people's educational thinking but also serve as automatic safety valves for contemporary society."[104] Apart from such proponents of public moral uplift, the constituency for city planning was mostly limited to local officials faced with inadequate infrastructure and to manufacturers eager to separate their factories from workers' housing so as to minimize complaints about poor conditions.[105] Even though the reach of the City Planning Law was extended in phases to every city and many towns and villages by 1933, the six largest cities were the chief targets; as of 1930 only twenty-one others had adopted zoning plans, presumably because of the attendant red tape, cost, and oversight from the metropole.[106]

The law explicitly recognized the need for more urban parklands by requiring municipalities to reserve 3 percent of the area in city planning districts for parks and scenic landscapes. Scenic landscapes were pleasant places long enjoyed by local residents and needed few if any improvements, so it is no surprise that by 1980 officials had recognized 732 of them in 215 cities.[107] Parks were another matter entirely; surveys carried out by the Home Ministry in 1919 and 1921 showed that, apart from Tokyo, almost no cities regarded parks as modern facilities. Many localities used old-style amusement districts, castle ruins, or temple and shrine grounds for patriotic ceremonies without investing in Western-style spaces modeled after Hibiya.[108]

Cemeteries formed another key component of green space design beginning in the early 1920s. Tokyo's planning, now driven by Gotō Shinpei (1857–1929) as mayor, took advantage of the City Planning Law to obtain one million yen in 1921 from the Home Ministry, which Gotō had headed

Tama Cemetery, founded in 1921 in Tokyo's western suburbs.

from 1916 to 1918, to purchase extensive lands to establish Tama Cemetery in suburban Fuchū.[109] The largest metropolitan cemetery in Tokyo, this graveyard now covers 128 hectares of lawns, trees, and shrubs and holds the remains of hundreds of notable persons, as does its immediate ancestor, Zōshigaya Cemetery in northwestern Tokyo, dating to 1874.[110] Most potentially contentious, although currently subdued, is Chidorigafuchi National Cemetery overlooking the Imperial Palace moat in central Tokyo. This quiet spot of repose contains the remains of more than 350,000 unidentified Japanese civilians and military personnel from World War Two.[111] Proposals to relocate the spirits of war dead from the nearby Yasukuni Shrine, which holds no remains, to Chidorigafuchi so as to defuse historical controversies swirling around the shrine have thus far gained little traction.

The City Planning Law fell far short of controlling urban growth, and its chief legacy for park development was confined to a few areas within the biggest cities. By one reckoning, as of 1910 Japan operated 288 city parks, a figure that rose to 406 by 1920.[112] For want of funds and initiative, very few of the 406 were newly built to the modern standards sought by Mori Ōgai, Abe Isoo, Katayama Sen, or Gotō Shinpei. For all its efforts at civic improvement since 1888, the city of Tokyo on the eve of the 1923 earthquake and fires counted only twenty-nine parks, most of them small and few of them up to date, for a population well above two million; at that point Osaka City had fifteen, nearly all measuring less than one hectare.[113] These numbers represented a very modest achievement for the project of building modern urban parks that began in earnest with Tokyo civic improvements in the mid-1880s. Not until the Kanto earthquake and fires did city parks gain the systematic attention their proponents had sought for nearly four decades. At the same time, urban parklands now had to compete for attention and funds with a growing movement in the Diet to designate national parks in some of Japan's most treasured scenery in the mountains and at the shore. The national park clamor, the earthquake and fires, and eventually World War Two all cast long shadows over the effort to provide a well-developed modern park system for Japan's cities, delaying it until deep into the post–World War Two era. The next chapters take up each of these developments in turn.

CHAPTER 2

National Parks for Wealth,
Health, and Empire

The national park as an idea in Japan traces to the 1870s, initially without the backing of government that city parks received. While the authorities were busy creating public space in the form of urban parklands—a few of them tantamount to nation's parks—elites outside the ruling group adapted another mode of spatial modernity from Western models: the concept of national spaces mapped as public parks in the mountains and at the seaside. Both these modes of public land management reinscribed human beings' interactions with their nonhuman surroundings; in the twentieth century urban and national parks sometimes competed for resources but more often complemented each other in function and impact. Despite their differences in scale, finances, and environmental context, it is significant that since 1873 the Japanese government, recognizing their many similarities, has consistently labeled both urban and national parks as *kōen* (public parks).

Imagining National Spaces

Like many peoples, Japanese in premodern times felt strong local identities but had a much weaker consciousness of the country as a whole. Individuals identified with the crossroads shrine, the village, and perhaps the feudal domain—the realm of personal experience—but seldom with the entire homeland unless they were high-born and learned. The same was true of villagers' consciousness of the nonhuman environment; intensely familiar with local geography, weather patterns, plants, and animals, they were only dimly aware of far-off geophysical features such as Mount Fuji, Nachi Falls, or the scenic vistas extolled by poets. Travel guides published in the Edo period began to expand the geographical horizons of those who could read them, mainly for religious pilgrimages, but life for most was routinely confined to the home region, celebrated in the variety of ballads and work songs unique to localities throughout the country.

When Japan encountered industrial modernity in the later nineteenth century, ingenuity and effort were required to stir an awareness of national spaces among people securely rooted in loyalties to hometowns. A unified central state, rapid industrialization and urbanization, common obligations of schooling, taxes, and conscription, and the rise of mass transit and media created shared experiences for new generations of citizen-subjects, but even in big cities spatial identities remained surprisingly localized, confined to residence, workplace, and perhaps nearby park—and to rural hometown in memory or imagination. To conceptualize a national park or national forest required psychic mobility away from one's immediate sensate environment to an abstraction, the larger ecosystem of the country as a whole.

The seeds of the national park idea came to Japan from abroad but sprouted in the Meiji period in ways more indigenous than was true of the modern Japanese urban park. The wish to simulate a Western spatial practice partly prompted the early national park movement in the 1870s, but for many of its champions the purpose was less to civilize the public or showcase Japan's modernity to the world than to affirm the distinctiveness of the land and its people. Geographers, botanists, and vocal devotees of the new sport of mountain climbing provided ideological underpinnings for this affirmation starting in the 1890s. These partisans sought to protect and promote "Japan's natural landscape" so as "to continue improving Japanese culture in the future,"[1] thus establishing clear difference, as they saw it, from the vast new national parks being opened in the United States.

Although they developed no concrete proposals and signed no petitions, key scientists laid the intellectual groundwork for Japan's national parks through their studies of geography and ecology. Uchimura Kanzō (1861–1930), famous as a nondenominational Christian, was also a fisheries scientist, teacher, and journalist who publicized the geographic thought of Alexander von Humboldt (1769–1859) and Karl Ritter (1779–1859) in *Chirigakukō* (Geography, 1894).[2] Nine years later Makiguchi Tsunesaburō (1871–1944), the future founder of the lay Buddhist movement Sōka Gakkai (Value Creation Society, est. 1930), came out with a 995-page compendium titled *Jinsei chirigaku* (Human geography, 1903), edited and annotated by his friend Shiga Shigetaka from an original manuscript of two thousand pages.[3] This volume focused mainly on local geographical features and contained fewer insights from abroad than either Uchimura's or Shiga's writings, although Makiguchi emphasized the importance of maintaining forests near cities.[4] He wrote about local communities and the value humans placed on them; he criticized the state for its emphasis on cult gods connected to the emperor, a viewpoint he shared with the folklorist Yanagita Kunio (1875–1962).[5] No link can be discerned between the geographical writings of either Uchimura or Makiguchi and their later careers as religious leaders, nor were their outlooks on Japan's physical environment especially concordant. Through their teaching and writing, each provided a new generation of Japanese with perspectives on their nonhuman surroundings, particularly Japan's terrestrial inheritance.

Also opposed to the government's tightening grip on localities and their geographical features was the biologist and folklorist Minakata Kumagusu (1867–1941), who tirelessly resisted the Home Ministry's shrine merger program of 1906–1912. Minakata worried that the trees surrounding former shrines would be felled for lumber or fuel, as eventually many were; he pointed out that forest fragmentation harmed birds, increased insects, and disposed farmers to use insecticides that ran off into the sea and harmed fish and those who ate them. He is thought to have introduced the term "ecology" to Japan in a protest letter dated November 19, 1911.[6]

The best-known Meiji-era scientist to develop the idea of national space, in contrast to the local distinctiveness favored by Makiguchi, Minakata, and Yanagita, was the geographer Shiga Shigetaka. Shiga traveled to the South Pacific, where he witnessed the miseries colonialism inflicted on subaltern peoples and grew determined to help Japan remain independent amid the struggle of powerful nations to dominate East Asia.[7] In some respects his *Nihon fūkeiron* (Japanese landscapes, 1894) indulged in bioregionalism, celebrating the distinctive features of the Japanese islands and romantically judging them superior to, not just different from, those in the West—what David Harvey calls a "green theory of value" driven by national identity.[8] Shiga was the first scientist to grasp Japan in its entirety from the country's geophysical infrastructure of mountains, oceans, rivers, valleys, and meteorology, not just from its superstructure as a political space defined by the government. Because of his wide travels, he understood how his scholarship as a physical geographer might connect with Japan's colonial policies, but he was far more interested in national distinctiveness than in state imperialism.[9]

To be sure, Shiga emphasized the aesthetic beauties of Japan's landscapes, but unlike most poets and painters he did so from scientific evidence and historical fact. Many critics have discerned a nationalist or even imperialist message in *Nihon fūkeiron,* noting its contribution to national essence discourses then in vogue,[10] but others are properly cautious about overreading Shiga.[11] This hugely popular book was reprinted fifteen times within eight years and helped foster a consciousness of Japan as a whole. In the same way that the Meiji state produced public space by proclaiming city parks, Shiga's systematic geographical descriptions helped the public see the entire archipelago as a picturesque landscape evoking pride, one that was better than scenery in other countries not merely because it was Japan's but also because it was, he declared, superior in scientific fact.

Although Shiga did not directly engage the nascent movement to authorize national parks in the 1890s, he favored conservation for anthropocentric reasons: to protect Japan's distinctive beauty for human appreciation, not to preserve the nonhuman for its own sake. Enjoying the outdoors, he said, would help the traveler grow fond of the terrain and recognize qualities about it that Shiga assured were not found in other countries.[12] A signal way to become aware of Japan's scenery, he believed, was the new sport of mountaineering—even though Shiga himself was not much of a climber. His descriptions of Japanese mountains were drawn mainly from the 1891 edition of Basil H. Chamberlain and W. B. Mason's *Handbook for Travellers in Japan,* making him an "armchair alpinist."[13] Shiga and his follower, the young banker Kojima Usui (1873–1948), lauded climbing amid the grandeur of mountain-filled landscapes as a vigorous group endeavor for scientifically minded moderns—a metaphor for an up-to-date Japan competing for acceptance in the comity of nations.[14]

Unlike famous vistas long revered because they evoked nostalgia for the past, the Japanese people, Shiga believed, should understand mountains and other aspects of Japan's superb topography as key elements of modernity and national exceptionalism in an age beset with international rivalries. Although Shiga was clearly a patriot, he was well-traveled abroad and international in outlook. Nonetheless, in the early twentieth century "geography was pressed into the service of the political, economic, and military elite as a means of fostering legal subjects of the state—rather than good citizens."[15] This was an outcome very different from the groundwork of ideas about the ecosystem laid by Uchimura Kanzō, Makiguchi Tsunesaburō, Minakata Kumagusu, Yanagita Kunio, Shiga Shigetaka, and many other late Meiji scientists and writers. Ever since Shiga, mountains in Japan have been a synecdoche for the nonhuman in general and, since their inception in 1931, for national parks in particular. To visit a national park, most Japanese assume, is to tour mountains, hike in the woods, and enjoy noodles topped with mountain vegetables—even though Japan also boasts impressive parklands at the shore and on islands and peninsulas far from the country's most spectacular mountain ranges.

Petitions for National Parks

One of the progenitors of Japan's national parks, the bureaucrat and landscape designer Tamura Tsuyoshi (1890–1979), credited the Meiji peer and future justice minister Okabe Nagamoto (1855–1925) with introducing the concept of the national park after visiting Yellowstone (est. 1872) during his stay in the United States from 1875 to 1882.[16] The earliest concrete discussions of a national park for Japan emanated in the late 1870s from Nikkō, a town in rugged mountains 120 kilometers north of Tokyo best known for its Tōshōgū Shrine, completed in 1636 to honor the memory of Tokugawa Ieyasu (1542–1616, r. 1603–1605). A Diet petition to authorize "grand state parks" in 1911 was the apex of a local movement originating at Nikkō, prompted in part by Okabe's reports about Yellowstone. Nikkō residents sought a "great imperial park" for their region, largely to regulate the steady growth of tourism at the shrines, temples, lake, waterfall, and uplands in the area.[17]

At the same time Hakone, only half as far from Tokyo as Nikkō, was growing into a tourist destination in the late 1870s in the hands of private land developers. In 1901 Kanagawa prefectural officials discussed turning the area into a "world park" for international tourists. Four years later Iwasaki Yanosuke (1851–1908), chief of the Mitsubishi enterprises, began agitating to establish Hakone as a national park, both to protect its environment and to draw foreign tourists.[18] Nearby Mount Fuji was discussed as a possible national park as well, but mainly for reasons of national pride, not emulation of the foreign. The statist implications of the national park concept became clear to Japanese during the Russo-Japanese War of 1904–1905; they had not been clear when Nikkō's leaders spoke of an imperial park in 1887. Advocates in and out of government believed that national parks would not only confer a distinct national identity at home but also project imperial power abroad by creating parks in the colonies.[19] The forthright Buddhist scholar Anesaki Masaharu (1873–1949), for example, called for "the establishment of national parks from an ultra-nationalistic viewpoint."[20] In this view, to adapt the American national park meant not merely recalibrating to the smaller scale and distinctive terrain of Japan; it also meant identifying indigenous scenic characteristics of the sublime, as Shiga had argued, in order to persuade and reassure Japanese that their physical environment surpassed that of other countries.

Business opportunities were an equally powerful engine of the national park movement in Japan. Kinoshita Yoshio (1874–1923), a railway specialist in the Communications Ministry, proposed creating national parks with the expected Russian compensation payments, which never came, after Japan's military victory in 1905. Kinoshita wanted to promote tourism to earn foreign exchange in the new age of international rail travel symbolized by the just-completed Trans-Siberian Railway. He sought to market Japan's scenic beauties to foreigners by establishing national parks—thus profiting the government railways, the tourist industry, and Japan's foreign exchange.[21] The marketing opportunities for this growing network would burgeon, Kinoshita recognized, if national parks were created to lure tourists, especially from overseas, now that European and American travel agents were publicizing round-the-world trips for the wealthy.[22] Through his ties to Gotō Shinpei, who headed the Postal Ministry from 1908 to 1911, Kinoshita was asked to testify to a House of Representatives committee in the Diet about national park management when lawmakers were considering the February 1911 petition to designate Nikkō as a park.[23] He backed the proposal largely on economic grounds, adding Fuji and the Seto Inland Sea to the list of potential parklands. Kinoshita also helped form the Japan Tourist Bureau in 1912 to promote travel to Japan by international visitors, whose spending would help lift the country out of recession following the costly military victory over Russia.[24]

Diet members in 1911 who favored parks for Nikkō, Hakone, and Mount Fuji spoke most often of protecting old religious properties, especially at Nikkō, and developing international tourism at all three. Park supporters cited preserving beautiful scenery and also improving people's health, one of the few expressed motives they shared with proponents of city parks. The lower-house committee endorsed national parks in principle, with particular sentiment for Mount Fuji; the cabinet formalized its approval on March 11, 1911, without any plan or appropriation to implement the parks. More petitions asking the government to actualize

Mount Nikkō at Nikkō National Park (est. 1934), among the most visited in the country since the 1870s because of its shrine to Tokugawa Ieyasu (1542–1616) and its mountain scenery. Courtesy Itō Taiichi.

national parks arrived in 1912, including an impassioned request from Nikkō mayor Nishiyama Shinpei,[25] but the matter languished along with similar plans for more city parks. After the Meiji emperor died in 1912, building the Meiji Shrine and Outer Garden took priority, a further setback for the national park movement.[26]

Despite the torpor about turning Nikkō into a park, sightseeing there steadily increased in the 1910s, as did sightseeing at Fuji, Hakone, Unzen, and many other scenic locations. Yamanashi Prefecture, just north of Mount Fuji, clamored for a national park there in 1916 and found a receptive response, but no subsidies, from the Home Ministry.[27] Two years later Tamura Tsuyoshi, a student of Honda Seiroku's, published *Zōen gairon* (Introduction to landscape design, 1918), which the government's official history of environmental protection considers a pathbreaking treatise on constructing national parks.[28] In 1918 Tamura, Honda, Uehara Keiji (1889–1981), and others started the Garden Society of Japan, which became a powerful lobby for integrating landscape architecture into the Home Ministry's sporadic future planning of national parks. Despite persistent financial problems, the diversions of the Meiji Shrine and monuments projects, and a lack of government leadership on the subject, the Diet continued to receive petitions and requests for parks steadily throughout the 1910s and 1920s—more than 120 of them by 1931 when the National Parks Law was finally enacted.[29] Some came spontaneously from localities eager for tourists; others were quietly developed internally by government officials and routed to the Diet through outside channels, taking advantage of a relatively favorable public attitude toward establishing national parks after World War One.

However strong the desires both to showcase and to safeguard picturesque places such as Nikkō and Fuji, three major structural problems dimmed the prospects for national parks. One was that much of the needed land, especially in the lower mountains, was in private hands. Finding the funds to purchase the most vital parcels for the public domain, and persuading landowners to accept restrictions on how they could use portions that remained private, were barriers too daunting to be overcome until well into the 1930s. Even in the early twenty-first century, 58 percent of Japan's forests are in private hands, mainly in small parcels of fewer than a hundred hectares managed by their owners. Land privatization in the

The forester, bureaucrat, and landscape designer Tamura Tsuyoshi (1890–1979) in 1956. Tamura was Japan's leading proponent of establishing national parks from 1918 through the enactment of the National Parks Law in 1931. He helped to administer the country's first national parks starting in 1934 and also advocated national parks for colonial Taiwan. Courtesy Kyōdō Tsūshinsha.

1870s fragmented forest holdings, and land reform in 1946 further splintered them; the average private forest is just 3.7 hectares and usually belongs to a nearby farm family. Timber and mining companies own a minority of the private forests but do not necessarily harvest their holdings; the amount extracted depends on market conditions. Local governments own 11 percent of the country's total forest areas, and the remaining 31 percent are national forest.[30] The latter presented a second structural problem a century ago: much of the land suggested for national park status already had been protected, however weakly, by the national Forest Law of 1897, diminishing lawmakers' appetites for making outlays for national parks. Moreover, bureaucratic imperatives within the Forestry Bureau dictated caution toward proposals to establish a parallel unit to administer parks that almost invariably would include national forest tracts within their borders.

A third structural difficulty was posed by a separate initiative starting in 1906 to protect tangible cultural properties long valued by local residents, eventually leading the Diet in 1919 to enact a Law for the Preservation of Historic, Scenic, and Natural Monuments. Although the items proposed for protection often seemed essentialist—favorite trees, waterfalls, rocks, local scenic spots, Buddhist sculptures, flora and fauna, and old buildings or ruins associated with premodern times—the idea of preservation came to Japan principally from the writings of the German geographer Alexander von Humboldt. Nonetheless the drift of the movement for monuments was retrogressive, culturally protectionist, perhaps even anti-Western, whereas supporters of national parks urged the state to sanction a new Japanese spatial modernity worthy of display to citizens and foreign visitors alike. This modernity, patterned partly after national parks in the United States, would be extensive in scale and would celebrate Japan's geological as well as biotic legacies. The 1919 monuments law applied to both public and private lands, but the sites designated for protection were mostly small, government-owned spots, not entire regions, and quite economical to operate. In the sere prose of the Environment Agency's official history, "it was a fiscal inevitability that Japan was limited to a system in which lands that should be protected could not be turned into publicly owned lands for public use."[31] Faced with the choice, it was easy for Diet members in 1919 to opt for low-cost monuments rather than expensive national parks, believing the national treasury could not afford to purchase broad parklands that ideally should be protected for future public use. When the Kanto earthquake and fires devastated the Tokyo-Yokohama region in September 1923, the cabinet leaped into crisis mode and mandated that the nation's fiscal priorities be recalculated from top to bottom—a further setback to the partisans of national parks, but one that was quickly overcome.

Forests and Monuments

With two thirds of its land area covered by forests, Japan has long been greener than most other countries. First-growth forests were cleared in many parts of western Japan when wet-rice agriculture entered from Asia during the Yayoi period (300 B.C.E. to 300 C.E.). Great stands of cryptomeria were felled to erect public buildings in the Nara (710–784) and Heian (794–1185) eras, with predictable soil erosion, riparian flooding, and silted estuaries.[32] Largely ineffectual edicts were issued in the fourteenth and sixteenth centuries to slow the exploitation of woodlands. Regenerative plantation forestry in Japan's young volcanic soils, mainly fast-growing cryptomeria, began in the Kisō district of today's Nagano Prefecture during the great population boom of the late seventeenth century, at least as early as German scientific forestry.[33] Edo-era restrictions on use and government policies to enable afforestation sought both to protect trees and to produce lumber, an early version of forest conservation as advocated in the United States starting in 1907. As Conrad Totman points out, Japan's "abundant verdure is not a monument to nature's benevolence and Japanese aesthetic sensibilities but the hard-earned result of generations of human toil that have converted the archipelago into one great forest preserve."[34]

Industrialization and urbanization in the Meiji era demanded ever more timber, felled from government and private forests alike, forcing woodland managers to replenish stocks via plantations.[35] Partly in response, the Forest Law of 1897 specified twelve categories of protected forests and scenic areas, mainly in the 40 percent of Japan's forests that were in public hands, but also covering certain contiguous private timberlands. The first national forests were identified two years later by the Forestry Bureau, established within the Home Ministry in 1879 and shifted two years later to the Agriculture and Commerce Ministry, the successor of which still supervises it. A second Forest Law in 1907 more vigorously boosted output of wood, but within two decades the rising use of coal for heating, chemical fertilizers for farming, and lumber sawn in Japan's colonies led to an actual decline in demand for Japanese-grown logs.[36]

Under the 1897 law the Forestry Bureau also began designating special zones within national forests for preservation. As a result, various mountainous areas that might have been candidates for national parks were now protected instead as national forests,[37] their ancient flora and rare fauna sometimes slated for preservation and some of their best scenery already tagged for recognition. Protection, preservation, and scenery were three of many agenda also embraced by advocates for parks, but their hug was weakened by the countervailing pull of the Forestry Bureau. And because they touted tourism and the development of modern facilities in would-be parklands, supporters from Nikkō, Hakone, Fuji, and elsewhere risked seeming to oppose protection and even, in today's terms, to be antienvironmentalist. This paradox plagued the national parks movement for three decades, heightened by bureaucratic sectionalism among the Forestry Bureau, Hygiene Bureau of the Home Ministry, Finance Ministry, and Railway Bureau of the Communications Ministry, the latter upgraded to Railway Agency and shifted to the Prime Minister's Office in 1908.

Another paradox of the age was that preservationists sought to shield favored historical sites against encroachments from industrial society, yet the monuments law they achieved in 1919 contained big loopholes for developing mines, lumbering, railways, roads, and hydroelectric dams—the very disruptions that helped propel the movement for monuments in the first place.[38] If people visit a ruin "to hold on to a disappearing past," offsetting a sense of loss by reconstructing the site in the mind's eye,[39] surely this holds true of viewing ancient Japanese shrines and temples, which were protected by a preservation law effective in 1897, as well as seeing secular historical ruins, imperial tombs, and even places once visited by the Meiji emperor. Beginning in the 1880s, such locations offered people who felt uprooted or disconcerted by societal change some familiar anchors amid the strong currents of Western-inspired industrialism and urbanism. Paralleling the calls for historical conservation, the botanist and pioneering ecologist Miyoshi Manabu (1862–1939) was among the first in Japan to argue for protecting the nonhuman environment. Perhaps unwittingly, he also contributed to the neoconservative movement to preserve monuments to the past when he introduced Humboldt's idea of the "monuments of nature" that the German had found in the South American tropics. Miyoshi's motive was cosmopolitan and scientific, but in the hands of others his proposal tapped nationalist sentiments brewed by the Russo-Japanese War. He spoke in favor of a proposal submitted to the upper house in 1911 by Marquis Tokugawa Yorimichi (1872–1925) and 117 other Peers to preserve historical and natural monuments.[40]

Marquis Tokugawa argued successfully that sites of historical and natural importance faced "destruction" and "now is the time to plan their preservation."[41] The Peers agreed forthwith, supporting the bill on the same day the cabinet gave its final approval in principle to establishing national parks. Neither vote was translated into immediate action: eight years elapsed before both houses of the Diet and the cabinet agreed on a monuments law. When it was finally enacted in 1919, the law protected small spots but hardly contributed to safeguarding Japan's physical environment or to an awareness of national space.[42] Its main effect was to invigorate local tourism by conferring official imprimaturs on out-of-town sites of cultural or aesthetic interest.[43] Little private land was required for most monuments, in contrast with the large tracts proposed for national parks, so supporting the monuments law was seen by the cabinet as fiscally responsible as well as good for business. The confected historicity to which the law aspired seemed aimed at marshaling public support in the countryside for nationalist policies during a relatively international moment in Japan's urban history, often characterized as Taishō liberalism. National funds to support monuments were sparse, leading the ministry to charge local owners with "a moral and social duty" to preserve them and to claim "that the work of preservation is in a [*sic*] large measure accomplished voluntarily"[44]—a foretaste of the volunteerism on which public parks increasingly rely in the 2000s.

In the long run, the prospect of profits through tourism led legislators to support both monuments and national parks regardless of whether they were drawn to the patriotic nostalgia implicit in historic monuments or to the forward-looking pride in the country's geophysical distinctiveness and aesthetic superiority popularized by Shiga Shigetaka. In this sense, both parks and the national state itself were spaces brokered by capitalism in Japan no less than in other industrializing countries.

Creating Desires for National Parks

"An incomprehensible popular movement seems to have cropped up" over the past few years, the forestry expert Uehara Keiji wrote with dismay in 1924: a public clamor to set up national parks throughout the country, even as Tokyo and Yokohama struggled to rebuild after the earthquake and fires of September 1923 (see chapter 3). Supporters of national parks, Uehara complained, were talking about land speculation, local prosperity, railways, buses, and tourist facilities, encouraged by the Hygiene Bureau of the Home Ministry. "Clearly this is becoming a pork barrel" for ministry officials and representatives in the lower house of the Diet, he lamented.[45] A distinguished botanist and a leader among Japan's landscape architects, Uehara stoutly advocated protecting the nonhuman environment; his ideological adversary in the early 1920s, Tamura Tsuyoshi of the Hygiene Bureau, favored establishing national parks to make prudent use of the country's outdoor resources. This same inescapable discussion of protection and use—never a simple binary in theory or practice—plagued national parks in the United States and many other countries throughout the twentieth century. Switzerland, Germany, Russia, and other states emphasized ecological preservation and scientific study in their national reserves; the United States, Canada, and many African countries generally prioritized tourism and made their national parks widely available to visitors, without sacrificing protections for wild animals in the case of Africa.[46] For Japan, where human activity for millennia has left few enclaves of the pristine, the question facing advocates of national parks was never whether, but instead how, these new public spaces best should be used. As with city parks, protection mattered but access mattered more, from the earliest petitions for national parks in the 1880s and the debates of the 1920s to the present.

The battle to institute national parks in Japan, which had ended in 1911 victoriously in principle but moot in practice, was joined with renewed energy in 1921 in bureaucratic conflict between two units of the Home Ministry. The Geography Section of the ministry headquarters supported environmental protection based on the monuments law of 1919, while the Public Health Section of the Hygiene Bureau wanted to establish national parks to encourage exercise and strong physiques.[47] The question was finally settled by force majeure: the countrywide demand from land developers, railway companies, and tourism operators to open parks that would invigorate prefectural economies, especially after the world depression struck in October 1929. In contrast to the social elites who had upheld historic preservation of a romanticized past through the monuments law, out-of-town boosterism by regional transportation companies and local entrepreneurs fanned the public fervor to push the Public Health Section's proposals for national parks through the Diet in 1931. Along the way much more was said about prospective use of the parks than about protecting their environmental assets.

The debates between Uehara Keiji and Tamura Tsuyoshi about national parks took place amid a noisy clatter of petitions and calls to rescue local economies, and eventually the national balance of payments, by promoting tourism. Many other reasons were adduced by advocates, but the snowballing movement to establish national parks owed even more to the developmentalist arguments of the Japan Tourist Bureau leader Kinoshita Yoshio than to Shiga Shigetaka's writings praising Japan's terrestrial distinctiveness. Certainly both Kinoshita and Shiga were moderns who tried to increase citizens' awareness of Japan as a national space. It was the supporters of the monuments law who upheld truly conservative, even essentialist, outlooks on protecting historical, scenic, and natural sites to which they retrospectively imputed great value—and thus they showed reluctance about national parks unless their main purpose was preservation, not recreation and enjoyment.

Tamura's *Zōen gairon* drew extensively on America's experience with national parks to argue that everyone should be able to enjoy them, and so both beautification and tourist facilities were needed.[48] Hired by the Public Health Section in 1920 to investigate national parks abroad and find ways to establish them at home, Tamura wrote in 1921 that the gorgeous scenery of the Japan Alps alone didn't make them a park; lodgings, amusements, hot springs, golf, tennis, riding, and theater—in other words, a resort—would turn a national park into something entirely different from a monument.[49] Tamura agreed with Shiga that mountains were Japan's most representative landscapes and recommended placing many relatively small national parks, averaging one hundred square kilometers each, all over the country. Everyone of every age, he argued, could enjoy the health benefits of outdoor exercise in parks.[50] That same year Honda Seiroku wrote that economic development of prospective park sites was desirable, even though "some damage to natural monuments and to scenery is inevitable."[51] The not-so-subtle subtext in Tamura's and Honda's writings was that some degree of use should receive priority because private land would have to be included within national parks. To them the question was not whether capitalist development should occur but under what conditions it should be regulated, including special protection of the most ecologically fragile spots within parks.

Uehara Keiji, Tamura's chief critic, was likewise a forester, landscape architect, and student of Honda's with close ties to the Home Ministry, but to its Geography Section rather than Tamura's Public Health Section. In 1922 he contended that national parks, if established, should function as protection zones for natural monuments on a vast scale, in contrast with the small spaces recognized under the monuments law of 1919. Uehara argued forcefully that "no matter what, national parks must first and foremost protect and preserve nature."[52] Smaller people's parks could be provided for popular recreation, entirely separate from huge national parks to which the public would have access only if engaged in scientific or educational research.[53] By 1924, sensing defeat for his position at the hands of developmentalists in the Public Health Section, Uehara called on government to cooperate with private opponents of development so as to restrict, rather than encourage, use of protected environments.[54] Three years later Uehara, now little heeded in the discussions about national parks, warned against "the growing unreasonable demand for the economic uses of nature"—roads, hydroelectric power, deforestation—and called for systematic preservation of landscapes.[55] This admonition, however prescient, received more lip service than respect in the next decades because big corporations and tourism entrepreneurs in Japan were little hampered by the eventual National Parks Law, the more so because the parks included private as well as public lands.

Tamura's and Uehara's outlooks captured the discordant views of the Home Ministry's Public Health and Geography Sections in the 1920s. The ministry's Hygiene Bureau, of which the Public Health Section was a part, had been in charge of public parks since the Grand Council order of 1873, and it saw protecting people's health as their main purpose. The Geography Section, which was newly responsible for monuments under the 1919 law, was chiefly concerned with safeguarding scenic, historical, and geophysical places of cultural significance. While the Public Health Section was choosing sixteen potential park sites for further scrutiny in 1923, the Geography Section preferred a few huge mountain parks resembling

German-style forest preserves for scientific purposes, shielded from wide public use, such as Fuji, Mount Aso, and Kirishima.

Tamura recognized that giant parks such as Yellowstone were out of reach for Japan and instead focused on models such as Hot Springs and Lafayette (now Acadia) National Parks, both of which were small and contained private lands.[56] Tamura and Honda reached out to supporters of the recent monuments law by touting conventional scenery preferred by Japanese for generations as best for new national parks: smaller places such as Lake Biwa and Lake Suwa. In 1923 the Forestry Bureau, abandoning its earlier caution, decided to support the Public Health Section's position in favor of publicly accessible parklands, because zoning within the proposed national parks seemed likely to secure the country's woodlands more firmly.[57] As a result, in Japan there was little of the ongoing antagonism that arose in the United States between the National Forest Service and the National Park Service when the latter was created in 1916.[58] With the Forestry Bureau now on board, Tamura and his former colleagues in the Public Health Section eventually compromised with the preservationists by accepting a number of candidates for parks from the Geography Section's list of large sites. This step gave Tamura and the Public Health Section unstoppable momentum in steering parks policy from 1927 onward. It was clear that the Home Ministry, not the Forestry Bureau, would administer the national parks once they were created; the parks would cover more than just national forest lands, and the Forestry Bureau had little interest in recreation or tourism.[59]

Looking back in 1981 on the debates about parklands, the official history of the Environment Agency (since 2001, Environment Ministry) noted with wry understatement that "the Tamura-Uehara dispute was rather removed from public reality."[60] The reality was that municipal governments and tourist businesses continued to agitate for national parks to lure visitors to their regions of the country. Business councils and village governments lobbied for parks through their Diet representatives of both major parties, as did private railways and bus companies. Local people wanted parks for their own areas, not necessarily a nationwide network, but Honda Seiroku pointed out that "the rise of a national rail network justified systematizing national parks."[61] Both Tamura and Honda accepted modern mechanical culture and saw a need for people to have direct contact with the nonhuman through a revolution in outdoor recreation.[62]

The February 1921 proposal to create national parks had been the first serious legislative attempt to revive the matter since 1911. Bureaucratic rivalries between the Geography and Public Health Sections derailed the bill, but dozens of petitions and proposals for Diet action on national parks arrived during the next eight years. Some of the lobbying was initiated locally; some reflected the efforts of Tamura and his colleagues to stimulate interest in tourism in towns and villages near prospective parks already on the Public Health Section's list of candidates. The petitions created ongoing chatter in the Diet in favor of the bill but had no immediate impact on which parks were selected or in what order they opened.[63] The press added to the drumbeat for national parks in the spring of 1927 when the *Osaka mainichi shinbun* held a contest backed by transportation companies to identify the eight best landscapes in the country. Within a month the newspaper received 93.4 million postcards, many generated by local groups eager to have their areas chosen for national parks, perhaps out of a desire for protection but certainly for tourism. The eight new landscapes selected by readers mostly featured rugged mountain beauty with the appeal of the unfamiliar and the supposedly untrodden, as lionized by Shiga Shigetaka and the Japan Alpine Club a generation earlier.[64]

Tamura Tsuyoshi and Honda Seiroku worked closely with the Public Health Section from mid-1927 onward to build an irresistible consensus in favor of a law establishing national parks. Without abandoning his commitment to public access and appropriate tourist facilities, Tamura now acknowledged the need to isolate zones of perpetual ecological preservation separate from parklands open to tourists, and he increasingly spoke in favor of environmental protection, especially because residents at a number of the locations chosen in 1923 as prospective parks seemed anxious that uncontrolled development by tourist and other companies would harm their scenery. He conceded that despite the pressure in favor of parks from many local tourism boosters, resort developers would prefer not to see national parks established in some areas because of the restrictions a law might impose.[65] Another step toward consensus was Tamura's emphasis on building national parks cheaply through mixed public and private ownership of land, a model found also in Italy that was soon adopted in Japan and remains in effect today. By making national forests, imperial lands, and other public properties the core, then adding appropriate privately held lands as part of the parks without depriving landlords of their ownership, the government could avoid the great cost of purchasing real estate. The tradeoff was that public parks would have to permit a good deal of private business activity, although owners also had to accept certain regulations on how they could use their lands.[66]

To speed the national parks movement forward, in December 1927 the Hygiene Bureau of the Home Ministry formed a quasi-official policy group, the National Parks Association. Tamura, Honda, and Uehara Keiji all played major roles in this umbrella organization, which aimed to publicize national parks, sway reluctant Diet representatives, and win passage of the National Parks Law, a goal finally attained in 1931 amid worldwide depression. The association's elite membership included grandees from the peerage, members of the lower house, government bureaucrats, and representatives of business and the Japan Tourist Bureau. Big businesses with a hand in tourism such as Mitsui, Mitsubishi, Nihon Yūsen, and Osaka Shōsen lent their support by contributing funds to the association.[67] This carefully constructed coalition of interests also included Shiga Shigetaka, the folklorist Yanagita Kunio, and writers from the conservative Romantic School, who were fond of an idealized "nature." The ecologist Miyoshi Manabu, who had been active in the effort to establish historical monuments, came aboard as well.[68] The association sponsored tours to would-be park sites to whet enthusiasm for the proposed legislation. Despite its rainbow of perspectives and the concessions Tamura and Honda had begun to make to preservationists, the association oriented itself primarily toward regulated development of parklands so as to attract large numbers of visitors, especially well-to-do tourists from overseas.

The chief reason offered in favor of national parks by the end of the 1920s was tourism, yet without the world depression not even the lure of visitors' money might have been enough to win a majority in the Diet. In 1929 the Japan Chamber of Commerce and Industry lobbied Diet members to find ways to earn foreign exchange, one of which was establishing national parks. The government agreed that drawing more foreign visitors was essential, and in April 1930 it set up a Board of Tourist Industry representing various agencies led by the government railways.[69] A report from the National Parks Association in 1931 underscored that the parks law "has an economic mission to improve our balance of international payments by attracting foreign visitors."[70] But clearly the overriding motive for promoting tourism in national parks was political—to rescue depressed local economies and woo their voters—rather than simply bulking up Japan's international finances. Regionalism, in the form of hoped-for cash injections through local tourism, was more significant an element than nationalism in winning legislative votes.

A second major argument in favor of national parks was one cited on behalf of city parks thirty years earlier: the collective health and stamina of the people. The National Parks Bill was drafted late in 1930 by the Public Health Section, whose leaders continued to emphasize hygiene, exercise, and recreation as goals of the parks, even though the version that went before the Diet early the next year was justified abundantly on economic grounds by its supporters. From the Public Health Section's standpoint, according to Home Minister Adachi Kenzō (1864–1948), "positive steps are needed to increase people's physical strength" by utilizing national parks.[71] Speaking before the Diet in favor of the National Parks Bill on February 24, 1931, Adachi said that the parks would bring "protection and development of places with grand and superb scenic beauty" to promote "the health, recreation, and education of the nation."[72] An ancillary rationale to win the support of the major parties, Minseitō and Seiyūkai, involved what could be called ideological health: national parks might inoculate citizens against radical ideas from the Soviet Union.[73] Unlike tourism, the public health of body or mind was a justification by elites for elites and had little to do with the eagerness of localities throughout the country to have their various mountain or seaside sites picked for national parks.

A third element in building a consensus for the National Parks Bill was environmental protection, something long advocated by partisans of historic and scenic monuments and more recently embraced by Tamura, Honda, and the otherwise prodevelopment National Parks Association. The National Parks Bill was coordinated with the Forest Law of 1897, as amended, and the monuments law of 1919. It called, paradoxically but realistically, for the public enjoyment of parklands and the protection of scenic beauty.[74] As resolutely as the Home Ministry and others in the government supported tourism in the prospective national parks, establishing them would also regulate development and thus forestall environmental damage, especially from great hydroelectric dams. Two separate power companies had built dams and generating stations on the Azusa River at Kamikōchi, which tourists began to reach by bus in 1929 on a road carved into the mountainside three years earlier by dam contractors. Visitors were drawn partly by Kamikōchi's designation in 1928 as a natural monument, which provided some legal protection for part of the district. By 1931 at least 70,000 tourists were making the trip each year—a clear sign of how dams spurred sightseeing despite the preservationist intent of the monuments law.[75]

Tamura Tsuyoshi conditionally opposed the hydroelectric dams on the Kurobe River, arguing that the monuments law was toothless and that a national parks law was needed to control big business' penchant for destroying the landscape.[76] Uno Tasuku, a senior official in the Environment Agency, conceded in 1972 that there was no way to stop damming the Kurobe in the 1920s, given Japan's need for electricity, yet Kurobe remained a headache for the authorities in 1953 when a fourth hydroelectricity plant was proposed upstream from the existing three.[77] Dams and other threats sparked sharp questions in both houses of the Diet about protecting the environment when the National Parks Bill was debated in 1931, particularly in the light of long-term pollution from the Ashio copper mine, which had poisoned the flooded Watarase River in 1890.[78] Nonetheless, last-minute maneuvering by utilities companies managed to exempt dams and mines from being included in national parks. On the other hand, protectionists won a small victory in Article 8 of the National Parks Law, which called on the relevant ministers (Home Ministry and Agriculture and Forestry Ministry) "to designate special zones for preserving natural scenery in planning national parks."[79] Nonetheless, no mention could be found in the 1931 law of preserving landscapes in national parklands outside the special zones. Even today the twenty-nine national parks contain only five special preservation zones to protect features considered pristine, as called for in Article 8. Otherwise, as Roderick Nash says of both Japan and France, "environmental control is nearly total"[80]—that is, nature is managed.

The National Parks Law ended up being approved unanimously and was promulgated on April 1, 1931. Home Minister Adachi Kenzō noted at the time that more prefectural governments were now taking steps to build parks on their own, creating an urgent need to bring order and system to what could easily become chaotic.[81] Even though the voices of prospective park users were almost unheard throughout two decades of debate, these stirrings from the outlands represented a challenge, possibly even a threat, to the city elites from business, bureaucracy, political parties, and the peerage who managed the legislative process but were unable fully to control the desires for national parks in provincial Japan. In this respect, the national park idea arose, as in the United States, among urban establishmentarians, but in Japan it became a regional and local movement beyond the ability of the metropole to contain.

Picking the Parks

Once the National Parks Law took effect, many practical questions remained. One was how to assure sustainable development of recreation while curbing damage to wildlife or the physical landscape. Another was how best to incorporate privately owned lands into the parks. Most important was finding the wherewithal to pay for the new entities, the more so given the financial claims of the many hundreds of new city parks established during the rapid urbanization of the 1930s. None of these problems were fully resolved during the brief window between 1934, when the first national parks were approved, and 1937, when mobilization for war with China slowed, and finally halted, the momentum to open more such parklands.

The law defined national parks in words of compromise, not clarity: "National parks are parks established by the national government to protect and develop our great natural scenery and at the same time to advance our people's health, relaxation, and education."[82] How to balance these imperatives was left unstated, giving a free hand to park planners in dealing with private land holdings, protecting the nonhuman while encouraging tourism, and finding revenues to operate the parks. The law permitted the government to incorporate private lands into public parks through expropriation, with just compensation to landlords, but in the midst of depression no funds could be found for this purpose. Instead, the Home Ministry took two steps to skirt the thorny problem of land seizure. First, it pared the original list of sixteen prospective national parks to twelve sites containing just 13 percent private property.[83] Six of the twelve were based almost entirely on government-owned lands, and nearly all except Yoshino-Kumano were in high mountains where including private tracts made little practical difference, at least initially.[84] Second, the ministry followed Italian practice in turning most of the national parks into regional mosaics covering an entire area, including both public and private holdings, thus achieving a degree of protection in the public lands—many of which were already restricted under the Forest Law of 1897—while permitting continued development, under controlled conditions, in the privately owned portions.

In effect, the planners of Japan's national parks opportunistically adapted their designs to the existing patchwork of government-owned and privately held lands while cleverly citing European models for safeguarding regions meant to showcase Japanese distinctiveness. From the start Japanese officials regarded the national parks in the United States as

Kappa Bridge over the Azusa River at Kamikōchi in Chūbu-Sangaku National Park (est. 1934) in the Japan Alps. Courtesy Itō Taiichi.

"public works," that is, facilities operated by central authorities, in contrast to the regional model covering public and private lands in an entire area that was employed in most of Japan's national parks—even though nearly all national parks in both countries included at least some private land. By this reasoning, most city parks in Japan were in principle also considered public works. Technically, Japan since 1931 has had no formal national park system, whereas the United States has had one since 1916, but in practice the Environment Ministry manages all twenty-nine national parks as a single entity.[85]

The twelve national parks established between March 1934 and February 1936 were chosen for their extensive scenery, suitability for recreational use, accessibility to the public, and compatibility with the regional model, with little likelihood of clashes between public and private interests. A number of them also featured historical and scenic sites of particular interest to preservationists as well as tourists.[86] Three northern candidates from the original 1923 list were dropped before the law was passed in 1931, and three others in the Japan Alps were combined into a single park, Chūbu

Hokkaido's Daisetsuzan National Park (est. 1934), at 2,309 square kilometers, is Japan's largest natural park. Courtesy Itō Taiichi.

Sangaku (Middle mountains), a name seemingly more authentic and less foreign than Alps.[87] Daisetsuzan in Hokkaido, although not appearing on any original list of candidates, was added to offset dropping nearby sites at Ōnuma and Noboribetsu, bringing the total created before World War Two to twelve. Daisetsuzan, Japan's largest park, was spread over 2,309 square kilometers in central Hokkaido accessible by the Ishikita Railway. It was apparently favored because it resembled a large American national park and contained relatively unspoiled landscapes.[88] Fuji and Hakone were merged into a single unit from the beginning; the Izu Peninsula was added to this most popular of all Japanese national parks after World War Two. Altogether the dozen parks created from 1934 to 1936 accounted for 2.7 percent of the national land area,[89] an important start toward the 14.3 percent covered by Japan's 394 natural parks today.[90]

The public-private model for national parks posed great dilemmas for ecological protection, as the Environment Agency's official chronicle notes: the regional scheme "was extremely important, the start of a complex and difficult park system."[91] If the parks were serious about protection in the 1930s, the reason was usually to safeguard local scenic assets for tourism. Regional parks were hard to administer because private landholders resisted giving up their customary fishing, logging, hunting, and farming practices, many of which were restricted by the 1931 law. Owners of steep interior tracts welcomed the parks and sought roads that would raise their land values, but the traffic also harmed the surroundings. In a time of economic doldrums few private owners could resist the siren songs of tourism and development, creating environmental difficulties and regulatory disputes that threatened the publicly owned portions of parks.[92]

Under these conditions it was almost inevitable that recreational and corporate needs prevailed, the more so since both state and citizens had a low awareness of environmental issues at the time. On the other hand, nine tenths of the land in the original twelve national parks established in the 1930s consisted of forests, mainly publicly owned.[93] Harvesting was still done mostly by hand, and sustainable forestry proved compatible with public parks until the lumber demands of World War Two brought about a huge increase in logging.[94] At that point tensions began to emerge between the Forestry Bureau, which imposed relatively loose regulation on the national forests, and the Physical Strength Bureau of the Welfare

Ministry, which was founded in 1938 and immediately took over supervision of national parks from the Home Ministry but did little to enhance them until after 1945. Felling trees on national forest lands within national parks during wartime caused environmental disruptions that the Welfare Ministry found difficult to halt.[95]

The biggest problem facing the new parks was financial, the result of another conundrum: the national parks were supposed to bring in revenue for Japan, yet to build them cost money the government was loath to provide. The National Parks Association noted in 1933 that national parks were considered "essential for the health and culture of the nation, at the same time not forgetting their importance as a source of revenue" from foreign tourists.[96] The organ of the International Tourism Association, a unit of the government railways' Board of Tourist Industry, wrote in 1938 that "it is also difficult to conceal the pleasure of inviting to Japan friendly foreign guests whose expenditures would offer some measure of relief in this time of economic emergency."[97] Such blandishments amounted to little more than a pipe dream; although domestic tourism thrived throughout the 1930s, international travel to Japan experienced little more than an uptick in the middle of the decade, constrained by hard times in the global economy and Japan's growing reputation as an international bully, particularly after the onset of all-out war with China in 1937.

In any case, the national parks established from 1934 to 1936 had little short-term impact on tourism. Staffing and funding were so meager that one authority concluded, "Japan's national park system in the 1930s was one in name only."[98] No regular, recurring budget existed for national parks, let alone enterprise revenues or an endowment. Instead the home minister (after 1938, welfare minister) had to seek one-time appropriations from the Diet each year as the central government's contribution to the costs of facilities and personnel associated with the parks. In practice, until 1938 national parks received about ¥100,000 annually for capital improvements, after which time war with China dried up the allocations. Personnel appropriations ran about ¥80,000 a year from 1934 to 1938, then were slashed to little more than ¥50,000 annually from 1939 to 1941, with prefectures and localities obliged to pay the rest of staffing costs.[99]

By the end of the decade, parks policy was clearly subordinated to the needs of the mobilized imperial state. While Japanese armies fought on in

China and prepared to battle Soviet forces at Nomonhan in Inner Mongolia, the Board of Tourist Industry's subsidiary for international tourism deadpanned in April 1939, "in line with national policy, we need to draw in foreign cash from the foreign guests whom we entice to Japan. . . . the great task of international tourism, as one wing of this holy war, is to propagate both abroad and domestically the true image of our youthful Japan with an old history."[100] Unfortunately for the Tourist Board, the national parks sat on magnificent old lands but were too juvenile in their development to attract much international cash or respect for Japan's "true image"— despite efforts to create "nature" both in parks and in imagery.

National Parks in Imperial Spaces

Rural landscape parks, urban parks, and city planning are some of the many institutions modern colonial empires routinely impose on subject peoples. These forms of regulated public space project the power of the metropole to enhance the governmentality or "governmental rationality"[101] of the colony, sharpening the focus of transplanted colonial administrators on "seeing like a state"[102] by increasing the legibility and subordination of the colonized. In the case of national parks, colonial regimes sometimes stake out boundaries to "preserve" an imagined or material "nature" from the modernizing efforts of local residents. "The European appropriation of the African landscape for aesthetic consumption" via national parks treated the nonhuman landscape as a scenic vision and a source of premodern aesthetic value to be preserved for its wild Otherness.[103] At other times, when colonizer and colonized are less culturally distant from each other, the hegemon can use public space to create sameness, not separateness, as a way to integrate subject peoples into the empire.

The latter was usually the case with city and national parks in Japan's overseas imperium from 1895 to 1945. In China the Japanese resident community established Rokusan Garden at Shanghai, with its small shrine and teahouse, in 1896, soon followed by Yamato Park in the Japanese concession at Tianjin built after the Boxer Rebellion of 1899–1901.[104] Yamato Park resembled a modern city park, the more so because Chinese could use it freely unlike most foreign concessions, but it primarily served overseas Japanese at a time when Japan was not yet a semicolonial power in China.

Taiwan was the scene of Japan's first planned imperial spaces from the moment Japan made it a colony after defeating China in the Sino-Japanese War of 1894–1895.

General Kodama Gentarō (1852–1906), vice chief of the army general staff, was sent to head the Japanese administration in Taiwan and took with him Gotō Shinpei, the chief of the Hygiene Bureau of the Home Ministry, to oversee public health on the island. In 1898, the year Kodama became governor general, Gotō was promoted to chief of welfare in the colonial administration, prompting his interest in city planning for the next three decades, during which time he burnished his fame for sweeping aside all obstacles in accomplishing feats of civic engineering.[105] Honda Seiroku was likewise sent to Taiwan in September 1896 to assess its forests.[106] Even before Gotō proclaimed a city planning process for Taibei (Jpn. Taihoku) in 1900, a narrow riverside space there known as Maruyama Kōen became the colony's first urban park in 1897. Shinto shrines were soon scattered in small green spaces throughout Taiwan.[107] Taibei Park, dating in principle to 1899, became a centerpiece of Japanese city planning under Gotō's design. A Japanese visitor marveled in 1913, "it is truly Taiwan's number-one park,"[108] similar to but smaller than Hibiya Park in Tokyo. Nearby was the Taibei Nursery Garden, opened in 1900 and renamed Taibei Botanical Garden in 1912. In line with Japan's colonial strategy of acculturation, the public was admitted to visit its compact but lush grounds and accompanying mini-zoo.[109] The garden's juxtaposition of plant specimens from throughout Japan's empire suggested cultural contiguity but not yet hybridity—the latter a goal the Japanese sought largely in vain both in Taiwan and in Korea during World War Two.

Well aware of the petitions to create national parks in Japan, Kanehira Ryōzō (1882–1948), a tropical botanist in the Taiwan colonial administration, urged the governor general in 1923 to protect and develop scenic landscapes by establishing national parks throughout the island.[110] Two years later the Home Ministry stated publicly that recreational parks should serve the people not only in Japan but also in its colonies, Korea, Taiwan, and even Karafuto (southern Sakhalin).[111] Tamura Tsuyoshi visited Taiwan to prepare a detailed plan for a national park at Alishan, then came back in 1932 to survey and report on another at Taroko. Honda Seiroku returned to the island in 1928 to assess the Yangmingshan and Dadunshan area just north of Taibei as the site of a third park. Recapping his sojourns in Taiwan, Tamura wrote in 1936 that he assumed Japanese-style national parks would soon be built in both Taiwan and Korea, now that the National Parks Law of 1931 was in force. He pointed out that most lands at Alishan and Taroko were government owned, with no major obstacles to protecting their environments. The much smaller Dadunshan site, with just ninety-four square kilometers, contained more private land, "but it has little worth mentioning by way of industrial value," so development could be tightly controlled at all three locations.[112]

Fortified with recommendations from Honda and Tamura, the colonial administration fostered local support groups to press for national parks in their respective areas.[113] These ritual organizations, although hardly necessary under the authoritarian rule of the colonial regime, nonetheless established parallels, if not quite sameness, with the parks-formation process in the homeland, steps evidently deemed important by colonial administrators in order to be taken seriously in Tokyo by demonstrating popular demand in Taiwan. In September 1935 the Government General in Taibei decreed that it would enforce the National Parks Law of 1931 in the colony, evidently eager to assure "that Taiwan would thus precede Korea and Sakhalin in establishing national parks" and to assert that the island's proposed sites compared favorably with Japanese national parks in their beauty.[114] Kohama Seikō, vice president of the Taiwan National Parks Association, boasted in 1936 that Taroko would become "Japan's largest national park" at 2,726 square kilometers and that Alishan, covering 1,860 square kilometers, would be third behind Daisetsuzan.[115] The faux triumphalism expressed by both the Government General and the Japanese resident community seemed geared to win Tokyo's attention and approval, a motive presumably bred of anxiety that Taiwan was becoming marginal as the Colonial Development Ministry increasingly prioritized Korea and, after 1931, Japan's informal colony in Manchuria.

The three sites chosen for national parks were all in the mountains, closely resembling the rugged highlands found in most of the twelve national parks created in Japan from 1934 to 1936. Unlike European parks in Africa, the national parks in Taiwan were meant to establish similarity with the metropole, and the local users were expected to learn civic duties as imperial subjects while visiting them. The paleontologist Hayasaka Ichirō (1891–1977) chafed at this emphasis on sameness, pointing out in 1936 that Taiwan was distinctive in its tropical vegetation and wildlife, yet the Japanese "have given this fact no consideration at all."[116] He sought to protect both tropical seaside landscapes and mountain areas for biological investigation, while also encouraging local people to use the parks, with a view toward "disciplining the bodies and minds of our future fellow citizens," the Taiwanese.[117]

Alishan, Taroko, and Dadunshan, totaling 4,668 square kilometers or 13 percent of the island, were declared national parks by the governor general in December 1937, just days after Japanese forces across the Taiwan Strait laid waste to Nanjing in a massacre that still reverberates—parks and armies each representing imperial might. Only sixty-two square kilometers of the new parks, fifty-six of them at Dadunshan, were in private hands,[118] yet because of the Sino-Japanese War raging on the mainland, nothing was done to develop these three impressive regions until long after Japan's defeat and Taiwan's ensuing occupation by mainlanders under Chiang Kai-shek's Nationalist government starting in 1948. Like Tamura during his first visit to Taiwan, the Taiwan National Parks Association claimed as late as 1939 that "we must recognize the true value of Taiwan for tourism"[119] as well as for security and economic development. But a year earlier Yamagata Saburō, head of the Government General's Internal Affairs Bureau, zeroed in on the rationale for national parks as the colonial overlord saw it: (1) "to promote national spirit" and develop patriotism, (2) "to improve people's physiques and hygiene," (3) "to develop the ideal of protecting nature," and (4) to educate people about flora and fauna.[120] Clearly the national parks project in Taiwan represented a projection of mainland goals;[121] although mobilization for total war prevented the nascent Taiwanese national parks from serving these purposes, Japanese-designed city parks on the island represented imperial values on a much less colossal scale but with immediacy and frequency.[122]

Japan's colonial administration in Korea, by contrast, built no national parks at all during its rule from 1910 to 1945. The Diamond Mountains (Kŭmgangsan) were a beacon for Japanese tourist operators during the colonial period and briefly appeared on a list of potential national parks compiled within the Japanese Home Ministry in the early 1920s.[123] Unlike the three parks in Taiwan, the Diamond Mountains had been a locus of Buddhist and Confucian practice since the eighth century, chronicled in premodern Korean texts as a cultural icon. When Japanese colonial tourism developed the area, it "manufactured a space where imperial desire and nationalist imperatives clashed."[124] The Korean writer Yi Kwangsu (1892–1950) and other patriots urgently sought to reclaim the mountains from foreign capitalist exploitation. Their opposition posed unexpected obstacles—duplicated at other potential sites on the peninsula—to designating them as national parks under Japan's dominion.

The Japanese National Parks Law of 1931 was not extended to cover Korea as it had Taiwan; the Republic of Korea established its first national park when Mount Jiri was approved in 1967.[125] In cities and towns, on the other hand, small parks were often attached to Shinto shrines built for resident Japanese, the earliest dating to 1882. The shrines and their parklands existed to meet contemporary needs, not nostalgic yearning for the past; they were means of "unifying popular sentiment,"[126] primarily that of Japanese settlers. More broadly, Japanese planners reconfigured the royal capital of Seoul both to civilize local residents (as with city parks in Japan) and to acculturate them (as with those in Taiwan)[127]—twin objectives of imperial control when colonizer and colonized are culturally closer than they are distant.

The Government General promulgated regulations in 1916 to preserve historical remains, doubtless a reflection of the drive for a monuments law then taking place in Japan. This led to a 1933 Law to Preserve Korean Treasures, Historic Sites, Scenic Vistas, and Natural Monuments, which had the effect of protecting certain locations that might be candidates for national parks in the postliberation era.[128] The Japanese authorities also adopted goals for city parks in 1930 as a part of land use planning for open areas, including both firebreaks and green spaces.[129] These ambitions were not realized because of worldwide economic depression, the diversion of resources and personnel to Manchuria after 1931, and full-scale war with China starting in 1937. In occupied areas of Manchuria and north China, on the other hand, Japanese planners accomplished more sweeping urban redevelopment than at home "because of the powerful authority they wielded there"[130]—and doubtless met less resistance than in Korea or even in Taiwan.

Taiwan, more prosperous but politically and industrially less prominent than Korea during the colonial period, perhaps had more reason to wish for the attention national parks might bring. With scenic landscapes equal in beauty to those in Taiwan, but larger in scale, Korea from 1910 to 1945 enjoyed a good deal of Japanese tourism even without national parks. Most important were the Government General's successive policies of social management and eventual efforts at integrating Koreans more fully into the empire, leaving no place for the costly enterprise of building national parks. Instead, city planning was the key Japanese spatial strategy deployed in Korea from the end of the nineteenth century until liberation in 1945.

On the brink of all-out war in 1937, neither Japan nor its colonies could boast of national parks in more than infancy, even though tourism to some of their most scenic locations was well developed. Wartime had adverse effects on both city and national parklands, bringing major changes to each, yet the frameworks for both carried over to the post-1945 period, when public space was renegotiated and reconfigured for a new era of pacifism, democracy, economic growth, and consumerism that is still salient today.

CHAPTER 3

Visions of a Green Tokyo

While Japan wrestled with defining and constructing public park-lands as national spaces in the 1920s and 1930s, planners in the Home Ministry and Tokyo prefectural government crafted two visionary designs for the future metropolitan landscape, incorporating public parks and other open spaces on a scale hardly imagined during the city's early years as the imperial capital. The first of these top-down plans was set in motion by the Kanto earthquake and fires of September 1923 but was partly thwarted by insufficient budget allocations and flagging political zeal for remaking the face of Tokyo. The second, the Green Space Plan of 1939, was greatly compromised by wartime mobilization, but many of its aims were accomplished unexpectedly through emergency measures for air raid defense. In the long run each vision left a clear imprint on Tokyo and cities elsewhere in Japan, especially for city planning in the postwar period.

The Kanto Disaster and City Parks

Half a century of state formation, rapid industrialization, and haphazard city planning had turned Tokyo by midsummer 1923 into a vibrant city-scape of four million people, one of the world's great urban magnets, where hundreds of thousands of students, writers, artists, and businesspeople from colonial Korea and Taiwan, semicolonial China, and elsewhere gathered to experience Japan as exemplar of a new Asian modernity, similar to but distinct from that of the great Western powers.[1] Then, "quite un-expectedly the fifty years of Tokyo culture," according to the authorized history of the event, "met with a terrible catastrophe on September 1, 1923, when earthquake and fire, unprecedented in history, dealt the city an almost fatal blow. Nearly one half of the entire city was completely reduced to ashes, and the once busy and prosperous Tokyo changed into a devastated field in a single day."[2] More than 115,000 lost their lives in the Kanto region, another 43,000 went missing, 128,000 houses were destroyed by the earthquake, and 381,090 households were listed as entirely burned out by fires that continued for three days.[3] In florid but heartfelt neo-Edwardian prose, the official narrative lamented that "the greater portion of the Capital, which had boasted till then of its architectural beauty and the magnificence of its civic life, lay in a miserable destruction; a mere wilderness of smoking embers . . . in the whole history of man, never had there been such colossal havoc wrought by a single convulsion of Nature, of such short a duration"[4]—although aftershocks kept survivors on edge for the next month.

Devastating as the disaster was, it provided a completely unanticipated opportunity to redefine public space in the capital region, including carving out more city parks in underserved neighborhoods. The principle that governed Tokyo's reconstruction, wrote the art historian Dan Inō (1892–1973) in 1931, was to build "the most solid structure with least possible expense,"[5] a paradoxical prescription that yielded little scopic satisfaction and much drabness. The same want of aesthetic imagination informed plans and designs for city parks during the seven-year rehabilitation period, partly because Home Minister Gotō Shinpei's extravagant initial proposals to remake Tokyo into an impressive imperial capital were emasculated by the cabinet, which cut his budget by seven eighths. What funding remained mainly was allotted to rebuilding roads, port facilities, and other infrastructural needs to restore the region's economy. Despite these priorities, Gotō and other "social bureaucrats"[6] mobilized appropriations for city parks in Tokyo and Yokohama totaling ¥23.86 million, nearly 3 percent of overall government outlays for reconstruction down to 1930.[7] With these funds both cities repaired their existing parks and built new ones that had long been envisioned but had become sidetracked when other needs prevailed. The destruction of the capital and the heightened importance of parks as refuges and firebreaks prompted gifts of new urban parklands to Tokyo during the next decade and more. Suburbanization resulting from the disaster and further industrial growth in the 1930s led to a much wider variety of urban parks and other green areas, both in the capital region and beyond.

Critics of Tokyo's recovery effort both then and since often have assailed Japan's leaders for failing to impose Haussmann-like civic engineering on the ravaged region, instead allowing Tokyo, Yokohama, and other damaged areas to re-establish their jumbled cityscapes after mainly cosmetic intervention. Many residents at the time were disappointed that the authorities did not do more, but it seems doubtful that Japan had the funds, technical know-how, experience with urban planning, and political will for a major re-engineering.[8] There was no Louis Napoléon to commandeer resources, nor was Gotō Shinpei nearly so imposing a figure as Baron Haussmann. At a time of fragile party cabinets, urban-rural tensions, and economic uncertainties, cautious consensus rather than bold imperiousness was the preferred approach to rebuilding a capital region for which many Japanese elsewhere in the country had little taste.

Advised by the American economist Charles A. Beard, Gotō seized the moment to map out great boulevards for central Tokyo, and he argued that more small parks would serve as particularly effective firebreaks in future calamities, as well as improve residential life in congested low-lying areas of the city.[9] Beard and Gotō were right that Tokyo's twenty-eight public parks had helped to stop the spread of structure fires, even though twelve parks were destroyed and five partly burned; the rest were damaged by some of the estimated 1.57 million persons who took temporary refuge in Tokyo city parks, so that almost all twenty-eight had to be repaired.[10] The Capital Reconstruction Board, established by imperial decree on September 12, 1923, with Gotō as chair, estimated that 46 percent of buildings in Tokyo City and 78 percent of those in Yokohama had been destroyed, mainly by fires, driving more than two thirds of the newly homeless to city parks and most of the rest to suburbs or rural hometowns.[11]

Fleeing to open spaces did not always assure safety; on the treeless grounds of a former army clothing depot at Honjo, the belongings refugees brought with them caught fire, and as many as 38,000 people died in the appalling conflagration.[12] A memorial hall for those who died in the earthquake and fires was established not far away, at Yokoamichō, in 1930. The best that can be said of parks as evacuation sites in 1923 is that

for most people they were temporary assembly points, not places for organized disaster relief such as Tokyo eventually began to plan in 1978 and
the Construction Ministry finally ordered in 1998, three years after Kobe
was devastated in the Hanshin earthquake.[13]

Rumors quickly spread after the 1923 earthquake and fires that Korean residents of the Kanto district were looting or otherwise taking advantage of the chaos. Although the authorities took at least three thousand
Korean residents into protective custody, thousands of Koreans perished
at the hands of Japanese vigilantes and police officers, as did some Chinese
residents. While abhorring such racial violence, certain Japanese scolds
called the earthquake and fires a national wake-up call to reform wasteful
urban consumer habits and lax morals. Even the socialist reformer Abe
Isoo called for both spiritual cleansing, by ending alcohol abuse and pros-
titution, and material renovation, through improved hygiene, sewerage,
transport, and parks;[14] unsurprisingly, Abe eagerly supported the grand
schemes of the Capital Reconstruction Board.

Gotō Shinpei decided to use the emergency to build a new city worthy
of the empire whose overseas interests he had administered during ten
years as a city planner in Taiwan, then as the first president of the South
Manchuria Railway Company from 1906 to 1908. He sought ¥4 billion to
kick-start his daring proposal, known as the big carryall, to provide monumental public buildings, broad avenues, abundant transit, and inviting
public spaces.[15] Gotō pressed this proposal through the Capital Reconstruction Board but ran into fierce opposition from fiscal conservatives
in the cabinet and out-of-town politicians in the Diet. The board's initial
budget was just ¥11 million, with two thirds earmarked for roads, yet Gotō
set aside nearly 3 percent for parks, the rationale being that they were de-
monstrably vital for fire defense and emergency refuge.[16]

Despite a series of budget shortfalls and a lack of any master plan to
reify the board's vision, Gotō successfully put forward a scheme in November 1923 to repair the damage to Tokyo's twenty-eight existing parks, then
construct three new large ones and fifty-two mini-parks in the hardest hit
areas of the city. A Special City Planning Law passed in December 1923
allowed reconstruction authorities to rebuild damaged areas through land
readjustment, a practice followed since the 1870s for improving farmlands
by pooling scattered private holdings and contributing as much as three

tenths for improvements that benefited the community, such as roads. Under the Special City Planning Law, which remained in effect until 1955, government planners could take as much as 10 percent of private land-holdings without compensation for projects benefiting the public good, including roads, parks, and stores, on the assumption that the improvements increased the value of the affected properties. Under a companion land expropriation law the state could take a larger proportion of private plots by paying proper compensation for the share above 10 percent.[17] But because of local resistance and scaled-down planning, only 9 percent of the devastated areas originally tagged for land readjustment actually were adjusted for public purposes other than roads, and many of the new parks

Never one to hide his light under a bushel, Gotō Shinpei (1857–1929), a physician who became civilian governor of Taiwan and president of the South Manchuria Railway, later served as foreign minister and home minister, then as mayor of Tokyo. Gotō led the reconstruction of Tokyo and Yokohama after the earthquake and fires of September 1, 1923, then retired from public office to become president of the Boy Scouts of Japan. Here he reviews a parade of scouts in the late 1920s. Courtesy Kyōdō Tsūshinsha.

were built instead on government- or city-owned properties. This meant that adjustment and expropriation were much discussed but little used for adding parklands to Tokyo and Yokohama during the official reconstruction period, from 1923 to 1930.[18]

The Capital Reconstruction Board was downgraded to Capital Reconstruction Bureau and placed under the Home Ministry in January 1924, whereupon Gotō resigned. His great carryall, although shrunken by seven eighths in yen terms, became a small but potent toolkit from 1924 to 1930; the bureau built sturdy civic infrastructure in central Tokyo, almost doubling the number of roads and tripling the number of public parks, although parklands increased in area by just 16 percent.[19] The bureau focused its bulldozer-like efforts on the most devastated low-lying areas of the city where the changes made a sizable impact, especially through improvements to streets and a handful of boulevards. In the confusion of post–World War Two recovery and high-speed growth, some of the most beautiful boulevards were topped with unsightly expressways, and many of the mini-parks were replaced by elementary schools, so that surprisingly little remains today of the green spaces added after 1923.[20]

Why city parks ranked relatively high among rebuilding priorities is recorded in the *Fukkō keikaku* (Reconstruction plan) of November 1923: "Reasons for establishing parks—in ordinary times, public health, rest, and relaxation; in emergencies, fire prevention, evacuation, and relief. . . . to date it has been completely impossible to implement ideal park plans for reasons relating to the national treasury."[21] As with their proposals for national parks at this same time, Home Ministry bureaucrats focused mainly on health and exercise and emphasized that "physical strength is national strength," adding a statist purpose to the democratization of sports and the demand for athletic facilities in public parks that were sweeping the country in the 1920s.[22] Writing in 1930 as the reconstruction of Tokyo and Yokohama was ending, Ōya Reijō (1890–1934), a specialist in park design, summarized the rationale for adding parks: public health, rest and recreation, city beautification, fire prevention, offsetting the effects of urban growth, education, and the economic benefit of lifting the value of nearby real estate.[23] Nowhere in this official rhetoric was any mention of physical strength for potential military purposes.

Instead the context was relatively internationalist and pacific, although focused on social improvement and public benefit. As recommended by Charles Beard, the mini-parks built near elementary schools typically had Western-style plazas for lectures, concerts, and meetings, a participatory if not outright democratic idea learned from Chicago. Playgrounds for children were inspired by German examples and by American child psychology of the 1910s.[24] Inoshita Kiyoshi (1884–1973), the Tokyo parks chief, made certain to avoid standardized designs for the new mini-parks scattered throughout the low-lying parts of the city most affected by fires.[25] Modified European-style station plazas also appeared during the reconstruction of Tokyo at Ueno, the Marunouchi side of Tokyo Station, and the Mansei intersection.

Of the three large parks added in Tokyo after 1923, the riverfront Sumida Park most resembled an Edo-era famous vista. The embankment was widened from eleven to thirty-three meters and planted with three rows of cherries. Most of the space for the project was contributed jointly by the national and city governments; the central government paid three quarters of the ¥7.5 million cost of land and construction, with Tokyo covering the rest.[26] Orishimo Yoshinobu, the national government's lead designer of urban space, modeled Kinshi Park after an inner-city counterpart in Chicago, with a running track and playing fields for workers in the nearby factories and a well-equipped playground for children. His advanced design, with users' needs foremost, was a rarity for Japan; he was doubtless able to exercise great latitude because the six-hectare location, on the site of a former army quartermaster depot, was in a run-down part of the city. Hamachō, the third new large park, became a popular oasis near the Nihonbashi business district. Justified as an emergency evacuation site, this four-hectare park was laid out with a plaza, walking path, playground, pool that doubled as an emergency reservoir, benches, and open areas for sports.[27] In these ways the scaled-back reconstruction program installed modern parks, generally resembling those in Western countries, in some of the neediest neighborhoods that had been largely untouched by the Grand Council parks of 1873, the Tokyo City Improvement Plan of 1888–1889, or the planning districts formed under the City Planning Law of 1919.

Mindful that public parks continued to serve as shelters for the needy, Inoshita Kiyoshi wrote in 1932 that the homeless spent more time there than other users and enjoyed the freedom they found in the open. He cited a Tokyo survey in late 1930 that identified 1,799 homeless persons in the city, 48 percent of whom spent the night at Asakusa, Ueno, and eighteen other of Tokyo's ninety urban parks. Inoshita noted that ordinary park visitors "don't like, and feel fear of," the homeless, but he pointed out that homeless people were citizens with full rights to use the parks. He called on parks officials to create a comfortable atmosphere for all park visitors,[28] a challenge of social management still unmet eighty years later.

Reconstruction money also financed two new large parks in Yokohama, with the central government paying 75 percent and the municipality 25 percent of the costs, the same basis as in Tokyo. These parks drew on modern design features from Hibiya Park and mainly from urban models in the West, but whatever aesthetic success they attained came mostly from their settings on hilltops or near waterways. Yokohama turned its stone memorial to the late feudal reformer Sakuma Shōzan (1811–1864)

Yamashita Park in Yokohama was Japan's first public seaside park, built atop rubble from the 1923 earthquake and fires.

into Nogeyama Park and zoo, a seven-hectare space surrounded by merchant villas and much verdure on Azuma Hill. Yokohama also added a well-planted swath on seven hectares beside the harbor and named it Yamashita Park, a pet project of Orishimo Yoshinobu mainly because it was Japan's first seaside park.[29] Ironically, Yamashita is vulnerable to earthquakes because it sits atop a landfill of rubble from the 1923 disaster.

Bank of Japan estimates put the total damage from the earthquake and fires at ¥4.57 billion ($2.28 billion at the time), triple Japan's national budget, although the actual amount was at least ¥2 billion higher.[30] When reconstruction officially ended in 1930, governments at all levels had spent ¥820 million to rebuild Tokyo and Yokohama. Additional outlays during the 1930s brought the final tally much higher; for Yokohama, which had just one tenth the population of Tokyo when the earthquake struck, rebuilding eventually soaked up ¥273.9 million in public monies.[31] The remaining costs fell on private insurers, businesses, and individuals or were met by long-term economic growth. Immediately after the earthquake the population of Tokyo City temporarily fell from 2.49 million to 1.53 million; the innermost districts never regained their density because many residents and factories relocated permanently to the suburbs.[32] The exodus accelerated the rapid suburbanization already taking place; the population in towns just outside Tokyo doubled between 1922 and 1930 to 2.9 million,[33] with railway and real estate conglomerates such as Tōkyū and Seibu enriched from erecting single-family "cultural residences" in tightly platted developments along their commuter lines. Haphazard local park development followed in the early 1930s. However inadequate the rebuilding efforts may have been, Tokyo City itself did not languish. Its economy steadily recovered and its population quickly rebounded and swelled to five million by 1932, partly because some of the suburbs were absorbed into the city that year when twenty wards were added to the original fifteen. With slight expansion at the edges in 1935 the city thereafter covered about the same area as the twenty-three wards of today.[34]

Private Gifts to the Public

An indirect result of the 1923 earthquake and fires was a steady stream of private land donations for public use throughout the metropolitan region, mainly to boost the number of urban parks. A half-century or more after daimyo and religious lands were turned into Grand Council parklands, the new gifts represented a second stage of converting private properties to common civic ownership. By donating estates to Tokyo, both the imperial household and leading business families helped to answer the public need for more green spaces throughout the sprawling region.

Conveying private real estate to an agency of government in Japan was well-nigh impossible before the linked concepts of public state and private property were clearly established in law and tax policy at the beginning of the Meiji period. Even before Inoshita Kiyoshi began soliciting the donations of private property that added thirty-four new parks to Tokyo between 1923 and 1946, family gardens and other green spaces had started to open to the public throughout the country. The Yokohama banker Hara Tomitarō (1868–1939) made his family garden available to visitors starting in 1906;[35] six years later General Nogi Maresuke (1849–1912) gave his residence to Tokyo for a park before he and his wife killed themselves in 1912.[36] Another early gift was the donation in 1913 of imperial estates west

A swan glides on pedal power at Inokashira Park in western Tokyo, granted by the imperial family in 1913.

of Tokyo that became Inokashira, Japan's first suburban park, two years later. The city planned the park with the promise to provide public access while also protecting the lake's watershed, a key source of drinking water. Later, faced with wartime shortages of timber, the government felled 15,000 trees—mainly cryptomeria—around the lake in 1944.[37] Today the restored woods serve, inter alia, as outdoor studios for musicians to practice brass and woodwinds.

Inoshita Kiyoshi, who became head of Tokyo's Parks Department in 1923, tirelessly cultivated rich donors to give the city lands for public betterment.[38] The imperial family, nominally to mark Crown Prince Hirohito's wedding, in 1924 returned Ueno Park to Tokyo's supervision and donated the Shiba Detached Estate and the Sarue Imperial Estate as city parks. The palace granted these lands barely four months after the earthquake and fires as a gesture of accommodation to city residents; part of the purpose was also to give Tokyo unquestioned control of open spaces in future emergencies.[39] The Shiba site immediately became a public park, known as the Kyū Shiba Rikyū Gardens, a landscape in the Japanese style originally commissioned by the Kii Tokugawa family in the Edo period. Part of the garden was taken over to construct a World Trade Center at Hamamatsuchō, opened in March 1970, which at 152 meters towers over the remainder of the park. Sarue, east of the Sumida River, was a lumber warehouse for the Tokugawa family during the Edo era.[40] Kinoshita turned it into a regular neighborhood park for parents with small children, teenagers playing soccer and baseball, and old people enjoying the outdoors. Another notable imperial donation arrived in 1934 when Prince Takamatsu (1905–1987), the younger brother of the Shōwa emperor, gave the core land for Prince Arisugawa Memorial Park.[41] Today its seven hectares include a hillside fishing pond, four tennis courts, and the well-used Tokyo Metropolitan Central Library.

Some of the largest gifts of city parklands during the 1930s were meticulously crafted former daimyo gardens in the capital and the castle towns of the 265 domains during the Edo period, as well as some lavish gardens in cities under direct Tokugawa control such as Nagoya, Kyoto, Osaka, and Nagasaki.[42] After the Meiji Restoration many of the finest daimyo gardens in Tokyo fell into private hands, mainly those of entrepreneurs who led Japan's new commercial and industrial enterprises. But a number

Sarue Park was donated to Tokyo by the imperial family in 1924 as a gesture of support after the earthquake and fires of 1923. Park benches at Sarue are segmented to deter visitors from reclining.

have become public parks, usually with nominal admission fees, of which Koishikawa Kōrakuen (1629), Hama Rikyū (1654), and Rikugien (1695) are notable examples.

Koishikawa Kōrakuen in central Tokyo was built by Tokugawa Yorifusa (1603–1661) starting in 1629 as a Chinese-style garden designed by Zhu Shunsui (1600–1682), a Ming refugee.[43] Its layout suggested a peaceful, stable order for Edo society, but after 1868 the new government reduced the garden to seven hectares and turned most of the property into a munitions factory. The compact garden, which resembled in terrain and vegetation the crowded residential housing outside its gates, became a public park in 1938 after the weapons factory was relocated to Kokura (Kitakyushu).[44] Koishikawa Kōrakuen remains Tokyo's oldest garden and one of its most serene public parks, attracting relatively few users considering its central location.

Hama Rikyū, a broad space in the shadow of bland skyscrapers at Shiodome, originated as a villa for Matsudaira Tsunashige (1644–1678), then became a bayside excursion site for the imperial family after 1868 and was converted to a public park shortly after World War Two. The Nakajima teahouse overlooking its Japanese garden proved useful for entertaining foreign dignitaries during the late nineteenth century.[45] Air defense trenches were dug and antiaircraft guns installed there during World War Two, but American bombers destroyed the teahouse and other park structures during an air raid on November 29, 1944. A year later the imperial household turned the space over to the Tokyo Metropolitan Government, which opened it as a public park the following April and eventually rebuilt the teahouse in 1982.[46]

Perhaps the last of the great daimyo gardens to be built in Edo before tight finances curbed the fief lords' horticultural ambitions was Rikugien, founded in 1695 by Yanagisawa Yoshiyasu (1658–1714).[47] This nine-hectare strolling garden, thickly planted with trees and shrubs surrounding a pond with aged koi and turtles, was laid out by Yoshiyasu with eighty-eight notable spots marked by stones to commemorate famous locations, poems, and customs in both China and Japan (only thirty-two markers survive). Whereas Koishikawa Kōrakuen used Chinese design principles to draw together representations of scenic vistas throughout Japan, Rikugien symbolically united Chinese and Japanese spatial culture through unmistakably Japanese landscaping. Iwasaki Yatarō (1835–1885) bought Rikugien in 1878 as a villa for his family, the founders of the Mitsubishi enterprises. In 1938 the family donated Rikugien to Tokyo City, which immediately opened it to the public as a park. Rikugien suffered little war damage and apparently was not used for growing vegetables, as was common in other city parks during the conflict and its immediate aftermath. Its administrators eliminated entrance fees in 1972 as a gesture toward broadening Tokyo's civic benefits, but in time the park became overwhelmed by visitors, so the fees were reinstated in 1979.[48] The small cost has not greatly discouraged attendance; Rikugien remains one of Tokyo's most appreciated amenities despite a location further from the city center than either Koishikawa Kōrakuen or Hama Rikyū.[49]

Perhaps the most nearly public of the late-Edo gardens was Mukōjima Hyakkaen, Tokyo's oldest small park founded by a commoner, for use by anyone who enjoyed flowers. This one-hectare property, near the banks of the Sumida River in an out-of-the-way corner of northeastern Edo, was

Rikugien (1695), a former daimyo garden donated to Tokyo by the Iwasaki family and opened as a public park in 1938.

built in stages starting in 1804 by the aesthete, tea connoisseur, and high-end antiques dealer Sahara Kikuu (1762–1831). Sahara chose shrubs and flowers mentioned in the Chinese *Shijing* (Book of poetry, 600 B.C.E.) and the Japanese *Man'yōshū* (Collection of ten thousand leaves, 8th c.), and he installed twenty-nine monuments honoring various writers. In 1938 Mukōjima Hyakkaen's owner donated the park to Tokyo City, which continued to operate it as a facility open to the public for a small fee.[50] Other private gifts of land intended for parks arrived steadily in the 1920s and 1930s, thanks to Inoshita's skill in cultivating donors but also to the costly burden of maintenance borne by the heirs of wealthy private entrepreneurs. Descendants of Yasuda Zenjirō (1838–1921), the baron of banking and insurance, donated his one-time daimyo garden in Yokoamichō to the city in 1922. It opened as Yasuda Garden Park in 1926 after damage caused by the earthquake had been repaired. Iwasaki Hisaya (1865–1955), the third president of the Mitsubishi holdings, gave five garden hectares of his Fukagawa residence in 1924 as public parkland. The city opened the property as Kiyosumi Garden Park in 1932 and added three hectares in 1977.[51]

The first year of national general mobilization for war, 1938, was a bountiful moment for parkland donations, driven by a combination of family financial stringency and Inoshita's entreaties to add more open spaces to Tokyo now that Japan and China were embroiled in chronic warfare that started in July 1937. The family of Finance Minister Takahashi Korekiyo (1854–1936), who was assassinated in a failed rightist coup, conveyed his

Kiyosumi Garden Park, built by a Tokyo merchant in the 1720s, opened to the public in 1932.

property in the Akasaka district to Tokyo in 1938, and it was soon turned into a public park. During the 1930s Inoshita Kiyoshi also built Sayama Park around the watershed of the Murayama Reservoir in western Tokyo Prefecture, took over control of Koishikawa Botanical Garden from the Education Ministry, and accepted many of the thirty-four properties he accumulated as gifts to the city between the 1923 earthquake and his retirement in 1946.[52] One of his last acquisitions was Tetsugakudō (Philosophy Hall), a small but lush park atop Wada Hill in Nakano Ward, Tokyo, featuring a classical "temple to moral philosophy," in the words of its founder, Inoue Enryō (1858–1919).[53] Inoue intended this oddly handsome memorial, built from 1904 to 1920, to exalt Buddha, Confucius, Socrates, and Kant as guides to youth for leading a moral life. The Inoue family gave the property to the city in March 1944. An abutting parcel donated in 1946 combined with the Inoue gift to form a fine park for a large population in northwestern Tokyo. Much grander is the Old Furukawa Garden, on three hectares north of Komagome Station in Tokyo. Originally the home of the Meiji diplomat Mutsu Munemitsu (1844–1897), this park was given to the city in 1956 and contains a formidable Western-style house and garden designed by Josiah Conder, as well as an adjacent Japanese garden by Ogawa Jihei (Niwashi Ueji, 1860–1933).[54]

By 1973, when Tokyo celebrated the hundredth anniversary of its first public parks, the city had accepted eighty-eight gifts of private land totaling 93 hectares, starting with Shimizudani Park in 1890. Together with existing city-owned parcels and additional purchases, the donations were turned into parks covering 167 hectares.[55] The motives for the gifts usually were cloaked from view but often seem to have involved family matters, especially deaths, rather than tax abatements or magnanimous outbursts of civic spirit. Commemorating a deceased relative in parkland brought more lasting attention than a grave marker, especially when the new park was named after the individual. Giving away real estate no longer needed by the family brought renown, if not cash, but at least it relieved the owners of maintenance expenses by transferring costs to the city parks department. Charitable gifts, even from family foundations, conferred few tax advantages on the donors because of the well-established principle in Japan that expenditures for the common good were the responsibility of government, not private citizens.[56] The impulse to contribute land to the

Tetsugakudō (completed 1920) is a "temple to moral philosophy," according to its founder, Inoue Enryō (1858–1919). His family donated the property to Tokyo for a public park, opened in 1946.

city during national general mobilization starting in April 1938 may have been heightened by prospective air defense needs in wartime, although a more likely explanation for the spate of gifts that year is Inoshita's charm in educating donors about Tokyo's ongoing green space plan, first discussed in 1932 and finally announced in 1939. Behind-the-scenes personal connections with bureaucrats and politicians doubtless played some role in stimulating the gifts as well. Even with allowances for the occasional unwanted donation, the city and its residents benefited considerably from the new public spaces, particularly because they were widely distributed in underserved neighborhoods.

The Home Ministry and City Parks in the 1930s

Within Japan the 1930s were a time of economic retrenchment, suppression of dissent, political violence, and increasing militarization of government from the Hirota Cabinet of March 1936 onward. Internationally the country engaged in tariff wars with its trade partners, withdrew from long-standing multilateral security and commercial treaties, and tightened the grip on its overseas colonies after the imperial army seized Manchuria in 1931, then engaged in all-out war with China starting in July 1937. The decade was also one of population growth for the biggest Japanese cities, especially in suburbs once war production partly relocated there after 1937. Tokyo Prefecture counted 5.4 million residents in 1930 and almost 7.4 million in 1940, double its 3.7 million just twenty years earlier.[57] Osaka in 1940 stood at 3 million, and Yokohama, Nagoya, and Kobe each approached 1 million.[58]

Tokyo, now the world's second-largest metropolis after New York, added 103 new city parks from 1931 to 1940, increasing the area of parklands within the thirty-five wards by half.[59] The Home Ministry required set-asides of 3 percent for parks in all 545 city planning districts nationwide starting in 1933, with particular results in suburban areas, although the greatest impact was felt after 1945. The 3 percent rule was carried forward in the Land Readjustment Law of 1954 and remains in effect for city planning districts, even though everyone agrees that 3 percent is far too low to meet people's needs.[60]

Nationwide more than five hundred new city parks were established in the mid-1930s, nearly all quite small.[61] Nagoya was the trailblazer and today, together with Tokyo and Fukuoka, remains one of Japan's greenest cities. In the late 1920s Nagoya used land readjustment in its city planning districts to build new neighborhood parks totaling thirty-four hectares, then by 1937 added another eighteen hectares of parkland "to commemorate the birth of Crown Prince Akihito" in 1933.[62] Osaka doubled its number of city parks from 1927 to 1938 by adding at least twenty-one new ones, averaging 1.5 hectares each, although its 1928 urban plan drafted by Seki Hajime had called for far more: forty-six parks on 560 hectares.[63] Nagoya and Osaka were also the first Japanese cities to put green belts and green spaces into practice, notably the Hattori and Tsurumi green areas in Osaka, completed in 1941.[64]

Tokyo too used land readjustment techniques to put together parcels for many of the parks it added during the 1930s.[65] Land readjustment cut into farmland at the city's edges and often profited private landowners, foreshadowing the post–World War Two era when land readjustment was a tool for landlords to raise their property values by developing private housing. Land readjustment in the 1930s helped municipal authorities stockpile real estate for potential parks but did not prove to be a refined instrument for their placement or development.[66] The City Planning Law also authorized cities to select certain areas, usually with attractive plantings, as scenic districts that could not be developed without approval from prefectural governors and the Home Ministry—a simple and inexpensive way to protect open lands from development. These districts were contemporary landscapes important to current residents for the relief from the city they afforded, quite distinct from the retrogressive famous vistas evoking a romanticized past that were provided for in the monuments law of 1919.

Some scenic districts created in the 1930s later were partly converted to parks with facilities to serve their neighborhoods, such as Zenpukuji scenic district in western Tokyo. The nearby Shakujii area around Sanpōji Temple was designated a scenic district in 1930, then partly turned into a public park from 1957 to 1959, with a long, narrow lake for boating and fishing overlooked by large homes of the wealthy.[67] More storied than these fine local parks was Senzoku Ike (Foot-washing pond) Park in southern Tokyo, where the radical Buddhist priest Nichiren (1222–1282) is said to have washed his hands and feet in 1282 shortly before he died.[68] Beginning in 1966 cities were also authorized to nominate sites of particular national significance as historical and cultural preservation districts. As of 2003 there were more than two dozen of these, covering 155 square kilometers. In addition, three prefectures where premodern capitals once stood have created special historical-cultural preservation districts: Nara (imperial government, 710–784), Kyoto (Heian imperial government, 794–1185), and Kanagawa (Kamakura military government, 1192–1333). These special districts preserve simulacra of the nation's political history.[69]

Tokyo's recovery from the earthquake and fires of 1923 jump-started a flurry of laws, regulations, donations, and planning that by 1940 added 142 city parks to the 28 that were in the capital when the earthquake struck.[70] Yokohama likewise benefited from reconstruction funding in expanding its city parks. Nationally the full effects of the 1919 City Planning Law were felt in a steep increase in urban parklands during the 1930s, although they were more subject to Home Ministry specifications than before. The rationales for providing more public spaces expressed both by officials and by private advocates remained divergent, sometimes contradictory, focused more on collective goals for a better society than on individual benefit. Despite ¥23 million in central government support for city parks during the reconstruction of Kanto, the pay-as-you-play principle laid down for the Grand Council parks in 1873 remained in effect; the parks were expected to generate enough revenues, mainly from rents and concessions, to pay their own way. Only after World War Two did the central government begin to make regular budget provisions for city parks, at a time when it also had to support the new national parks that were approved by the Diet in 1931.

A Green Belt for the Capital

Shortly after the Diet passed the National Parks Law of 1931, Japan's thinking about urban open spaces took a turn toward the suburbs when the Home Ministry and Tokyo formed the Tokyo Green Space Planning Commission, inspired partly by the 1924 International City Planning Conference held in Amsterdam, to develop a green space plan for the entire area within a fifty-kilometer radius of Tokyo Station, covering nearly ten thousand square kilometers and a population of five million. The commission thus recalibrated the scope of Japanese metropolitan design away from small city planning districts toward conceptualizing the capital region as a whole. This first attempt at regional planning in Japan involved representatives from the Home Ministry, Tokyo City, police, railways, construction, traffic, religious institutions, and the three neighboring prefectures of Kanagawa, Saitama, and Chiba. The goals were to protect selected suburban environments from rampant development, provide more spaces for sports and recreation, and, most quixotic, stop urban creep into the suburbs.[71] Rather than building retrospectively on the 1919 City Planning Law, the commission acted prospectively as a guidepost to the postwar era, anticipating fresh legislation for the entire megalopolis that was enacted in the 1950s. Its recommendations, published after much deliberation in 1939, guided other prefectures in seeking green spaces to belt their cities against relentless spread.

Inoshita Kiyoshi, the Tokyo parks chief, was a key actor in the Green Space Commission along with the urban planner Kitamura Tokutarō (1886–1968). Kitamura is often credited with being the first to use the term "green space" (*ryokuchi*), translating the German *Grünfläche* (green surface) in 1924; at about the same time the urban administration specialist Ikeda Hiroshi (1881–1939) drew on the French idea of *espace libre* to create its Japanese equivalent, *jiyū kūchi* (free open space). Honda Seiroku and Uehara Keiji, occasional antagonists in the debates over national parks, began to use "open space" in 1924, expanding their horizon of vegetation beyond the sometimes stark city parks of the reconstructed Tokyo.[72] Reflecting these international concepts as mediated by Japanese practice, the Green Space Commission consistently defined green spaces as eternally open land, never to be built on, always available for the public to enjoy. The term "green space" meanwhile took on certain romantic colorations in Japan during the 1930s, connoting something closer to the nonhuman environment than merely empty spaces as before.[73]

While the commission's deliberations dragged on, Japan's eight-year war in China began with due patriotic pride on the home front, tempered by puzzlement about why the skirmish outside Beijing on July 7, 1937, unlike other battles after Japan seized Manchuria in September 1931, did not end in a quick settlement between the imperial army and Chiang Kai-shek's Nationalist government. Instead the fighting bogged down, then dilated into total war with the Western Allies starting with Japan's attacks on Pearl Harbor, the Philippines, and Hong Kong on December 8, 1941, Tokyo time. The multifront conflict turned against Japan in mid-1942 and ended three years later in deep public disillusionment, vast ecological damage, and utter military disaster.

An Air Defense Law enacted in April 1937 authorized fire-prevention green zones that eventually helped implement both the Green Space Commission's recommendations in 1939 and revisions to the City Planning Law in 1940 to account for air defense. By the time the Green Space Commission reported to the mayor of Tokyo in 1939, the case for adding more green areas was bolstered by wartime needs to train young people's physiques, emplace antiaircraft guns, and create emergency evacuation grounds. The commission's report became a major element in the cabinet's Air Defense Open Space Plan of 1943, which anticipated the massive air raids by U.S. Army Air Corps B-24s and B-29s that obliterated more than half the structures in sixty-six Japanese cities between November 1944 and August 1945.[74] Despite these developments, the main arguments in the commission's report remained squarely civilian: environmental protection, enhanced recreation, and guarding against urban sprawl.[75]

The 1939 Tokyo Green Space Plan dwarfed in scope if not in cost Gotō Shinpei's first grand design for remaking Tokyo after the 1923 earthquake and fires. The 1939 proposal identified three types of green areas: (1) ordinary open spaces such as parks, cemeteries, temple and shrine grounds, botanical gardens, schoolyards, community vegetable plots, and amusement parks; (2) built green environments, such as tree plantations, dairies, airfields, farms, and fisheries; and (3) other properties such as formal gardens and protected scenic and historical monuments. The plan named forty potential parks and wooded areas, covering seventeen square kilometers, and twenty-seven mini-parks to be distributed from the Yamanote area of Tokyo City outward to the fifty-kilometer boundary of the capital district. The commission's enthusiasm was so great that it extended its compass, informally but persuasively, as far as one hundred kilometers west of the city to the mountains. Included were vacant private properties with the huge total of 2,891 square kilometers that could be purchased and turned into large green preservation zones, for recreation, rest, and enjoyment of the surroundings.[76] Starting in 1950 most of these preservation zones ended up in the Chichibu-Tama-Kai National Park, the Tanzawa Daizan Quasi-National Park, or prefectural parks. Overall the plan called for 3,579 square kilometers of green space at a cost of more than ¥100 million (U.S. $25 million), including land acquisition and improvements.[77]

But the central feature of the 1939 design repeated the city's earlier efforts to control expansion: a green girdle intended "to serve as one step in blocking the unlimited growth and excessive size of greater Tokyo," according to the commission's notes.[78] The plan projected a circumferential belt of open land, one to two kilometers in width, stretching 72 kilometers in a great arc from the Tama River and Kinuta in western Setagaya, along the Zenpukuji River, through Ogikubo and following today's Kanpachi Boulevard to Senkawa, then along the Toda River to the Edo and Ara Rivers. Such a giant swath would occupy 134 square kilometers of great potential value to their owners and to the developers who sought this land in

The upper Ara River in Chichibu-Tama-Kai National Park, established in 1950 (Kai was added in 2000). Courtesy Karen L. Thornber.

the postwar period. This visionary plan recommended that the prefecture buy 110 square kilometers of these properties within five years, assisted by funds available under the Air Defense Law and separate monies tagged for purchasing parks to commemorate the supposed 2,600th anniversary of the nation's founding in 1940. As of 1939 about 80 of these 145 square kilometers were farms and forests, known as productive green spaces.

Eventually the projected green belt, renamed the nation's only air defense green belt in 1943, was expanded to 145 square kilometers, including 15 square kilometers devoted to public beautification and 25 to parks.[79]

In some ways the Tokyo Green Space Plan was ill-timed, yet it appeared at a fortuitous moment for the history of urban parks in Japan. The bad timing, in the thick of a major war in China, precluded winning the funds needed to implement the plan, which was endorsed by the mayor and forwarded to the home minister but never sent to the cabinet for approval. Moreover, to the extent that containing population within the green belt was a genuine aim, the plan came too late and with too few teeth to stop the continual expansion of housing into the suburbs, especially because local governments during wartime lacked the cash to buy up farmlands for parks and other green spaces. Despite the vicissitudes of war and defeat, Tokyo's population by 1949 swelled to nine million, bursting through the ring of open land to settle into ever more distant suburbs.[80] It proved hard to institutionalize green belts in the largest cities because both land owners and developers, sensing profits, took full advantage of Japan's lack of clear land policies, and thus much of the 1939 Green Space Plan came to naught. Even the new City Planning Law of 1968, which tried to limit urbanization of the suburbs, was eviscerated or even ignored under the incessant demand for land in the 1970s and 1980s.[81]

On the other hand, the Green Space Plan of 1939 appeared in time to function as the Tokyo region's first informal master plan, sketching the outlines of parks and other open lands that took concrete shape in the second half of the century. The plan also rode the worldwide wave of interest in sports and recreation during the 1930s, especially once the Physical Strength Bureau of the new Welfare Ministry (est. 1938) began promoting vigorous exercise, now with support from the army. The Welfare Ministry, formed mainly from the Hygiene Bureau of the Home Ministry, was responsible for stabilizing people's livelihoods and for "cultivating people's spiritual and physical capacities through promoting their health for the industrial economy and, in emergency times, for national defense."[82] Parks, athletic fields, and other open spaces such as those advocated in the Green Space Plan were indispensable for this purpose, and led by Tamura Tsuyoshi the Physical Strength Bureau pressed hard for more of them.

The Welfare Ministry allocated ¥400,000 in 1939 for new sports facilities in fourteen big cities and another ¥100,000 to refurbish existing ones, so that as Japan plunged ever deeper into war, athletics for both males and females figured more and more conspicuously in planning for parks and other green spaces.[83] In 1940 the ministry nearly quintupled its outlay for sports, to ¥1.9 million,[84] then in 1941 increased it by another ¥1 million.[85] By then group exercises and physical education had become de rigueur in schools, factories, and offices in both Japan and the colonies. Under National General Mobilization, sports for youths and adults, as with children's playgrounds during the war, were intended for collective "control and order," not free play.[86] The much-anticipated Tokyo Olympics of 1940 also triggered great public interest in athletics until the games were postponed, to be held there under far more pacific circumstances in 1964.[87] Coupled with the Air Defense Law of 1937 and the celebrations of Japan's 2,600th anniversary in 1940, the otherwise beleaguered Green Space Plan helped to identify a number of important Tokyo parklands that, through a convoluted process, became available for fuller development as key social investments after World War Two.

In the Nation's Service

Long before plunging into war with China in 1937, Tokyo planned to host three major events for national prestige in 1940: the Olympics, a world exposition, and a ceremony in the Imperial Palace plaza marking the 2,600th anniversary of the country's founding.

Because of World War Two, only the latter went forward as scheduled in November 1940, together with East Asian Games in Tokyo involving athletes from throughout the empire, Southeast Asia, and Hawai'i. For the anniversary ceremony the palace outer plaza was replanted with black pines, still visible today, suggesting longevity of the imperial line. As a part of the anniversary, the central government underwrote half the costs of acquiring vacant land in twenty-six cities to serve as commemorative parks. The Tokyo assembly in February 1940 approved a ¥25 million budget to establish seven of these, all of them open areas identified in the Green Space Plan of 1939.[88] Six anniversary green spaces were jointly purchased by Tokyo and the central government, adding 584 hectares of suburban open lands with riverside woods, paddies, dry fields, and orchards from Kinuta in the southwest clockwise through Jindai, Koganei, Toneri, and Mizumoto to Shinozaki in eastern Tokyo. The seventh, at Ōizumi, was regained from U.S. military forces in 1972–1973.

Most of these parcels were not developed as parks during the war but were instead rented out as farmland, making them vulnerable to land reform when American officials imposed economic democratization starting in October 1946. The proportion lost to land reform ranged from 43 percent at Koganei and 44 percent at Kinuta to 95 percent at Toneri, forcing the metropolitan government to repurchase the most crucial forfeited portions when it set about reconfiguring the six into scaled-back city parks.[89] Eventually all seven parks became handsome public spaces with extensive botanical beds, broad open meadows, flowering trees, and in most cases athletic fields. To a lesser degree the 559 hectares of anniversary parklands acquired by Osaka and the 535 hectares acquired by Nagoya, after going through land reform and selective repurchase, similarly became parklands appealing to many age groups.[90] In short, although the

Tokyo's Palace Outer Garden, with black pines in the plaza planted in 1940.

imperial anniversary eventually produced some much-needed parks nationally, in Tokyo the tonic was far less immediate than with the royal grants of imperial estates at Inokashira in 1913 and Ueno, Sarue, and the Kyū Shiba Rikyū property in 1924.

Yet the most important legacy of wartime for Japan's city parks after 1945 was a long-term outcome of the 1937 Air Defense Law, particularly after it was amended in 1941 to let cities designate firebreaks. The law encouraged strategic industries to scatter to suburbs far outside the capital, where they would be less vulnerable to bombs and ensuing fires. The resulting exodus created a need for outlying parks that the Green Space Plan did not fully address, and it also created a need for open spaces to protect against the spread of fire. Closer to Tokyo, relentless suburbanization encroached on or leaped right over much of the green belt set forth in the 1939 plan, so that the Air Defense Law and follow-up legislation became major implements for carving out open spaces, especially in regions outside city planning districts. This legal cascade made it easier for city officials around the country to open up public spaces: "land was expropriated for parks and green spaces on a vast scale hitherto unknown in Japan."[91] Some were converted to permanent parklands after 1945, but in the immediate context of 1940 urban parks and other green spaces now existed to serve the state to a degree not previously seen or foreseen.

By recognizing air defense as a legitimate function of city parks, the government freed up money from the Home Ministry to allow Japan's largest cities to purchase at least four thousand hectares in addition to the several thousand acquired jointly with central and prefectural monies to mark the 2,600th anniversary.[92] By 1943, air defense parks were established in forty-six cities,[93] meaning that large chunks of open real estate were frozen by the militarized state and unavailable to others, removed from the everyday transactions of the civilian economy and no longer subject to routine sale and purchase in a free market. Yet after 1945 this emergency commandeering of land greatly benefited farmers through land reform, developers as the cities repopulated, and in certain cases municipal authorities eager to add new parklands.

Despite the ravages of bombings, postwar malnutrition, severe inflation, and land reform, Tokyo retained or repurchased sizable portions of its air defense green space for development as parks. In addition to the seven anniversary parks, downsized air defense tracts were revamped and newly reopened as city parks at Komazawa in time for the 1964 Olympics, as well as at Wadabori, Shakujii, Zenpukuji, and many other places. Among prewar facilities that were part of the air defense network, Inokashira Park lost about 15 percent of its area to land reform but remained a popular venue for residents of the western suburbs. In sum, even though parks and other green areas in Tokyo were put to hard labor during the national emergency, wartime left a solid foundation for expanding the city's open spaces once the country began to repair war damage. This little-recognized inheritance from the darkest era of Japan's modern history stands shoulder to shoulder with the Grand Council directive of 1873 and Gotō Shinpei's reconstruction of the city in 1923 as decisive elements in the growth of a much greener capital during the past half-century.

Parks and Society from War to Peace

Arising between these elaborate land use plans and the postwar metamorphosis of green spaces into city parks were their wartime functions amid national peril. By 1943 both Tokyo and Osaka had seized all remaining vacant lots to prevent construction and keep them ready as firebreaks. The Wartime Emergency Law of February 1943, announced as Japanese forces fell back after fierce fighting in the South Pacific, brought a halt to city planning and construction of city parks and green spaces. Historic, scenic, and natural monuments were closed, followed by national parks the next year. Schools, shrines, and parks were stripped of metal objects requisitioned as scrap for war matériel. Parks and other green areas not only served as passive firebreaks but also hosted both students and soldiers for drill; near the end of the war housewives and the elderly worked out there with bamboo spears, practicing with grim resolve to repel an expected enemy invasion.

The American air raids from Pacific bases on Saipan and Tinian during the last nine months of the war caused vast damage by conventional high explosives and unconventional napalm fire bombs well before the atomic devastation of Hiroshima and Nagasaki in August 1945. Ten million people, including three million from the Tokyo area, evacuated the cities for temporary refuge with rural relatives or at inns in the mountains or at the shore. Nationally, 115 cities suffered the worst bombings and fires, which destroyed 632 square kilometers and burned 2.3 million homes.[94] The bombings and fires killed considerably more than 100,000 people in the Tokyo wards and destroyed 759,000 homes, roughly half the city's housing at that time.[95] City parks and green spaces were not prime bombing targets, but those with antiaircraft artillery often were attacked as soon as they gave away their camouflaged positions by firing at the American planes, which could spot the gunbursts from three thousand meters or more in the air.[96]

Open areas, including city parks, were effective firebreaks during all but the most severe incendiary bombings of residential neighborhoods. As intended, they also served as meeting points for families driven from their homes and as temporary overnight refuges, but the number of survivors immediately accommodated in city parks was far smaller than during the earthquake and fires of September 1, 1923. The reasons are clear: (1) citizens were well prepared for the air raids and during bombings often stayed in their home shelters, which were usually trenches in their yards, then emerged to staff bucket brigades for putting out fires in the largely wooden neighborhood housing; and (2) the 1923 earthquake struck the entire region at once, without warning, whereas the American attacks generally hit only selected targets in major cities on any given day. Three well-known exceptions were the massive firebombing of twenty-five square kilometers of low-lying areas in Tokyo on the night of March 9–10, 1945, Hiroshima on August 6, 1945, and Nagasaki three days later. The special role of parks for sheltering the newly homeless was long term; as of 1946, Tokyo still maintained temporary barrack-style housing in fifty city parks, housing nearly three thousand families,[97] while many thousands more fended for themselves in parks, beneath bridges, and along rail lines in the capital and throughout the country.

After the air raids local people began to plant sweet potatoes and pumpkins in Ueno and many other parks; Shinobazu Pond was used for growing rice.[98] The itinerant population chopped down some of Ueno's noted cherries for firewood, but springtime crowds returned in 1946 to view the blossoms on those that remained. Two years later a local civic group undertook to plant 250 new cherry trees in the park, with hopes of adding 750 more in future years.[99]

Even grimmer was the function of city parks as temporary burial sites for people killed in the air raids. Tokyo was overwhelmed by nearly 100,000 fatalities in the March 10, 1945, firebombing, when more than 12,000 bodies were placed in mass graves at Kinshi Park, an equal number at Sarue, and more than 8,000 at Ueno.[100] Part of the large cryptomeria forest at Inokashira Park was cut down to make coffins for those killed in air attacks. After the war the central government paid half the costs of restoring parks and exhuming bodies from temporary graves for a three-year period. About 7,000 corpses were identified and claimed by relatives; more than 100,000 others were cremated and placed in urns at the memorial hall for victims of the 1923 earthquake and fires, which was renamed the Tokyo Metropolitan Memorial Hall in 1951.[101]

The American military occupation of Japan from August 1945 to April 1952 changed so much about Japan, and yet so little. Nonetheless there is no doubt, as the historian John W. Dower puts it, that the Americans imposed "a neocolonial revolution from above" on Japan.[102] Public parks in city and country were buffeted by many changes right after the war, including some setbacks needing much time to repair, but overall they served as sources of institutional continuity from prewar to postwar. Even though 1,700 hectares of city parks were built under urban programs to repair war damage,[103] between 1945 and 1955 the country suffered a net loss of 163 city parks and 307 hectares of parkland, not taking into account new public facilities built inside parks such as an office building for City Hall in Kobe. These conditions led the Diet to enact a new City Parks Law in 1956 to assure the financial and spatial health of urban green areas (see chapter 4).[104]

A minor element in the net loss was that the American occupation requisitioned parks in several Japanese cities, but with its general headquarters in the Daiichi Building facing the Imperial Palace in Tokyo, the burden fell most heavily on that city. The Americans took over the baseball field, public hall, and other facilities and land at Hibiya but left most of the park available to the public. Nine other Tokyo parks were commandeered during the occupation, as well as a section of the Chōfu green space in the suburbs, covering parts of the airfield and residential area. The Americans gave back all 106 hectares of requisitioned city parks and green areas to Tokyo by the end of the occupation in 1952 except Yasuda

Garden Park, which they abandoned in July 1954, and the Chōfu property, returned to Tokyo's administration in 1973–1974 as part of a general re-alignment of American military facilities in the wake of Okinawa's rever-sion to Japanese authority on May 15, 1972.[105] The temporary loss of these public facilities at a time when park space was in decline for other reasons doubtless rankled, but the actual disruptions to people's everyday lives were relatively minor.

More permanent were the encroachments on parks caused by the ur-gent need for new houses, schools, and places of entertainment. As Tokyo repopulated from its August 1945 low point of 2.8 million in the ward area, a huge shortage of houses caused by wartime air raids led city of-ficials to allow fifty-three small parks totaling sixty hectares to be con-verted to new residences, yielding nearly three thousand homes. Although the area ceded to housing represented only 4 percent of Tokyo's public

Food became scarce in Japan in 1944 and even scarcer during the winter of 1945–1946, and city parks were partly plowed under to grow grain and vegetables. These well-dressed students tend a plot in Tokyo's Hibiya Park. Courtesy Tokyo Metropolitan Park Association.

parklands at the end of the war, more than a third of the loss occurred at a single location, Toyama Park in Shinjuku Ward, which according to the city parks administrator Ueda Yasuyuki "has never been restored to its planned glory."[106] Parks and other green spaces were natural targets for planners seeking construction sites for schools, causing the conversion of eighteen hectares in Tokyo alone.[107] Another seventeen hectares were used up by construction of new public and semipublic buildings, but the largest demand of all came from entrepreneurs of horse, bicycle, and auto racing, whose new enterprises provided popular entertainments for shared public and private profit at Ōi, Fuchū, Tachikawa, and Tokyo Keiōkaku, built on former green spaces totaling eighty-four hectares.[108]

Far more widespread was the loss of public open space to land reform, primarily green spaces not yet developed as city parks. When food grew desperately scarce during late 1945 and 1946, prefectural governors were urged to use parks and other green areas as temporary farmlands.[109] Nationwide more than a thousand hectares of city parkland and other green spaces are thought to have been used for cereals or vegetables from 1943 to 1946, after which most of these farmed parcels were sold to tenants through the land reform program. As a result, land reform claimed three large green space districts in Osaka and caused the forced sale or long-term lease of roughly five hundred hectares of Tokyo's open lands,[110] almost entirely open green spaces in the suburbs that had been rented out to tenant farmers, not land lost from established city parks. In effect, the cities represented the kind of big landlord that the reform was meant to humble through forced sale to tenants for a small fraction of the land's market value. The food crisis and the need to help tenants were urgent, but the lost area, at 33 percent of Tokyo's total city parks and green spaces in 1945,[111] was a harsh blow to the green belt planners and the Welfare Ministry officials who sought far more public spaces for the capital region.

Another change affecting land use in Japan was the separation of religion and state that was reconfirmed in the new constitution of May 1947. The separation, foreshadowed in the guarantee of religious freedom in the 1889 Meiji Constitution, meant that temple and shrine real estate, heretofore considered public-use property, was now returned to private religious use without restriction. As a result, between 1947 and 1955 roughly

410 hectares of temple and shrine precincts once considered public park-land were subtracted from the 963 hectares of city parks remaining in the capital after land reform,[112] completing the secularization of public space from its religious origins within the properties of temples and shrines as of 1868.

Mitigating these losses of public parks was a 1948 law allowing former Japanese military bases to "be leased to local public bodies free of charge . . . when used by public bodies for parks and green spaces."[113] By 1961 about 660 hectares of new city parks had been built on former Japanese bases not needed by the American occupation.[114] Osaka, Nagoya, Hakodate, and Utsunomiya were immediate beneficiaries of base conversion, but Tokyo's turn was delayed by the occupation and subsequent diplomacy. Because the American forces took over most imperial Japanese army and navy facilities in the Kanto region, then retained many of them under the terms of the Security Treaty of 1952, metropolitan Tokyo waited until the 1970s before receiving sizable military areas for use as city parks. In 1973 the United States returned about 860 hectares to Japan, including a large base at Tachikawa, one third of which was developed into the 180-hectare Shōwa Memorial Park under national auspices in 1983.[115] Tokyo Metropolis also was able to create city parks on 195 hectares of other army and air force bases returned by the United States during the 1960s and 1970s. The most central of these was Yoyogi Park on the site of the imperial army drill ground next to the Meiji Shrine at Harajuku. This base was renamed Washington Heights by the occupation and used for military housing before being partly converted to a village for Olympic athletes in 1964. Most of the other city parks established on former military grounds were opened in western suburbs such as Ōizumi, Musashino, Fuchū, and Higashi Yamato between 1981 and 2000,[116] finally fulfilling part of the promise of the Tokyo Green Space Plan of 1939. Including Shōwa Memorial Park, which functions as a city park, base conversion added 375 hectares to Tokyo's stock of urban parklands, a belated and partial offset of the 497 hectares lost to land reform from 1946 to 1952. Given the shrinkage of city park areas both in Tokyo and nationally in the decade following surrender, clearly new methods and new funds were required to create more open spaces for ballooning urban populations after 1955.

Rebuilding

The narrative of Japanese city parks from 1945 to 1955 was mainly one of restoring damaged areas in existing parks and building small new ones, on public land if possible, through purchase if feasible, or at times through land readjustment. Local civic groups contributed uncounted hours to clearing rubble, replanting, and installing what equipment they could afford. Residents in Hiroshima donated their time and skills to help create the Peace Memorial Park, built starting in 1949 as a combined project of citizens and governments at many levels. Parks that charged fees reopened fast: Ueno Zoo drew a throng of 98,879 on a Sunday in April 1949, which would be a banner crowd three decades later at a Tokyo department store or a half-century later at Tokyo Disneyland.[117] Restoration and reconstruction were watchwords, but without much long-term vision from planners or vocal constituency from park users. Even with the recovery of former imperial military bases temporarily taken over by the Americans, most Japanese cities barely managed to refurbish their prewar parklands by 1955, let alone add significantly to their green spaces.

The national government established a War Damage Reconstruction Board in late 1945 and approved a Basic Reconstruction Policy soon thereafter for the 115 cities hardest hit by air raids. Among the policy's many agenda items was the idealistic target of reserving at least 10 percent by area of urban reconstruction districts for parks, playgrounds, green belts, and other open spaces.[118] A Special City Planning Law passed by the Diet in September 1946, together with legislation in 1949 to create peace parks at Hiroshima and Nagasaki, provided a streamlined legal basis for carrying out the rebuilding nationally. The 1946 law recognized green zones totaling 314 square kilometers in the ten largest cities, including 92 square kilometers in Tokyo Metropolis, providing a degree of protection for suburban open lands even if they were later subjected to land reform. In a vain effort to prevent a headlong rush of people back to the largest cities, the Basic Reconstruction Policy and the Special City Planning Law prioritized smaller cities between 1946 and 1949, compounding the financial hurdles faced by the largest metropolitan areas when they repopulated even faster than expected.[119]

Tokyo's 1946 reconstruction plan at first embraced the entire Kanto plain, but for want of legal jurisdiction in other prefectures it was soon cut back to Tokyo Metropolis. Its quixotic goal was to keep the population of the ward area at its December 1945 level of 3.5 million, and it allowed for an additional 5 million in suburbs lying beyond the green belt that had been proposed in 1939 and incorporated into the Air Defense Open Space Plan of 1943. The reconstruction of Tokyo, led by chief planner Ishikawa Hideaki (1893–1955), was meant to accomplish much that Gotō Shinpei's rebuilding project had failed to do in 1923: remake parks, roads, parkways, transit, and residential districts to relieve congestion, provide more fire-breaks, and plant trees, shrubs, and flowers. The plan sought to produce 33 square kilometers of parklands in bombed-out districts of Tokyo, but only 5 square kilometers were actually completed, nearly all in existing parks that were restored.[120] Altogether the plan identified 180 square kilometers for rebuilding with appropriate green spaces, yet only 14 square kilometers were finally incorporated into the reconstruction of Tokyo, mostly through land readjustment near major transit hubs.[121] The Special City Planning Law of 1946 carried forward the principle of land readjustment, but only 6 percent of the planned areas actually were adjusted in the capital,[122] mainly because landlords resisted the uncompensated forfeitures and the occupation was cool to land readjustment as a mechanism.[123]

Both Ishikawa Hideaki's vision and the renewal efforts in other cities sputtered for reasons like those that reduced Tokyo's recovery plans in 1923 to the basics. As in 1923, the Reconstruction Board was prematurely terminated and its functions were dispersed to a number of agencies. In both the mid-1920s and the late 1940s, the central city and the suburbs grew so fast that green space planning was overwhelmed by demands for new housing and other amenities; the ward area of Tokyo swelled from a population of 3.5 million in December 1945 to 5.4 million in 1950, then kept on growing throughout the 1950s.[124] The government abandoned green belts in 1968, finally agreeing that they were unworkable. The preference given to small cities in reconstruction from 1946 to 1949 shows that local political antagonism toward the biggest cities, expressed in the Diet and elsewhere, hampered funding for Tokyo and Yokohama after World War Two, much as it had in 1923.[125] By 1949, partly because of a retrenchment known as the

Dodge plan to stifle inflation and stabilize revenues, Tokyo's share of the national budget for reconstruction had fallen to less than 11 percent.[126] The Basic Reconstruction Policy was scaled back in 1950, with plans for green spaces along roadways and rail lines abandoned altogether.[127]

Unbowed by these legal and financial complexities, Tokyo authorities took several steps to enhance their green assets in the early and mid-1950s. They managed to gain a financial commitment for city planning from the central government when the Diet passed a National Capital Construction Law in 1950.[128] Tokyo also won protection from 1950 to 1953 for a number of scenic and historical sites under the 1919 monuments law and the 1946 Special City Planning Law, and it revived the commemoration rubric when it announced plans in 1956 to celebrate five hundred years since Ōta Dōkan (1432–1486) designed Edo castle, surrounded by pines near the Sumida River—considered Tokyo's founding event. The chief spatial legacy of this anniversary was Jindai Botanical Park in suburban Chōfu, opened in 1961 on forty-seven hectares. Jindai emblematized the revival of green space planning and the unremitting westward shift of Tokyo's population in the 1950s, and together with Kinuta Family Park represented initial steps toward a more comprehensive network of parks for the capital region in the 1970s and 1980s.

Many Japanese continue to see the wartime era as a valley of darkness lying between the peaks of emerging national prominence in the early twentieth century and unimagined economic prosperity starting in the 1960s. Without doubt the period from 1937 to 1945 was materially harsh and emotionally draining for most Japanese, but as a group they suffered much less than the populations victimized by Japan's imperialism in Asia or the many embattled peoples trapped in the European theater of World War Two. Japanese public amenities such as city and national parks underwent severe financial cutbacks during the war, and their roles were redefined by mobilization for the eight-year national emergency. Although urban parklands in many cities were badly damaged by bombing raids, evacuees seeking shelter, and forced conversion to vegetable plots and graveyards, the aggregate area devoted to public open spaces benefited in the long run from planning for air defense and from the 1940 celebrations of the country's founding. The first decade after Japan's surrender in 1945 nevertheless shows that, as with Tokyo and Yokohama in 1923, most of the recovery in city parks nationwide was carried out locally, often privately by residents and merchants, without much overall design or state intervention to shape how public spaces of all kinds were produced. Under the circumstances, pre-existing city parks and other green areas came through the era adequately repaired, but insufficiently updated to meet the needs of a new generation of postwar city residents. Like many elements of business and society, Japan's public parks served as agents of institutional continuity amid the political gyrations from prewar pluralism through wartime authoritarianism to postwar democracy. Many years were required to overcome the harm wartime inflicted on parks, yet the configurations of public green spaces in Japan today can be traced in surprising detail to decisions taken during wartime and its immediate aftermath.

CHAPTER 4

Parks and Prosperity, 1950s–1980s

"In a land with so much scenic beauty and with such a high degree of appreciation of the cultural values of scenery as Japan, [it is disappointing] to find so few areas which are properly preserved and set aside for public recreation and enjoyment."[1] With these measured words combining protection and praxis, Charles A. Richey, a senior planner in the United States National Park Service, gave the occupation's imprimatur in 1948 to the goal of Japan's national parks from their birth: conserving the country's abundant nonhuman resources by balancing desires for outdoor recreation against the need to protect the environment for future generations. Richey's doctrine, known to Americans as sustainable use, was no less anthropocentric than most other human interactions with the nonhuman throughout Japan's recorded history, and doubtless long before. In this view both city and national parks were meant to satisfy people's wishes for exercise, relaxation, and aesthetic appreciation, and environmental concerns were actually concerns about how human beings were affected by ecological degradation. In short, sustainable use meant putting the nonhuman at the service of the nation.

A skein of interrelated events powered the public demand for both national and city parks in Japan from the end of the occupation in 1952 until the economic slowdown of the early 1990s. Rapid industrial growth led to unprecedented urbanization and residential crowding, which drove citizens to seek public spaces both near and far for relief, relaxation, and recreation. Higher household incomes particularly affected attendance at national parks because for the first time in a generation many people could afford to travel to Japan's scenic land- and seascapes. But the heaviest burden of visitors fell on city parks, which like the nation as a whole had barely recovered their pre-1937 vigor when a cascade of newcomers flooded the largest urban centers seeking educations and incomes, in hopes of a new lifestyle stirred, but not promised, by dreams of postwar democracy.

The four decades after Richey's report in 1948 were a bullish era for both Japan's urban and national parks. The latter, together with quasi-national and prefectural parks, were collectively renamed natural parks when the National Parks Law of 1931 was supplanted by a Natural Parks Law in 1957. Partly because the Americans showed more interest in national parks than in city parks, during the occupation the original dozen national parks were joined by five new ones, all but one of which were established between May 1949 and September 1950 despite the Dodge retrenchment, which hindered funding for city parks far more than for national ones.[2] Two more national parks were opened in 1955, the baseline year for the country's era of high-speed economic growth that peaked in 1973; four were added in the early 1960s and four more in the early 1970s. Only two have been established since, Kushiro Shitsugen (Hokkaido) in 1987 and Oze (near Nikkō) in 2007, bringing the total to twenty-nine. Most of Japan's fifty-six current quasi-national parks also were founded between 1949 and the early 1970s, as were various other kinds of public spaces straddling the line between city and national parks.

Rising household incomes, temporary escape from ever more crowded cities, new transport and lodging, pride in Japan's geophysical and biotic endowment, the worldwide interest in outdoor recreation, and the government's ever-present hope to draw more international tourists all played a part in developing natural parks during this period, but so did a growing interest, consonant with international trends, in protecting the environment from an ecological and not just anthropocentric standpoint. Environmental concerns at times spilled over into protests and outright resistance to government policies, followed by negotiation, compromise, and cooperation once the Environment Agency, founded within the Prime Minister's Office in 1971, replaced the Welfare Ministry as overseer of natural parklands. Nonetheless, the imperatives of economic development regained top priority in natural parks more often than not during the 1980s.

The decades from 1960 to 1990 also were a golden era for city planners in general and park designers in particular as Japan wrestled with how to produce more green spaces for urban newcomers. The country began investing as never before in more and better-equipped city parks. To justify the outlays, Tokyo and other cities marshaled the same arguments long cited by prewar advocates of urban parks: public health, exercise, fire safety, disaster mitigation, civic betterment, and relief from residential crowding. The Welfare Ministry and the Environment Agency, drawing on well-established policies of social management, increasingly regarded access to parks as a fundamental right of urban citizenship—what Tokyo Metropolis called a "civil minimum" standard for all residents. Officials frequently cited statistics from European and American cities with abundant parklands to argue for more open spaces so that Japan could catch up to its international counterparts. Environmental concerns expressed by neighborhood groups beginning in the mid-1960s added to the clamor for more green spaces in the cities. The result was a greater expansion of urban parks between 1960 and 1990 than in the entire period from the Grand Council decree of 1873 through the 1950s.

New Parks for a Democratic Nation

Most of the impetus for building more national parks in Japan after 1945 came from uncorking local ambitions for tourism that had been bottled up during wartime. The discourse about parks right after the war was almost identical with that of the 1930s, as Tamura Tsuyoshi wrote in 1948: "Recreation and education are the two main effects of parks on the people." City parks emphasize recreation more, whereas national parks provide "the spiritual uplift of natural beauty."[3] Originally a bold advocate for drawing more visitors, Tamura now worried that "at present our national parks are in a phase of only being recognized as objects for the tourism business." He wanted his country to recognize that parks were important resources for the future but lamented that "our people's knowledge of national parks is unexpectedly poor, and neither is their interest in them very great."[4] Of course Tamura was wrong about the lack of interest. In 1948 Azuma

Ryōzō (1879–1980) said that attracting foreigners to national parks "will help restore Japan's place in international relations" and that "parks will also develop our Japanese spirit in a healthy international direction."[5] Clearly the contact with overseas visitors and with Japan's environment in these public spaces would stimulate positive attitudes, he believed, in a society grappling with the meaning of postwar democracy.

Japan under national general mobilization after 1938 had greatly exploited its green resources, including timberlands in the colonies, to support the war effort. Tamura, who had quit his bureaucratic position before being fired, said after the war that he had been "called unpatriotic for battling to preserve scenic spots" from the logger's axe.[6] The damage to forests continued during the occupation because Japan faced massive demand for wood products to rebuild its cities. The Forestry Bureau of the Agriculture and Forestry Ministry, upgraded to a semi-independent Forestry Agency in 1947, relaxed rules on clear-cutting within protected areas during the 1950s to increase log output, creating frictions with the Welfare Ministry's officials in charge of national parks. A new Forest Law in 1951 authorized plantation silviculture to replenish woodlands depleted during the previous thirteen years. Not even the Natural Parks Law, enacted in 1957, managed to reduce the rapid pace of felling within national and quasi-national parks in the late 1950s.[7]

If democratization meant access, the early postwar years were the first time large numbers of citizens flocked to national parks, even though they remained under development and were still incompletely outfitted with amenities. The effort to draw visitors to the country's seventeen national parks was well underway by 1950, when attendance reached fifty million,[8] and robust domestic tourism was clearly the main stimulus of the travel and hotel industries by the end of the occupation in April 1952. During the American occupation democratization also opened three former imperial properties as national people's parks, turning private lands of the newly secularized throne into public spaces. The Imperial Palace Outer Garden in Tokyo, formally created in 1940 to commemorate the 2,600th anniversary of the country's founding, became a national people's park in 1947, as did the 65-hectare Kyoto Imperial Palace Outer Garden. Two years later the imperial garden at Shinjuku, with 58 hectares, was opened to the public. The Tokyo Outer Garden, a vast and slightly sterile 115 hectares east of the inner palace, was augmented in 1968 by the newly opened East Garden of the palace and the next year by the Kitanomaru forest to the north.[9]

Shinjuku Imperial Garden national people's park is the historical seed-bed of Shinjuku, Tokyo's largest and most variegated commercial, governmental, transportation, and business district. Originally the estate of the Takatō daimyo, Naitō Kiyonari (1555–1608), it was taken over by the Meiji government and turned into the Shinjuku Imperial Botanical Garden in 1879.[10] There the horticulturalist Fukuba Hayato (1856–1921) juxtaposed European and Japanese design elements that in time came to accord well with each other. Seeds and cuttings from the imperial garden's collection were used to populate parks, plazas, and roadways with trees throughout Tokyo and colonial Taiwan starting in 1907. The people of Taiwan are said to have reciprocated through the gift of a lakeside pavilion, installed in 1930 on the southern side of the park.[11] Like Hibiya, the Shinjuku garden was expensive to restore after the huge American air raid on May 25, 1945,

Shinjuku Imperial Garden became a public park in 1949 after a half-century as an imperial recreation retreat in the heart of Tokyo. Skyscrapers began to loom above the park in 1971.

which burned nearly everything except the Taiwan pavilion and an imperial rest house. Along with other city parks, the Shinjuku garden was used to grow potatoes and green-leaf vegetables during the acute food shortages from 1945 to 1947.[12]

Democratization also meant equal access to energy, mineral, and timber resources in the mountains as well as a greater chance to engage in recreation. Four dozen new dams to provide hydroelectricity were underway or planned as of 1951, with adverse consequences for certain parks, while a revised Mining Law in February 1951 affected national parks and forests by enabling the extraction of nonferrous minerals.[13] As these demands for recreation and resources suggest, the high-speed growth of the mid-1950s and thereafter had a considerable impact on Japan's parks and overall environmental heritage. In an attempt to reconcile contending viewpoints, the Diet unanimously passed a Natural Parks Law that took effect in June 1957, replacing the 1931 National Parks Law as amended in 1949.[14] In most respects the 1957 law gruntled the same interests as before. Ink was spilled to reassure preservationists that the environment would be protected, yet promoting tourism clearly was the main purpose; "designating natural parks is intended for nature tourism," Ueda Yasuyuki, a career parks administrator, bluntly declared.[15] If campers and sightseers represented a soft form of environmental use, miners, loggers, and other businesses who were favorably treated in the 1957 law represented harder-edged exploitation. In this way the law's instrumentalist approach to parklands assured that both tourism and natural resource extraction would thrive within national, regional, and local parks, risking "a fateful clash between protection and development."[16] Under the law, special preservation zones were to remain open for scientific research but otherwise left alone; all other parklands could undergo changes in use provided the impact on scenery was minimal.[17]

The Natural Parks Law of 1957 recognized three types of parks: national parks, quasi-national parks as first authorized in the revised National Parks Law of 1949, and prefectural and local parks outside the large cities. Quasi-national parks were smaller and thought to be less scenic than full-scale national ones. Prefectural and local natural parks, comparable to state parks in the United States, proliferated after World War Two because they did not require central government approval. As with national and quasi-national parks, their purpose was primarily economic: to boost regional tourism by catering to the growing demand for recreation areas, often by converting a historic or scenic landscape into a larger park. As of 1957 Japan counted 203 prefectural or local natural parks as well as a dozen quasi-national and 17 national ones,[18] now loosely coordinated within a single legal framework.

Quasi-national parks, the Welfare Ministry announced in 1950, were meant to "preserve superb nature for people in the future" in locations near cities easily visited by public transit.[19] Two decades later the Japan Travel Bureau, no longer bothering to nod toward environmental protection, frankly acknowledged that quasi-national parks played a key recreational role for city residents, offering access to millions who might not be able to travel to a national park.[20] Quasi-national parks also were hedged by fewer restrictions on development and administered with less central oversight than full national parks, although the central government supported half the cost of improving their facilities.[21] Beginning in 1950 with Lake Biwa and two others, twenty quasi-national parks had been established as of 1960 and twenty-four more were established during the next decade. Only a dozen have been added since 1970, presumably because the catch-up from earlier insufficient parkland was considered complete.[22]

Perhaps the most popular quasi-national park, and one of the most controversial, was Meiji no Mori Takao Kokutei Kōen, widely known as Takaosan for its main feature, 599-meter Mount Takao. The park, reached in less than an hour by train from central Tokyo, each year attracts an estimated 2.5 million people, mainly to make the ninety-minute climb past ancient temples to the summit but also to see its rare plants, wild grasses, and a five-hundred-year-old cryptomeria with "octopus roots." As with most quasi-national parks, the emphasis is on recreation, from camping and hiking to nature education and crafts, as well as clearing underbrush.[23] Despite sustained protests by residents and environmentalists, backed by extensive but fruitless litigation, two ten-meter-wide tunnels are being drilled through Mount Takao to extend a suburban ring road further south.[24] The legal and political battles over the tunnels have become a well-publicized if largely symbolic node in the resistance to the full-blown construction state that Japan became in the 1960s but has shown hints of cutting back under Democratic Party rule.

Whooper swans at Lake Kussharo, a large caldera in Akan National Park (est. 1934) in Hokkaido. Courtesy Itō Taiichi.

While bowing to the inevitable flood of tourists visiting Japan's natural parks, the veteran forester and parks administrator Senge Tetsumaro pointed out in 1962 that "most of the national parks in Japan are indispensable and important places for the study of human and cultural sciences."[25] Scientific sites that proved most popular among tourists included Aso-Kuju National Park in Kyushu, a caldera formation measuring sixteen by twenty-three kilometers with five volcanic cones; Lake Towada in

Towada-Hachimantai National Park (est. 1936) in northern Honshu. Courtesy Itō Taiichi.

Towada-Hachimantai National Park, comparable in size to Crater Lake, Oregon; and Lake Mashu in Hokkaido's Akan National Park, 212 meters deep and transparent to a depth of 41.6 meters when measured in 1931, a clarity not known to be matched elsewhere. Understandably, officials at Lake Mashu made much of its round *marimo* algae, which sometimes grew twenty to thirty centimeters in diameter, at their largest the size of a soccer ball. Nearby is Lake Kussharo, the world's largest caldera at twenty by twenty-six kilometers.[26] Side by side with the usual curiosities found in unfamiliar terrain, the broader access to national parks and other protected lands after the late 1950s provided important open spaces for hands-on science education for Japan's public at large.

The City Parks Law of 1956 and Planning the Capital Region

Urban sprawl was a nemesis to Japan's cities no less than to other global metropolitan centers in the mid-twentieth century. The quarter-century after 1950 witnessed the fastest expansion of space devoted to Japanese cities ever, from 1 percent of the country's total land area to 2.2 percent by 1975. The urbanized portions of Tokyo, Kanagawa, Saitama, and Chiba prefectures more than doubled at the same time,[27] lifting their share of the national population to 19 percent. In response to the torrent of newcomers, starting in 1950 private developers rushed to erect residential buildings in and around the biggest cities, aided by low-interest financing from the Housing Loan Corporation established by the government that year. As in-city tenements and suburban farmlands yielded to contractors' bulldozers, the urgency of planning open spaces both in city centers and on the edges led to a new City Parks Law in 1956, as well as authorization the same year for a Capital Region Development Plan that was finalized in 1958.[28]

Despite its vague definition of city parks as "parks established and administered by local public bodies,"[29] the new City Parks Law gave prefectural and municipal administrators a firmer hand in operating their parks and in protecting them from competing uses of park spaces, no matter how worthy.[30] Before World War Two the central government owned the land on which many urban parks sat, but the 1956 law gave localities the right to purchase properties and establish their own city parks, with the promise of partial subventions from the state. It decreed that only 2 percent of a park's area could be used for concessions, toilets, and administrative buildings (5 percent in the case of cultural facilities) and stipulated that not more than half of a park could be devoted to athletic fields and facilities. The law also set targets of three square meters of city park space per resident in built-up areas and six square meters in residential districts,

Purchased in 1941 as air defense green space and used as a golf course after World War Two, Kinuta Family Park opened to the public in 1957. The broad lawns are dotted with giant cherries and ringed by a fine power-walking path.

ambitious goals for cities that averaged just 2.1 square meters per capita nationally in 1956.[31]

The Capital Region Development Plan of 1958 drew on the Green Space Plan of 1939 but doubled its statutory radius from fifty to one hundred kilometers outward from Tokyo Station. Modeled in part after the 1944 design for Greater London by the architect Sir Patrick Abercrombie (1879–1957), this plan called for a green ring fifteen to twenty-five kilometers from the city center, with residential suburbs beyond it and industrial and commercial development consigned to distant subcenters. It also proposed adding 130 playgrounds, 27 neighborhood parks, and 34 large community parks during the next ten years.[32] If this proposal had surfaced right after the war, it might have accomplished its goals of dispersing factories and offices to satellite cities while also controlling the growth of suburbs, but in 1958 urbanization soon overwhelmed the plan. The Japan Housing Corporation, established in 1955, was already building large apartment blocks in parts of the green belt, creating an impasse with the law's ban on development there. Moreover, almost no central government funds were available to purchase parcels for preservation or to compensate private landlords for constraints on how properties in the green belt could be used.[33] In 1965 this ineffectual plan was scaled back to a fifty-kilometer radius, and the green belt was redesignated as a development zone to accommodate more housing tracts,[34] a frank recognition of the power of capitalism to impinge on urban green spaces as well as on Japan's natural parks.[35] Four more capital region plans emerged between 1968 and 1999, each trying without much success to disperse central city functions to multiple subcenters on the periphery.[36] Still, whatever their drawbacks, the City Parks Law of 1956 and the various plans and laws targeting the capital region brought about almost a tripling of the number of city parks nationwide by 1971.[37]

Partly in response to pressure from environmentalists, a Capital Region Suburban Green Space Protection Law was approved in 1966 to do what the 1958 plan largely failed to accomplish: provide funds to purchase lands for public use or to compensate landlords for curbs on using their lands within locally chosen suburban protection zones. Some of the zones soon succumbed to housing projects, particularly those protection zones the Finance Ministry deemed too expensive to acquire.[38] Nonetheless eighteen of these zones covering 157 square kilometers had been established as of 1980, mostly outside the choicest development areas, and thus they were embraced with enthusiasm by local officials and residents.[39] This little-noticed law, if not a sea change in how space planning took place in Japan, at least started an ebb of central state command and a corresponding flood of local initiatives that continue today.

Within this legal and planning framework, Tokyo in the late 1950s and 1960s also expanded its parklands by searching for green spaces in various spots once put to other uses: former military bases, scientific reserves, abandoned factories, and riverside and bayside locations. Yoyogi Park, built in stages after 1963 next to the Meiji Shrine at Harajuku, is probably the city's most heavily used open space among the many parks that use former military bases. Left deliberately free of facilities, in keeping with worldwide ideas of open-space design in the 1960s, its extensive lawns are surrounded by more than a hundred thousand trees and a small bird sanctuary, recently colonized by large crows.[40] Yoyogi has always been a park for free spirits, with as broad a variety of visitors, nationalities, and street performers as any in the capital. Hikarigaoka, Toyama, and Shōwa Memorial Parks are other leading examples of bases converted to parklands in the capital, and many others are found in cities elsewhere.

Large reserves for botanical and zoological study in Tokyo grew increasingly popular as they became available to the public after World War Two; most of the reserves have conformed to the provisions of the City Parks Law since 1956. The National Institute for Nature Study at Shirokane, open since 1949 as a branch of the National Science Museum, is noted for its evergreen oaks atop sixteenth-century military earthworks.[41] The Meguro Experimental Forestry Station, established by the government in 1900, has been open since 1989, displaying its nearly seven thousand tall trees of fifteen meters or more, many exceeding three meters in circumference.[42] Botanical gardens are especially popular sites for visitors interested in scientific study. The gem in Tokyo is Koishikawa Botanical Garden, established in 1681 to grow medicinal herbs and converted to a botanical laboratory when the predecessor to Tokyo Imperial University

Yoyogi Park, on fifty-five hectares next to Tokyo's Meiji Shrine. A true people's park, it consists of open lawns, thick forests, a rose garden, and a bird sanctuary.

took it over in 1877. The main collection holds five thousand plant species from China, Japan, Korea, and Taiwan, including specimens of two thousand tropical and subtropical species in greenhouses.[43] In Sapporo the Hokkaido University Botanical Garden, created in 1886 by Professor Miyabe Kingo (1860–1951), is famous for its conifers as well as its Japanese oaks, elms, and maples. This small public park also contains 180 species in its ethnobotanical collection, including plants used by Ainu for food, clothing, building, and medicine.[44]

In addition to former military bases and current scientific preserves, waterside locations and former industrial properties were turned into public parklands under the City Parks Law after 1956. Part of the motive was to clean up polluted rivers and bays and beautify sites fouled by factory emissions. Rising land prices also prompted Tokyo to turn to underused spaces. Starting in 1965 the city began reconfiguring the dry floodplains within the dikes of the Naka, Ara, and Edo Rivers as playing fields and open parks, without large trees or structures because in springtime the rivers occasionally swelled partway up their concrete levees. A disadvantage of this strategy is that cormorant habitats along lakeshores and rivers "have been eliminated by Japan's ubiquitous and ill-conceived river impoundment projects, which usually replace the original riparian vegetation with baseball fields and golf courses."[45] As early as 1959 the government limited the expansion of both factories and universities in the Tokyo and Osaka core regions, so a number of firms sold their in-city properties and relocated to suburbs where there were fewer size or environmental restrictions. Some of these abandoned industrial sites were recycled into parklands, including Kameido Central Park on the grounds of a disused Hitachi plant and Kiba, a Japanese government park in a warehouse area formerly used by lumberyards.[46] At the same time the Factory Location Law, revised in 1974, required owners of newly built industrial plants to include green spaces, a provision met with much reluctance.[47]

Like the capital district, both the Osaka and Nagoya areas engaged in broad-based regional planning after 1956, buoyed by the City Parks Law and companion legislation to improve infrastructure and promote economic development. The resulting Osaka Regional Plan of 1961 sought to expand park areas in Osaka Prefecture from ten to fifty square kilometers by 1975 and to preserve nearby mountains as green spaces, but housing projects soon consumed most of these open lands.[48] Somewhat more successful were efforts in the Osaka region to identify preservation districts under the Historical Landscape Conservation Law of 1966. Osaka, Nara, and Kyoto established twenty-one preservation districts in or near ancient capitals in the Kinki region between 1966 and 1980, while also agreeing to set aside more than eight hundred square kilometers during the same period as suburban green spaces. Tokyo, by contrast, was able to protect only eighty-two hectares as suburban green spaces under the 1973 Urban Green Space Protection Law that authorized the practice.[49]

Nagoya, which was already a national leader in opening new city parks during the 1950s, emulated Osaka in designating suburban green spaces for conservation, including nearby mountainous areas unsuitable for development.[50] Nagoya also used the Land Readjustment Act of 1954 more extensively than did other major cities in developing new housing, carefully observing the requirement to reserve 3 percent of the adjustment district for city parks. However, as a part of the environmental movement of the late 1960s, citizens' groups arose around the country to defend green spaces, rights to sunlight, and residential districts from land readjustment that would bring large condominiums, called mansions, to thinly settled neighborhoods. In 1968 a national liaison association of voters opposed to land readjustment issued newsletters, books, and petitions resisting the practice as disruptive and contrary to the public interest. The group was credited with influencing how land readjustment was implemented in many cities, although less so in Nagoya than elsewhere.[51] Its advocacy on behalf of citizens resisting the state and big business continues today through publications from the Local Government Research Institute.

Some clues to how the new parks were being used emerged from a cabinet survey of adult city residents throughout Japan conducted in 1966. In the survey, 58 percent of respondents said they visited a city park or private amusement park on typical weekends and 23 percent on weekdays. The most commonly chosen reason for visiting a city park was leisurely strolling and enjoying the scenery (59 percent), followed by caring for children (42 percent).[52] Both the high attendance on weekends and the large proportion of people caring for children typified local playgrounds and wayside parks in family-oriented residential areas. The passive preferences expressed by respondents (only 6 percent mentioned sports) varied considerably from the professed aims of park leaders to provide open spaces for enhancing health, hygiene, and physical vigor.

Parks and National Development

The 1960s were the peak years of Japan's high-speed growth and a time of ever greater pressures on the country's natural parks from developers and tourists alike. The average annual growth rate of the nation's gross domestic product, adjusted for inflation, was nearly 11 percent from 1955 until the first Arab oil embargo in 1973. From then until 1991 the average growth was more than 5 percent per year, very high for a mature economy that ranked third behind the United States and the Soviet Union in output throughout the 1970s and 1980s. This newfound affluence helps to explain why both city and national parks grew dramatically in number, as well as attendance, during these decades. At the same time, neither the Natural Parks Law of 1957 nor the Basic Forestry Law of 1964 posed major obstacles to businesses seeking to answer the energy and resource needs of a robust national economy. Yet by the end of the 1960s severe environmental degradation provoked a torrent of citizen protests and demands for greater protection of ecosystems inside and outside the national parks.[53]

Even before the steep rise in household incomes took hold, the early 1960s were a surprisingly powerful springboard for discretionary travel in Japan. The Prime Minister's Office reported that visitors to national parks grew from 90 million in 1960 to 161 million in 1964, a rise only partly attributable to the increase in number of parks from nineteen to twenty-three during these years; at the same time attendance at quasi-national parks rose from 52 million to 90 million.[54] On the other hand, a 1965 survey by the Capital Region Development Committee showed that public amenities such as parks, civic athletic fields, and open green spaces were used by only one quarter as many persons as were private facilities such as driving ranges, batting cages, tennis courts, swim pools, ski slopes, sports venues within amusement parks, and company-owned athletic fields. The finding that public facilities were relatively less well used was odd, inasmuch as parks at that point already accounted for 12 percent of national land area (today the figure is 14 percent), so for the most part the infrastructure for experiencing the outdoors was already in place.[55]

The energy and resource requirements of Japan's fired-up economy were even more hazardous to natural parks and their contiguous forests than the steady footfalls of tourists. The travails of Lake Biwa Quasi-National Park from industrial sources and the inadvertent introduction of harmful species were well known, but the park most affected by manufacturing plants was Seto Inland Sea National Park, ringed with major industrial centers and victimized by expropriation of some of its supposedly protected land areas for factory sites. Scenic roads through national parks exacted a toll from the environment as well as from drivers' wallets, starting with the Bandai-Asahi Skyline in 1959. Another highway, the Fuji Subaru Skyline, led motorists 2,350 meters high in the Fuji-Hakone-Izu National Park for spectacular views of Fuji out one window and the sparkling Pacific out the other, but its exhaust pollution was also blamed for blighting twenty thousand first-growth trees in the park. Such expressways often benefited logging companies, as with the controversial Southern Alps Forest Superhighway, which was finally permitted to open in 1981 over objections from environmentalists, local residents, and parkgoers.[56]

The Basic Forestry Law passed in 1964 was intended to increase the output of logs and lift the incomes of timber companies, including woodcutters on national forestlands within natural parks. A secondary goal was protecting watersheds, soils, and habitats. By 1999 two fifths of all Japanese forests were monoculture tree farms, mostly cryptomeria still in their first generation.[57] In general, such plantations harmed forests and natural parks by driving out the undergrowth that supported birds and ground animals and helped the soil retain rainwater, leading to erosion and river silting.[58] Lumbering caused forest fragmentation that prevented various avian species from nesting; at the same time, broadleaf trees that were unsuitable for lumber or pulp were often neglected, especially as villagers no longer scoured the undergrowth for fuel and fertilizer because of petroleum- and chemical-based alternatives. The timber industry was wounded by cheaper foreign competition after import restrictions ended in 1961; by 1969 half of Japan's consumption consisted of wood from abroad. As a result, reforestation fell from 4,300 square kilometers in 1954 to just 339 square kilometers in 1999.[59]

Led by the botanist Numata Makoto, ecologists and environmentalists in the 1960s addressed the overuse of forests in general and national parks in particular by tourists, backpackers, utilities, and timber and mining corporations. The Nature Conservation Society of Japan, founded in 1951 amid protests against plans for dams and hydroelectric plants at Oze in Nikkō and other national parks, joined in a number of movements in the 1960s to slow the degradation of parks and woodlands. Dams for hydroelectricity on the Kurobe River in Chūbu-Sangaku National Park, controversial since the early 1920s, have released water for nearly four months each summer ever since 1961 to replenish the parched lower river in the dry season, a recognition by Kansai Electric Power Company that serious downriver effects of damming persist. Prompted by the writings of the novelist-activist Ishimure Michiko,[60] Japanese environmentalists have long assailed the Ichifusa Dam on the Kuma River, which was built in 1960 and created a lake that buried the village of Mizukami in Kumamoto Prefecture. Nearby, the Kawabe River Dam at Itsuki has provoked bitter protests since it was first proposed in 1966; construction for the $3.6 billion project is currently underway, but it may never be finished because Kabashima Ikuo in 2008 became the first governor of Kumamoto Prefecture publicly to oppose the dam.[61] Such acts of resistance were largely symbolic, for by 2000 the government had already dammed 110 of Japan's 113 major rivers, poured concrete retaining walls on 60 percent of the country's seashores, and lined the bed and banks of nearly every river, creek, and stream wider than one meter, including those in natural parks, with thick concrete to control flooding.[62]

The putative short-term benefits of damming rivers could not mask the likely long-term damage to their ecosystems, a myopic conundrum common to many environmental crises.[63] Park roadways, too, were a favorite target of protest because building them meant felling trees and completing them meant more truck traffic for hard-edged resource exploitation and more buses and cars for softer-edged tourism. Local businesspeople were torn; some welcomed the improved access as good for business, but others believed that damaged environments would drive visitors away. Most of the resistance to tourism and economic development came from people outside the parks, who were unaware of how often those living on private lands within park boundaries could overlook the environmental damage occurring around them because they relied on visitors and industries for their livelihoods. As was true of antipollution efforts in the

1960s throughout the country, the courts were increasingly employed to settle disputes about forests and natural parks arising between development-minded government agencies and private citizens. A media favorite was Tarōsugi, an ancient cryptomeria spared by the Tokyo Higher Court from being cut down outside Nikkō's Tōshōgū Shrine for road improvements, which were first announced in 1963.[64] Plans for forest roads in the Shirakami Mountains of northern Honshu were dropped when twenty thousand letters of opposition poured in; the region later became a World Heritage site.[65]

In sum, national, quasi-national, and prefectural natural parks in the 1960s enjoyed growing favor with tourists who sought both simple sightseeing and more engaged recreation, taxing park staffs and facilities to the extreme. Parks and forests also faced severe pressures from corporations eager to profit from a fast-expanding economy with a great appetite for primary resources such as timber and minerals. Resistance from environmentalists and some local populations gathered momentum late in the decade, in tandem with antipollution efforts in Minamata, Toyama, Yokkaichi, and the largest cities. By then, thanks in good measure to publicity in the press, many visitors to Japan's natural parks wondered just how wise the doctrine of sustainable use really was.

Limited Environmental Protections

During the prime ministership of Satō Eisaku (1901–1975, P.M. 1964–1972) the government supported economic growth and cooperation with the United States but also reacted shrewdly to antiestablishment protests by students over university governance, by unionists and intellectuals over allowing the Japan-U.S. Mutual Security Treaty to continue automatically in 1970, by farmers and leftists over building a new airport at Narita, and by a wide spectrum of citizens over Japan's material support for the American war against communist revolutionaries in Southeast Asia. Perhaps the most successful legacy of the Satō Cabinet was building a consensus among business, the bureaucracy, and the Liberal Democratic Party (LDP) in favor of broad environmental legislation in the "pollution Diet" of 1970. His government's policies were reactive, responding to media attention and unprecedented citizen and consumer movements stirred by serious environmental degradation nationwide since the mid-1960s. The environmental crisis of the late 1960s legitimized citizens' opposition to their government's domestic policies and spurred their collective action more effectively than any issue before or since.[66]

Japan's civic environmental movement of the mid- and late 1960s differed in leadership, organization, and aims from the demonstrations led by what Patricia Steinhoff has termed the "national protest cartel," starting soon after 1945 and culminating from 1965 to 1975.[67] Directed by the Japan Socialist Party and the Japan Communist Party, the cartel sponsored wide-ranging political protests, drawing their strength from union members, university students, antinuclear groups, Burakumin outcastes, and women's organizations, and the demonstrations often involved anti-state violence. In contrast, the environmental movement was egalitarian in command, based in local residents' and consumers' associations, and usually targeted a limited set of objectives, not the displacement of Liberal Democratic Party rule.[68] The civic antipollution efforts, although mainly focused on industrial pollutants, were important elements in spurring a new City Planning Law in 1968 and special legislation in 1972 mandating five-year master plans for city parks.

The new City Planning Law, replacing the original law dating to 1919, paradoxically sought to foster systematic urban development without impairing "sound harmony with agriculture, forestry and fishing"[69]—the same delicate blend of use and protection faced by the country's natural parks. The new law yielded mixed results for city parks and other green spaces, but the master plans for city parks beginning in 1972 provided sinews, and cash, for vigorous growth of urban parklands after the mid-1970s. The 1968 City Planning Law was sometimes known as the line-drawing law because it drew a boundary between urbanization-development and urbanization-control districts, the latter intended to preserve open spaces. Nationwide about 13,000 square kilometers were duly classified for promoting urbanization and 36,000 for restrictions on further development.[70] The law nominally delegated responsibility for city planning from the Construction Ministry to prefectural or local officials, although central government controls over taxes and income transfers kept top-down planning largely intact.[71] Slightly more than half of the areas identified as green belts in the 1958 Capital Region Development Plan were now classified for urbanization and no longer for protection. Within Tokyo Metropolis, 95 percent of the ward area and nearly 60 percent of the rest of the prefecture were considered fair game for promoting urbanization.[72] In urbanization-control districts throughout the country, environmental protections were surprisingly weak. Projects under 1,000 square meters were exempt, so builders executed many small-scale developments.[73] Within the urbanization-development districts, the new City Planning Law ended the earlier practice of requiring permits to build two-story buildings in parks within planning districts.[74] To mitigate complaints about a lack of consultation during the planning process, the law called for public hearings, explanatory conferences, and written comments from the public before construction was approved, but in practice the meetings mainly consisted of one-way information sessions without input from citizens. Once the Building Standards Law was amended in 1970, local residents gained more voice in deciding which areas should be designated as urbanization-development districts or as urbanization-control districts.[75]

When the economist Minobe Ryōkichi (1904–1984, gov. 1967–1979) was elected governor of Tokyo Metropolis, he sought various public amenities for residents, including safety, medical care facilities, leisure activities, and urban parks. He cited a 1966 survey showing that 20 percent of children's play areas were on city streets, not playgrounds, schoolyards, or parks.[76] Once the new City Planning Law of 1968 took hold, Minobe's deputies cobbled together the Tokyo Medium-term Plan '69, which sought to double the area assigned to city parks and open spaces by 1985 to 3 square meters per capita—a benchmark that was met before that year and raised to 4.6 square meters per person by 1993.[77] In comparison, Osaka Prefecture increased its per capita parks and open spaces from 1.7 square meters in 1966 to 3.5 in 1985 for its six million residents.[78] As Tokyo added new parks under Article 12 of the City Planning Law, it phased out its green belt districts and inserted more parks in residential areas. As a result, the metropolis greatly increased its stock of fully developed parklands from 380 hectares in 1970 to 1,030 hectares in 1980, including some private donations.[79]

These additions, which were matched in a number of other city planning districts nationwide, took place despite a dropoff of environmental activism by private citizens after the first Arab oil embargo of 1973–1974 led to a brief economic downturn. Although the cabinet reverted to developmentalist policies following the oil shock, national bureaucratic agencies neither abandoned the antipollution laws passed since the late 1960s nor left city park implementation entirely to the whims of localities. The Environment Agency, established in 1971, took particular pride in natural parks but was also sympathetic to the Construction Ministry's attempts to use the City Planning Law to promote new urban parks, partly justified by the time-honored rationale of disaster prevention. Reformist mayors and governors in Tokyo, Osaka, Kyoto, and Kobe likewise provided momentum for expanding parklands during the 1970s.[80] But land prices continued to spiral upward, big cities kept on sprawling outward, and the beleaguered City Planning Law proved inadequate for providing the new parks or protecting the open spaces envisaged by its framers.

Instead, what made the 1970s and 1980s "the age of city parks"[81] in Japan was the Law for Emergency Measures to Develop City Parks, passed in 1972 at the initiative of the Construction Ministry partly to balance the regional development projects advocated by Prime Minister Tanaka Kakuei (1918–1993, P.M. 1972–1974) in his *Nihon rettō kaizōron* (Reconstructing the Japanese archipelago), published in June of that year.[82]

The main purpose of the emergency measures law was to put improvements of city parks on the same five-year planning and funding cycles as upgrades to roads, waterways, housing, sewerage, and trash management. The overall goal was "improvement of the urban environment" so as "to promote healthy urban growth and preserve and enhance the physical and mental health of city residents"[83]—unexceptionable shibboleths voiced by government officials ever since Nagayo Sensai in 1885 (see chapter 1).[84]

The five-year plans deployed a panoply of techniques to uncover more city parklands: purchase, lease, land readjustment, center city renewal, and takeover of former factory sites and military bases as well as developing vacant public lands along rivers and bays.[85] Prefectural and municipal governments selected new parcels for parks, then applied to the national treasury for assistance with land acquisition and capital costs of facilities. The national government reimbursed 40 percent of these expenditures under the first five-year plan, from 1972 to 1975, then raised the rate to 48 percent for the second plan from 1976 to 1980.[86] National treasury aid for maintaining city parks doubled by 1976 to 16 percent of operating costs.[87]

Given this rich infusion of national government cash, it is understandable that the Construction Ministry in 1972 began to encourage partnerships among local governments, private businesses, and nongovernmental organizations to support parks,[88] along the lines of the successful private-public sponsorship of Expo '70 in Osaka two years earlier. Partnerships were slow to take off but by today have become standard options for acquiring city parklands and administering them.

The 1972 emergency measures law greatly speeded the upward trajectory of spending on urban parklands. National and local outlays for land purchases, refurbishing existing facilities, and adding new ones in city parks nationwide rose from ¥4.6 billion ($12.8 million) in 1960 to ¥58.0 billion in 1970, then leaped another sixfold to ¥357 billion in 1980. Residential land prices in Tokyo rose 2,000 percent between 1960 and 1980, so property owners fought any restrictions that would reduce real estate values and held out for abundant compensation when public bodies sought land for parks or green spaces. Faced with ever-higher land costs as well as outspoken demands for civic facilities from residents in the 1980s, governments found themselves spending ¥910 billion annually for city park upgrades by 1990. The peak year for city park additions and improvements was 1995, when costs reached ¥1,261 billion ($10.5 billion), after which mini-recessions, stagnant tax revenues, and a large national budget deficit brought about a steady contraction in capital expenditures by governments for parks, shrinking outlays in half by 2003.[89] As the number of parks, visitors, and facilities soared, the costs of running city parks nationwide rose from ¥5.9 billion in 1965 to ¥271 billion in 1990, peaking at ¥407 billion in 1997 before falling back to about ¥275 billion in the year ending in March 2005.[90]

Important as the countrywide agitation by environmentalists was for stimulating city park planning, it had an even greater effect on regulating the use of Japan's natural parks. Facing acute pollution within their borders, Hokkaido, Kagawa, and Nagano prefectures passed environmental ordinances in 1970 and 1971, which quickly prodded the central government to do the same in a political culture highly resistant to local usurpations of central powers. The first citizens' conference for environmental conservation held in Japan took place in the rain on May 17, 1970, at Tokyo's Shimizudani Park, a familiar site of antiwar protests, to seek not only antipollution measures but also the restoration of fragile ecosystems.[91] Representatives of seventy-seven antipollution and conservation groups met in 1971 to form the Japan Union for Nature Conservation to press for further protections.[92] By that point many Japanese corporations, like those in other countries, had decided it was good business to reduce pollution. The Satō Cabinet and the Diet made just enough concessions to the widespread public concern about foul air, water, and terrain to take the sting out of the agitation without much collateral damage to domestic business and industry.

One outcome of the antipollution movement and resulting legislation was the creation of the Environment Agency in 1971 to enforce the laws and police industrial behavior. The agency took over responsibility for natural parks from the Welfare Ministry and absorbed the Forestry Agency's duties in protecting wildlife. Its main charge was to protect public health, not the nonhuman surroundings, yet advocates for the natural parks rejoiced when the medical doctor and politician Ōishi Buichi (1909–2003) became the first director of the agency. Ōishi showed a strong preference for protection over recreational or industrial use of the national parks, despite unremitting pressures from ever more visitors on the one hand and energy companies and resource-extraction corporations on the other.[93] His stance alienated local residents and businesses who sought infrastructure and development for their regions, and meanwhile the environmental legislation from the 1970 Diet session made it more difficult to establish new natural parks because tougher standards now had to be met. As in other countries, some private owners inside existing parklands, angered at regulations on using their properties, talked of seceding from their parks.[94] In contrast, as during the 1930s, others saw danger in having their lands included in new parks because real estate and tourist businesses would rush in.[95] The prediction was accurate; even under the new laws and agency, approvals to develop private businesses within national parks—ranging from ski, golf, and swim facilities to dams, electricity plants, and lumbering operations—continued to be pro forma and were granted almost automatically.[96]

To give the Environment Agency a firmer legal foundation, as well as to respond to strong pressures from the Wild Bird Society, Japan Science Council, Union for Nature Conservation, and other environmental groups and academic scientists, the Diet passed a watered-down Nature Protection Law in 1972 that subsumed parts of the Natural Parks Law of 1957. It established nature protection zones within natural parks with three basic classifications: (1) special-preservation zones with supposedly primeval lands, where all human activity except scientific research was banned, such as volcano vents or mountain summits; (2) special regions, with considerable protection of flora and fauna but allowing limited felling; and (3) ordinary regions, where normal activities were permitted but permission from the prefectural governor was required to build large structures, create landfills, or bulldoze earth if it changed the topography. Water parks were included to protect coral, other seas creatures, and marine scenery.[97] The goal was to safeguard species diversity, the first major legislative attempt to do so in Japan and one much affected by the U.S. Wilderness Act of 1964. Jurisdictional disputes among the Construction Ministry, Forestry Agency, Welfare Ministry, and Ministry of International Trade and Industry prevented the application of the Nature Protection Law to other green spaces, but at least it laid a basis for prefectural protection of parklands.[98] From the start the Environment Agency had a generally positive, if mixed, impact on national and quasi-national parks. The agency became enmeshed in intraparty factionalism when its second director, the future LDP prime minister Miki Takeo (1907–1988), underwent tenacious questioning in the Diet on March 2, 1973, from another future premier, Hashimoto Ryūtarō (1937–2006), concerning the agency's effectiveness. Hashimoto pressed for protecting animals, eventually forcing Miki to take greater steps toward preserving the living environment both inside and outside the public parklands.[99]

Problems of land acquisition and use, finance, and resort development plagued the parks throughout these decades of prosperity, increasing leisure-time travel, political corruption, and speculative excess. The most ecologically fragile regions deserving special preservation status usually lay within national forests where they were beyond the Environment Agency's jurisdiction and less well secured by law and practice than would be ideal. For the lands within its own direct purview, the Environment Agency had few weapons for punishing even the most egregious violators of special regions because criminal penalties were so light as to seem "sweet."[100] The Forestry Agency managed to evade serious new legislative oversight and continued to use the Basic Forest Law of 1964 as a means of supporting the timber industry. The reality was that natural parks "were exploited under the pretext of recreational development for the public health."[101]

Serving as intermediate spaces between natural and city parks was another category of large-scale public park that was largely exempt from the Nature Protection Law of 1972: Japanese government parks, authorized in 1974 and incorporated into the revised City Parks Law of 1976. Their purpose was recreation, not environmental protection. Built by the powerful Construction Ministry mainly near major population centers, Japanese government parks were designed to be three hundred hectares or more in size; today they number seventeen, all but one fully open to the public, drawing about twenty-eight million visitors a year.[102] In contrast with the inadequate financing available for natural parks from the Environment Agency and local governments, these spaces-in-between were directly operated by a semipublic foundation that tapped funds from the national postal savings accounts and insurance companies.[103]

Musashi Hills Woodland Park, authorized in 1968 and completed in 1974, was the first government park to open. The park's operators say it "was built to enjoy relaxation and recreation amid nature's abundant greenery"[104] for persons on day trips from the capital. Closer to central Tokyo is another government park on part of the former American air base at Tachikawa, the 180-hectare Shōwa Memorial Park, marking the fiftieth anniversary of the emperor's accession in 1926. Known as "the king of Tokyo's parks,"[105] Shōwa Memorial Park began drawing 2.5 million visitors annually almost as soon as it opened in 1983.[106] Comfortably supported by central state monies, the government parks took some of the demand for recreational spaces away from the much less well-funded natural parks, and they also met the needs of urban residents for nearby outdoor experiences, however artificial, that the inadequate city parks were unable to meet.

Nonetheless, growing household incomes meant that the stream of visitors to national, quasi-national, and prefectural natural parks turned into a flood in the 1970s, attracting tourism entrepreneurs like flies to honey. By 1978 the government estimated that the annual number of natural park visitors had reached about 317 million in the twenty-seven national parks, 271 million at fifty-one quasi-national parks, and 228 million at prefectural natural parks,[107] levels that have risen only 11 percent since. That same year the Environment Agency faced lawsuits by local governments for lowering protections against nitrogen oxide and protests from the Japan Union for Nature Conservation for truckling to developers while doing too little to preserve the nonhuman environment. Nonetheless, the second Arab oil embargo in 1979 shocked the government into proposing a new round of 200 new atomic, coal-fueled, hydroelectric, and geothermal plants for generating electricity, 119 of them to be sited partly or entirely in natural parks. After loud protests from environmentalists, a scaled-back Alternative Energy Law was passed in 1980 that added more plants to the 20 percent of all electric power stations that were already located within the parks.[108]

The modest environmental safeguards of the Nature Protection Law of 1972, although vitiated by pressures from park visitors and industrial projects, represented a degree of progress toward species conservation in certain natural parks, as reflected in the successive green censuses carried out since 1973. But overall the national, quasi-national, and prefectural parks experienced relentless demands that overwhelmed the small staff responsible for environmental protection. The central government's reimbursements to prefectures for upgrading facilities in the natural parks leveled off after 1979 and as of 1988 stood at ¥2,474 million, roughly 40 percent of the total spent by the prefectures on improvements to the natural parks within their borders. This total expenditure, equivalent to $48 million, was exceedingly small for a country with more than 900 million visitors annually to its natural parks.[109]

Contrasted with this weak public investment was perhaps the stiffest blow to environmentalism and the greatest symbol of excessive national affluence, the resort law of 1987. Mountain or seaside resorts where exercise and fitness, not alcohol, were the motifs became locales in the 1980s for individuals and small groups to develop a third space beyond home and workplace. The resort law, stemming from the broad Reaganesque program of deregulation and privatization carried out by the Nakasone Yasuhiro Cabinet (1982–1987), potentially could turn nearly forty thousand square kilometers, or 11 percent of Japan's land area, into resort zones, many of them in national parks. It gave developers tax breaks and other means to obtain land cheaply and provided ¥10 trillion ($69 billion) in public funds to advance private resort construction. Close ties among construction and real estate companies, the LDP members most beholden to them for campaign contributions, and the Construction Ministry bulldozed the law through the Diet, but dissenters within the ruling party such as Hashimoto Ryūtarō expressed skepticism about the effects of such massive development on Japan's forests.[110] The resort law assumed that more than ¥100 trillion would be invested by public and private sources in resort zones by the end of the century, but the contraction of real estate values after 1991 and slow-growth economy thereafter curtailed many entrepreneurs' hopes that had been engendered by this law.[111]

The gold-plated resort law was a glittering symbol of how national authorities favored business interests over environmental protection for most of the period from Charles Richey's fence-sitting endorsement of conservation for public enjoyment in 1948 through the decade of consumer bounty in the 1980s. To be sure, environmentalists made some important gains from the late 1960s until the oil shock of 1973, especially in curbing pollution and in protecting the most vulnerable zones in the natural parks. For the most part, however, commercial and industrial development triumphed over the public interest in guarding the parks against overuse by businesses and tourists alike. Yet the indifferent economic performance of the 1990s and a new wave of environmentalism have led to a new, more complex experience for Japan's natural parks since the early 1990s.

Urban Green Spaces in the Affluent 1970s and 1980s

Despite the weighty sums invested in city parks during the 1970s under the first two five-year plans, officials were well aware that as of 1978 nearly three times as much space nationwide still was being used for golf courses, most of them private, as for city parks.[112] On the other hand, the payoff from the first two plans was evident in each of the largest cities except Yokohama, which had a huge population influx in the 1970s. Kobe more than doubled its city park area per resident between 1971 and 1981, Fukuoka nearly doubled its area, and Sapporo raised its parkland per capita by 58 percent. The national average gain for cities covered by the five-year plans between 1971 and 1981 was 59 percent.[113] The third plan, covering

1981 through 1985, showed the effects of ever-steeper land prices; ¥2.88 trillion was budgeted and 12,000 hectares of city parklands were added, triple the cost for 27 percent less land than under the first plan.[114]

The new parks were so popular that Prime Minister Nakasone Yasuhiro murmured in the mid-1980s about a green space doubling plan, in obvious mimesis of the enormously popular income doubling plan announced in 1960 by Premier Ikeda Hayato (1899–1965, P.M. 1960–1964).[115] Nakasone's motive, catering to the construction and real estate industries, was to deregulate city planning, but bureaucratic officials feared a loss of influence and citizens' groups resisted any retrenchment of local planning powers. Still the fourth five-year plan, from 1986 to 1990, increased expenditures for parks by only 10 percent, well below the rise in land prices, and anticipated adding 22 percent fewer hectares than its predecessor. The fourth plan shifted focus from quantitative measures of progress to qualitative agenda items, such as "green fitness parks, urban ecology parks, craft parks for creative leisure, and event parks," with programming to fit these community-building goals.[116]

This trend toward choices of activities and local options about how parks should be used was fortified when the City Planning Law of 1968 was revised in 1989 via a new Basic Land Law requiring consultation with residents before planning could be finalized. Throughout, the Construction Ministry cleverly maintained that the chief reason for building more city parks was to stockpile disaster relief zones, a rationale difficult to rebut during Diet funding debates.[117] Both qualitatively and quantitatively, Japan's city parks were at new peaks of variety, accessibility, and scale when the fourth plan ended in early 1991, having nearly tripled the number of city parks since 1976 and more than doubled their area since 1973. Under the five-year plans, Tokyo tripled the area of its city parklands between 1971 and 1993.[118] The total annual expenditures on Tokyo's city parks in 1992 ran to ¥135.3 billion, including land acquisition, improvements, maintenance, administration, equipment, facilities, reserves, and miscellany, with a payroll of six thousand employees to operate nearly ten thousand parks of all sizes and a small number of zoos and cemeteries within the metropolis.[119] These were huge numbers for creating public spaces on a scale unimagined in the Tokyo City Improvement Plan a century earlier.

As should be expected from the leaders of a country rocketing toward unprecedented prosperity, proposals for further development and national land utilization sometimes seemed to counter the well-funded five-year plans for expanding Japan's city parks during the 1970s and 1980s. Two national development plans in 1969 and 1975 and a new National Land-use Planning Law in 1974 foundered in the face of rapidly rising land prices, a problem that plagued natural parks as well. The land use law emphasized environmental safeguards, tried to limit the growth of city populations, and required the prefectures to develop land use plans. It attempted to extend city planning principles to the entire country, but despite the Diet's clear intent to have the land use law supersede earlier legislation affecting forests and parks, the Forestry Agency, Construction Ministry, and Environment Agency all reasserted their determination to use national forests, city parks, and natural parks as they saw fit. Like many earlier pieces of legislation, its effect was diminished because the thrust was restrictive, forbidding various forms of land use without incentives to encourage desirable alternatives to urban sprawl.[120]

At cross-purposes with, if not contrary to, the national development plans and the land use law was the Urban Green Space Protection Law of 1973. This law tried to safeguard existing open spaces and called for green space planning in tandem with the five-year plans for city parks that began one year earlier. Until this point Governor Minobe and other champions of public space had emphasized "greenery in the midst of the city," but henceforth national policy began shifting to "the city in the midst of greenery."[121] The Urban Green Space Protection Law required prefectures and municipal governments to purchase any lands proposed for development within the green space districts and to keep them open to the public indefinitely—another in a long list of unfunded mandates from the Diet. Prefectures understandably were reluctant to establish green space districts where developers planned to cut trees or build, given the high cost of buying the properties and the loss of potential tax revenues. Although the Urban Green Space Protection Law fell short of a comprehensive national plan and depended on prefectures to carry it out, the prevailing philosophy after 1973 clearly was that urban green space was valued as unreservedly good, an outlook codified in official policy without explanation or rationale.

As called for in the law, prefectures began to produce green master plans in 1977, and by 1982 about 270 of the 300 big-city green space planning districts had completed their master plans and begun putting them into effect, including Tokyo's highly detailed plan of 1981.[122] Other prefectures continued to do so until the master plans were succeeded by basic green space plans in 1994. The principle to be followed was civic reconstruction (*machizukuri*), a buzzword of city planning in Japan since the 1960s implying citizen involvement in neighborhood improvements, an ideal seldom realized before the 1990s (see chapter 5). In their basic green space plans after 1994 local bodies were expected to engage residents in green censuses, social needs surveys, and other kinds of environmental assessments before finalizing their master plans. The Construction Ministry set a benchmark of twenty square meters of green space per city resident by 2000 and urged the local green space districts to assure that 30 percent of built-up areas in their jurisdictions be devoted to parks and open spaces, both highly unrealistic goals.[123]

In Tokyo Prefecture, 1980 marked the first time that housing accounted for a majority of the metropolis' urbanized land area (52 percent of 960 square kilometers), nearly double the proportion just twenty-five years earlier. The area devoted to farmland, meanwhile, fell from 36 percent in 1955 to 16 percent in 1980 as new residential developments gobbled up some of the extensive open spaces cherished by the authors of the long-obsolete Tokyo Green Space Plan of 1939.[124] Urbanization rates give some idea of how crowded Japan's cities had become by the 1980s, but numbers cannot capture the claustrophobia of urban commuting, shopping, and neighborhood living felt by many city people during these prosperous years, particularly newcomers accustomed to more space in the countryside. The term *midori* for green space was a favorite of campaigning politicians of the left and right by the mid-1980s. They were aware of surveys such as Tokyo's in 1986 that found residents listing more green space as their highest desideratum for making the city more livable, ahead of sunshine, fresh air, or quiet.[125]

Tokyo's 1981 green space plan and follow-up protocols accurately anticipated doubling the per capita parkland and open space by 2000. To supplement its own funds and national government reimbursements for expanding parks and other open spaces, Tokyo set up an Urban Green Space Foundation in 1985 to attract private donations, with limited tax advantages for businesses that contributed, to be used to add small parks and other forms of beautification around civic facilities.[126] Japan's National Trust movement, which began in 1969 after citizens in Kamakura rallied to stop a housing development in 1964 behind the Tsurugaoka Hachiman Shrine, gained momentum in the mid-1980s by soliciting private gifts to install trees and preserve forests. Similar public-private partnerships in Tokyo helped the metropolis add ginkgos, plane trees, Chinese maples, weeping willows, and zelkovas to the estimated 3.5 million trees over three meters tall in the ward area identified in the green census of 1983.[127] Tokyo and other prefectures also established tree contracts with owners of private woodlots, excusing their fixed-asset taxes and reducing their inheritance taxes for terms of five to twenty years in return for allowing the public to use these green spaces. If a landlord later wanted the land back, the municipality was forced either to buy it or face an outcry from citizens who used it. By 2004 this joint public-private system, managed by volunteers, had expanded to cover 7,441 square kilometers of leased woods nationwide, with nearly three fourths of the contracts in the Tokyo region.[128]

Through April 2004, more than three hundred new green sites had been purchased within cities and suburbs through the master planning required of the nation's green space districts under the Urban Green Space Protection Law. Nearly half of the sites were in Nagoya and Fukuoka, whereas Tokyo had only six because land was too expensive and its open-space planning was already far advanced. The ¥103.5 billion invested in these new city and suburban green space sites was less than a tenth of the ¥1,261 billion spent on Japan's city parks in 1995 alone, but the two are difficult to compare. City parks involved more extensive and more costly land purchases, facilities, equipment, and upkeep. Park users greatly outnumbered visitors to green spaces, and programming, maintenance, and administrative expenses were vastly greater for parks. Yet both parks and green spaces gave emergency officials the disaster-prevention zones they needed, city planners the aesthetic values they sought to relieve commercial crowding and residential blandness, and citizens the open areas they desired for exercise, diversion from routines, or simple enjoyment of the nonhuman, no matter how controlled the environments of these government-produced spaces.

CHAPTER 5

Parks and New Eco-Regimes

Japan in the 1990s and early 2000s was washed by the same tides of emergent ecological consciousness as other countries with postindustrial economies and rich environmental legacies. Like their global counterparts, civic-minded Japanese increasingly engaged with ecological issues in general and open-space planning in particular, in both city and natural parks. Despite the tangled complexities and Croesian cost of adding more parks, green spaces, and open lands, Japan devotes two thirds of its surface to forests and for more than a generation has reserved one seventh of its land area as urban greenery and national, quasi-national, and prefectural natural parks. Attendance at natural parks and recreation grounds within government forests peaked in the early 1990s and official funding leveled off shortly thereafter, yet these legally protected spaces continue to be vital to the national imaginary about, and practical experience of, the nonhuman environment.

In urban Japan a grand five-year plan, beginning in 1991, attempted to pare the government's budget surplus through large investments in social amenities such as housing, sewerage, and city parks. The surplus quickly became a deficit, but money kept flowing to the parks. Allocations were ¥5 trillion from 1991 to 1995, up 60 percent from the previous plan, and rose another ¥2.2 trillion during the seven-year period from 1996 to 2002.[1] Given the time required from initial planning until parks were ready for use, it was not surprising that despite an indifferent national economy Japan added another 29,592 city parks between 1991 and 2005—more than it had established during the century from 1873 to 1972. Put another way, the decades of heaviest investment in city parks from 1972 to 2005 added

76,997 parks with 828 square kilometers, an expansion not even Gotō Shinpei could have imagined three quarters of a century earlier. Urban populations kept on growing throughout this golden age of park development, but thanks to careful planning and budgeting, the city park space per resident nationwide rose even faster, from 3.4 square meters in 1976 to 8.9 in 2005—a notable 161 percent increase, although 8.9 square meters per capita was still quite low by international standards.[2]

Why Japan continued to invest in urban green spaces despite its economic woes and budget deficits after 1992 is traceable partly to pump priming via public works overseen by the Construction Ministry and partly to a perception that the nation's environmental health outside the cities was rosy. Although the extent of Japan's vegetation is difficult for city residents or urban visitors to imagine, the Environment Ministry considers 95 percent of Japan's surface green. This includes two thirds devoted to forests and parks, nearly a quarter to farms and orchards, 5 percent to grasslands, and 1 percent to inland water, figures that have remained stable for many decades. Cities, roads, and the built environment account for nearly all the rest.[3] These figures help explain why Japanese leaders since World War Two have devoted such extraordinary resources to bringing green spaces to their cities and relatively fewer to protecting the nation's seemingly abundant countryside environment.

Although bureaucrats extolled rural Japan as extensive and ecologically sound, private groups sought to preserve patches of wildness, volunteers conducted green censuses to tabulate flora and fauna, and endangered species were identified and shielded by law in the 1990s and early 2000s. National parks and other landscapes achieved international recognition as World Heritage sites and Ramsar Convention wetlands, even though the number of rangers and other specialized personnel to oversee these scenic locations remained surprisingly small. Road and dam construction continued to threaten natural parks, pollution remained a menace, and laws intended to restrict game hunting met with indifferent enforcement. A vigorous movement to restore rural interfaces between farms and forests gained momentum during the national economic slowdown of the 1990s that saw the annual growth rate in gross domestic product fall to about 1 percent between 1992 and 2004, during which the country experienced four brief recessions. Both natural and city parks depended increasingly on volunteer staffing in the early 2000s, a time when most environmental groups found themselves working with the national government rather than against it, even as the Environment Ministry, upgraded from an agency in 2001, began promoting ecotours to some of Japan's most environmentally fragile spots. As has been true since the first Forest Law of 1897, the precarious balance between protection and use remains ambiguous, but often tilted toward the latter.

Natural Parks and Wildlife Protection

Just 56 square kilometers within Japan's national parks are special preservation zones containing "primeval" lands where all human activity apart from scientific study is prohibited. Within quasi-national and prefectural parks, natural environment preservation districts cover 216 square kilometers.[4] Another 763 square kilometers are recognized as prefectural protection areas, of which about one third are special regions with considerable wildlife conservation but some controlled felling of trees. Normal timber cutting and construction are allowed in nearly half of these protected areas, meaning that just 552 square kilometers enjoy more than nominal environmental protection—about 1 percent of the total area covered by Japan's 394 natural parks today.

To oversee twenty-eight national and fifty-five quasi-national parks as of 2000, the Environment Agency employed just 205 officials in regional field offices and another 67 at local service points, staffing so lean as to be virtually invisible to the estimated 675 million persons who visit a national or quasi-national park each year.[5] Fuji-Hakone-Izu remains the most popular, drawing about 100 million visitors a year, followed by the Seto Inland Sea at 38 million. Lake Biwa continues to top the quasi-national parks in attendance, with 29 million.[6] In 2000 the central government paid ¥17.6 billion toward the operating costs of national and quasi-national parks, down from the all-time high of ¥18.4 billion in 1998. By March 2008 the figure had dropped to ¥11.8 billion, reflecting tighter budgets in Tokyo as well as the government's devolution policy of making localities more responsible for their own incomes and outlays.[7] One way to increase local revenues was to approve applications to use the parks for taxpaying commercial purposes.[8] If by the early twenty-first century the whine of the chain saw was relatively muted as logging waned within the natural parks, the thump of the construction hammer and nail gun grew louder as subventions from Tokyo grew scarcer.

Outside the natural parks prefectural governors were also free to use the Wildlife Protection and Hunting Law of 1918 to designate other wildlife conservation areas,[9] many of which were established to control hunting or small-scale cutting of bamboo and other trees by local residents. By the 1980s this law protected 477 species of birds and 62 species of mammals from hunting or trapping, of which the Environment Agency considered 38 avian and 14 mammalian species endangered.[10] In 1992 the government passed a Law for Conservation of Endangered Species of Wild Fauna and Flora intended to protect entire ecosystems, not just threatened species.[11] This legislation signaled Japan's greater eagerness than in the past to conform to international ecological standards.

Since 1972 the Nature Conservation Law has required the Environment Agency (since 2001, Ministry) to carry out an elaborate green census every five years to survey the country's topography, species distribution, wildlife habitats, and scenic vistas as a guide to biodiversity for policy makers and the general public.[12] Focused entirely on named species, the results from 2004 identified 1,400 vertebrate and 35,000 invertebrate animal species, as well as nearly 32,000 plant species.[13] A previous green census completed in 1989 identified 668 species of birds in Japan, nearly two thirds migratory. Almost 10 percent of the national surface was designated as bird-protection areas in 2004, including more than six hundred special sanctuaries in national forests, natural parks, and reserves where hunting, trapping, and egg pilfering were forbidden.[14] Perhaps best-known is the fate of the Japanese red-crested crane, the most prized of the country's six crane species, at the Kushiro Shitsugen National Park and environs in Hokkaido. The Kushiro marsh has shrunk by at least 30 percent during the past half-century, and without winter corn at feeding stations run by private citizens and the prefectural government, nearly all the one thousand cranes there likely would starve.[15] Many other government partnerships with private citizens to protect flora as well as fauna, based on data from green censuses, have helped the Environment Ministry enforce the lenient provisions of the Nature Conservation Law and the much tougher Endangered Species Law of 1992. A watered-down Environmental Impact

Assessment Law took effect in 1997, aiding conservation groups in law-suits alleging that agencies and private developers were shirking statutory requirements.

Despite the flurry of regulations and a much higher public conscious-ness of ecological matters, the early 2000s were marked by deep environ-mental concerns affecting natural parks and other preserves. An endemic problem facing birds and their host trees is forest fragmentation, mainly caused by suburbanization but also by roads and power-line corridors in deep forests. As birds that consume leaf-eating caterpillars disappear for want of habitat, the remaining trees suffer great damage.[16] Global warm-ing has apparently caused seedling trees to take root in two subalpine marshes in Aso-Kuju National Park in Kyushu. Local residents carry out controlled burns every spring to clear volunteer saplings from the moors, which draw an estimated five million visitors each year to see azaleas in June and brilliant autumn leaves in November.[17] Mount Jizo in Zao Quasi-National Park was famous as recently as 1977 for its frost-silvered trees four months each winter, but thirty years later the silver freeze lasted just two months. Park leaders worry that if global temperatures rise two more degrees centigrade no frost will form at all.[18]

Although Japan since 1970 has crafted an environmental success story in controlling many forms of pollution, its record in protecting threat-ened and endangered species, both in and out of natural parks, has been smudged by the demands of tourist entrepreneurs and resource develop-ers, by recreational pressures on both mountains and seashores, and by a partially decentralized system of parks administration that burdens local governments with hefty financial loads. As a result, few Japanese environ-mentalists were surprised in 2005 when the Virginia-based organization Conservation International identified their country as one of thirty-four global "biodiversity hotspots" where humans and their constructions threatened the nonhuman environment.[19]

National Parks and International Recognition

Eager since at least 1905 to draw foreign visitors to the country's scenic landscapes, and proud host in 1997 of the Kyoto Protocol, Japan was un-derstandably chagrined to be labeled a biodiversity hotspot. On the other hand, officials were gratified to have some of Japan's most important natural parks, geophysical features, and historical buildings recognized by international conventions and commissions. In 1972 member states of UNESCO adopted the Convention for the Protection of the World Cultural and Natural Heritage, which Japan belatedly ratified in 1992 as part of a larger effort to attain legitimacy in the global community.[20] The World Heritage program proved to be a boon for tourism because the publicity surrounding Japan's newly designated locations lured huge numbers of domestic visitors.

World Natural Heritage sites were quickly approved at Yakushima in Kirishima-Yakushima National Park in Kyushu and the Shirakami Mountains bordering Tsugaru Quasi-National Park in Akita Prefecture, both in 1993. Shiretoko National Park in northeastern Hokkaido was added as a natural heritage site in 2005. Eleven other locations in Japan are listed as World Cultural Heritage sites, including Itsukushima in the Seto Inland Sea National Park, shrines and temples in Nikkō National Park, and pilgrimage routes in Yoshino-Kumano National Park. At other sites, local citizens' organizations such as the Ogimachi Society to Protect the Natural Environment at the Shirakawa cultural heritage village in Gifu Prefecture negotiate between the government and residents to preserve old architecture while also attracting tourists through nostalgia for a bygone rural lifestyle that never quite existed.[21] In the government's eyes, Japan's three natural heritage sites and eleven cultural heritage sites are embarrassingly few in relation to the worldwide totals of 176 natural areas and 689 cultural ones as of 2009.[22]

Often seen as Japan's wildest frontier because of its spectacular winter sea ice, glittering lakes, and beautiful hiking scenery, the Shiretoko peninsula also has 123 dams on 44 rivers, abundant concrete and asphalt along its roads and waterways, and mounds of shoreline garbage drifting in from the Sea of Okhotsk. City-based environmentalists, local residents in Shari Town, and the Environment Agency forged an effective partnership in 1977 to protect deep stands of oaks and firs at Shiretoko, and despite logging pressures from the Forestry Agency in the early 1980s, the private-public alliance remained effective.[23] When the Switzerland-based World Conservation Union (IUCN) evaluated the park in 2004, it demanded— and Japan agreed—that the Forestry Agency remove some of the dams and install fishways around the remaining ones so that salmon and trout could run the rivers in summer and autumn. The survey team noted that fish were essential food sources for brown bears before the bears hibernated, as well as for red foxes and wild birds. Although UNESCO seeks to maintain its natural heritage locations in pristine condition, this is hardly possible at a national park drawing hundreds of thousands of visitors a year,[24] especially from other Asian countries. In 2009 Japan also gained recognition for three of its natural parks as UNESCO Geoparks under a program established in 2004 that grew to sixty-three locations worldwide.[25]

The Japanese government in 1980 accepted the Convention on Wetlands of International Significance, a pact to protect migratory birds and their habitats originally signed at Ramsar, Iran, in 1971. The Kushiro marsh was immediately approved as a Ramsar wetland, followed by a dozen more up to 2002, at which point the government adopted a new biodiversity strategy to preserve and restore ecologically sensitive areas. Perhaps chagrined that Great Britain had ten times as many Ramsar wetlands, the Environment Ministry then campaigned to add more sites, bringing the total to thirty-seven by 2008.[26] Among the marshes was part of Akan National Park in Hokkaido, which together with nearby Daisetsuzan National Park may be even wilder than Shiretoko, and the well-known Oze swampland, which became Japan's twenty-ninth national park in August 2007. The Ramsar site at Oze spreads across eighty-seven square kilometers, nearly three quarters of which is privately owned, mainly by Tokyo Electric Power Company. Plans to build a hydroelectric dam there, initially broached in 1903, eventually triggered Japan's first conservation movement, led by the League to Assure Preservation of Oze starting in 1949. Since the 1970s visitors have been required to carry their trash home with them, and no soap is allowed in Oze's upland huts. The Environment Agency acknowledged the effectiveness of conservationists by recognizing the Oze Protection Foundation in 1995, the first local organization to administer a park area in Japan. The power company partially abandoned its dam project in 1996.[27] The emperor decided in 2007 "to share nature with the public" by transferring almost half of his 1,200-hectare villa at Nasu, Tochigi Prefecture, to Nikkō National Park as a de facto offset when Oze was split off to become its own national park later that summer.[28]

One of many waterfalls at Shiretoko National Park (est. 1964) in northeastern Hokkaido, considered Japan's wildest natural park. Courtesy Itō Taiichi.

Japan's skill at mixing performance and the environment achieved international recognition through the World Expo Aichi 2005, held on the outskirts of Nagoya with the theme "nature's wisdom." The slogan was an ironic choice by planners, who originally sought to use the entire 530-hectare Kaisho Forest, supposedly "unspoiled natural surroundings," but were forced by local activists to cut back to fifteen forest hectares plus surrounding land in Seto City, a famous pottery center.[29] Kaisho is a carefully restored interface between human settlements and the nonhuman environment, discreetly managed with a view toward protecting trees, watersheds, and wildlife as well as peripheral paddies. The volunteers who took care of this rural restoration zone formed a preservation group in 2004 backed by the Japanese Nature Conservation and Wild Bird Societies to fight the expo and follow-up plans for housing within the forest. When nesting goshawks were discovered there, even the International Bureau of Expositions in Paris criticized the prefecture and local planners. The combination of local and global criticism in advance of the event revealed changed outlooks on the environment and development, even if the exposition itself only partly fulfilled the hopes of activists.

Pavilions were built from recycled or recyclable materials, and visitors were warned to use public transportation, not private automobiles. Unlike the Osaka Expo '70, which featured Japan's high-speed growth, the scaled-down Aichi Expo nominally focused on global environmental problems, demonstrations of solar energy projects, and woodcrafts and rope making led by members of the Kaisho preservation group. Yet well-attended displays of high technology and robotics somewhat dimmed the green theme. The most popular venue was the Chinese pavilion featuring its own success at rapid economic prosperity, and when this "natural" exposition closed its gates in September 2005, it had cleared the astonishing sum of ¥10 billion thanks to its corporate sponsors, brisk sales of high-profit logo toys, and a total fee-paying gate of twenty-two million people, seven million higher than initial projections.[30] The ¥10 billion profit was almost as great a sum as the central government's share of annual operating costs of all the national and quasi-national parks in the country.

A New Forest Culture

As imports of wood products rose and staffing levels fell, the Forestry Agency suffered declining income and a loss of prestige in the 1970s, despite its unflagging support of Japanese foresters and its new skiing and camping facilities for the public that opened in 1967. In response to the environmental movements of the late 1960s, the agency began touting the public benefits of forests in an attempt to lure visitors to the recreation areas within national forests. The new forest culture meant that public woodlands should benefit the people, not merely extractive industries. Selective preservation was now an authentic watchword. The agency clearly recognized that the "social roles of forests are becoming more and more important worldwide"[31]—implicitly confirming Maki Fumihiko's conception of inner spatial depth. Then the old forest culture made a partial comeback: the agency received large infusions of cash in the mid-1990s as the central government, under pressure from the United States, began to spend massively on public works to stimulate the low-growth national economy. Despite long-standing criticism from ecologists and environmentalists, the agency projected in 1994 that forest roads, many of them traversing natural parks, would more than double by 2025 to 97,000 kilometers in length.[32] It brushed aside objections that more roads would cut off the normal ranges of ground animals, fragment forests, drive deep-forest birds away, and allow new species to enter.

Nonetheless, between 1990 and 1997 the Forestry Agency mollified some of its critics by establishing two dozen zones within national forests as biodiversity reserves open only to scientific investigators, bringing the total pristine area outside natural parks to 3,200 square kilometers.[33] In 1998 the agency barred timber cutting in 80 percent of national forest lands and opened about one fourth of total forest areas for use by local residents. It also promoted its many public recreation sites, which attracted 162 million visitors in the year ending March 2000.[34] Clearly the government still intended the forests to be put to human use, although now less to serve the needs of loggers and more to satisfy the desires of campers, backpackers, skiers, and nature photographers in search of renewal in the outdoors.

The cabinet in April 2009 approved a plan to thin 200,000 hectares of trees annually for the next five years to promote forests' absorption of carbon dioxide, as well as to preserve biodiversity. A government white paper on forestry appearing the following month called for burning wooden biomass fuel because it emits fewer greenhouse gases than coal and heavy oil. Occasionally, replanting happened for local environmental reasons; since 1996 a nonprofit organization of hundreds of volunteers each year has reforested sections of mountains near the Ashio copper mill in Tochigi Prefecture, where the last mine was abandoned in 1972. The surrounding woodlands still contain sulfur from smoke emitted by the copper refinery starting in 1877.[35]

Forests, mainly national ones, make up about nine tenths of Japan's natural parks and share many of the problems of overcrowding, competing demands, underfunding, deteriorating maintenance, and human-animal contacts that plague managed reserves open to the public everywhere. Complaints about dams remained endemic in the 1990s, even though plans to build ninety-two new ones were abandoned after 1996 because of reduced water consumption and stiff local opposition. Japan has more than 2,700 river dams, with several hundred under construction or design, although the Hatoyama Yukio Cabinet called for a thorough review of dam projects in late 2009. The default rationale for building them, as well as for lining river banks and shorelines in concrete, remains flood control, although much evidence indicates that concrete channels are more prone to flash flooding.[36] With more than three dozen additional hydroelectric plants now planned, some of them in national parks or forests, a number of Japanese environmentalists favor wind turbines as alternatives, an option endorsed by an advisory panel to the Environment Ministry in December 2003.

Japan's new forest culture of greater public access steadily eroded the perimeters between the human and nonhuman. Contact with bears increased in the 1990s as more visitors gathered nuts and wild mushrooms in natural parks and backpackers intruded on animal habitats in forest recreation districts. Plantations of coniferous trees, as well as declining log harvests because of imports, led to the neglect of forests and a dropoff in food for bears. Thousands of oaks killed by uncontrolled boring beetles deprived bears of acorns for mast. As rural villages depopulated, the animals feasted on abandoned orchards; when people left garbage near bear ranges the chances of encounters increased. A brief bear hunting season begins each year on November 15, but environmentalists have generally urged the government to reduce the kill limits and instead to restore habitats so that bears will not wander so often into areas thickly settled by humans.[37]

Protected at various times by both national and prefectural regulations, deer and goat antelopes (serows) spread into natural parks and nearby farmlands in the 1990s and early 2000s, doing considerable damage to young trees and crops. Warmer weather allowed more animals to survive the winter, and clear-cutting forest tracts followed by monoculture regeneration left many seedlings and shrubs vulnerable to predation. As a result, the replanted areas, as well as well-foraged understories beneath mature trees, were subject to erosion in heavy rains, which clogged rivers and sluices. Japan's vast plantations of cryptomeria are the chief suspects in outbreaks of pollen allergy, similar to hay fever, suffered by 20 percent of the population south of Hokkaido each spring.

Tightly controlled by law and local custom, the number of hunting licenses fell off from a peak of 400,000 in the 1970s to fewer than 200,000 today, mainly issued to males over age thirty. Even though more than 110,000 deer were killed by hunters in 1999 alone, culling, sport hunting, and trapping were insufficient to thin the populations of deer, serows, and wild boars that increasingly ate or trampled human plantings.[38] Wild monkeys likewise encroached fearlessly on suburban truck farms to plunder potatoes, persimmons, rice, and other crops.

Commenting on Japan's new forest culture of ecological awareness, the Kyoto forester Takayanagi Atsushi asks rhetorically, "Do you kill serows or fence your crops against them?" Different prefectures use different methods of dealing with pestiferous wildlife, but Takayanagi concludes that "for coexistence [by people] with wildlife in nature, cultural backgrounds are more necessary than resource control."[39] This consciousness is reflected in the growing numbers of volunteers helping to manage Japan's natural parks and especially in the movement to restore neglected spaces on the margins between farms and woodlands, particularly those near natural parks.

Eco-Regimes: Volunteers and Rural Restoration

As in many mature democratic societies, Japan's age of ecovolunteers and nonprofit organizations began in the 1990s and gathered even more momentum in the new century, with no hint of abating. By the time the Diet passed a Law to Promote Specified Nonprofit Activities (nonprofit organization law) in 1998, many thousands of nongovernmental organizations (NGOs) of all kinds existed throughout the country.[40] Through them an estimated 400,000 Japanese volunteered in 2006, four times the number in 1985.[41] Without volunteers, the natural parks, national forest recreation areas, and countless other public services could barely function. They began serving in national parks in 1980 as subrangers responsible for such varied tasks as environmental education and trash management. By 1988 the Environment Agency estimated that two thousand volunteers were assisting in national parks leading bird-watching tours, observing terrestrial animals, educating tourists, and working with the media to promote responsible use by visitors. At that point only nine of Japan's twenty-eight national parks had ranger stations; the rest depended on a handful of licensed professional guides and mainly on part-time local volunteers to shepherd the several hundred million parkgoers each year.[42] As recently as 2001 Japan had just 150 natural park and forest rangers, known as nature protection officers, to train and supervise about three thousand volunteer guides in national and quasi-national parks, where another two thousand volunteers staffed visitor centers and maintained trails and campgrounds. Despite the minuscule staffing provided by central government budgets, the level of cooperation among national officials, prefectural bureaucrats, and local citizens is considered healthy, if underfunded.[43]

Shortly after the Environment Agency was upgraded to a ministry in 2001 it instituted a Green Worker program to train volunteers systematically in environmental protection and to begin paying them small stipends, for which it budgeted ¥200 million for 2002. A Natural Parks Foundation was established to implement the Green Worker plan, with particular attention to plant and animal protection, campground cleanups, and regulating snowmobiles in national parks.[44] Part of the reason for the program was to give the Environment Ministry greater control over park management, but another factor was that heretofore only licensed guides could be paid, and most of them preferred to work in cities where incomes were greater. Apart from the Green Workers, more than a thousand volunteer groups served in Japan's forests as of 2003, consisting of roughly thirty thousand individuals from the cities who enjoyed the exercise and had a good level of technical knowledge. They only partly replaced professional foresters, whose numbers dropped a remarkable 60 percent between 1990 and 2000. Still, the environmental critic Tanaka Atsuo contends that "forest volunteers will not save the trees. When they bring groundless expectations that it will be easy, they face reality and are disillusioned."[45]

Although many Japanese have a high awareness of ecological problems, most of the estimated eight thousand environmental groups active as of 2003 focused on single locations or issues, conducted little research, and were more concerned with education than with policy changes. The political scientist Wilhelm Vosse points out that most such organizations were consensual: "rather than an opposition movement, the environmental movement became a partner in the Japanese political system"[46]—as the volunteers in natural parks and forests confirm.

A number of conservation organizations since the mid-1980s have been less concerned with preserving park habitats than with the rural restoration movement on the borderlands between forests and farms. Volunteers have rehabilitated quasi-forested woodlands that farmers once maintained for charcoal, mulch, and fodder, but which fell into disuse and became overgrown when households converted to fossil fuels and synthetic fertilizers in the 1950s. Thereafter a number of these marginal landscapes spontaneously reforested, bringing animals closer to village residents.[47] The restoration movement developed as a volunteer land management effort to renew these places in-between so people could grow mushrooms, revive open-canopy forest bottoms, re-establish diversity of plants and ground animals, control erosion, and purify watersheds. Yet for many participants the restoration zones became spaces of an urban imaginary as much as of a rural reality. Many of the sixty-nine restoration organizations active in 1996 were dominated by city dwellers interested in landscape aesthetics and sometimes in re-establishing a romanticized rural culture abandoned by villagers after World War Two.[48] Whether nostalgic or simply naturalist in outlook, weekend participants sought a sustainable society based on organic resources by reviving intermediate lands where people and nonhuman surroundings formerly interacted daily, before village farming and woodland maintenance went into a tailspin during the era of high-speed economic growth.

Entire shelves in major Japanese bookstores burgeoned with titles on the rural restoration movement after the photographer Inamori Mitsuhiko published *Satoyama monogatari* (Tale of rural restoration) in 1995, documenting farm and forest reclamation in Ogi, on Lake Biwa near Ōtsu in Shiga Prefecture.[49] The largest restoration project in the Tokyo region is Shishitsuka, one hundred hectares of mostly private land near Tsuchiura

Station in Ibaraki Prefecture. This site has been managed since 1989 by the Shishitsuka Nature and History Society, whose goal is "to hand over to our children this valuable restored land,"[50] hoping that the next generation will be equally interested in environmental sustainability. Despite a quarter-century of earnest forest restoration, many critics fear that depending on volunteers may not be a reliable long-term method of maintaining these lands.[51]

Ecology and Commerce

Eager to capitalize on a new wave of environmental profitability, the Environment Ministry in 2003 began planning ecotours to some of Japan's most treasured landscapes, including Shiretoko, Yakushima, Shirakawago, and Urabandai, where natural parks or national forests contained pristine areas supposedly protected against intrusion. Aware of the income to be reaped by showcasing science-based contacts with the nonhuman, the Diet passed a law in June 2007 to promote ecotourism, the most recent of the ever-hopeful campaigns to draw international visitors that date at least to Kinoshita Yoshio in 1905. One travel agency, Reborn, offered outings to clean garbage on Fuji, weed organic vegetable plots, and run marathons through forests. Some businesses began to choose ecotours as part of their company training programs,[52] much as they once put their new management employees through Zen meditation or street-corner oratory. Kyoto, although "a natural fit for eco-tourism and the slow life movement,"[53] was already too thronged with visitors to bother with this market, but Michelin's *Le Guide Vert, Japon* nonetheless awarded the city three stars in its first edition, released in 2009.

To meet its ever-receding targets to reduce greenhouse gas emissions under the Kyoto Protocol of 1997, the Japanese government in 2004 floated the idea of imposing an environment tax on the consumption of fossil fuels. Opinion surveys conducted during the next three years revealed mixed public reactions, and no decision was taken. Then the steep downturn of world credit and equities markets in 2008 led the government to delay any new taxes; instead it proposed renaming the current gasoline and other energy taxes as environment taxes, ideally redirecting the revenues from road development to environmental conservation.[54] The Japan Business

Federation (Nippon Keidanren) joined the green movement in January 2009 by seeking economic recovery partly through energy-saving technologies.[55] The government has also conceded that Japan's natural parks and forests cannot help reduce greenhouse gases so greatly as originally projected when the Kyoto Protocol was adopted. The Environment Ministry periodically seeks to recover more of its costs in operating national and quasi-national parks by imposing entrance fees at parks that lack them.[56] Admission charges presumably also would reduce attendance, cut automobile emissions, and relieve stress on ecosystems. But such fees have been implemented only piecemeal because of jurisdictional disputes with the Forestry Agency, the presence of private lands within natural parks, and the ongoing negotiation of use and protection.

The Nature Conservation Society of Japan, a nongovernmental organization dating to 1951, pointed out in 2000 that despite the more stringent environmental laws adopted in the 1990s, the additional World Heritage sites, and the newly designated Ramsar wetlands, "the basic role played by national parks has not changed. Are the management operations and legal basis of the national parks grounded in a context of up-to-date natural-environment preservation?"[57] A follow-up report in 2001 criticized park administrators for catering to tourists by focusing too much on beautiful scenery and urged them instead to develop a deeper ecological awareness of their park environments. It recommended reorienting park management via zoning, monitoring for overuse, and assessing impacts of enterprises within parks. The society called for better environmental education, more professional training for staff, higher quality public contacts with the non-human, and a more solid financial footing for national and quasi-national parks. These steps would win greater international respect for Japan's efforts at environmental protection, including its newfound forest culture, growing volunteerism, and energetic rural restoration movement. The key, the report concluded, was a reorientation of outlook by park administrators and national leaders toward a new consciousness of ecological order and biodiversity.[58] This consciousness has been well established among the Japanese scientific community for nearly a half-century and has begun to take root in the natural parks, where demands from extractive industries are on the wane, tourism businesses are adjusting to environmentalism, and many visitors seek deeper, better-informed engagement with their nonhuman surroundings. Whether such an outlook will come to prevail over the doctrine of sustainable development in Japanese policy decisions cannot yet be forecast with any accuracy.

Laws from Above, Plans from Below

In support of its ill-starred bid to host the 2016 summer Olympics, Tokyo announced a ten-year master plan in 2006 called Tokyo's Big Change, one goal of which was to "have Tokyo become the city with the lowest environmental load in the world," presumably per capita, through steps that included adding more parks, trees, and green spaces.[59] Actually the Big Change was less an emulation of Beijing's Green Olympics of 2008 than a warmed-over version of the Tokyo Megalopolis Concept, announced in 2001, which mainly sought to build more highways and train lines.[60] Another key aim of the Big Change was "to increase goodwill toward other Asian cities" whose well-to-do residents flocked to Japan's scenic highlights early in the new millennium, helping to pump up local tourist businesses. The metropolitan government soon put in motion a ¥1.7 trillion three-year plan starting in 2008 to restore the waterfront, double roadside trees to one million, add a thousand hectares of green space, try once again to braid a greenbelt from the Tama to the Ara Rivers, and revitalize stale Ueno Park as a "cultural forest" for residents and tourists.[61] Tokyo optimistically sought to make its Ecolympics the first-ever "carbon-minus Games," but the International Olympic Committee paid scant heed and instead selected Rio de Janeiro in late 2009. Nonetheless, like earthquakes, fires, air raids, and the 1964 Olympics, the possibility of holding the 2016 event gave Tokyo added leverage in prying loose funds from both the national government and corporate sponsors to carry out city planning projects long on hold for want of sufficient budgets.

The true big changes for Japan's city parks in the early 2000s arrived incrementally and often below the radar of media attention, yet collectively they represented novel approaches to the uses and functions of public space. The 1993 amendments to the City Parks Law were based on "the idea of turning the city itself into a park,"[62] with greater attention to open spaces of all kinds rather than conventional parks alone. Recognizing the graying of society, the new law redefined children's playgrounds as street-side parks, with sandboxes and cute animal rides gradually replaced by benches and shrubbery.[63] After the Hanshin earthquake and fires of 1995, the City Parks Law was revised again so that heliports, water tanks, and storehouses of emergency supplies could be built in city parks—the latest chapter in a long saga of disaster prevention and relief.[64] At their most ambitious, the step-by-step innovations of the early 2000s reinscribed the urban park as an institution of civic culture, no longer primarily an instrument of social control. In 2004 the semiofficial Japan Parks and Green Space Association acknowledged that open spaces were needed in cities so that people could interact with the nonhuman environment, nurture their spirits by enjoying biodiversity and seasonal changes, assure their own safety from disasters, and "enjoy multifunctional green spaces during their leisure hours, in response to changing times"[65]—a remarkably different discursive script from earlier generations of nation-first ideology, when vigorous exercise, freedom from disease, and building public identity and citizenship were marquee goals.

Legislative and fiscal authority over urban open space in Japan was highly centralized from the moment the Grand Council of State created city parks by fiat in 1873. Various amendments to the City Parks Law of 1956 and the new City Planning Law of 1968 permitted a whiff of consultation between officials responsible for parks and citizens who used them. But, ironically, not until the cabinet took the most top-down of legal steps—issuing basic laws with the effect of executive orders, without parliamentary action—was bottom-up participation by the general public mandated for planning future urban parks. In 1993 a cabinet-approved Basic Environmental Law took effect, followed a year later by an equally ex cathedra Basic Environmental Plan, both of which established in fundamental law the principles of citizen participation in environmental planning and human coexistence with the nonhuman. The changes derived from a large package of administrative and political reforms adopted by a coalition of non-LDP parties that came to power in 1993, weakening the grip of the Construction Ministry on land use policy until the LDP regained control in 1995. Socialists, Communists, and other opposition politicians criticized the ministry for insufficiently emphasizing parks, which doubtless received lower priority because they were less lucrative for landowners, contractors, and their LDP supporters than were large-scale public works.[66]

The City Planning Law was duly amended in 1999 to conform with the Basic Environmental Law and Plan, simplifying decisions in city planning districts while providing for consent by neighborhood residents to actions that affected them. More revisions in 2000 allowed citizens to bring their ideas for city planning to upper-tier government offices. But the real change was making city planning a statutory function of prefectural and municipal governments, no longer one delegated from the national government. How consistently local mayors consulted their constituencies before finalizing plans is uncertain; what is clear is that the 1999–2000 amendments did not include specific protections for green spaces or provide enough financial independence to municipalities to implement the new city parks and other open spaces they were obligated to plan.[67]

Major revisions to the Urban Green Space Protection Law of 1973 coordinated scenic planning and green space planning at the local level, effective in 2004. The City Parks Law also was amended in 2004 to let nonprofit organizations operate city parks, and a Third Scenic Green Space Law, enacted the same year, entrusted planning and administering scenic green spaces to local government bodies and required more input by local residents in the process; it also authorized local nonprofits to carry out small-scale improvements within scenic districts.[68] Yet in April 2006 the national government decreed that municipalities could ease the green space requirements for factories from 20 percent of a proposed site to 10 percent in a bid to attract more industry and improve local economies;[69] no locality dared not do so if it wished to compete, both economically and bureaucratically.

At the same time, scientists and city planners began to extol parks and other green areas for their environmental benefits in reducing urban temperatures. Now parks were more and more appreciated for improving air quality, serving as windbreaks, humidifying neighborhoods during autumn and winter dry seasons, absorbing carbon dioxide, and helping to reduce global warming. Personal benefits of visiting parks included both physical well-being and "psychological stability"[70] by reducing stress, partly through inhaling the aromas of plants and trees. These considerations were almost always yoked to the economic advantages conferred by parks in attracting tourists, reducing energy demand through their cooling effect, and raising real estate values for condominiums with handsome views of green spaces.[71]

Tokyo and its neighboring prefectures developed four more regional development plans through 1999 with increasing attention to civic amenities, including parks and green spaces, rather than economic growth alone. The metropolis had poured a great deal of its own money into capital improvements for city parks ever since the 1980s, cresting at ¥126 billion in 1988,[72] but the ensuing economic slowdown forced Tokyo to cut back on its operations budget for city parks: with 1997 as 100, the index of outlays for city park administration and upkeep fell to 70 in 2001 and was projected to slide to just 52, or ¥37 billion, in the year ending in March 2006.[73] In spite of these vicissitudes, Tokyo Metropolis in the face of relentless population growth was able to double its city park space per capita between 1960 and 1975, then more than double it again between 1975 and 1993.[74] Between 1993 and 2003 the metropolis added another 1,315 city parks and eight square kilometers of parkland, lifting the per capita figure to 5.0 square meters.[75] Undeterred by such statistics, the environmental critic Aoki Kōichirō commented in 1998 that "even though parks are increasing, green space is decreasing—a puzzle."[76] Of course it was no puzzle at all, as Aoki knew; housing, roads, schools, and other buildings were consuming genuine open areas faster than the authorities could produce artificial space in the form of city parks.

Contributions, commerce, privatization, and volunteerism steadily seeped into thinking about urban public parks after 2000, all with a view toward decreasing the burden of operating costs borne by prefectures and municipalities. Starting in 2003, donors from a dozen prefectures contributed ¥150,000 to ¥200,000 each to install memorial benches with personalized messages in Tokyo's major parks,[77] signaling a new form of self-expression by individuals and, more important, an increasing sense of ownership of civic space by the public. Tokyo Metropolis also sought to augment revenues by imposing entrance fees at more public parks and installing more concessions. More than ten million people paid entrance fees averaging ¥200 to use fifteen of Tokyo's most renowned parks, zoos, and aquaria in the year ending in March 2008, with Ueno Zoo at 3.5

million easily the most popular.[78] The Tokyo Metropolitan Park Association, established by the metropolis in 1954 to manage most of the city's large parks, operated an academy at Hibiya Park to train volunteers to assist the paid staff in the eighty-three parks, gardens, cemeteries, and other locations under its aegis.[79]

More direct forms of privatization included a Private Finance Initiative bill introduced in the Diet in 1998, patterned after British practice, to encourage outside entities to take over various functions previously considered the government's responsibility. Starting in 2001, the Land, Infrastructure, Transport, and Tourism Ministry (successor to the Construction Ministry) exhorted park managers to contract with private firms not merely to operate concessions and restaurants but also to renew aging facilities, plan new parks, and manage some parks outright.[80] The 2006 report implementing the 2001 Megalopolis Concept extolled parks established by the private sector for the public good, so as to inveigle companies into preserving undeveloped lots for conversion to green spaces rather than subdividing them for commerce or residences. It invited individuals and businesses to contribute to a Tokyo Metropolitan Urban Green Space Fund, and it also urged citizens to serve as volunteers in the parks and as advocates via the Internet[81]—in effect appealing to private companies and individuals to take ownership of public green spaces through their buy-in for the common good.

Cities in the new millennium began to adopt the European practice of constructing roof gardens on buildings to help cool the occupants and surrounding neighborhoods. Starting in the 1990s a consensus held that Japan's largest cities were radiant "heat islands" where roads, factories, rooftops, and air conditioners gave off warmth long after sundown. Residents of even the tiniest houses and apartments in Japan have long placed bonsai and other potted plants on roofs, balconies, and window boxes for beautification by creating the illusion of space, so everyone could have the hint of a yard garden. Green roofs and cascades of sidewall vegetation on both public and private buildings—the ultimate in top-down constructions of the nonhuman environment—show how Japanese cities since the 1990s have tried to draw businesses, planners, and residents into partnerships to add green spaces while reducing heating and cooling loads and cutting storm water runoff. A forerunner was the nine-story Shindai Building near Osaka Station, completed in 1964 with several thousand trees and shrubs planted in a Japanese garden. Rooftop greenery first came to Tokyo on government buildings, then spread to other public structures, business complexes, and apartment towers when metropolitan officials started giving "administrative guidance" to developers in the 1990s.

Suasion turned into law in April 2001 through a Tokyo ordinance requiring new buildings on lots of a thousand square meters or more to devote 20 percent of the exterior grounds and 20 percent of the accessible roofs to green spaces,[82] in return for tax abatements. Part of the rationale for requiring roof gardens was aesthetic, but the main impetus was the finding by Tokyo Metropolitan University that Tokyo's average year-round temperature increased by 2.9 degrees C between 1900 and 2000, five times greater than global warming. Other data showed that the number of days per year with temperatures above 30 degrees C doubled between 1993

Rooftop gardens and wall curtains of vines and other climbing vegetation became common in Japanese cities early in the 2000s to reduce the heat-island effects of reflected and radiated heat. The distinctive towers that ventilated the below-grade shopping plazas and parking lots at Shinjuku Station's west exit were clad in symbolic coats of ivy.

175

and 2003. Vegetation could cool not only building interiors but also the city, especially at night when conventional roofs and walls radiated heat absorbed during the day. Another benefit was dampening outdoor sounds in the city center, particularly from construction and road traffic.[83]

Yet when developers fragmented the public park, deracinating it from its terrestrial context, and reconstructed it in small patches on urban rooftops, they added only cosmetic social meaning since most such green roofs were gazed gardens, seen from other buildings and not enjoyed by strolling.[84] Building managers in Japan found that roof gardens desiccated easily in the wind and required careful water management as well as impeccable drainage systems and structural reinforcement, all of which drove up installation costs. Architectural critics sometimes complained that building designers used buzzwords such as "ecology," "biotope," or "coexistence with nature" while creating environmentally disruptive structures, and landscape designers occasionally came under fire for not installing simple flowers along with the exotic plants they chose for rooftops, a charge levied against park managers as well. All parties agreed that cities, like seaside beaches, cooled best when onshore breezes blew off the water in the afternoons.[85]

Urban Parks and Their Residents

Ueno and thousands of other city parks were handmaidens of Japan's modern narrative of state formation, social betterment, and civic community, yet it is both poignant and ironic that some of the public parks most identified with prewar imperialism and postwar social management have become semipermanent homes to thousands of people squeezed to the edges of Japan's centrifugal social system. The plight of urban homeless people drew fresh public notice during the economic turbidity of the 1990s and led to greater activism by advocates, negotiated agreements with bureaucrats, and more recently a ramrod official posture toward the homeless who took shelter in public parks. Many park dwellers beneath blue tarps denied their own marginality and believed they were contributing to family and nation by living on their own, not relying excessively on relatives or the state to survive. Some homeless men even considered themselves "samurai," brave, selfless, and persistent in the face of adversity.[86]

Although Tokyo Metropolis banned park tents in 2004 and moved most of their residents into publicly subsidized apartments, many soon sought the greater freedom of the streets and parks, getting by on pensions and aid from support groups when day jobs formerly open to them increasingly were filled by young part-timers.

As in other countries, nearby residents sometimes stayed away because they believed parks harbored vandalism, crime, trash, or unpleasantness attributable to the homeless. The National Police Agency listed 12,769 reported instances of crime in city parks nationwide in the year ending in March 2001, which if accurate meant a single incident per year in one park of every seven. No one knew with certainty how many homeless lived in parks, but even if they sheltered many of the fifty thousand or more persons estimated by nonprofit organizations to be without homes, it would mean an average of one individual for every two parks.[87] Clearly the perception that parks were overpopulated with distasteful or

Tucked away down a side pathway inside Tokyo's Ueno Park are blue and green vinyl tents of homeless residents, screened off for a degree of privacy.

dangerous residents, a flame fanned periodically by mass media, at times overwhelmed statistical reality. Yoshihara Satoshi, director of Toyama Park in Tokyo, pointed out in 2002 that it was very difficult to evict people from public parks, regardless of minatory signboards or complaints from neighbors. Nearby residents organized community safety patrols, on bicycle and foot, with a keen focus on parks that housed homeless persons, and mothers supervised "let's play" gatherings there for as many as a hundred children, only to find that the homeless almost never caused difficulties. For their part, the tent dwellers complained that outsiders discarded trash, scribbled graffiti, brought in weapons, and cut off the park lights after dark to engage in intimacies.[88] Despite the self-image as samurai and the alternative communities they formed in the parks, homeless people were marginalized actors who seldom indulged in outright resistance to the authorities; whatever limited agency they exerted stemmed mainly from long-standing legal precedents protecting tenants' rights through an elaborate eviction process predisposed in favor of those already settled in dwellings of any kind.

Nonprofit organizations such as Second Harvest food bank, founded in 1999, distributed hundreds of hot meals each week at Ueno and other parks throughout the country, as well as nonperishables twice a month, but city authorities were reluctant to let other nonprofits use parks even for charitable purposes. The biweekly street magazine *Big Issue,* originating in the United Kingdom in 1991 to encourage self-help, was sold in a Japanese edition by more than a hundred homeless street vendors starting in 2003, reaching a circulation of 29,000 in late 2007.[89] Nonetheless, the resources and support services for the homeless in Japan seemed unpredictable, if not parsimonious, by international standards. Park dwellers in Osaka were backed by a cadre of sympathizers when the police evicted residents from Osaka Castle Park in early 2006, ironically to prepare the site for a national urban greenery fair (Hanasaisai) and a world rose convention later that spring. With Japan's largest homeless population, the city was further burdened in October 2008 when the supreme court ruled that Yamauchi Yūji, who had lived in Ogimachi Park since 1998, could not use his tent as his registered address in order to join the national medical insurance plan, vote, apply for a job, get a driver's license, or seek a passport.[90]

Homeless persons such as he could register their addresses, however, if they moved to city shelters.

Tokyo officials in the 1990s pulled up the grass and paved over Ōkubo Park, just north of the steamy Kabukichō entertainment quarters in Shinjuku, to make it less comfortable for those camped there in cardboard cartons. By 2007 the city had removed basketball hoops, soccer goals, four trees, and two dozen stone stools, reducing the park to a blank cityscape devoid of flowers, recreation, or a place to sit.[91] Despite such inimical measures, homeless people were probably safer in Japan's city parks than their counterparts in most other countries, but occasional physical attacks against them suggest that they faced more adversity in parks than did the nearby residents who found their presence so distasteful. The plight of homeless persons, including laid-off workers evicted from company housing during the deep recession of 2008–2009, came under intense scrutiny from the press when more than three hundred persons constituting a "precariat" (precarious proletariat)[92] flocked to a temporary tent city set up over the 2009 New Year's holiday in Hibiya Park directly across from the elegant Imperial Hotel. Yuasa Makoto, who founded the nongovernmental organization Moyai in 2001, led the effort to establish the campground but came under attack for not distancing himself from businesses that profited from sales to the poor. Party politics intervened when Sakamoto Tetsushi, the LDP parliamentary secretary for internal affairs and communications, compared the tent villagers to student radicals in the late 1960s and questioned their will to work (he soon expressed remorse for his remarks).[93] Within days the Health, Labor, and Welfare Ministry offered loans and monthly payments to many of the jobless, while also easing the criteria for receiving benefits. At the same time, nongovernmental organizations in Saitama, Aichi, and Osaka prefectures took steps to feed and find shelter for the homeless in their areas. To conserve commodities, a Tokyo-based group stepped up its *mottainai* (lit., "wasteful") campaign in 2009 to curtail wasted foodstuffs, estimated at nearly 20 million tons annually in Japan—almost as great as the amount of world food aid.[94] The metropolitan government sheltered 833 jobless persons at the Olympic Youth Village during the 2010 New Year's holiday. Both the quick official response and the outspoken critical discourse clearly showed that by 2010 poverty in Japan, which affected more than 15 percent of the population, was a social and not just an individual problem.

Eco-Regimes: Community Partners

Municipal governments in the new century invited citizens more fully into planning parks and green zones, encouraged volunteers to help operate them, as was also true of Japan's natural parks, and turned cautiously but firmly to private management models for public parklands. In line with national government policies since the late 1990s, the devolution of more fiscal and management duties to local governments made a noticeable dent in the older top-down style of administering city parks. A civic reconstruction movement to involve residents in planning, implementing, and operating neighborhood amenities was embraced by officials at many levels and became a staple of citizen influence over parks and green spaces

Tokyo's Ōkubo Park in 2007 after officials had removed basketball hoops, four trees, and all places to sit, rendering it a barren asphalt cityscape and an eyesore to occupants of nearby offices, apartments, hotels, and Metropolitan Ōkubo Hospital.

as society matured and the needs of the old as well as the young grew conspicuous. In response, streetside parks all over Japan started revamping their grounds from kickball for children to gateball for the elderly, a small change that symbolized how civic space had begun to elude the noose of predictability and develop greater diversity of functions, turning into a shifting middle ground of continual discussion between citizens and their rulers.

Civic reconstruction as a partnership of officials and neighborhood residents for urban improvements took place in big cities and small towns throughout Japan, variously to rebuild locations maimed by pollution such as Minamata in Kumamoto Prefecture, to revive picturesque mountain communities to attract tourists, or to add amenities to crowded residential blocks in the largest metropolises. The civic reconstruction movement arose in Nagoya and Kobe in the 1960s, then gathered momentum through progressive politics in various big cities during the 1970s. When the City Planning Law of 1968 was amended in 1980, civic reconstruction for parks and other improvements acquired a firmer legal basis. The technique may also have served to reduce the influence of neighborhood associations and other old-time local organizations.[95] Further amendments to the City Planning Law in 1992 required local authorities to include private citizens in drafting municipal master plans, making civic reconstruction a standard practice for the first time.[96]

Seeking a larger purpose for civic reconstruction, a number of scholars and critics no longer addressed participatory planning in terms of economic development but instead in the rhetoric of human relations with nonhuman surroundings. Writing in 1990, historian Kimura Shōzaburō emphasized community sustainability and remarked that civic reconstruction was instrumental for a new life culture that was "no longer human-centered but nature-centered,"[97] although few signs of Kimura's hoped-for recentering appeared during the next two decades. Esashi Yōji, a forestry professor, compared civic reconstruction to the miniaturization that produced individual bonsai trees, arguing that each neighborhood had different needs and that trees, shrubs, and flowers gave each city space distinctiveness.[98] Landscape architect Shinji Isoya wrote in 2008 that the "keys to *machizukuri* [civic reconstruction] are safety, freedom from worry, and stability" in people's contacts with the environment.[99] Civic reconstruction was not an ideology but a cluster of practices for neighbors to take planning and operating community facilities into their own hands. This meant many different things for urban parks, depending on location, needs, and level of public engagement in negotiating with bureaucrats. It is true that "the roles of urban parks in urban environmental sustainability [have] been little researched, but their importance to livability seems clear."[100] Thus nearly all civic reconstruction activities shared an anthropocentric vision of the social functions of parks and green spaces, not a focus on environmental preservation or ecological revitalization.

The Hanshin earthquake and fires of January 17, 1995, provided an indirect push for changes in how city parks were managed in Japan by confirming that local leaders were much quicker than the central government to adapt to new spatial needs. The catastrophe also forced the famously hierarchical city government of Kobe to obey the 1992 revisions of the City Planning Law by using civic reconstruction councils to design the rebuilding of 1,200 damaged hectares. Residents' greater interest in parks and other green spaces in Kobe after 1995 implied better neighborhood relations, which helps to explain "why the process of participation" in civic reconstruction "often seems to be more valued than the outcome."[101] The Hanshin disaster also helped spawn new nonprofits around the country; more than 16,000 nongovernmental groups filed initial paperwork with the government for tax-exempt status after the nonprofit organization law of 1998 was adopted, 80 percent of them volunteer units without paid staff.[102] In the late 1990s park administration began a steady but incomplete turn from Ōkubo Park–style bureaucratism toward engaging communities in planning and operating parklands. The Decentralization Promotion Act of 1995 and Omnibus Decentralization Law of 1999 laid a legal foundation for shifting more national government functions to prefectures and municipalities, as well as authorizing private involvement in public administration through NPOs, some of which were active with city parks and others with environmental conservation.[103]

After nonprofits were legalized in 1998, localities such as Musashino in Tokyo held civic reconstruction workshops for citizens on building green partnerships, protecting the environment, and improving nearby parks.[104] By the time the Local Self-Government and City Parks Laws were revised in 2003, green space planning was a core goal of civic reconstruction groups throughout the country, sometimes less for its own sake than as a means of building community. Diverse rather than standardized vegetation in city parks was now favored, in accord with local topography and residents' preferences.[105] Greater input into decisions also meant a larger citizen responsibility for park management, much of which was unglamorous sanitation and cleanup. Civic reconstruction groups were needed daily to make certain the parks were open, clean, and safe. The operative theme was subjectivity by "involving society in management," no longer objectivity through social management by bureaucrats, as during much of the twentieth century. If, as Shinji hoped, parks under civic reconstruction management turned into "outdoor community centers," their volunteers risked becoming more and more routinized through membership in NGOs hired by local governments to operate public parks.[106]

Civic reconstruction activism helped local residents enable various new uses of parks and green spaces in the early 2000s. Citizens implemented the Law for Barrier-Free Transport, effective in 2000, by altering public parks and gardens to make them accessible to wheelchair users.

Jindai Botanical Park, opened in 1961 in Tokyo's western suburbs, contains a vast barrier-free rose garden.

Ōizumi Park in northwestern Tokyo was an early example, with a universal-design garden. Nakazawa Makoto, who founded the consulting firm Barrier-Free in 2001, became a leading advocate for universal-design green spaces. These sites for nature therapy through encounters with the nonhuman environment were so important in Japan's aging demographic pyramid, Setagaya officials decided, that they made all the ward's public parks accessible to the disabled.[107] Partnerships between local residents and municipal authorities also produced community gardens modeled after the National Garden Scheme of Great Britain. Civic reconstruction groups felt even more empowered after the supreme court in 2008 decided in favor of residents in Hamamatsu, Shizuoka Prefecture, who sought to block a rezoning plan in the initial stages, rather than waiting until the plan was finalized to appeal a fait accompli.[108] The ruling seemed likely to give local citizens a stronger role in city planning and in the operation of public facilities.

Many localities nonetheless found it hard to match their needs for public space with the Lincolnesque aspiration of the Omnibus Decentralization Law (1999) for "local decisions and local responsibility based on local residents"[109] because they still depended on government financing and technical expertise. Some relief arrived via the Municipal Mergers Law of 1998, which brought about Japan's latest wave of local government consolidation from 1999 to 2006, shrinking the number of jurisdictions from 3,232 to 1,820. Part of the enticement to merge was the central government's irresistible promise to pay 70 percent of the costs of new public works for ten years, including city parks. Once the expensive public works subsidies ended, national officials expected to save ¥1.8 trillion annually in efficiencies from the mergers.[110]

NPOs and individual volunteers began taking up more of the slack once the Local Self-Government Law and the City Parks Law were amended in 2003 to privatize many aspects of park planning and operations through contracts with nonprofits or even private firms, changes that opinion surveys showed were warmly endorsed by most park users.[111] Further aid for neighborhood development arrived in 2005 when the Land, Infrastructure, Transport, and Tourism Ministry began subsidizing localities through community design funds, of which the Setagaya Trust and Community Design (est. 1992) was the precursor. A Decentralization

Reform Promotion Law, approved in 2006 to replace the 1995 Decentralization Promotion Act, was intended by the cabinet to cut both central and local government costs without surrendering further control from the center, but prefectures and municipalities hoped the law would serve as a lever to pry them freer of legislative and administrative direction from Tokyo without fostering wide gaps between rich and poor prefectures.[112] As a result of decentralization, Mayor Tsuchiya Kimiyasu of Yamato City, a Tokyo suburb, turned many public services over to neighborhood associations, local self-governing groups, or private vendors, a model followed also in Sanjō City (Nagano Prefecture), Shiki (Saitama Prefecture), Setagaya Ward (Tokyo), and elsewhere.[113] Although local social services and civic amenities such as parks generally operated effectively with staffing by NPOs and individual volunteers, they continued to need funds for materials, equipment, updates, and expansion. They unavoidably were buffeted by ongoing jousts between central and local authorities, in which national officials still held the fattest purse, porous though it was from servicing the nation's enormous public debt.

Whether Tokyo undergoes its Big Change cannot yet be known, but the steady shift of agency from bureaucratic fiat to decisions jointly taken with local citizens has begun to readjust the relationships among national officials, local authorities, and private citizens to a degree unimagined a generation earlier. Japan's experience with both urban and natural parks starting in the 1990s suggested that these institutions of civic culture were vibrant public spaces, not inert open lands, to be put to varied uses as society's needs changed. Much like the environmentalists concerned with national parks and forests, supporters of urban parklands gradually grew less confrontational and more cooperative with the authorities as both law and practice became more accommodating to the interests of park users. Not yet clear is whether civic reconstruction groups will end up as agents of the political system, like many environmental organizations, or whether they will move beyond their anthropocentric focus to a deeper engagement with the animals, plants, and terrestrial landscapes that comprise Japan's ecosystems.

Parks, the Public, and the Environment in Japan

"We would like to cut down the trees with nature in mind," declared Suzuki Takehiko, chair of the Shōsenkyō Tourism Association of Yamanashi Prefecture in 2008. The seeming illogic of Suzuki's entreaty, with which the Environment Ministry apparently concurred, was easily explained: Shōsenkyō Gorge billed itself as "Japan's most beautiful valley," a sightseeing highlight of Chichibu-Tama-Kai National Park, but recently trees had grown up to spoil the view. The trees posed no threat to the nonhuman environment in Shōsenkyō, but in anthropocentric terms they imperiled tourism in the economically struggling region.[1] This episode illustrates an ongoing dilemma faced by societies since antiquity: Under what circumstances, and for what purposes, do governments intervene in human interactions with the nonhuman? For more than a millennium Japan's leaders usually have been conscious of the need to guard water, timber, and marine resources from overuse, but the new age of spatial modernity that accompanied imperial state formation after 1868 radically recast the relationships among the people, their government, and the nonhuman environment by introducing capitalism, industrialization, social integration, and the concept of public space. More than a century later, the paradoxes of ecological modernity surfaced in Suzuki Takehiko's appeal to a government environmental protection ministry to let arborists clear trees that menaced private commerce in a public reservation—some core themes of this book in cameo.

Both city parks and nonurban parks—national, quasi-national, and prefectural preserves, since 1957 collectively called natural parks—formed key components of Japan's modern spatial culture. This culture was first produced by decree from the Grand Council of State in 1873, passed through stages of negotiation among government officials, private interests, and the public that used (and sometimes abused) the parklands, and then entered the twenty-first century in deeply altered circumstances stemming from hyperurbanization, postindustrial capitalism, increasing ecological consciousness, and growing if still unequal partnerships among citizens, businesses, and the state. Starting with the Grand Council and the Iwakura Mission in the early 1870s, leaders seemed to agree that to be modern was to enjoy the hygienic, civilizing uplift imparted by green spaces open to all members of the now legally egalitarian public, on terms dictated by high-modernist bureaucrats projecting statist norms. The central authorities produced landscapes of power that imposed visual and spatial order on a potentially unruly society only recently liberated from fixed statuses defined by the Edo polity. Hibiya Park, opened in 1903, seemed to apotheosize European-style spatial modernity, but within two years it became an occasional landscape of representation as well as of power when enraged citizens defied the police and occupied the park to protest terms of the Portsmouth Treaty that ended the Russo-Japanese War. In the century since, a number of nodal urban parks throughout the country have evolved as sites of public assembly and engagement between authorities and the people, spaces controlled by neither state nor citizen, yet both.

Writers, scientists, and legislators in the 1890s began to call for national parks to showcase Japan's distinctive environmental endowment to citizens and international visitors alike. Urban elites played up the public health and recreational benefits of visiting both city and national parks, but local leaders in the areas targeted for national parks were far more interested in the potential impact of tourism on their communities. Timber, mining, and hydroelectric businesses, as well as other private owners of properties to be included within park boundaries, lobbied successfully to protect their rights against undue restrictions, so that from the start national parks were aggregations of regional interests as much as displays of nationwide spatial pride. Unlike some European states, Japan paid scant attention to preserving supposedly pristine ecosystems for scientific study;

even today barely twenty small sections of natural parks enjoy rigorous bans on all human activity except research—which itself might harm the environment. Instead the dominant modality of park management has been to balance environmental conservation against public recreational desires and private business requirements, to assure that the needs of both current and future generations are met—the controversial doctrine of sustainability that has undergone continual reinterpretation by government, corporations, and citizens around the world over how to treat these public spaces most responsibly.

Although public parklands in both city and countryside displayed the command of the central state, they also revealed certain egalitarian realities characteristic of modern, socially mobilized states, whether imperial, republican, or democratic. City parks from the start were meant for all residents, however much the state sought to modify their behavior to fit defined norms. Hibiya and similar spaces attracted the supposedly civilized social upper echelons but also the ordinary and humble. Urban elites proved unable fully to control the movement for national parks, which instead took on a regional flavor that was confirmed in the Natural Parks Law of 1957. The American occupation of Japan secularized open spaces associated with temples and shrines and eventually led to the demilitarization of large tracts that became available to all. In this way, parks emblematized Japan's postwar ideal of a secular, pacifist, democratic society.

The bedrock of social stability was economic prosperity, and capitalism in the form of tourism was a driving engine of the national park movement from 1905 onward, led by railway, hotel, and real estate companies. Although some lawmakers and other patricians saw in national parks the expression of Japan's topographical distinctiveness, aesthetic superiority, and imperial self-assurance, the quest for profits and foreign exchange through tourism was the single most important factor convincing the Diet to approve a National Parks Law amid the worldwide depression in 1931. Postwar capitalist democracy meant that energy, logging, and mining businesses had equal access to resources in national parks, just when the public had its first major chance to visit them for recreation. During the prosperous 1960s and 1970s, as energy companies and resource extraction businesses upped their demands and ever more visitors overwhelmed national, quasi-national, and prefectural natural parks, administrators faced new pressures from environmentalists and some local residents to safeguard these public reserves from overuse.

Protecting the nation's scenic landscapes was mandated in the National Parks Law of 1931, reflecting decades of concern about mines, dams, and logging, and reiterated in the Natural Parks Law of 1957, but neither act provided effective sanctions. Gradually protections of the nonhuman gathered strength in law as well as practice, but more important in curbing the rapacious potential of the 1987 resort law was the national economic slowdown starting in the early 1990s. Still, the lure of cash from abroad continued to affect park policy, evident when the government set up the Japan Tourism Agency in 2008 to attract more free-spending visitors from elsewhere in Asia, many of whom sought out supposedly wild areas such as Shiretoko National Park. After three quarters of a century, Japanese officials continued to struggle with defining the optimal uses of natural parks, balancing conflicting demands from businesses, tourists, and environmentalists that defied easy resolution or much satisfaction.

The effort to increase international tourism, in which Japan ranked last among developed nations in 2009, has concentrated mainly on metropolitan centers. The Koizumi Cabinet, eager to create a country that is "good living, good visiting," commissioned a study on luring foreign tourists, which reported in 2003 that "most people in the world long for cities. In order to beautify Japan's cities we need to develop a citizens' movement to 'make our streets beautiful.'"[2] The recommendations were folded into the Third Scenic Green Space Law of 2004, intended to curb outdoor advertising, restrict building design, and increase green spaces by offering incentives to architects and contractors to incorporate more mini-parks and open areas into their projects. Both the nascent Green Party and the staid Japan Communist Party supported environmental laws as wise policy with broad voter appeal.[3] In 2006 the new prime minister, Abe Shinzō, unwittingly discouraged international visitors with his nationalistic vision of creating a "beautiful Japan" reminiscent of the novelist Kawabata Yasunari (1899–1972), whose speech when accepting the 1968 Nobel Prize in literature was titled "Myself from Beautiful Japan." Abe's successor, Fukuda Yasuo, quietly closed the office Abe had established for pursuing this diversionary project. One pleasing city space tourists often saw was Tokyo's Miyashita Park along the inner Yamanote train line between Harajuku and Shibuya. In late 2008 the future of this green strip was threatened when Shibuya Ward invited bids for naming rights from Nike and Adidas, prompting an outcry from advocates for the homeless as well as from citizens fearful that the park might charge fees or even lose its public character[4]—another of the many contests over the nation's green spaces continually taking place among public, private, and government interests.

The first public-private partnerships for parklands in Japan date to the National Parks Law of 1931, which institutionalized regional parks consisting of both government-owned and privately owned property. This hybridity sapped the strength of national bureaucrats and placed great responsibility on prefectures to finance major portions of natural parks, and it also limited the effectiveness of environmental controls because of respect for landlords' rights. For their part, private landowners within parks had to accept restrictions on how they could use their lands, although through the 1990s permission was almost routinely granted for both residential and commercial construction unless it was grossly disruptive to the environment. For city parks, Expo '70 in Osaka was a textbook example of public-private partnerships that have continued since. At less lofty levels of financial power, the Capital Region Suburban Green Space Protection Law of 1966 marked the beginning of local initiatives for city parks and open spaces, the first hint of an ebb of central government autonomy in planning parks.

Beginning in the 1980s ordinary citizens engaged vigorously both in rural reclamation of the contact zones between fields and forests and in urban park design and maintenance through a process of community building called civic reconstruction. In the first decade of the new millennium the National Forestry Agency as well as natural park officials promoted a new forest culture of heightened ecological awareness, environmental protection, and greater variety of recreational and educational experiences for the one billion or more persons who visited natural parks and national forests each year. City parks likewise reflected significant changes in function as they became bona fide institutions of civic culture rather than just social management. No longer designed by cookie cutter, they hosted a wide range of activities depending on the demographics of the neighborhoods they served. As city park services were privatized to both nonprofits and management companies, conflicts between the two occasionally invited intervention and negotiation by municipal or prefectural officials. For parks and most other amenities of civic life in Japan the era of top-down planning faded with the end of the twentieth century, although central government command of finances yielded only slowly to the principle of devolution adopted in the late 1990s.

Nearly all Japanese in 2010 were aware of basic environmental matters, yet by that year their country had fallen far behind its pledges under the 1997 Kyoto Protocol to help slow global warming, and the government lowered its estimate of how effectively its parks and forests could serve as sinks to remove carbon dioxide and other air pollutants.[5] In United Nations climate talks held in December 2008 Japan was criticized more severely than all other countries except Canada for helping to scuttle an agreement among a group of industrialized nations that would have set stiff goals for reducing greenhouse gas emissions by 2020. In response, Environment Minister Saitō Tetsuo hardly reassured other countries with his tepid statement that "Japan is by no means negative about fighting global warming."[6] On the other hand, in late 2008 Edahiro Junko, executive director of the volunteer network Japan for Sustainability and translator of Al Gore's *An Inconvenient Truth* (2006), found both government and business more receptive to environmental activism now that most nongovernmental organizations were less confrontational and less driven by ideological commitment.[7] The same was true of civic groups that planned and operated city parks, although the danger of co-optation by the bureaucratic establishment lurked when neighborhood organizations let down their guard.

Ever since the Grand Council established city parks by fiat in 1873 and various writers, scientists, economists, landscape architects, and government officials offered multiple discourses to justify more public spaces, urbanization has been as crucial to the rationale for city parks as tourism has been for justifying national parks. Despite earthquakes, fires, and wartime bombings, economic growth meant that Japan's cities continued to expand to the point where nearly 80 percent of the nation's population was urbanized, creating an overpowering demand for leisure, recreation, and environmental experiences both near at hand and in more distant natural parks. For many decades the greatest blinder to recognizing the centrality of public spaces in Japan was the bureaucratic attitude that city parks were entities to be protected from their users. Today citizens are much more involved in defining and implementing the uses of parks, both natural and urban, imparting many meanings and greater permanence to these public spaces. Educators such as Hara Takeshi, who tirelessly promotes sustainability through the Waseda School of Environment, help to increase consciousness of relationships between human beings and their surroundings by focusing on how citizens interact with local government.[8] Yet at present it is still uncertain whether Japan's well-established ecological awareness, by inviting humility and respect toward the diverse terrain, habitats, and ecosystems of which humanity is a part, will gradually erode the anthropocentrism of park policies in particular and society's approach to the nonhuman environment in general.

Notes

Introduction

1. Shiga Shigetaka, *Nihon fūkeiron* (Tokyo: Iwanami, 1937), p. 272. Originally published in Tokyo by Seikyōsha in 1894.
2. Shirahata Yōzaburō, "Kōen nante mō iranai," *Chūō kōron* no. 1272 (1991): pp. 195–196. See Seta Nobuya, *Saiseisuru kokuritsu kōen: Nihon no shizen to fūkei o mamori, sasaeru hitotachi* (Tokyo: Asahi Bīru, 2009), p. 8. For park ideology in the United States, see Galen Cranz, *The Politics of Park Design: A History of Urban Parks in America* (Cambridge, Mass.: MIT Press, 1982), pp. 207–212.
3. In a 2008 study by Columbia and Yale researchers, Japan ranked 21st in overall environmental performance on a list of 149 countries headed by Switzerland and other European nations, even though it rated 84th in addressing climate change, including its per capita greenhouse gas emissions. *Japan Today* online, January 24, 2008.
4. Kankyōshō, *Kankyō tōkeishū* (Tokyo: Kankyōshō, 2008), pp. 261–262. Throughout, I use "natural park" for *shizen kōen,* in keeping with common (but not universal) practice in English-language works published in Japan. The term might equally be translated "nature park."
5. Ibid., pp. 272–273; Tokyoto Kensetsukyoku Kōen Ryokuchibu, ed., *Tokyoto no kōen ryokuchi mappu 2009* (Tokyo: Tokyoto, 2009). For a critical view, see Ian G. Simmons, *Environmental History: A Concise Introduction* (Oxford, Eng.: Blackwell, 1993), p. 155.
6. Kevin Short, *Nature in Tokyo: A Guide to Plants and Animals in and around Tokyo* (Tokyo: Kodansha International, 2000), p. 13; Yabe Tomoko, ed., *Tokyo kōen sanpo* (Tokyo: Burūsu Intāakushonzu, 2009), p. 4.
7. Ishikawa Mikiko, *Toshi to ryokuchi* (Tokyo: Iwanami, 2001), p. 307.
8. Itō Yukio, ed., *Ima, kōen de nani ga okite iru ka* (Tokyo: Gyōsei, 2002), p. 220. The figure is for Tokyo Prefecture. *NHK World* online, January 3, 2010.
9. *Japan Times* online, June 30, 2008.

10. See Rebecca Solnit, *Savage Dreams: A Journey into the Hidden Wars of the American West* (San Francisco: Sierra Club, 1994), p. 265; Mark Overmyer-Velázquez, "Visions of the Emerald City: Politics, Culture, and Alternative Modernities in Oaxaca City, Mexico, 1877–1920" (PhD dissertation, Yale University, 2002), p. 32; Karen Laura Thornber, *Empire of Texts in Motion: Chinese, Korean, and Taiwanese Transculturations of Japanese Literature* (Cambridge, Mass.: Harvard University Asia Center and Harvard-Yenching Institute, 2009), pp. 2–5, 11–14.

11. See Henri Lefebvre, *The Production of Space,* trans. Donald Nicholson-Smith (Cambridge, Mass.: Blackwell, 1991), esp. pp. 31–33; Saskia Sassen, ed., *Deciphering the Global: Its Scales, Spaces and Subjects* (New York: Routledge, 2007); David Harvey, *Justice, Nature, and the Geography of Difference* (Cambridge, Mass.: Blackwell, 1996); James C. Scott, *Seeing Like a State: How Certain Schemes to Improve the Human Condition Have Failed* (New Haven, Conn.: Yale University Press, 1998); Paul Carter, *The Road to Botany Bay: An Essay in Spatial History* (Boston: Faber and Faber, 1987).

12. Timothy Morton, *Ecology without Nature: Rethinking Environmental Aesthetics* (Cambridge, Mass.: Harvard University Press, 2007), p. 11. See also pp. 84–85; Harvey, *Justice,* pp. 10, 207–210, 262, 293–294.

13. Timothy Mitchell, *Colonising Egypt* (Berkeley: University of California Press, 1991), p. xi.

14. Harvey, *Justice,* p. 112.

15. See Scott, *Seeing Like a State,* pp. 4–5; Harvey, *Justice,* pp. 109–112; Shin Yongcheol, *Toshi kōen seisaku keiseishi: Kyōdōkei shakai ni okeru midori to ōpun supēsu no genten* (Tokyo: Hōsei Daigaku Shuppankyoku, 2004), pp. 2–3; Todd A. Henry, "Respatializing Chosŏn's Royal Capital: The Politics of Japanese Urban Reforms in Early Colonial Seoul, 1905–1919," in Timothy Tangherlini and Sallie Yea, eds., *Sitings: Critical Approaches to Korean Geography* (Honolulu: University of Hawai'i Press and Center for Korean Studies, University of Hawai'i, 2008), pp. 15–17; Timothy Tangherlini and Sallie Yea, "Introduction," in Timothy Tangherlini and Sallie Yea, eds., *Sitings: Critical Approaches to Korean Geography* (Honolulu: University of Hawai'i Press and Center for Korean Studies, University of Hawai'i, 2008), pp. 3–4; Werner Sollers, *Neither Black nor White yet Both: Thematic Explorations of Interracial Literature* (Cambridge, Mass.: Harvard University Press, 1997), pp. 3–4; Karen R. Jones and John Wills, *The Invention of the Park from the Garden of Eden to Disney's Magic Kingdom* (Cambridge, Eng.: Polity Press, 2005), p. 171.

16. Cf. Herbert Muschamp, "Looking Beyond Vision," in Herbert Muschamp et al., *The Once and Future Park* (New York: Princeton Architectural Press, 1993), p. 13; Miodrag Mitrašinović, *Total Landscape, Theme Parks, Public Space* (Aldershot, Eng.: Ashgate, 2006), pp. 20–24; Roderick P. Neumann, *Imposing Wilderness: Struggles over Livelihood and Nature Preservation in Africa* (Berkeley: University of California Press, 1998), pp. 24–28; Scott, *Seeing Like a State,* p. 92.

17. Neil Smith, *Uneven Development: Nature, Capital and the Production of Space* (New York: Blackwell, 1984), p. 57.

18. Cf. Roderick F. Nash, ed., *American Environmentalism* (New York: McGraw-Hill, 1990), pp. 1–2; Morton, *Ecology,* pp. 15, 125, 173; Harvey, *Justice,* p. 118. For a thoughtful discussion of "nature" in Japan, see Julia Adeney Thomas, *Reconfiguring Modernity: Concepts of Nature in Japanese Political Ideology* (Berkeley: University of California Press, 2001), esp. pp. 3–7, 179.

19. Mary Sutherland and Dorothy Britton, *National Parks of Japan* (Tokyo: Kodansha, 1980), p. 6. See John Hanson Mitchell, *The Wildest Place on Earth: Italian Gardens and the Invention of Wilderness* (Washington, D.C.: Counterpoint, 2001), p. 52.

20. Mitchell, *Wildest Place,* p. 53; Jones and Wills, *Invention of the Park,* pp. 12–18; Charles E. Doell and Gerald B. Fitzgerald, *A Brief History of Parks and Recreation in the United States* (Chicago: Athletic Institute, 1954), p. 7; Masao Maruyama, *Studies in the Intellectual History of Tokugawa Japan,* trans. Mikiso Hane (Tokyo: University of Tokyo Press, 1974); Thomas, *Reconfiguring Modernity,* pp. 174–175.

21. See James A. Fujii, "Introduction," in Maeda Ai, *Text and the City: Essays on Japanese Modernity,* ed. James A. Fujii (Durham, N.C.: Duke University Press, 2004), pp. 3, 14.

22. Solnit, *Savage Dreams,* pp. 251–252; Leo Marx, *The Machine in the Garden: Technology and the Pastoral Ideal in America* (New York: Oxford University Press, 1964), p. 89.

23. Jones and Wills, *Invention of the Park,* pp. 25–27; Solnit, *Savage Dreams,* pp. 254–255. See Michele Marra [Michael F. Marra], trans. and ed., *A History of Modern Japanese Aesthetics* (Honolulu: University of Hawai'i Press, 2001); Neumann, *Imposing Wilderness,* p. 19.

24. George F. Chadwick, *The Park and the Town: Public Landscape in the 19th and 20th Centuries* (New York: Praeger, 1966), pp. 44, 49.

25. Alexander Garvin, *The American City: What Works, What Doesn't,* 2nd ed. (New York: McGraw-Hill, 2002), pp. 32, 45; Alan Tate, *Great City Parks* (London: Spon Press, 2001), pp. 1, 73, 83; Chadwick, *Park and the Town,* pp. 111–112; Jones and Wills, *Invention of the Park,* pp. 46–47.

26. Sam Bass Warner, Jr., "Public Park Inventions: Past and Future," in Herbert Muschamp et al., *The Once and Future Park* (New York: Princeton Architectural Press, 1993), pp. 17–18; Chadwick, *Park and the Town,* p. 71.

27. David P. Jordan, *Transforming Paris: The Life and Labors of Baron Haussmann* (New York: Free Press, 1995), p. 172. See pp. 155–157, 171, 277–285; Doell and Fitzgerald, *Brief History,* p. 20; Chadwick, *Park and the Town,* pp. 152–154; Garvin, *American City,* p. 47.

28. Jones and Wills, *Invention of the Park,* p. 52. See p. 54; Cranz, *Politics of Park Design,* pp. 15, 61–65, 86, 91, 101–106, 183, 203–205, 236; Mitrašinović, *Total Landscape,* p. 28; Garvin, *American City,* pp. 13, 39; Chadwick, *Park and the Town,* pp. 216–217; Doell and Fitzgerald, *Brief History,* p. 37.

29. Cranz, *Politics of Park Design,* p. 240.

30. Ibid., pp. 107, 135–145, 186, 205, 237–238; Jones and Wills, *Invention of the Park*, pp. 58–60; Tate, *Great City Parks*, p. 1; Garvin, *American City*, pp. 41–42; David Louwerse, "Why Talk About Park Design," in Andreu Arriola et al., *Modern Park Design: Recent Trends* (Amsterdam: Thoth, 1993), pp. 9–13.

31. Whitney North Seymour, Jr., ed., *Small Urban Spaces: The Philosophy, Design, Sociology, and Politics of Vest-pocket Parks and Other Small Urban Spaces* (New York: New York University Press, 1969), pp. 1–5; Garvin, *American City*, pp. 40–41; Tate, *Great City Parks*, p. 1; *Boston Globe* online, February 12, 2007; *New York Times* online, June 5, 2008.

32. Ian G. Simmons, *Earth, Air and Water: Resources and Environment in the Late 20th Century* (London: Edward Arnold, 1991), pp. 147–148.

33. Roderick Nash, *Wilderness and the American Mind*, 4th ed. (New Haven, Conn.: Yale University Press, 2001), p. xi. See pp. 24–25, 33–36; Mitchell, *Wildest Place*, pp. 13–16, 61; Robert J. Brulle, *Agency, Democracy, and Nature: The U.S. Environmental Movement from a Critical Theory Perspective* (Cambridge, Mass.: MIT Press, 2000), pp. 115–117; Roger L. DiSilvestro, *Reclaiming the Last Wild Places: A New Agenda for Biodiversity* (New York: John Wiley & Sons, 1993), pp. 35–37.

34. William Cronon, *Changes in the Land: Indians, Colonists, and the Ecology of New England* (New York: Hill and Wang, 1985), p. 3; James Morton Turner, "From Woodcraft to 'Leave no Trace': Wilderness, Consumerism, and Environmentalism in Twentieth-Century America," *Environmental History* 7, no. 3 (2002): p. 463; *New York Times*, September 2, 2003, pp. D1–D2; Max Oelschlaeger, *The Idea of Wilderness: From Prehistory to the Age of Ecology* (New Haven, Conn.: Yale University Press, 1991), p. 4; Nash, *Wilderness*, pp. 44–47, 85–106; Neumann, *Imposing Wilderness*, pp. 21–23; William Cronon, "The Trouble with Wilderness; or, Getting Back to the Wrong Nature," in William Cronon, ed., *Uncommon Ground: Rethinking the Human Place in Nature* (New York: W. W. Norton, 1995), pp. 69–76.

35. Susanna Hecht and Alexander Cockburn, *Fate of the Forest: Developers, Destroyers and Defenders of the Amazon* (London: Verso, 1989), pp. 15, 27.

36. Neumann, *Imposing Wilderness*, p. 31.

37. Nature or the natural was *tennen*, later *shizen*.

38. Solnit, *Savage Dreams*, p. 247. For a recent summary, see Michael P. Nelson and J. Baird Callicott, eds., *The Wilderness Debate Rages On* (Athens: University of Georgia Press, 2008). See also Alfred Runte, *National Parks: The American Experience*, 3rd ed. (Lincoln: University of Nebraska Press, 1997), pp. 11–14; Alfred Runte, "Preservation Heritage: The Origin of the Park Idea in the United States," in John R. Stilgoe, Roderick Nash, and Alfred Runte, *Perceptions of the Landscape and Its Preservation* (Indianapolis: Indiana Historical Society, 1984), pp. 54–55; Jones and Wills, *Invention of the Park*, pp. 67–71; Norman T. Newton, *Design on the Land: The Development of Landscape Architecture* (Cambridge, Mass.: Harvard University Press, 1971), pp. 524–525.

39. Runte, "Preservation Heritage," pp. 62–63; Dyan Zaslowsky and T. H. Watkins, *These American Lands: Parks, Wilderness, and the Public Lands* (Washington, D.C.: Island Press, 1994), pp. 17–18; Nash, *Wilderness*, p. 108; DiSilvestro, *Reclaiming*, p. 151.

40. Roderick Nash, "The Roots of American Environmentalism," in John R. Stilgoe, Roderick Nash, and Alfred Runte, *Perceptions of the Landscape and Its Preservation* (Indianapolis: Indiana Historical Society, 1984), p. 38. See Nash, ed., *American Environmentalism*, pp. 6, 10, 38, 53, 59, 71, 90–112; Brulle, *Agency, Democracy, and Nature*, pp. 119–120, 133, 146–153; Runte, *National Parks*, pp. 69–70; Zaslowsky and Watkins, *These American Lands*, pp. 58, 71–73; Scott, *Seeing Like a State*, pp. 14–15, 20.

41. Nash, *Wilderness*, pp. 325–327. See p. viii, 254, 317–319; Turner, "From Woodcraft," pp. 468–469; Linda Flint McClelland, *Building the National Parks: Historic Landscape Design and Construction* (Baltimore: The Johns Hopkins University Press, 1998), pp. 478–479; DiSilvestro, *Reclaiming*, p. 161; Zaslowsky and Watkins, *These American Lands*, pp. 36–38; Runte, "Preservation Heritage," p. 72; Michael Frome, *Regreening the National Parks* (Tucson: University of Arizona Press, 1992), pp. 69–71.

42. See Brulle, *Agency, Democracy, and Nature*, pp. 126–130, 156–160, 173–185, 190–192; DiSilvestro, *Reclaiming*, pp. 23–25.

43. Numata Makoto, *Seitaigaku hōhōron* (Tokyo: Kokon Shoin, 1967).

44. For comparable developments in the United States, see DiSilvestro, *Reclaiming*, pp. 18–19, 162–168, 179; Mitchell, *Wildest Place*, p. 21; *New York Times* online, September 10, 2006. The *Boston Sunday Globe*, December 3, 2006, p. A24, reported that visits to U.S. national parks peaked in 1996 (four years after the downturn in Japan) and attributed the decline to a "nature-deficit disorder" among minorities and the young.

45. See Andrew Barshay, *State and Intellectual in Imperial Japan: The Public Man in Crisis* (Berkeley: University of California Press, 1988), pp. 5–6. For similar ideas in Japan's administration of Korea, see Henry, "Respatializing Chosŏn's Royal Capital," pp. 31–32. Edo amusement districts were called *sakariba*.

46. See Maruyama Hiroshi, *Kindai Nihon kōenshi no kenkyū* (Kyoto: Shibunkan Shuppan, 1994), pp. 8–10; see also David L. Howell, *Geographies of Identity in Nineteenth-century Japan* (Berkeley: University of California Press, 2005).

47. Maki Fumihiko, quoted in Alexandra Munroe, ed., *New Public Architecture: Recent Projects by Fumihiko Maki and Arata Isozaki* (New York: Japan Society, 1985), p. 16. See Maki Fumihiko, *Miegakuresuru toshi: Edo kara Tokyo e* (Tokyo: Kajima Shuppankai, 1980).

48. Lefebvre, *The Production of Space*; Michel Foucault, *The Foucault Reader*, ed. Paul Rabinow (New York: Pantheon, 1984); Jean Baudrillard, *The Mirror of Production*, trans. Mark Poster (St. Louis, Mo.: Telos Press, 1975); Jürgen Habermas, *The Structural Transformation of the Public Sphere*, trans. Thomas Burger (Cambridge, Mass.: MIT Press, 1989). On the haziness of ideas about public space, see Mitrašinović, *Total Landscape*, pp. 29–30.

49. Scott, *Seeing Like a State*, p. 2. See pp. 89–93, 121; Overmyer-Velázquez, "Visions of the Emerald City," pp. 136–137.

50. *New York Times*, May 30, 2008, p. A17; Itō Taiichi, personal communication, May 17, 2006. See Zaslowsky and Watkins, *These American Lands*, pp. 2–3, 27–29.
51. See Mitrašinović, *Total Landscape*, pp. 14, 18; Tangherlini and Yea, "Introduction," p. 7.
52. Jones and Wills, *Invention of the Park*, p. 8. See pp. 1–7; Cranz, *Politics of Park Design*, pp. x, 213; Muschamp, "Looking Beyond Vision," pp. 12–13.
53. Shinji Isoya, "Kōen no rekishi," in Suzuki Tetsu, Higuchi Tadahiko, Shinji Isoya, Kobayashi Haruto, and Takano Fumiaki, *Kōenzukuri o kangaeru* (Tokyo: Gihōdō, 1993), p. 90.
54. Shin, *Toshi kōen*, pp. 9, 14.
55. Cf. Runte, *National Parks*, p. xxii.
56. Suzuki Satoshi and Sawada Seiichirō, *Kōen no hanashi* (Tokyo: Gihōdō, 1993), pp. 6–7.
57. See Motoko Oyadomari, "The Politics of National Parks in Japan" (PhD dissertation, University of Wisconsin, Madison, 1985), pp. 65–66.
58. Civic reconstruction is *machizukuri*; rural reclamation is *satoyama*.
59. For the United States, see Cranz, *Politics of Park Design*, pp. 214–215.
60. Shirahata, "Kōen nante mō iranai," pp. 196–197; Diana Balmori, "Park Redefinitions," in Herbert Muschamp et al., *The Once and Future Park* (New York: Princeton Architectural Press, 1993), p. 39; Warner, "Public Park Inventions," pp. 19–20; Tate, *Great City Parks*, p. 194.
61. See Jane Jacobs' pathbreaking antimodernist critique in *The Death and Life of Great American Cities* (New York: Random House, 1961).
62. Shin, *Toshi kōen*, p. 3.
63. Ibid., pp. 3–4; Ono Ryōhei, *Kōen no tanjō* (Tokyo: Yoshikawa Kōbunkan, 2003), pp. 1–2.
64. Robert A. Askins, personal communication, April 6, 2004.
65. E.g., Ian J. Miller, "Didactic Nature: Exhibiting Nation and Empire at the Ueno Zoological Gardens," in Gregory M. Pflugfelder and Brett L. Walker, eds., *JAPANimals: History and Culture in Japan's Animal Life* (Ann Arbor: University of Michigan Center for Japanese Studies, 2005), pp. 273–313; Alice Y. Tseng, *Imperial Museums of Meiji Japan: Architecture and the Art of the Nation* (Seattle: University of Washington Press, 2008); John K. Nelson, *Enduring Identities: The Guise of Shinto in Contemporary Japan* (Honolulu: University of Hawai'i Press, 2000).
66. Victor Brombert, *In Praise of Antiheroes* (Chicago: University of Chicago Press, 1999), p. 1.

Chapter 1: From Private Lands to Public Spaces

1. Ichikawa Hiroo, *Bunka to shite no toshi kūkan* (Tokyo: Chikura Shobō, 2007), pp. 120–121, 129; Tokyo Metropolitan Government, *A Hundred Years of Tokyo City*

Planning (Tokyo: Tokyo Metropolitan Government, 1994), p. 2. See Fukukawa Shinji and Ichikawa Hiroo, eds., *Gurōbaru furonto Tokyo* (Tokyo: Toshi Shuppan, 2008); Roman Cybriwsky, *Tokyo: The Shogun's City at the Twenty-First Century* (New York: John Wiley & Sons, 1998), p. 60.

2. Shiojima Dai, *Midori no chōsen* (Tokyo: Kajima Shuppankai, 1982), pp. 6–7; Shin, *Toshi kōen,* pp. 35–39; Ono, *Kōen no tanjō,* p. 3; Sakamoto Shintarō, *Nihon no toshi kōen: Sono seibi no rekishi* (Tokyo: Intarakushon, 2005), pp. 3–5; Shinji, "Kōen no rekishi," pp. 49–57; Ide Hisato, ed., *Ryokuchi kankyō kagaku* (Tokyo: Asanuma Shoten, 1997), pp. 3–8; André Sorensen, *The Making of Urban Japan: Cities and Planning from Edo to the Twenty-first Century* (London: Routledge, 2002), pp. 30–31, 43; Suzuki and Sawada, *Kōen no hanashi,* pp. 3, 133; Satō Akira and Shimoyama Shigemaru, *Landscape Planning and Recreation in Japan* (Tokyo: Nihon Kōen Ryokuchi Kyōkai, 1985), p. 44; Hidenobu Jinnai, *Tokyo: A Spatial Anthropology,* trans. Kimiko Nishimura (Berkeley: University of California Press, 1995), p. 101. By ancient custom, rural villagers had access to common lands (*iriaichi*) where diversion was permitted. Popular pleasure is *kōraku.*

3. Max Horkheimer and Theodor W. Adorno, *Dialectic of Enlightenment,* trans. John Cumming (New York: Herder and Herder, 1972). See Amino Yoshihiko, *Muen, kugai, raku: Nihon chūsei no jiyū to heiwa,* expanded ed. (Tokyo: Heibonsha, 1987); Nam-lin Hur, *Prayer and Play in Late Tokugawa Japan: Asakusa Sensōji and Edo Society* (Cambridge, Mass.: Harvard University Asia Center, 2000), esp. pp. 47–72, 98–99. "Stretching the spirit" is *kinobashi.*

4. Ishikawa, *Toshi,* p. 192.

5. Yamakawa Kikue, *Women of the Mito Domain: Recollections of Samurai Family Life,* trans. Kate Wildman Nakai (Tokyo: University of Tokyo Press, 1992), p. 78; Ishikawa, *Toshi,* p. 192; Ibarakiken Kankō Kyōkai, ed., *Kōdōkan to Kairakuen* (Mito: Ibarakiken Kankō Kyōkai, 1962), p. 77; Suzuki and Sawada, *Kōen no hanashi,* p. 4.

6. Shirahata Yōzaburō, *Kindai toshi kōenshi no kenkyū: Ōka no keifu* (Kyoto: Shibunkan Shuppan, 1995), p. 175; Narumi Masayasu, *Yokohama Yamate Kōen monogatari* (Yokohama: Yūrindō, 2004), p. 38.

7. Hyōgoken Engei Kōen Kyōkai, ed., *Hyōgo Kenritsu Maiko Kōen hyakunenshi* (Akashi: Hyōgoken Engei Kōen Kyōkai, 2001), p. 7. See Tatsumi Shin'ya, *Kōbe kara no kōen bunka: Hyōgo no kōen 1868–2000* (Osaka: Burēn Sentā, 2000), pp. 14, 27.

8. Shirahata, *Kindai,* p. 176; Tanaka Yoshio, *Yokohama kōen monogatari* (Tokyo: Chūō Kōronsha, 2000), pp. 17, 26, 30; Narumi, *Yokohama,* pp. 20, 37–38, 47, 52, 83, 115, 166, 182–183; Ishikawa, *Toshi,* pp. 192, 206; Harigaya Shōkichi, *Bunmei kaika to kōen* (Tokyo: Tokyo Nōgyō Daigaku Shuppankai, 1990), pp. 53–54; Katō Yūzō, ed., *Yokohama Past and Present* (Yokohama: Yokohama City University, 1990), p. 45.

9. Shirahata, *Kindai,* pp. 168–169; Suzuki and Sawada, *Kōen no hanashi,* p. 4.

10. Kume Kunitake, *Tokumei zenken taishi: Beiō kairan jikki,* vol. 1 (Tokyo: Hakubunsha, 1878), quoted in "Japan's First Ambassadors to the US," http://jasgp.org/content/view/431/179/ (accessed June 30, 2009). See Itō Taiichi, "The Influence of the American

Concept of a National Park on Japan's National Park Movement," in *National Park Ideas, Part 4* (Yellowstone National Park, Wyo.: National Park Service, 2004), pp. 196–197.

11. Kume freely interchanged the terms *teien* (formal garden) and *kōen* (public garden) for "park." *Kōen* was first used for "park" in 1832 to describe an archery ground in Tsuwano, in today's Shimane Prefecture. From 1853 to 1868 *yūen* and *kōen* were both used. The latter was the standard term used in government documents from 1873 on. See Uchiyama Masao, ed., *Toshi ryokuchi no keikaku to sekkei* (Tokyo: Shōkokusha, 1987), pp. 175, 178; Harigaya, *Bunmei*, pp. 48–49. See also Shin, *Toshi kōen*, pp. 35–37; Ian Nish, ed., *The Iwakura Mission in America and Europe: A New Assessment* (Richmond, Surrey, Eng.: Japan Library, 1998), p. 114; "Illustration of Industrial World Exposition Site in Austria," http://jpimg.digital.archives.go.jp/kouseisai/category/drawing/austria_e.html (accessed June 30, 2009).

12. Ichikawa, *Bunka,* p. 121. The Grand Council of State is Dajōkan.

13. Shin, *Toshi kōen,* pp. 39–42, 142–143; Ono, *Kōen no tanjō,* pp. 3–4, 12–13; Oyadomari, "Politics," pp. 100–101; Sanada Junko, *Toshi no midori wa dō arubeki ka* (Tokyo: Gihōdō, 2007), p. 17; Ueda Yasuyuki, *Midori no toshi keikaku* (Tokyo: Gyōsei, 2004), p. 79; Shinji, "Kōen no rekishi," p. 74; Hyōgoken, *Hyōgo,* p. 7; Roderick Wilson, "From *Sakariba* to City Parks: Public Space in Meiji-Period Tokyo" (unpublished paper, Stanford University, 2003), pp. 10–11.

14. Dajōkan Directive No. 16, January 15, 1873, reprinted in Ono, *Kōen no tanjō,* pp. 10–11.

15. Trent E. Maxey, "Defining the 'Greatest Problem': Religion and State Formation in Meiji Japan," lecture, Harvard University, October 17, 2008.

16. Kankyōchō Shizen Hogokyoku, *Shizen hogo gyōsei no ayumi* (Tokyo: Daiichi Hōki Shuppan, 1981), pp. 39–40; Shin, *Toshi kōen,* pp. 39–42, 57, 65–66; Hyōgoken, *Hyōgo,* p. 7; Tanaka Kōtarō, ed., *Ueno Kōen to sono shūhen me de miru hyakunen no ayumi* (Tokyo: Ueno Kankō Renmei, 1973), p. 14; Tokyoto Kōen Kyōkai, ed., *Tokyo no kōen* (Tokyo: Tokyoto Kensetsukyoku Kōen Ryokuchibu, 1995), pp. 1, 8–9; Ishikawa, *Toshi,* p. 193; Ono, *Kōen no tanjō,* pp. 11–12; Sanada, *Toshi,* p. 17; Nishimura Yukio, *Toshi hozen keikaku* (Tokyo: Tokyo Daigaku Shuppankai, 2004), p. 54; Oyadomari, "Politics," p. 107; Wilson, "From *Sakariba* to City Parks," p. 15.

17. Sōrifu Shingishitsu, ed., *Kankō gyōsei hyakunen to Kankō Seisaku Shingikai sanjūnen no ayumi* (Tokyo: Gyōsei, 1980), p. 34; Kankyōchō, *Shizen,* p. 42. See Aoi Akihito, *Shokuminchi jinja to teikoku Nihon* (Tokyo: Yoshikawa Kōbunkan, 2005), p. 138; Shirahata, *Kindai,* p. 185; Tawara Hiromi, *Midori no bunkashi: Shizen to ningen no kakawari o kangaeru* (Sapporo: Hokkaido Daigaku Tosho Kankōkai, 1991), pp. 133–134, 155; Ishikawa, *Toshi,* p. 12.

18. Ishikawa, *Toshi,* p. 194. See Kankyōchō, *Shizen,* p. 42; Ueda, *Midori,* p. 304; Hyōgoken, *Hyōgo,* p. 8; Nishimura, *Toshi,* p. 54.

19. Tokyoto, *Tokyo no kōen,* p. 428; Ishikawa, *Toshi,* pp. 198–199; Shin, *Toshi kōen,* p. 179.

20. Nihon Kōen Ryokuchi Kyōkai, ed., *Kōen ryokuchi manyuaru* (Tokyo: Nihon Kōen Ryokuchi Kyōkai, 2004), p. 9; Tokyoto, *Tokyo no kōen*, pp. 428–429; Uchiyama Masao and Minomo Toshitarō, *Tokyo no yūenchi* (Tokyo: Kyōgakusha, 1981), pp. 4–5; Abe Isoo, *Toshi mondai: Abe Isoo kōjutsu* (Tokyo: Waseda Daigaku Shuppankai, ca. 1910), p. 43. See Shirahata, *Kindai,* pp. 215–216; Shin, *Toshi kōen,* pp. 179–180; Ono, *Kōen no tanjō,* p. 12; Edward Seidensticker, *Low City, High City* (New York: Knopf, 1983), pp. 119–122; Ishikawa, *Toshi,* p. 199.

21. Uchiyama and Minomo, *Tokyo,* pp. 8, 11; Tokyoto, *Tokyo no kōen,* p. 430.

22. See Ueda, *Midori,* pp. 73–74; Sakamoto, *Nihon,* pp. 9–10.

23. Kobayashi Yasushige, *Ueno Kōen,* rev. ed. (Tokyo: Tokyoto Kōen Kyōkai, 1994), pp. i–ii. See Tanaka, *Ueno,* pp. 15–16; Toshima Hiroaki, *Ueno Kōen to sono fukin* (Tokyo: Hōshū Shoin, 1962), 4:8–9; Tokyoto Kōen Kyōkai, *Ueno Kōen monogatari: Kaien shikiten kara 120shūnen* (Tokyo: Tokyoto Kōen Kyōkai, 1996), pp. 10–11; Ishikawa, *Toshi,* p. 194.

24. Ishikawa, *Toshi,* p. 194; Kobayashi, *Ueno,* pp. 23–24; Suzuki and Sawada, *Kōen no hanashi,* p. 133; Seidensticker, *Low City,* p. 27; Tanaka, *Ueno,* p. 17; Club Smart Life, ed., *Tokyo yasuragi kūkan mappu* (Tokyo: Tokyo Shoseki, 2004), p. 64.

25. Tanaka, *Ueno,* pp. 25–26. See pp. 18–19; Kobayashi, *Ueno,* pp. 26–29; Toshima, *Ueno,* pp. 13–15; Maejima Yasuhiko, *Tokyo kōenshi banashi* (Tokyo: Tokyoto Kōen Kyōkai, 1989), pp. 30–31; Seidensticker, *Low City,* p. 117; Tokyo Metropolitan Government, *Twenty-Five Tales in Memory of Tokyo's Foreigners* (Tokyo: Tokyo Metropolitan Government, 1989), pp. 54–57. The Ministry of Military Affairs is Hyōbushō, predecessor to the Army and Navy ministries, which were established in 1872.

26. Kobayashi, *Ueno,* pp. 29–38; Maruyama, *Kindai,* p. 62. See Joseph R. Allen, "Taipei Park: Signs of Occupation," *The Journal of Asian Studies* 66, no. 1 (2007): p. 188. The Japan Academy is the Nihon Gakushiin.

27. See Tseng, *Imperial Museums,* p. 11.

28. Ono, *Kōen no tanjō,* pp. 105–117, 122–124; Kobayashi, *Ueno,* pp. 39–43, 52–53; Ishikawa, *Toshi,* p. 198; Maruyama, *Kindai,* p. 83. See Yoshimi Shun'ya, *Hakurankai no seijigaku* (Tokyo: Chūō Kōronsha, 1992); Taki Kōji, *Tennō no shozō* (Tokyo: Iwanami, 1988), p. 76; Takashi Fujitani, *Splendid Monarchy: Power and Pageantry in Modern Japan* (Berkeley: University of California Press, 1996).

29. Ueda, *Midori,* p. 305. See Miller, "Didactic Nature," pp. 273–275; Kobayashi, *Ueno,* p. 51.

30. Tanaka, *Ueno,* pp. 16, 23; Ono, *Kōen no tanjō,* pp. 104, 118, 122.

31. See Overmyer-Velázquez, "Visions of the Emerald City," pp. 97–99.

32. Maruyama, *Kindai,* p. 82; Kobayashi, *Ueno,* pp. 62–63; Ono, *Kōen no tanjō,* p. 129.

33. Maruyama, *Kindai,* p. 83. See Fujitani, *Splendid Monarchy,* p. 125; Ono, *Kōen no tanjō,* pp. 105, 133–137.

34. Pierre Bourdieu, *Distinction: A Social Critique of the Judgment of Taste,* trans. Richard Nice (Cambridge, Mass.: Harvard University Press, 1984), p. 7.

35. Nagayo Sensai draft, Tokyo City Improvement Commission, March 3, 1885, in Ono, *Kōen no tanjō*, p. 16. See also Fujimori Terunobu, *Meiji no Tokyo keikaku*, 3rd ed. (Tokyo: Iwanami, 2004).

36. Tokyo Metropolitan Government, *Hundred Years*, pp. 2, 10–12; Ono, *Kōen no tanjō*, pp. 13–16, 26–27. See Hoyt J. Long, "On Uneven Ground: Provincializing Cultural Production in Interwar Japan" (PhD dissertation, University of Michigan, 2007), pp. 244–259.

37. Shin, *Toshi kōen*, pp. 43–44; Ono, *Kōen no tanjō*, pp. 14, 26–29, 37–45; Ann Marie L. Davis, "Exporting (Double) Standards and Western Morality: Compulsory Venereal Disease Testing in the Japanese Treaty Ports, 1860–1890," lecture, Modern Japanese History Workshop, Waseda University, May 12, 2006. See Ruth Rogaski, *Hygienic Modernity: Meanings of Health and Disease in Treaty-Port China* (Berkeley: University of California Press, 2004), pp. 136–139, 153–154, 163–164.

38. Ichikawa, *Bunka*, p. 126; Tokyo Metropolitan Government, *Hundred Years*, pp. 2, 20; Ueda, *Midori*, pp. 80–81. The Council of Elders is Genrōin.

39. Ono, *Kōen no tanjō*, pp. 49–56. See Shin, *Toshi kōen*, pp. 43–44.

40. Ishikawa, *Toshi*, p. 7.

41. Tokyo Shiku Kaisei Shingikai, "Kōen" (April 21, 1885), reprinted in *Tokyo shiku kaiseihin kaichikukō shinsa giji hikki*, in Ono, *Kōen no tanjō*, p. 17. See Shiojima, *Midori*, p. 12.

42. Ishikawa, *Toshi*, pp. 7, 202; Shin, *Toshi kōen*, pp. 44–46; Tokyo Metropolitan Government, *Hundred Years*, pp. 18–20; David Schuyler, *The New Urban Landscape* (Baltimore: The Johns Hopkins University Press, 1986), pp. 151–152; Ueda, *Midori*, p. 82; Ono, *Kōen no tanjō*, pp. 14–15; Wilson, "From *Sakariba* to City Parks," p. 24; Suzuki and Sawada, *Kōen no hanashi*, p. 5.

43. Ichikawa, *Bunka*, p. 123; Ono, *Kōen no tanjō*, pp. 59–60; Sorensen, *Making of Urban Japan*, pp. 46, 69.

44. Ueda, *Midori*, p. 81. See Tanaka Masahiro, *Tokyo no kōen to genchikei* (Tokyo: Keyaki Shuppan, 2005), pp. 33–38; Mori Midori and Hibi Sadao, *Tokyo midori sansaku* (Osaka: Hoikusha, 1988), p. 34.

45. Quoted in Maruyama, *Kindai*, p. 165. See also pp. 163–164.

46. Ono, *Kōen no tanjō*, pp. 32–37; Shin, *Toshi*, p. 47; Ishida Yorifusa, *Nihon kindai toshi keikakushi kenkyū* (Tokyo: Kashiwa Shobō, 1987), p. 64.

47. Mori Ōgai and Koike Masanao, *Eisei shinpen* (Tokyo: Nankōdō, 1897), quoted in Maruyama, *Kindai*, p. 67. See p. 138; Shibata Tokue, *Nihon no toshi seisaku: Sono seiji keizaigakuteki kōsatsu* (Tokyo: Yūhikaku, 1978), pp. 33–37; Ishida Yorifusa, *Mori Ōgai no toshiron to sono jidai* (Tokyo: Nihon Keizai Hyōronsha, 1999), pp. iv, 93; Tokyo Metropolitan University, ed., *Tokyo, Urban Growth and Planning 1868–1968* (Tokyo: Tokyo Metropolitan University, 1988), p. 15. See also Shin, *Toshi kōen*, p. 68.

48. Shibata, *Nihon*, pp. 53–56; Tokyo Metropolitan University, *Tokyo*, p. 15.

49. Kunikida Doppo, "Musashino" (1898), in Kunikida Doppo, *Musashino* (Tokyo: Min'yūsha, 1901). See Sanada, *Toshi*, pp. 25–26.

50. Kōda Rohan, *Ikkoku no shuto: Hoka ippen* (Tokyo: Iwanami, 1993 [1899]), pp. 102–103.

51. Ibid., pp. 105–109. See Maruyama, *Kindai*, p. 139.

52. Katayama Sen, *Toshi shakaigaku* (Tokyo: Shakaishugi Toshokan, 1903), pp. 92, 95. See Shibata, *Nihon*, pp. 38–43; Shin, *Toshi kōen*, p. 71; Maruyama, *Kindai*, pp. 67–69.

53. Katayama, *Toshi shakaigaku*, p. 99. See p. 98.

54. Oyadomari, "Politics," p. 114; Maruyama, *Kindai*, p. 69.

55. Abe Isoo, *Ōyō shiseiron* (Tokyo: Nikkō Yūrindō, 1908), p. 224. See Shibata, *Nihon*, p. 47; Maruyama, *Kindai*, pp. 70–71; Shin, *Toshi kōen*, pp. 72, 96.

56. Abe, *Toshi mondai*, p. 44.

57. Ibid., p. 39.

58. Ibid., p. 40.

59. Ibid., p. 45.

60. Inoue Tomoichi, *Jichi yōgi* (Tokyo: Hakubunkan, 1909). See Shin, *Toshi kōen*, p. 69.

61. Vivian Blaxell, "Designs of Power," *The Asia-Pacific Journal* online 35, no. 2 (August 31, 2009): p. 9.

62. See Isoda Kōichi, *Shisō to shite no Tokyo: Rokumeikan no keifu* (Tokyo: Ozawa Shoten, 1991). See also Tokyoto, *Tokyoto no kōen*, p. 21; Shirahata, *Kindai*, p. 189; Ishida Yorifusa, *Nihon kindai toshi keikaku no hyakunen* (Tokyo: Jichitai Kenkyūsha, 1987), p. 44; Ueda, *Midori*, pp. 82–84; Suematsu Shirō, *Tokyo no kōen tsūshi*, expanded ed. (Tokyo: Tokyoto Kōen Kyōkai, 1996), 1:4; Suzuki and Sawada, *Kōen no hanashi*, p. 85; Seidensticker, *Low City*, pp. 122–123; Shirahata, "Kōen nante mō iranai," pp. 191–193.

63. Suematsu, *Tokyo*, 1:4. See *Hibiya 100* (Tokyo: Ueda Shoten, 1984), pp. 40, 46, 48.

64. Honda Seiroku, *Honda Seiroku taiken 85nen* (Tokyo: Kōdansha, 1952), quoted in Maejima Yasuhiko, *Hibiya Kōen*, rev. ed. (Tokyo: Tokyoto Kōen Kyōkai, 1994), p. 44. See Shirahata, *Kindai*, pp. 205–206.

65. Shirahata, *Kindai*, p. 193; Maejima, *Hibiya*, p. 46; Shin, *Toshi kōen*, p. 54.

66. Maejima, *Hibiya*, p. 56.

67. Sōrifu, *Kankō*, p. 34; Maejima, *Hibiya*, pp. 50, 72–74; Shiojima, *Midori*, p. 169. See Kashima Shigeru, "Hibiya Kōen o tsukutta Honda Seiroku to iu hito," *Tokyojin* 18, no. 11 (2003): p. 113.

68. Henry, "Respatializing Chosŏn's Royal Capital," pp. 33–35, notes that when Japanese colonial administrators opened Seoul's Pagoda Park in 1913, the flora were badly damaged by visitors. Officials then used Pagoda Park, like Hibiya, as a stage to foster "proper" civic behavior and public morality as defined by elites. See also Suzuki and Sawada, *Kōen no hanashi*, p. 86; Shirahata, *Kindai*, p. 224. Virtuous conduct is *kōtoku*.

69. *Tokyo nichi nichi shinbun*, June 1, 1903, quoted in *Hibiya 100*, p. 54.

70. Allen, "Taipei Park," p. 186. The performance occurred on August 1, 1905.

71. See Shirahata, *Kindai*, p. 221; Ueda, *Midori*, p. 86; Maejima, *Hibiya*, p. 56.

72. *Hibiya 100*, p. 55; Maejima, *Hibiya*, p. 57. Because visitors could freely enter the park, attendance statistics were mere estimates and provide no basis to profile park users.

73. Nishikawa Kōjirō, in *Shūkan heimin shinbun*, July 10, 1904, quoted in Maruyama, *Kindai*, p. 73. See also p. 72. Public park is *kōen*; government park is *kan'en*.

74. Maruyama, *Kindai*, pp. 72–73.

75. See Maruyama, *Kindai*, pp. 83–84.

76. Ono, *Kōen no tanjō*, pp. 160–161, 169–171; Suzuki and Sawada, *Kōen no hanashi*, pp. 86–87.

77. Shumpei Okamoto, *The Japanese Oligarchy and the Russo-Japanese War* (New York: Columbia University Press, 1970), esp. pp. 205–208. See also *Kodansha Encyclopedia of Japan* (Tokyo: Kōdansha, 1983), 3:129; Maruyama, *Kindai*, pp. 84–85; Ono, *Kōen no tanjō*, pp. 95, 175.

78. Andrew Gordon, *Labor and Imperial Democracy in Prewar Japan* (Berkeley: University of California Press, 1991), p. 32. See pp. 26–29; Naoko Shimazu, *Japanese Society at War: Death, Memory and the Russo-Japanese War* (Cambridge, Eng.: Cambridge University Press, 2009), pp. 50–51.

79. See Ono, *Kōen no tanjō*, pp. 171, 175; Maeda Ai, *Genkei no Meiji* (Tokyo: Asahi Shinbunsha, 1978).

80. Maruyama, *Kindai*, pp. 85–101. See Ono, *Kōen no tanjō*, pp. 177–178.

81. See Fujii, "Introduction," p. 2.

82. *New York Times*, June 30, 2009, p. B1.

83. *Japan Today* online, December 30, 2007.

84. Lefebvre, *Production of Space*, p. 222.

85. Tokyoto, *Tokyo no kōen*, p. 21; Ishikawa, *Toshi*, p. 204.

86. Calculated from data in Yasuo Masai, "The Human Environment of Tokyo," in Gideon S. Golany, Keisuke Hanaki, and Osamu Koide, eds., *Japanese Urban Environment* (Oxford, Eng.: Pergamon, 1998), p. 66.

87. Nakayama Tōru, *Osaka no midori o kangaeru* (Osaka: Tōhō Shuppan, 1994), p. 19. See Ishikawa, *Toshi*, pp. 210–211. Early "urban" parks included Itsukushima, Matsushima, and Unzen.

88. See Maruyama, *Kindai*, p. 6.

89. Suzuki and Sawada, *Kōen no hanashi*, p. 167; Aikawa Sadaharu and Fuse Rokurō, *Yoyogi Kōen* (Tokyo: Kyōgakusha, 1981), pp. 6, 10; Tokyo Metropolitan Government, *Hundred Years*, p. 20; Ishikawa, *Toshi*, pp. 218–219.

90. Kondō Mitsuo, *Toshi ryokuka tokuhon* (Tokyo: Enu Teī Esu, 2007), pp. 172–175.

91. Ueda, *Midori*, p. 184; Maejima Yasuhiko, *Inokashira Kōen*, rev. ed. (Tokyo: Tokyoto Kōen Kyōkai, 1995), p. 15; Aikawa and Fuse, *Yoyogi*, pp. 10–11; Shinji, "Kōen no rekishi," p. 50; Tokyo Metropolitan Government, *Hundred Years*, p. 20; Tokyoto, *Tokyoto no kōen*, p. 23.

92. Uchiyama Masao and Minomo Toshitarō, *Yoyogi no mori* (Tokyo: Kyōgakusha, 1981), p. iii, points out that at New Year's 1981 the Meiji Shrine was the most visited in Japan, at 3.9 million. The National Police Agency reported that a record 99.4 million

people made New Year's visits to temples and shrines in 2009, including Meiji Shrine (3.2 million), Naritasan (3.0 million), and Kawasaki Daishi (3.0 million). *Metropolis* online, January 23, 2009.

93. Tokyoto, *Tokyo no kōen*, p. 24; Ueda, *Midori*, p. 26; Tokyo Metropolitan Government, *Hundred Years*, p. 20; Ishikawa, *Toshi*, pp. 215–217; Suzuki and Sawada, *Kōen no hanashi*, pp. 168–169, 174–177.

94. *Japan Times* online, November 8, 2008. Some of the protestors bore placards reading "Takiji's voice is being heard," referring to the proletarian novelist Kobayashi Takiji (1903–1933).

95. Tokyo Metropolitan Government, *Tokyo: The Making of a Metropolis* (Tokyo: Tokyo Metropolitan Government, 1993), p. 32.

96. Watanabe Shun'ichi, "The State of the Art of Machizukuri," lecture, Harvard University, February 27, 2004.

97. Jeffrey E. Hanes, *The City as Subject: Seki Hajime and the Reinvention of Modern Osaka* (Berkeley: University of California Press, 2002), pp. 212–214, 225. See Shiojima, *Midori*, pp. 13–14; Ishida Yorifusa, "Local Initiatives and the Decentralization of Planning Power in Japan," in Carola Hein and Philippe Pelletier, eds., *Cities, Autonomy, and Decentralization in Japan* (London: Routledge, 2006), pp. 29–30; Sorensen, *Making of Urban Japan*, pp. 133–134.

98. Nishiyama Yasuo, "Western Influence on Urban Planning Administration in Japan: Focus on Land Management," in Haruo Nagamine, ed., *Urban Development Policies and Programmes* (Nagoya: United Nations Centre for Regional Development, 1986), p. 319; Sorensen, *Making of Urban Japan*, pp. 135–137; Thomas R. H. Havens, *Architects of Affluence: The Tsutsumi Family and the Seibu-Saison Enterprises in Twentieth-Century Japan* (Cambridge, Mass.: Harvard University Council on East Asian Studies, 1994), pp. 26–31.

99. Ishikawa, *Toshi*, p. 212; Sorensen, *Making of Urban Japan*, p. 115.

100. Ishikawa, *Toshi*, p. 212.

101. Shin, *Toshi kōen*, p. 82; *Kodansha Encyclopedia of Japan*, 8:180.

102. Tokyo Metropolitan Government, *Tokyo*, pp. 16–17; Tokyo Metropolitan Government, *Hundred Years*, p. 21; Maruyama, *Kindai*, p. 174.

103. Tokyo Shiyakusho Kōenka, ed., *Tokyoshi kōen gaikan* (Tokyo: Tokyo Shiyakusho, 1923), p. 3.

104. Ibid., pp. 3–4.

105. See Sorensen, *Making of Urban Japan*, pp. 89–90.

106. Ibid., pp. 117–118. See Shin, *Toshi kōen*, pp. 85–88; Maruyama, *Kindai*, pp. 6–7.

107. Satō and Shimoyama, *Landscape Planning*, p. 2. See Ishikawa, *Toshi*, p. 213; Sanada, *Toshi*, p. 16; Sakamoto, *Nihon*, p. 15; Shin, *Toshi kōen*, p. 83.

108. Maruyama, *Kindai*, pp. 166–167.

109. Shin, *Toshi kōen*, p. 181.

110. Spiro Kostof, *America by Design* (New York: Oxford University Press, 1987), p. 219; Club Smart Life, *Tokyo*, p. 176; Andrew Bernstein, *Modern Passings: Death Rites,*

Politics, and Social Change in Imperial Japan (Honolulu: University of Hawai'i Press, 2006), p. 107; Yokohama Gaikokujin Bochi, *Kōkai junro annaizu* (Yokohama: Yokohama Gaikokujin Bochi, n.d. [2007]), p. 1. The foreigners' cemetery high on the Bluff at Yokohama memorializes dozens of European and American businesspeople active in the Meiji period.

111. Ueda, *Midori*, p. 325; Itō, *Ima*, pp. 160–161; *Japan Times*, May 29, 2007, p. 2.
112. Nishimura, *Toshi*, pp. 57, 90. Of the 406 parks in 1920, 74 lay on former shrine or temple lands, 72 on old castle lands, 70 on open and mostly undeveloped open spaces, and 46 at scenic landscapes. Another 41 were memorial parks associated with wars or tours by the imperial family and 16 were private gardens converted to public parklands.
113. Ōbayashi Munetsugu, *Toshi shakai seisaku to shite no kōen mondai* (Tokyo: Ōhara Shakai Mondai Kenkyūjo, 1923), p. 51.

Chapter 2: National Parks for Wealth, Health, and Empire

1. Shiga, *Nihon fūkeiron*, p. 272.
2. Uchimura Kanzō, *Chirigakukō* (Tokyo: Keiseisha Shoten, 1894; reprinted by the same publisher as *Chijinron* in 1897).
3. Makiguchi Tsunesaburō, *Jinsei chirigaku* (Tokyo: Bunkaidō, 1903).
4. Makiguchi drew on the location theory of optimal propinquity of agriculture to urban centers in Johann Heinrich von Thünen (1783–1850), *Der Isolierte Staat* (Hamburg: F. Perthes, 1826).
5. Takeuchi Keiichi, "The Significance of Makiguchi Tsunesaburō's *Jinsei chirigaku* (Geography of Human Life) in the Intellectual History of Geography in Japan," *Journal of Oriental Studies* 14 (2004), *Special Series: The Spirit of India*, pp. 113, 119–127.
6. Katō Sadamichi, "The Three Ecologies in Minakata Kumagusu's Environmental Movement," *Organization & Environment* 12 (1999): pp. 86, 93; Roger Pulvers, "Japan's Wild Scientific Genius: Minakata Kumagusu," *Japan Focus* online, January 20, 2008.
7. Tawara Hiromi, "Shizen kōen no rekishi," in Fukutomi Hisao and Ishii Hiroshi, eds., *Midori no keikaku: Toshi kōen to shizen kōen* (Tokyo: Chikyūsha, 1985), p. 117; Masako Gavin, *Shiga Shigetaka, 1863–1927: The Forgotten Enlightener* (Richmond, Surrey, Eng.: Curzon, 2001), p. 44.
8. Harvey, *Justice*, p. 170. See Jennifer Robertson, *Native and Newcomer: Making and Remaking a Japanese City* (Berkeley: University of California Press, 1991), p. 18; Kenneth B. Pyle, *The New Generation in Meiji Japan: Problems of Cultural Identity, 1885–1895* (Stanford, Calif.: Stanford University Press, 1969), p. 161; Richard Okada, "'Landscape' and the Nation-State: A Reading of *Nihon fūkeiron*," in Helen Hardacre and Adam L. Kern, eds., *New Directions in the Study of Meiji Japan* (Leiden: Brill, 1997), pp. 90–107.

9. Taki, *Tennō*, p. 89; Gavin, *Shiga*, p. 27; Shiga, *Nihon fūkeiron*, pp. 273–275. See Miyoshi Manabu, *Shokubutsu seitai bikan* (Tokyo: Fuzanbō, 1902); Tawara, "Shizen," p. 118.

10. See, for example, Murakushi Nisaburō, *Kokuritsu kōen seiritsushi no kenkyū: Kaihatsu to shizen hogo no kakushitsu o chūshin ni* (Tokyo: Hōsei Daigaku Shuppankyoku, 2005), p. 20. Gavin, *Shiga*, p. 27, presents a forceful counterargument. See also Thomas, *Reconfiguring Modernity*, pp. 174–175, for an incisive evaluation of Karatani Kōjin's writings on landscapes in Meiji Japan. Shiga used the concrete, highly physical *fūkei* for "landscape" rather than the more abstract, humanistic *keikan*.

11. See Okada's cautionary remarks in "'Landscape' and the Nation-State," pp. 90–93.

12. Tawara, "Shizen," p. 118. See Gavin, *Shiga*, pp. 34–35, for a critique.

13. Kären Wigen, "Discovering the Japanese Alps: Meiji Mountaineering and the Quest for Geographical Enlightenment," *Journal of Japanese Studies* 31, no. 1 (2005): p. 15. See p. 14 for a discussion of Basil H. Chamberlain and W. B. Mason, *Handbook for Travellers in Japan*, 3rd ed. (Yokohama: Kelly & Walsh, 1891). Westerners such as the metallurgist and amateur archaeologist William Gowland (1842–1922) explored the Honshu mountains and named a northern portion of them the Japan Alps. The Rev. Walter Weston (1861–1940), based in Yokohama, admired the beauty of the Nagano Alps at Kamikōchi. Walter Weston, *Mountaineering and Exploration in the Japanese Alps* (London: J. Murray, 1896), p. viii.

14. Kojima Usui, *Nihon Arupusu*, 4 vols. (Tokyo: Maekawa Bun'eikaku, 1910–1915). See Tawara, "Shizen," p. 118. Kojima, Weston, and Takatō Shoku (1877–1958), who wrote *Nihon sangakushi* (Tokyo: Hakubunkan, 1906), helped to found the Japan Alpine Club in 1905. In 2009 the club proposed a new national holiday for October 14, Mountain Day. *Japan Today* online, December 16, 2009.

15. Takeuchi Keiichi, "Landscape, Language and Nationalism in Meiji Japan," *Hitotsubashi Journal of Social Studies* 20 (1988): p. 128. See Thomas, *Reconfiguring Modernity*, pp. 179, 183, 185, on ultranationalist uses of nature in Japan in the 1930s. See also Julia Adeney Thomas, "'To Become As One Dead': Nature and the Political Subject in Modern Japan," in Lorraine Daston and Fernando Vidal, eds., *The Moral Authority of Nature* (Chicago: University of Chicago Press, 2004), pp. 309–324, on the ideas of the political scientist Maruyama Masao (1914–1996) about politics and nature. Famous vistas are *meishō*.

16. Tamura Tsuyoshi, *Kokuritsu kōen kōwa* (Tokyo: Meiji Shoin, 1948), p. 48. Okabe used the term *kokuen* for national park. See Murakushi, *Kokuritsu*, p. 5; Itō, "American," p. 197; Sōrifu, *Kankō*, p. 30. U. S. Grant visited Nikkō in 1879 and suggested it be protected by law. The German physician Erwin Baelz (1849–1913) recommended that Nagasaki make Unzen volcano a prefectural park.

17. Murakushi, *Kokuritsu*, p. 6. The town counted 41,036 tourists in 1881, rising to 48,884 by 1884. Foreign visitors increased from 168 to 723 during the same period.

18. Kankyōchō, *Shizen*, pp. 45–46; Oyadomari, "Politics," p. 116; Murakushi, *Kokuritsu*, p. 8.

19. Maruyama, *Kindai*, pp. 269–270.

20. Itō, "American," p. 197.

21. Steven J. Ericson, *The Sound of the Whistle: Railroads and the State in Meiji Japan* (Cambridge, Mass.: Harvard University Council on East Asian Studies, 1996), p. 89. See Itō, "American," pp. 198–199; Murakushi, *Kokuritsu*, p. 9; Oyadomari, "Politics," pp. 135–137; Tanaka Masahiro, *Nihon no shizen kōen: Shizen hogo to fūkei hogo* (Tokyo: Sagami Shobō, 1981), p. 207.

22. Murakushi, *Kokuritsu*, p. 7.

23. On journalistic publicity, see ibid., p. 10.

24. See David R. Leheny, *The Rules of Play: National Identity and the Shaping of Japanese Leisure* (Ithaca, N.Y.: Cornell University Press, 2003), pp. 57–62; Murakushi, *Kokuritsu*, p. 10; Itō, "American," p. 200; Nomoto Kyōhachirō, *Meiji kinen Nihon daikōen sōsetsugi* (Tokyo: Nomoto Kyōhachirō, 1908); Tanaka, *Nihon no shizen*, p. 193. In October 2008 the Japanese government established a new unit, the Japan Tourism Agency, with the Foucauldian mission of serving as a "control tower" for attracting more international visitors, especially from Asia. Fukada Takahiro, "New Tourism Agency to Act as Policy 'Control Tower,'" *Japan Times* online, October 1, 2008.

25. Uno Tasuku, "Kokuritsu daikōen setchi ni kansuru kengi," *Kokuritsu kōen* 243 (1970): pp. 4–7; Maruyama, *Kindai*, pp. 297–299; Kankyōchō, *Shizen*, p. 45; Oyadomari, "Politics," pp. 121–126; Murakushi, *Kokuritsu*, pp. 3–7, 11–20.

26. Tanaka, *Nihon no shizen*, pp. 200–201, 206; Itō, "American," p. 200.

27. Murakushi, *Kokuritsu*, pp. 26–28.

28. Tamura Tsuyoshi, *Zōen gairon* (Tokyo: Seibidō Shoten, 1918). A second edition was issued by the same publisher in 1925, titled *Zōengaku gairon*. On the importance of this work see Kankyōchō, *Shizen*, p. 46.

29. Kankyōchō, *Shizen*, p. 46; Tanaka, *Nihon no shizen*, p. 192. The Garden Society of Japan is Nihon Teien Kyōkai.

30. Yoshiya Iwai, "Introduction," in Yoshiya Iwai, ed., *Forestry and the Forest Industry in Japan* (Vancouver: University of British Columbia Press, 2002), pp. xiv–xv; Kenichi Akao, "Private Forestry," in Yoshiya Iwai, ed., *Forestry and the Forest Industry in Japan* (Vancouver: University of British Columbia Press, 2002), pp. 24–25.

31. Kankyōchō, *Shizen*, p. 8. See p. 6; Kōdansha Sōgō Hensankyoku, ed., *Nihon no tennen kinenbutsu* (Tokyo: Kōdansha, 2003), p. 4.

32. Simmons, *Earth*, p. 82; Pradyumna P. Karan, *Japan in the 21st Century: Environment, Economy, and Society* (Lexington: University Press of Kentucky, 2005), pp. 25–26.

33. Jun'ichi Iwamoto, "The Development of Japanese Forestry," in Yoshiya Iwai, ed., *Forestry and the Forest Industry in Japan* (Vancouver: University of British Columbia Press, 2002), pp. 3–5; Conrad D. Totman, *Japan's Imperial Forest Goryōrin, 1889–1946* (Folkestone, Kent, Eng.: Global Oriental, 2007), p. xxvi; Conrad D. Totman, *The Green Archipelago: Forestry in Preindustrial Japan* (Berkeley: University of California Press, 1989), p. 6.

34. Totman, *Green Archipelago,* p. 1.

35. Totman, *Japan's Imperial Forest,* pp. 10–13, 35–36; Conrad D. Totman, "Unifying the Realm, Distressing the People: The Land-Tax Reform of 1871–1881" (unpublished manuscript, Yale University, 2001), pp. 11–14; Michael Jay Roy, "National Forest Management in Hokkaido, Japan: Biodiversity Conservation Considerations" (PhD dissertation, University of Montana, 1998), p. 62. See Atsushi Takayanagi, "Treatment of Forests and Wildlife in Modern Society," in Yoshiya Iwai, ed., *Forestry and the Forest Industry in Japan* (Vancouver: University of British Columbia Press, 2002), pp. 292–294; James Fisher, Noel Simon, and Jack Vincent, *Wildlife in Danger* (New York: Viking, 1969), pp. 193, 222–223.

36. Koji Matsushita and Kunihiro Hirata, "Forestry Owners' Associations," in Yoshiya Iwai, ed., *Forestry and the Forest Industry in Japan* (Vancouver: University of British Columbia Press, 2002), pp. 41–43; Conrad D. Totman, *A History of Japan* (Malden, Mass.: Blackwell, 2000), pp. 498–499.

37. Itō, "American," p. 200; Matsushita and Hirata, "Forestry Owners' Associations," pp. 41–42; Roy, "National Forest," p. 63; Totman, *Green Archipelago,* p. 195.

38. Bunkachō Bunkazai Hogobu, ed., *Tennen kinenbutsu jiten* (Tokyo: Daiichi Hōki Shuppan, 1971), p. 313; Murakushi, *Kokuritsu,* p. 24; Oyadomari, "Politics," pp. 137, 140, 152–153, 464–465.

39. Mark Neumann, *On the Rim: Looking for the Grand Canyon* (Minneapolis: University of Minnesota Press, 1999), p. 34. See Kamahori Miki, "Japan's Cultural Heritage Preservation Policy," *Japan Journal* online 4, no. 10 (2007).

40. Miyoshi's proposal to protect trees appears in *Tōyō gakugei zasshi* 23 (1906). See Bunkachō, *Tennen,* pp. 312–313; Kōdansha, *Nihon,* p. 4; Oyadomari, "Politics," p. 138; Murakushi, *Kokuritsu,* p. 24; Newton, *Design,* p. 525. The U.S. Antiquities Act, protecting monuments, was enacted in 1906.

41. Tokugawa Yorimichi, speech to House of Peers, March 11, 1911, quoted in Bunkachō, *Tennen,* p. 313.

42. Newton, *Design,* pp. 525–527; Nihon Shizen Hogo Kyōkai, *Yutaka na shizen, fukai fureai, pātonāshippu: 21seiki no kokuritsu kōen no arikata o kangaeru* (Tokyo: Nihon Shizen Hogo Kyōkai, 2000), pp. 7–8. See Oyadomari, "Politics," pp. 148–149, 151–153, 463–465; Kōdansha, *Nihon,* p. 4.

43. Bunkachō, *Tennen,* p. 315.

44. Naimushō, *Preservation of Natural Monuments in Japan* (Tokyo: Department of Home Affairs, 1926), pp. 2–4; Fisher, Simon, and Vincent, *Wildlife in Danger,* pp. 162, 185. By 1926 the Home Ministry had designated 166 historic, 47 scenic, 188 biological, and 19 geological monuments; as of 2004 the Cultural Agency recognized 1,495 historic sites, 289 scenic sites, and 927 natural monuments, mainly plant species. See Kankyōshō, *Kankyō hakusho* (Tokyo: Gyōsei, 2004), p. 142; Gaimushō, *Environment and Development: Japan's Experience and Achievement—Japan's National Report to UNCED 1992* (Tokyo: Gaimushō, 1991), p. 62. Kōdansha, *Nihon,* p. 4, gives slightly different figures for 2003.

45. Uehara Keiji, *Kokuritsu kōen no hanashi* (Tokyo: Shinkōsha, 1924), p. 104. See pp. 105–112 for petitions supporting legislation to establish national parks.

46. See Jones and Wills, *Invention of the Park*, pp. 73, 76, 82. See also Ōi Michio, "The Role of National Parks in Social and Economic Development Process," in Hugh Elliott, ed., *Second World Conference on National Parks* (Morges, Switz.: International Union for Conservation of Nature and Natural Resources, 1974), p. 4; Ōi Michio, *Fūkei e no banka: Watakushi no shizen hogoron* (Tokyo: Anvieru, 1978).

47. See Tanaka, *Nihon no shizen*, pp. 134–136.

48. Tamura, *Zōen gairon*.

49. Tamura Tsuyoshi, "Kokuritsu kōenron," *Tokyo asahi shinbun*, September 8, 1921, cited in Kankyōchō, *Shizen*, p. 47. See pp. 43–46; Murakushi, *Kokuritsu*, pp. 29–31.

50. Kankyōchō, *Shizen*, p. 48; Tawara, *Midori*, pp. 171–172.

51. Honda Seiroku, "Fūkei no riyō to tennen kinenbutsu ni taisuru yo no konponteki shuchō," *Shiseki meishō tennen kinenbutsu* 4, no. 8 (1921): p. 91, quoted in Murakushi, *Kokuritsu*, p. 50. See Tawara, *Midori*, p. 180.

52. Uehara Keiji, in *Tokyo asahi shinbun*, November 1922, in Uehara Keiji, *Zōen taikei* (Tokyo: Kashima Shoten, 1974), 2:29.

53. Kankyōchō, *Shizen*, p. 48; Murakushi, *Kokuritsu*, pp. 62–64.

54. Uehara, *Kokuritsu*, pp. 112–113.

55. Uehara, speech, Pan Pacific Conference, Honolulu, April 12, 1927, in Uehara, *Zōen taikei*, 4:40.

56. Itō, "American," p. 202.

57. Ibid., p. 203; Oyadomari, "Politics," p. 193; Murakushi, *Kokuritsu*, pp. 34–37, 44; Maruyama, *Kindai*, p. 142; Tanaka, *Nihon no shizen*, pp. 222–223.

58. Nash, *Wilderness*, p. 184.

59. Itō Taiichi, "Influence of Forestry on the Formation of National Park Policy in Japan," *Journal of Forest Planning* 2 (1996), p. 89. As of 1930 the Forestry Bureau had 193 offices and 1,500 employees throughout Japan, with ¥3.7 million in annual revenues.

60. Kankyōchō, *Shizen*, p. 50.

61. Honda Seiroku, "Kokuritsu kōen," in Teien Kyōkai, ed., *Toshi to kōen* (Tokyo: Seibidō, 1924), p. 9.

62. Maruyama, *Kindai*, pp. 143–144.

63. Murakushi, *Kokuritsu*, p. 42. See pp. 51–57; Tanaka, *Shizen*, pp. 209–215; Maruyama, *Kindai*, pp. 302–309.

64. Tanaka, *Shizen*, p. 209; Itō, "Forestry," p. 88; Oyadomari, "Politics," pp. 216–218. The three famous views were at Itsukushima, Amanohashidate, and Matsushima. The new choices were Unzen, Towada, Kiso, Kamikōchi, Kegon Falls at Nikkō, Karikachi, Beppu, and Muroto.

65. Kankyōchō, *Shizen*, p. 49; Murakushi, *Kokuritsu*, pp. 72–73, 76–79.

66. Murakushi, *Kokuritsu*, pp. 72, 78.

67. Maruyama, *Kindai*, pp. 7–8; Oyadomari, "Politics," p. 225.

68. Senge Tetsumaro, "Kokuritsu Kōen Kyōkai 50nen o kaerimite," *Kokuritsu kōen* 355 (1979): pp. 10–11; Kankyōchō, *Shizen*, p. 52; Murakushi, *Kokuritsu*, pp. 71, 79–82.

69. Nihon Shizen Hogo Kyōkai, *Yutaka*, p. 8; Senge, "Kokuritsu," p. 10; Itō Taiichi, personal communication, May 17, 2006; Murakushi, *Kokuritsu*, pp. 83–84; Ueda, *Midori*, p. 143.

70. Itō Takehiko, *Kokuritsu Kōenhō kaisetsu* (Tokyo: Kokuritsu Kōen Kyōkai, 1931), p. 26. See Nihon Shizen Hogo Kyōkai, *Yutaka*, p. 3.

71. Adachi Kenzō, "Kokuritsu kōen mondai ni tsuite," *Kokuritsu kōen* 3, no. 1 (1931): p. 1.

72. Adachi Kenzō, "Kokuritsu Kōen Hōan teian no riyū," *Kokuritsu kōen* 3, no. 3 (1931): p. 2.

73. Oyadomari, "Politics," p. 231. See pp. 228–230. Most other sources omit mention of antiradicalism as a significant factor in winning support for the National Parks Bill.

74. Nihon Shizen Hogo Kyōkai, *Yutaka*, pp. 8–9.

75. Tanaka, *Shizen*, pp. 179–183, 224–228; Murakushi, *Kokuritsu*, pp. 92–94.

76. Summarized in Murakushi, *Kokuritsu*, p. 92. See p. 72.

77. Uno Tasuku, "Kaihatsu to hogo no chōwa wa dono yō ni shite torarete kita ka," *Kankō* 7, no. 5 (1972): pp. 4–5.

78. Murakushi, *Kokuritsu*, pp. 111–112.

79. Quoted ibid., p. 119.

80. Nash, *Wilderness*, p. 379.

81. Adachi, "Kokuritsu Kōen Hōan," pp. 2–3.

82. Quoted in Itō, *Kokuritsu Kōenhō*, pp. 30–31.

83. Murakushi, *Kokuritsu*, p. 129; Itō, "American," p. 202.

84. Itō, "Forestry," p. 94; Murakushi, *Kokuritsu*, p. 129.

85. Nihon Shizen Hogo Kyōkai, *Yutaka*, p. 3; Tanaka, *Shizen*, pp. 223, 239–240; Murakushi, *Kokuritsu*, p. 122. This de facto central method can be traced to the recommendations of Charles A. Richey, a senior National Park Service officer, who conducted a survey of Japan's national parks for the American occupation authorities in 1948 (see chapter 3). Charles A. Richey, *A Study of the Japanese National Parks April–August 1948* (Tokyo: General Headquarters, Supreme Commander for the Allied Powers, Civil Information and Education Section, 50-page typescript and appendixes, 1948).

86. Murakushi, *Kokuritsu*, pp. 127–128. The twelve were authorized in three batches: Seto Inland Sea, Unzen, and Kirishima, all in southwestern Japan, in March 1934; Akan, Daisetsuzan, Nikkō, Chūbu Sangaku, and Aso, all in the mountains, in December 1934; and Towada, Fuji-Hakone, Yoshino-Kumano, and Ōyama (the smallest, at 124 sq. km) in February 1936. See Ueda, *Midori*, p. 143.

87. Ueda, *Midori*, p. 138.

88. Tanaka, *Shizen*, p. 219.

89. Waseda Daigaku Kankō Gakkai, *Kokuritsu kōen* (Tokyo: Waseda Daigaku Kankō Gakkai, 1966), p. 3; Seta, *Saiseisuru,* p. 8. See p. 182 for data on Japan's current twenty-nine national parks.

90. Maruyama, *Kindai,* p. 298. Twelve national parks were established in Japan and 103 others elsewhere during the 1930s, exceeded only by the 1950s when 120 were founded worldwide.

91. Kankyōchō, *Shizen,* p. 85.

92. See Tanaka, *Shizen,* pp. 240–246; Ishikawa, *Toshi,* p. 243; Murakushi, *Kokuritsu,* p. 137.

93. Totman, *Japan's Imperial Forest,* p. 3. In the 1930s about 56 percent of Japanese forestlands were privately owned.

94. Itō, "Forestry," pp. 85, 93.

95. Sōrifu, *Kankō,* p. 81; Zenkoku Shizen Hogo Rengō, ed., *Shizen hogo jiten,* expanded ed. (Tokyo: Ryokufū Shuppan, 1996), 1:265–266, 301–305; Kankyōchō, *Shizen,* p. 8.

96. Tsunashima Teiji, ed., *Nihon no kokuritsu kōen* (Tokyo: Nihon Kokuritsu Kōen Tosho Kankōkai, 1933), preface. See Yamamoto Tatsuo, "Jo," in Kokuritsu Kōen Kyōkai, *Kokuritsu kōen annai* (Tokyo: Kokuritsu Kōen Kyōkai, 1933).

97. *Kokusai kankō* 6:4 (1938), opening leaf, quoted in Barak Kushner, *The Thought War: Japanese Imperial Propaganda* (Honolulu: University of Hawai'i Press, 2006), pp. 34–35.

98. Murakushi, *Kokuritsu,* p. 123.

99. Tamura Tsuyoshi, ed., *Nihon no kokuritsu kōen* (Tokyo: Kokuritsu Kōen Kyōkai, 1951), p. 286; Murakushi, *Kokuritsu,* p. 125.

100. *Kokusai kankō* 7:2 (1939), p. 96, quoted in Kushner, *Thought War,* p. 35.

101. Colin Gordon, "Governmental Rationality: An Introduction," in Graham Burchell, Colin Gordon, and Peter Miller, eds., *The Foucault Effect: Studies in Governmentality with Two Lectures by and an Interview with Michel Foucault* (London: Harvester Wheatsheaf, 1991), pp. 1–51.

102. Scott, *Seeing Like a State,* pp. 4–5.

103. Neumann, *Imposing Wilderness,* pp. 9, 16–17.

104. Mark R. Peattie, "Japanese Treaty Port Settlements in China, 1895–1937," in Peter Duus, Ramon H. Myers, and Mark R. Peattie, eds., *The Japanese Informal Empire in China, 1895–1937* (Princeton, N.J.: Princeton University Press, 1989), p. 195; Rogaski, *Hygienic Modernity,* p. 199.

105. See Ueda, *Midori,* p. 87.

106. Honda, *Honda Seiroku,* p. 137. See Totman, *Japan's Imperial Forest,* p. 145. Taiwan was elevated to the status of a full province of China only in 1877.

107. Aoi, *Shokuminchi,* pp. 118–135.

108. Allen, "Taipei Park," pp. 172, 174, 177; Murasaki Nagaaki, *Taihoku shashinchō* (Taihoku: Shinkōdō Shoten, 1913), p. 6.

109. Hu Wenqing, *Taiwan de kungyuan* (Taibei: Yuanzu Wenhua, 2007), p. 190; Murasaki, *Taihoku shashinchō,* p. 24.

110. Chen Yuanyang, *Taiwan no genjūmin to kokka kōen* (Fukuoka: Kyushu Daigaku Shuppankai, 1999), pp. 91–92. See Huiyu Caroline Tsai, *Taiwan in Japan's Empire Building: An Institutional Approach to Colonial Engineering* (London: Routledge, 2009).

111. Oyadomari, "Politics," p. 214.

112. Tamura Tsuyoshi, "Taiwan kokuritsu kōen no shimei," *Taiwan no sanrin* 123 (1936): pp. 6–8. See Chen, *Taiwan*, p. 92.

113. Kōji Kanda, "Landscapes of National Parks in Taiwan During the Japanese Colonial Period," in Mizuuchi Toshio, ed., *Representing Local Places and Raising Voices from Below* (Osaka: Osaka City University, Department of Geography and Urban Culture Research Center, 2003), p. 113; Chen, *Taiwan*, p. 92.

114. Inagaki Ryūichi, "Taiwan ni okeru kokuritsu kōen mondai," *Kokuritsu kōen* 8, no. 1 (1936): pp. 7–9; Sōrifu, *Kankō*, p. 33; Chen, *Taiwan*, p. 92.

115. Kohama Seikō, "Kokuritsu kōen no shimei," *Taiwan no sanrin* 123 (1936): p. 4.

116. Hayasaka Ichirō, "Taiwan no kokuritsu kōen jigyō ni taisuru kibō," *Taiwan no sanrin* 123 (1936): p. 238.

117. Hayasaka Ichirō, "Taiwan no kokuritsu kōen," *Taiwan Hakubutsu Gakkai kaihō* 151 (1936): p. 189.

118. Ishikawa Sadatoshi, "Taiwan ni okeru kokuritsu kōen no enkaku," *Kokuritsu kōen* 10, no. 1 (1938): p. 7; Wei Hongjin, ed., *Taiwan de guojia kungyuan* (Taibei: Yuanzu Wenhua, 2002), p. 19; Yamagata Saburō, "Taiwan kokuritsu kōen no shitei ni atarite," *Kokuritsu kōen* 10, no. 1 (1938): p. 4; Iwata Shūkō, *Taiwan kokuritsu kōen gashū* (Taihoku: Taiwan Kokuritsu Kōen Kyōkai, 1940), preface.

119. Taiwan Kokuritsu Kōen Kyōkai, "Jo," in Okada Kōyō, *Taiwan kokuritsu kōen shashinshū* (Taihoku: Taiwan Kokuritsu Kōen Kyōkai, 1939), p. 1.

120. Yamagata, "Taiwan," pp. 4–5.

121. Kanda, "Landscapes," p. 113.

122. Wei, *Taiwan*, pp. 14–15; Kubo Mikio, "Taiwan no kokuritsu kōen," *Kokuritsu kōen* 386 (1982): p. 16; Wang Xianpu, "East Asia," in Jeffrey A. McNeely, Jeremy Harrison, and Paul R. Dingwell, eds., *Protecting Nature: Regional Reviews of Protected Areas* (Gland, Switz.: International Union for Conservation of Nature and Natural Resources, 1994), pp. 163, 165. Taiwan in 1972 enacted a law authorizing national parks and another establishing an Environment Agency. Alishan and Dadunshan (renamed Yangmingshan) became national parks in 1985, Taroko the next year, and others in the 1990s, including Jinmen (Quemoy) National Park in 1995. See Michael Szonyi, *Cold War Island: Quemoy on the Front Line* (New York: Cambridge University Press, 2008).

123. Tanaka, *Shizen*, p. 212. See Ellie Y. Choi, "Laying Claim to the Diamond Mountains: Travel and the Historical Imagination," paper, Association for Asian Studies Annual Meeting, Atlanta, Ga., April 3–6, 2008.

124. Ellie Y. Choi, "Space and National Identity: Yi Kwangsu's Vision of Korea during the Japanese Empire" (PhD dissertation, Harvard University, 2009), p. 30. See also pp. 200, 222.
125. Ishii Hiroshi and Woo Hyung Taek, "Kankoku no kokuritsu kōen (1)," *Kokuritsu kōen* 380 (1981), p. 6.
126. Aoi, *Shokuminchi,* p. 10. See pp. 150–151, 159–165 for data on shrines in Korea.
127. Henry, "Respatializing Chosŏn's Royal Capital," pp. 16–17.
128. Ishii and Woo, "Kankoku," p. 7.
129. Son Chŏng-mok [Sohn Jung Mok], *Nihon tōchika Chōsen toshi keikakushi kenkyū,* trans. Nishigaki Yasuhiko, Ichioka Miyuki, and Lee Jong Hee [Yi Chong-hŭi] (Tokyo: Kashiwa Shobō, 2004), pp. 121, 126–127; Woo Hyung Taek, "The Social Impacts of Land Use Planning in the National Parks of South Korea," in Patrick C. West and Steven R. Brechin, eds., *Resident Peoples and National Parks* (Tucson: University of Arizona Press, 1991), pp. 264–265. In South Korea a parks law in 1967 authorized national parks, and in 1980 a much broader Natural Parks Law was enacted. The country currently has eighteen national parks. In concert with private investors from the south, North Korea has undertaken development of the Diamond Mountains as a vacation spa long noted for its mineral waters and scenic beauty, as well as for its thousands of "slogan rocks" carved with sayings from President Kim Il-Sung (1912–1994) and his son and successor Kim Jong-il (1942–).
130. Ishida, *Nihon kindai toshi keikakushi kenkyū,* p. 199.

Chapter 3: Visions of a Green Tokyo

1. See Thornber, *Empire of Texts in Motion,* pp. 38–42, 46–58.
2. Tokyo Municipal Office, *The Reconstruction of Tokyo* (Tokyo: Tokyo Municipal Office, 1933), p. 3.
3. Ibid., p. 9; Tokyo Metropolitan Government, *Tokyo,* p. 32. See Gordon, *Labor and Imperial Democracy,* pp. 176–177.
4. Tokyo Municipal Office, *Reconstruction,* pp. 7–8.
5. Dan Inō, *The Reconstruction of Tokyo and Aesthetic Problems of Architecture* (Tokyo: Japan Council of the Institute of Pacific Relations, 1931), p. 4.
6. Sheldon Garon, *Molding Japanese Minds: The State in Everyday Life* (Princeton, N.J.: Princeton University Press, 1997), pp. 50–53.
7. Ishikawa, *Toshi,* p. 225. The figure includes ¥10 million for new park construction in Tokyo and ¥4.58 million in subventions from the national treasury. See Tokyo Municipal Office, *Reconstruction,* p. 294; Sally Ann Hastings, *Neighborhood and Nation in Tokyo, 1905–1937* (Pittsburgh: University of Pittsburgh Press, 1995), pp. 45–47.
8. See J. Charles Schencking, "The Great Kanto Earthquake and the Culture of Catastrophe and Reconstruction in 1920s Japan," *Journal of Japanese Studies* 34, no. 2 (2008): pp. 323–325.

9. Charles A. Beard, *The Administration and Politics of Tokyo: A Survey and Opinions* (New York: Macmillan, 1923), pp. 177–179.

10. Tokyo Municipal Office, *Reconstruction*, pp. 10, 288. According to *Teito fukkō jigyōshi*, in Nihon Toshi Sentā, *Toshi to kōen*, p. 55, Ueno Park hosted an estimated 500,000 evacuees, the Palace Outer Plaza 300,000, Shiba 200,000, and Hibiya 150,000; twelve others sheltered 420,000 persons. The total damage to Tokyo's twenty-eight city parks was estimated at ¥730,687.

11. *Teito fukkō jigyōshi*, quoted in Tokyoto, *Tokyo no kōen*, p. 23; Katō, *Yokohama*, p. 139; Shiojima, *Midori*, p. 14. See Uchiyama, *Toshi*, p. 179.

12. Ishikawa, *Toshi*, p. 222.

13. See Shin, *Toshi kōen*, pp. 161–162.

14. See Schencking, "Great Kanto Earthquake," pp. 295, 303, 316; Abe Isoo, "Teito no kensetsu to sōzōteki seishin," *Kaizō* 5, no. 11 (1923): pp. 49–71. For his *Toshi mondai*, see chapter 1.

15. Tokyoto, *Tokyo no kōen*, p. 23; Tokyo Metropolitan University, *Tokyo*, pp. 19–20; Ueda, *Midori*, pp. 88–89, 93–94; Tokyo Metropolitan Government, *Tokyo*, p. 34; Ichikawa, *Bunka*, p. 124. See Jordan Sand, *House and Home in Modern Japan: Architecture, Domestic Space, and Bourgeois Culture, 1880–1930* (Cambridge, Mass.: Harvard University Asia Center, 2003), pp. 203–221. Carryall is *furoshiki*.

16. Shin, *Toshi kōen*, p. 89.

17. Sorensen, *Making of Urban Japan*, pp. 122–123; Maruyama, *Kindai*, pp. 5–6. See Nishiyama, "Western Influence," pp. 318, 328–329; André Sorensen, *Land Readjustment and Metropolitan Growth: An Examination of Suburban Land Development and Urban Sprawl in the Tokyo Metropolitan Area* (Oxford, Eng.: Elsevier Science, 2000), p. 123.

18. Sorensen, *Making of Urban Japan*, pp. 122–123; Maruyama, *Kindai*, pp. 5–6. See Nishiyama, "Western Influence," pp. 318, 328–329; Tokyo Municipal Office, *Reconstruction*, p. 248; Ishikawa, *Toshi*, p. 229; Tokyo Metropolitan University, *Tokyo*, pp. 20–21.

19. Ichikawa, *Bunka*, p. 124; Tokyo Municipal Office, *Reconstruction*, pp. 115, 130; Maruyama, *Kindai*, p. 172; Kawamoto Akio, *Sumida Kōen* (Tokyo: Kyōgakusha, 1981), pp. 18–20; Watanabe Shun'ichi, "Planning History of the Capital Tokyo" (unpublished manuscript, Tokyo University of Science, 2005), p. 3.

20. Ichikawa, *Bunka*, pp. 124–126; Ueda, *Midori*, pp. 94–95; Ishikawa, *Toshi*, p. 229; Schencking, "Great Kanto Earthquake," pp. 323–325.

21. Teito Fukkōin, *Fukkō keikaku* (November 1923), quoted in Shiojima, *Midori*, p. 14. See Koshizawa Akira, *Fukkō keikaku: Bakumatsu no taika kara Hanshin Awaji daishinsai made* (Tokyo: Chūō Kōronsha, 2005).

22. Maruyama, *Kindai*, pp. 7, 149.

23. Ōya Reijō, *Kōen oyobi undōjō: Keikaku sekkei sekō* (Tokyo: Shōkabō, 1930), pp. 1–42.

24. Jinnai, *Tokyo*, pp. 198–199; Shirahata, *Kindai*, p. 229; Sanada, *Toshi*, pp. 37–44.

25. Ueda, *Midori*, p. 96; Takashi Itoh, "Design and Layout Plan of Bridges and Parks in Reconstruction Project after the Great Kanto Earthquake," in Tokyo Metropolitan University, ed., *Tokyo: Urban Growth and Planning* (Tokyo: Tokyo Metropolitan University, 1998), p. 98. Fifteen new parks were in today's Taitō Ward, eleven in Chūō, eight in Sumida, seven each in Kōtō and Chiyoda, and two each in Minato and Bunkyō.

26. Kawamoto, *Sumida*, pp. i, 25; Tokyo Municipal Office, *Reconstruction*, p. 293; Ishikawa, *Toshi*, p. 227; Ueda, *Midori*, p. 97.

27. Shin, *Toshi kōen*, pp. 92–93; Ishikawa, *Toshi*, p. 228; Sakamoto, *Nihon*, p. 18; Ueda, *Midori*, p. 97.

28. Inoshita Kiyoshi, *Inoshita Kiyoshi chosakushū toshi to midori* (Tokyo: Tokyoto Kōen Kyōkai, 1973), pp. 104–107, from a contribution to *Teien to fūkei* dated March 1932.

29. Katō, *Yokohama*, p. 145; Satō and Shimoyama, *Landscape Planning*, p. 2; Ishikawa, *Toshi*, pp. 225, 228; Ueda, *Midori*, p. 97; Itoh, "Design," p. 99; Tokyoto Zōen Kensetsu Jigyō Kyōdō Kumiai, ed., *Midori no Tokyoshi* (Tokyo: Shikōsha, 1979), p. 2.

30. Katō, *Yokohama*, p. 138; Tokyo Municipal Office, *Reconstruction*, p. 34; Schencking, "Great Kanto Earthquake," p. 296.

31. Dan, *Reconstruction*, p. 2; Katō, *Yokohama*, p. 142. Cf. budgeted figures for reconstruction in Tokyo Municipal Office, *Reconstruction*, pp. 166–167.

32. Tokyo Metropolitan Government, *Hundred Years*, p. 22; Nakabayashi Itsuki, "Concentration and Deconcentration in the Context of the Tokyo Capital Region Plan and Recent Cross-Border Networking Concepts," in Carola Hein and Philippe Pelletier, eds., *Cities, Autonomy, and Decentralization in Japan* (London: Routledge, 2006), p. 55.

33. Sorensen, *Making of Urban Japan*, p. 125.

34. Tokyo Metropolitan Government, *Tokyo*, p. 38.

35. Katō, *Yokohama*, pp. 264–265.

36. Shin, *Toshi kōen*, p. 117; Ueda, *Midori*, p. 306.

37. Maejima, *Inokashira*, pp. i–ii, 33–38, 107; Shin, *Toshi kōen*, p. 117; Ueda, *Midori*, pp. 97, 306, 309.

38. See data compiled by Inoshita Kiyoshi in 1931, reprinted in *Inoshita Kiyoshi chosakushū*, pp. 98–103; Ueda, *Midori*, pp. 122–124.

39. Suematsu, *Tokyo*, 2:50–51; Kobayashi, *Ueno*, p. 70; Tokyo Municipal Office, *Reconstruction*, p. 288.

40. Suematsu, *Tokyo*, 2:55–56; Tokyoto, *Tokyo no kōen*, p. 24; Kobayashi, *Ueno*, p. 70; Ueda, *Midori*, pp. 97–98, 307, 317.

41. Maejima, *Tokyo*, p. 234; Ueda, *Midori*, p. 124.

42. Ueda, *Midori*, pp. 61–63; Jinnai, *Tokyo*, pp. 32–33. See Thomas S. Hardy, "People of the Garden: Aesthetics in Everyday Life in a Tokyo Neighborhood" (PhD Dissertation, New School for Social Research, 1986), pp. 65–66.

43. Tokyo Metropolitan Park Association, *Koishikawa Korakuen Gardens* (Tokyo: Tokyo Metropolitan Park Association, 2005); *Koishikawa Kōrakuen*, wooden plaque outside main entrance to the park.

44. Tokyoto, *Tokyo no kōen*, p. 35; Yoshikawa Matsu and Takahashi Yasuo, *Koishikawa Kōrakuen*, 3rd ed. (Tokyo: Tokyoto Kōen Kyōkai, 2001), pp. 61–63.

45. Ueda, *Midori*, p. 304; Kosugi Takemi, *Hama Rikyū Teien*, rev. ed. (Tokyo: Tokyoto Kōen Kyōkai, 1994), pp. 4–5, 36–38, 43–44.

46. Ueda, *Midori*, p. 309; Kosugi, *Hama Rikyū Teien*, pp. iii, 36, 48–49, 55–62.

47. Morohashi Tetsuji, *Dai Kanwa jiten* (Tokyo: Taishūkan Shoten, 1956), 2:50–51; Tokyo Metropolitan Park Association, *Rikugien* (Tokyo: Tokyo Metropolitan Park Association, 2006); Mori Mamoru, *Rikugien*, 3rd ed. (Tokyo: Tokyoto Kōen Kyōkai, 2001), p. i; Club Smart Life, *Tokyo*, p. 62.

48. Ueda, *Midori*, p. 308; Mori, *Rikugien*, pp. 106–108, 120–124, 130.

49. Other daimyo properties that became public spaces include the Naitō house grounds where Shinjuku Imperial Garden Park now stands, the Aoyama family estate that was turned into Aoyama Cemetery, the Morioka Nanbu residence that was renamed Prince Arisugawa Memorial Park in 1934, the Hosokawa villa that is now the site of Shin Edogawa Park near Mejiro, and the vast Maeda holdings that became campuses of Tokyo University at Hongō and Komaba, including Komaba Park, with its excellent Library of Modern Japanese Literature. See Club Smart Life, *Tokyo*, pp. 32, 50–52; Jinnai, *Tokyo*, pp. 24–25.

50. Club Smart Life, *Tokyo*, p. 74; Tokyo Metropolitan Park Association, *Mukōjima Hyakkaen* (Tokyo: Tokyo Metropolitan Park Association, 2006).

51. Inoshita, *Inoshita Kiyoshi chosakushū*, p. 102; Maejima, *Tokyo*, pp. 184–188; Ueda, *Midori*, pp. 97–98; Shin, *Toshi kōen*, p. 118; Tokyo Metropolitan Park Association, *Kiyosumi Teien* (Tokyo: Tokyo Metropolitan Park Association, 2006). See Loraine E. Kuck, *World of the Japanese Garden: From Chinese Origins to Modern Landscape Art* (New York: Weatherhill, 1966), pp. 246–247.

52. Inoshita, *Inoshita Kiyoshi chosakushū*, pp. 102–103; Ueda, *Midori*, pp. 123–124; Tokyoto, *Tokyo no kōen*, pp. 32–33; Maejima, *Tokyo*, pp. 234–235.

53. Inoue Enryō, *Tetsugakudō annai*, rev. ed. (Tokyo: Tetsugakudō, 1924), p. 1. See Club Smart Life, *Tokyo*, p. 150; Ueda, *Midori*, p. 309; Okada Masahiko, "Taking a Walk around the Hall of Philosophy: Science, Philosophy and Religion in Modern Japan," lecture, University of Chicago, May 1, 2005, pp. 1–3.

54. *Kyū Furukawa Teien* (Tokyo: Tokyoto Kōen Kyōkai, 2004).

55. Suematsu, *Tokyo*, 2:55.

56. See Thomas R. H. Havens, *Artist and Patron in Postwar Japan: Dance, Music, Theater, and the Visual Arts, 1955–1980* (Princeton, N.J.: Princeton University Press, 1982), pp. 33–36.

57. Shin, *Toshi kōen*, p. 109.

58. Ishida, "Local," p. 34.

59. Kimura Hideo, *Toshi bōkū to ryokuchi kūchi* (Tokyo: Nihon Kōen Ryokuchi Kyōkai, 1990), p. 39.

60. Sakamoto, *Nihon*, p. 16; Nihon Toshi Sentā, *Toshi*, p. 87; Nihon Kōen Ryokuchi Kyōkai, ed., *Nihon no toshi kōen* (Tokyo: Nihon Kōen Ryokuchi Kyōkai, 1978), pp. 2–3, 144f.

61. Ishikawa, *Toshi*, p. 14. As of 1936, city planning districts nationwide covered 19,900 hectares, 370 hectares of which were parklands. At 1.9 percent, this fell short of the Home Ministry's modest goal of 3 percent.

62. Maruyama, *Kindai*, pp. 211–212; Shin, *Toshi*, p. 110.

63. Osaka Shiyakusho, *An Outline of Municipal Administration of the City of Osaka, 1930* (Osaka: Osaka Shiyakusho, 1930), pp. 69–72; Maruyama, *Kindai*, p. 214; Ishikawa, *Toshi*, pp. 235–237.

64. Nakayama, *Osaka*, p. 20; Ishikawa, *Toshi*, p. 237.

65. Kimura, *Toshi*, p. 39.

66. See Maruyama, *Kindai*, pp. 216–217; Hanayama Yuzuru, *Land Markets and Land Policy in a Metropolitan Area: A Case Study of Tokyo* (Boston: Oelgeschlager, Gunn & Hain, 1986), pp. 37–38, 41.

67. Tanaka, *Tokyo*, pp. 47–60; Ueda, *Midori*, p. 102; Kensetsushō, ed., *Nihon no toshi seisaku* (Tokyo: Gyōsei, 1984), p. 331; Nihon Kōen Ryokuchi Kyōkai, *Kōen ryokuchi manyuaru*, p. 394. Scenic districts are *fūchi*; famous vistas are *meishō*.

68. Club Smart Life, *Tokyo*, p. 112; Sumiko Enbutsu, "Drenched in History: Scenic Senzoku Pond," *Japan Times* online, October 3, 2003; Ueda, *Midori*, pp. 100–102.

69. Nihon Kōen Ryokuchi Kyōkai, *Kōen ryokuchi manyuaru*, pp. 402, 420; Kensetsushō, *Nihon no toshi seisaku*, p. 329. Historical and cultural preservation districts are *rekishiteki fūdo hozon kuiki*.

70. Kimura, *Toshi*, p. 39.

71. Tokyoto, *Tokyo no kōen*, p. 27; Tokyo Metropolitan University, *Tokyo*, p. 23; Ishikawa, *Toshi*, p. 244; Sanada, *Toshi*, pp. 110–111. The fifty-kilometer radius embraced 9,620 square kilometers.

72. Ueda, *Midori*, pp. 113–114; Hirano Kanzō, "Kitamura Tokutarō: Nihon no ryokuchi keikaku no paionia," *Randosukēpu kenkyū* 58, no. 1 (1994): pp. 1–2; Ishikawa, *Toshi*, pp. 233–234.

73. Ishikawa, *Toshi*, p. 247; Sanada, *Toshi*, p. 23.

74. Nihon Kōen Ryokuchi Kyōkai, *Kōen ryokuchi manyuaru*, p. 11; Tokyo Metropolitan University, *Tokyo*, p. 23.

75. Sanada, *Toshi*, pp. 110–111. On p. 25 Sanada questions whether military concerns about the health of recruits played much part in the discourse about the Green Space Plan.

76. Ishikawa, *Toshi*, pp. 248, 250; Tokyo Metropolitan University, *Tokyo*, p. 23; Ueda, *Midori*, pp. 108–109; Sanada, *Toshi*, p. 30; Ishida, *Nihon kindai toshi keikakushi kenkyū*, p. 205; Shin, *Toshi kōen*, pp. 112–113.

77. Ishikawa, *Toshi,* pp. 250–251; Ishida, *Nihon kindai toshi keikakushi kenkyū,* p. 206. The proposed 180 scenic roadways reached 3,824 kilometers in total length.

78. Tokyo Ryokuchi Keikaku Kyōgikai, *Jiko shūroku* (Tokyo: Tokyo Ryokuchi Keikaku Kyōgikai, 1939), quoted in Sanada, *Toshi,* p. 84.

79. Ishida, *Nihon kindai toshi keikakushi kenkyū,* p. 206; Sorensen, *Making of Urban Japan,* pp. 144–145; Watanabe, "Planning," p. 3; Tokyoto Toshi Seibikyoku Toshi Kibanbu Shisetsu Keikakuka Kōen Ryokuchi Tantō, ed., *Midori no shinsenryaku gaidorain* (Tokyo: Tokyoto, 2006), p. 50; Nihon Kōen Ryokuchi Kyōkai, *Kōen ryokuchi manyuaru,* pp. 16–17, 417; Ueda, *Midori,* p. 328. See Satō and Shimoyama, *Landscape Planning,* pp. 12–13. Other allocations within the 145 square kilometers were 15 for schoolyards, 10 for public organizations, 18 for residents' garden plots, 18 for small farms, and 9 for roads. Urban farmland is taxed at rates much lower than developed land, so that Tokyo Prefecture as of 2004 still had 38 square kilometers of farm plots.

80. Sanada, *Toshi,* pp. 9–10; Shin, *Toshi kōen,* p. 109.

81. Ono, *Kōen no tanjō,* pp. 185–186; Ishida, *Nihon kindai toshi keikakushi kenkyū,* pp. 199, 204.

82. Kōseishō statement, 1938, quoted in Shin, *Toshi kōen,* p. 124. See Maruyama, *Kindai,* p. 138, 149–151.

83. Shin, *Toshi kōen,* p. 128.

84. Maruyama, *Kindai,* p. 154.

85. Kimura, *Toshi,* p. 36.

86. Shin, *Toshi kōen,* p. 121.

87. Ibid., pp. 154–155; Sanada, *Toshi,* pp. 26–27, 33. See Sandra Collins, *The 1940 Tokyo Games: The Missing Olympics* (London: Routledge, 2007).

88. Satō and Shimoyama, *Landscape Planning,* p. 3; Ishiuchi Nobuyuki, *Kinuta Ryokuchi (Kinuta Fuamirī Pāku)* (Tokyo: Kyōgakusha, 1981), pp. 13–15. See Ueda, *Midori,* p. 125. The twenty-six cities gained a total of twenty-four square kilometers of commemorative parks. The ¥25 million Tokyo allocation in 1940 included ¥17.3 million for land acquisition across five years and ¥7.7 million for construction, facilities, equipment, administration, and contingencies.

89. Ishida, *Nihon kindai toshi keikakushi kenkyū,* p. 210; Ishiuchi, *Kinuta,* p. 56.

90. Tokyo Metropolitan Government, *Hundred Years,* pp. 36, 38; Ueda, *Midori,* p. 109; Satō and Shimoyama, *Landscape Planning,* p. 3.

91. Maruyama, *Kindai,* p. 176.

92. Tokyoto, *Tokyo no kōen,* p. 32; Ishikawa, *Toshi,* p. 14; Kimura, *Toshi,* p. 36; Sakamoto, *Nihon,* p. 22. The government allocated ¥10.6 million to buy vacant land in 1939, ¥15.7 million in 1940, and ¥24.5 million in 1941.

93. Tokyoto, *Tokyo no kōen,* pp. 30–33; Sakamoto, *Nihon,* p. 23. Tokyo City (Tokyoshi) and Tokyo Prefecture (Tokyofu) were merged in July 1943 into Tokyo Metropolis (Tokyoto), which functioned like a prefecture. The twenty-three special wards of Tokyo Metropolis, at 621 square kilometers, corresponded closely with the thirty-five

wards of Tokyo City in existence between 1932 and 1943. As of 1943 the metropolis directly administered 166 city parks. After the war many were transferred to the wards, so that the metropolis today administers 80. The wards also assumed responsibility for 173 small parks, including financing them. See Shin, *Toshi kōen*, pp. 197, 218.

94. Nakabayashi, "Concentration," p. 58.

95. Tokyo Metropolitan University, *Tokyo*, p. 25; Ichikawa, *Bunka*, p. 126.

96. Nihon Kōen Ryokuchi Kyōkai, *Kōen ryokuchi manyuaru*, p. 11.

97. Ibid., p. 12; Tokyoto, *Tokyo no kōen*, pp. 38–39. In 1946 the parks housed 2,865 families. For details of the air raids, see Thomas R. H. Havens, *Valley of Darkness: The Japanese People and World War Two* (Lanham, Md.: University Press of America, 1986), pp. 176–188.

98. Kobayashi, *Ueno*, pp. 76–78; Shinji Isoya, *"Nō" no jidai—surō na machizukuri* (Kyoto: Gakugei Shuppansha, 2003), pp. 129–130; Seidensticker, *Low City*, p. 137, notes that by August 1945 the largest animals remaining at the Ueno Zoo were three camels, two giraffes, and a water buffalo. Two elephants refused to eat poisoned food and were deliberately starved to death by the keepers.

99. Suzuki and Sawada, *Kōen no hanashi*, pp. 135–136.

100. Tokyoto Irei Kyōkai, ed., *Sensai ōshita kaisō jigyō shimatsuki* (Tokyo: Tokyoto Irei Kyōkai, 1985), pp. 38–40. See Kawamoto, *Sumida*, p. 30.

101. Kobayashi, *Ueno*, p. 80; Nihon Kōen Ryokuchi Kyōkai, *Kōen ryokuchi manyuaru*, p. 12; Shin, *Toshi kōen*, p. 182; Cary Caracas, "Remembering and Memorializing the Tokyo Air Raids" (unpublished manuscript, University of California, Berkeley, 2003), pp. 4, 9–10. In 2001 Ishihara Shintarō, governor of Tokyo, dedicated a peace monument at the Memorial Hall in Yokoamichō Park to honor the memory of those killed in the air raids.

102. John W. Dower, *Embracing Defeat: Japan in the Wake of World War II* (New York: W. W. Norton, 1999), p. 561.

103. Satō and Shimoyama, *Landscape Planning*, p. 4.

104. See Sakamoto, *Nihon*, p. 32.

105. Toshi Bōsai Bika Kyōkai, *Tokyoto ni okeru sengo 50nen no kōen ryokuchi no hensen ni kansuru chōsa* (Tokyo: Toshi Bōsai Bika Kyōkai, 1997), p. 10; Shin, *Toshi kōen*, p. 140.

106. Ueda, *Midori*, p. 133.

107. Suzuki and Sawada, *Kōen no hanashi*, pp. 5–6; Hanayama, *Land*, p. 23; Shin, *Toshi kōen*, p. 140.

108. Shin, *Toshi kōen*, p. 140.

109. Ibid., pp. 141–142. Converted lands for farming were limited to the lesser of 10 percent of a city planning district or three hectares.

110. Ueda, *Midori*, p. 129; Sōrifu, *Kankō*, p. 89.

111. Nihon Kōen Ryokuchi Kyōkai, *Kōen ryokuchi manyuaru*, p. 12. See Sakamoto, *Nihon*, pp. 27–28; Ishikawa, *Toshi*, p. 15.

112. Shin, *Toshi kōen*, p. 143; Tokyoto, *Tokyo no kōen*, p. 42; Sōrifu, *Kankō*, p. 90.

113. Kokuyū Zaisanhō, June 1948, quoted in Ueda, *Midori*, p. 120.

114. Shin, *Toshi kōen*, pp. 148–149; Sakamoto, *Nihon*, p. 27.

115. Ueda, *Midori*, p. 193.

116. Toshi Bōsai, *Tokyoto*, p. 20; Ueda, *Midori*, p. 194.

117. Ueda, *Midori*, pp. 147–148.

118. Sōrifu, *Kankō*, p. 90; Ishikawa, *Toshi*, pp. 260–261.

119. Nihon Toshi, *Toshi*, p. 88; Nihon Kōen Ryokuchi Kyōkai, *Kōen ryokuchi manyuaru*, pp. 14–15; Sakamoto, *Nihon*, p. 24; Ishida, "Local," pp. 35–36. For the text of the 1946 law, see Ueda, *Midori*, pp. 127–128. See also Itō Kunie, *Kōen no yō to bi* (Kyoto: Dōhōsha, 1988), pp. 2–5.

120. Suematsu, *Tokyo*, 2:41.

121. Ueda, *Midori*, pp. 310–311; Tokyo Metropolitan University, *Tokyo*, p. 27. See Nakabayashi, "Concentration," pp. 58–60; Carola Hein, "Visionary Plans and Planners: Japanese Traditions and Western Influences," in Nicholas Fiévé and Paul Waley, eds., *Japanese Capitals in Historical Perspective: Place, Power and Memory in Kyoto, Edo and Tokyo* (London: RoutledgeCurzon, 2003), p. 325; Sorensen, *Making of Urban Japan*, pp. 163–164.

122. Watanabe, "Planning," p. 304.

123. Ichikawa, *Bunka*, p. 127; Tokyo Metropolitan Government, *City Planning*, pp. 36, 114. Cf. Gerhard Larsson, *Land Readjustment: A Modern Approach to Urbanization* (Brookfield, Vt.: Avebury, 1993), pp. 18–19; Hanayama, *Land*, p. 43.

124. Nakabayashi, "Concentration," p. 61.

125. Toshi Bōsai, *Tokyoto*, p. 12. Tokyo's budget to operate parks in 1948 was just ¥13 million ($36,000), plus ¥3 million from concession and admission fees.

126. Sorensen, *Making of Urban Japan*, p. 165.

127. Ishikawa, *Toshi*, p. 263; Tokyo Metropolitan University, *Tokyo*, p. 27.

128. See Nakabayashi, "Concentration," p. 61.

Chapter 4: Parks and Prosperity, 1950s–1980s

1. Richey, *Study*, p. 11.

2. Tamura, *Nihon no kokuritsu kōen*, pp. 154–156, calculates that as of late 1950, about 18 percent of the area of Japanese national parks was privately owned. Natural park is *shizen kōen*.

3. Tamura, *Kokuritsu kōen kōwa*, p. 74.

4. Ibid., pp. 1, 3. The Mountain Village Promotion Law of 1970 sought, with indifferent results, to stimulate tourism in rapidly depopulating rural communities.

5. Azuma Ryōzō, *Amerika kokuritsu kōen kō* (Tokyo: Awaji Shobō, 1948), pp. 22–23.

6. Tamura, *Kokuritsu kōen kōwa*, p. 59. See Sōrifu, *Kankō*, p. 34; Koji Matsushita and Kunihiro Hirata, "Forestry Owners' Associations," in Yoshiya Iwai, ed., *Forestry and*

the *Forest Industry in Japan* (Vancouver: University of British Columbia Press, 2002), p. 43.

7. Koji Matsushita, "National Forest Management," in Yoshiya Iwai, ed., *Forestry and the Forest Industry in Japan* (Vancouver: University of British Columbia Press, 2002), p. 84; Itō, "Forestry," p. 94.

8. Sōrifu, *Kankō*, p. 83.

9. *Daily Yomiuri*, May 6, 2008, p. 3. National people's parks are *kokumin kōen*. West of the imperial castle, the Chidorigafuchi National Cemetery was established in 1953 on one hectare to honor Japan's unknown civilian and military dead from World War Two. Kankyōshō, *Kankyō hakusho*, p. 145; Tokyoto, *Tokyo no kōen*, p. 45; Sōrifu, *Kankō*, p. 83. See Shin, *Toshi kōen*, pp. 193–194.

10. *Japan Times* online, March 2, 2007. The Yodobashi water filtration plant was replaced by a newer facility at Wadabori, Ōhara, Setagaya Ward, in 1965. The Yodobashi site was developed as Tokyo's first skyscraper district after height restrictions were lifted in 1971 and includes Tange Kenzō's striking City Hall (1991). Shinjuku Imperial Garden is Shinjuku Gyoen.

11. Kanai Toshihiko, *Shinjuku Gyoen*, rev. ed. (Tokyo: Tokyoto Kōen Kyōkai, 1993), p. 39. See pp. 33–34; *Japan Times* online, December 25, 2003, November 12, 2004, March 2, 2007; Ishikawa, *Toshi*, p. 206; Ueda, *Midori*, p. 84.

12. Kanai, *Shinjuku*, pp. 46–49; Shin, *Toshi kōen*, p. 196.

13. Oyadomari, "Politics," pp. 294–295. See pp. 71–73 for details of jurisdictional disputes among the Welfare Ministry, Forestry Agency, Education Ministry, Transport Ministry, Land Development Agency, and Ministry of International Trade and Industry from the late 1940s until 1971. In the 1950s as much as 60 percent of sulfur produced in Japan was mined in national parks. Foreign visitors to Japan rose from 56,000 in 1951 to 212,000 in 1960. See Tamura, *Kokuritsu kōen kōwa*, p. 59.

14. Kokuritsu Kōen Kyōkai and Nihon Shizen Hogo Kyōkai, eds., *Nihon no shizen kōen* (Tokyo: Kōdansha, 1989), p. 8.

15. Ueda, *Midori*, p. 144.

16. Tawara Hiromi, *Hokkaido no shizen hogo: Sono rekishi to shisō*, expanded ed. (Sapporo: Hokkaido Daigaku Tosho Kankōkai, 1987), p. 237.

17. Ibid., p. 44. See Tawara, "Shizen," pp. 113–114.

18. Tokyoto, *Tokyo no kōen*, p. 49; Tokyoto Kensetsukyoku Kōen Ryokuchibu, *Tokyoto no shizen kōen: Sono genjō to shōrai* (Tokyo: Tokyoto Kensetsukyoku Kōen Ryokuchibu, 1966), pp. 3–4; Ueda, *Midori*, p. 142; Waseda, *Kokuritsu*, pp. 4–5. For a more favorable view of protections in the 1957 law, see Uchiyama, *Toshi*, p. 7.

19. Kōseishō Kokuritsu Kōenkyoku and Kokuritsu Kōen Kyōkai, *Nihon no kokuritsu kōen* (Osaka: Sanwa Ginkō, 1964), pp. 103–104. Quasi-national parks are *kokutei kōen*.

20. Nihon Kōtsū Kōsha, *Kokuritsu kōen to kokutei kōen* (Tokyo: Nihon Kōtsū Kōsha, 1970), p. 29.

21. Zenkoku, *Shizen,* 2:394; Shibano Kōichirō, *Kankyōchō* (Tokyo: Kyōikusha, 1975), p. 73.

22. Tawara, "Shizen," p. 128. See Tamura, *Nihon no kokuritsu kōen,* p. 257; Nihon Shizen Hogo Kyōkai, *Yutaka,* p. 13.

23. Takao Shinrin Sentā, *Mori e yōkoso* (Hachiōji: Rin'yachō Kanto Shinrin Kanrikyoku, 2005); "Takaosan ni Tonneru o Horasenai" Hyakumannin Shomei Jikkō Iinkai, *Kokutei kōen Takaosan no shizen o Ken'ōdō kara mamorō!!* (pamphlet distributed at Keiō Takaosanguchi Station, May 8, 2005); *Mainichi Daily News* online, April 14, 2008. Michelin gave Takaosan three stars in its 2007 guide, the same as Fuji, presumably for its exceptional flora. About three fifths of the park's 770 hectares are national forests.

24. "Takaosan ni," *Kokutei; Japan Times* online, April 23, 2004; *Daily Yomiuri,* July 8, 2007, p. 24.

25. Senge Tetsumaro, "The Educational Contributions of National Parks in Japan," in Alexander B. Adams, ed., *First World Conference on National Parks: Proceedings* (Washington, D.C.: National Park Service, U.S. Department of the Interior, 1962), p. 241.

26. Kokuritsu Kōen Kyōkai, comp., *National Parks of Japan* (Tokyo: Tokyo News Service, 1957), pp. 8, 12; Tamura Tsuyoshi, "Introduction," in Kokuritsu Kōen Kyōkai, comp., *National Parks of Japan* (Tokyo: Tokyo News Service, 1957), pp. 2–3; Carol Thornber, personal communication, November 18, 2005.

27. *Kokusei chōsa,* cited in Shiojima, *Midori,* p. 29. From 1950 to 1975 the four prefectures' urbanized area grew from 1,006 to 2,332 square kilometers and their combined population rose from 12.7 million in 1950 to 17.8 million in 1960.

28. Tokyo Metropolitan University, *Tokyo,* pp. 27–28.

29. Quoted in Ueda, *Midori,* p. 148.

30. Tawara, *Hokkaido,* p. 48.

31. Nihon Toshi Sentā, *Toshi,* p. 89; Sakamoto, *Nihon,* p. 32; Sōrifu, *Kankō,* p. 91; Shin, *Toshi kōen,* pp. 149–150. Tokyoto, *Tokyo no kōen,* p. 48, states that Tokyo in 1956 had 1.1 square meters of city parkland per capita, compared with 7.6 for Chicago, 11.9 for New York, 19.8 for Boston, and 45.3 for Washington, D.C. in 1940.

32. Shin, *Toshi kōen,* p. 165.

33. Ishikawa, *Toshi,* pp. 294–295; Tokyo Metropolitan University, *Tokyo,* p. 28.

34. Sanada, *Toshi,* p. 76.

35. *National Report of Japan Prepared for Habitat: United Nations Conference on Human Settlements* (Tokyo: Government of Japan, 1976), pp. 13–14. The National Land Development Plan, obsolete even before it was announced in 1962, called for fifteen new industrial cities and six industrial development zones.

36. Tokyo Metropolitan University, *Tokyo,* p. 29.

37. Tokyoto, *Tokyo no kōen,* p. 47.

38. Ueda, *Midori,* p. 165; Tokyoto, *Tokyo no kōen,* p. 47; Kōen Ryokuchi Iji Kanri Kenkyūkai, ed., *Kōen ryokuchi no iji kanri to sekisan,* 4th rev. ed. (Tokyo: Keizai

Chōsakai, 2005), pp. 28–29; Tokyoto Seikatsu Bunkakyoku Kokusai Kōryūbu Gaijika, *3rd Long-Term Plan for the Tokyo Metropolis* (Tokyo: Tokyo Metropolitan Government, 1991), preface; Tokyo Metropolitan University, *Tokyo*, pp. 32–33; Watanabe, "Planning," p. 5; Nakabayashi, "Concentration," pp. 68, 71–72; Tokyoto Toshi Keikakukyoku Sōmubu, ed., *Planning of Tokyo* (Tokyo: Tokyoto, 2002), p. 8. See Hanayama, *Land*, p. 25. The number of city parks rose from 4,479 in 1956 to 12,219 in 1971 and their area from 148 to 236 square kilometers. From 1982 to 1991 Tokyo came up with three long-term plans of its own, partly to offset successive capital region plans. The Capital Region Suburban Green Space Protection Law is Shutoken Kinkō Ryokuchi Hozenhō.

39. Sōrifu, *Kankō*, p. 93; Ishikawa, *Toshi*, p. 16; Satō and Shimoyama, *Landscape Planning*, p. 16; Ueda, *Midori*, p. 164. Ishikawa, *Toshi*, p. 295, argues that few green spaces were protected under the 1966 law.

40. Aikawa and Fuse, *Yoyogi*, pp. 7, 18; Tokyoto, *Tokyo no kōen*, p. 53; Ueda, *Midori*, pp. 183–184; Sumiko Enbutsu, "It's a Stroll in the Park to Find the Old Yoyogi," *Japan Times* online, December 3, 2004.

41. Club Smart Life, *Tokyo*, p. 34; National Science Museum, Tokyo, *The Institute for Nature Study* (Tokyo: National Science Museum, 1992).

42. Ibid., p. 88; Ueda, *Midori*, p. 192; *Japan Times* online, April 29, 2004.

43. Tokyo Daigaku Daigakuin Rigakukei Kenkyūka Fuzoku Shokubutsuen, ed., *Koishikawa Shokubutsuen to Nikkō Shokubutsuen* (Tokyo: Koishikawa Shokubutsuen Kōenkai, 2004), pp. 6–7, 20, 36, 42, 46, 68, 75–76; Kawakami Sachio, *Koishikawa Shokubutsuen* (Tokyo: Kyōgakusha, 1981), pp. i, 5, 7, 9; Club Smart Life, *Tokyo*, p. 60.

44. Hokkaido University, *The Botanic Garden Field Science Center for Northern Biosphere* (Sapporo: Hokkaido University, 2005).

45. Short, *Nature in Tokyo*, p. 55.

46. Ueda, *Midori*, p. 201.

47. Satō and Shimoyama, *Landscape Planning*, p. 26; Shin, *Toshi kōen*, p. 243.

48. Nakayama, *Osaka*, pp. 23–24.

49. Tokyo Metropolitan Government, *City Planning*, p. 97.

50. Ibid., p. 24; Satō and Shimoyama, *Landscape Planning*, pp. 7, 16.

51. Ishida, "Local," p. 38; Hanayama, *Land*, p. 109. The Local Government Research Institute is Jichitai Kenkyūsha.

52. Naikaku Sōridaijin Kanbō Kōhōshitsu, *Toshi kōen ni kansuru seron chōsa* (Tokyo: Naikaku, 1967), pp. 2–9.

53. Itō, "Forestry," p. 85. Figures are for 1971. On postwar economic policy, see Laura E. Hein, "Growth Versus Success: Japan's Economic Policy in Historical Perspective," in Andrew Gordon, ed., *Postwar Japan as History* (Berkeley: University of California Press, 1993), especially pp. 110–120.

54. Senge, "Educational," pp. 241–245; Kankyōchō, *Quality of the Environment in Japan 1980* (Tokyo: Ōkurashō Insatsukyoku, 1981), p. 300. In 1961 centrally appointed

park rangers numbered just fifty-two; only forty-seven more had been hired by 1980. Local governments hired their own rangers or relied on volunteers.

55. Shin, *Toshi kōen,* pp. 167–168; Waseda, *Kokuritsu,* p. 5.

56. Nihon Shizen Hogo Kyōkai, *Yutaka,* pp. 18–19; Oyadomari, "Politics," p. 344.

57. Shoji Mitsui, "National and Regional Forest Policies," in Yoshiya Iwai, ed., *Forestry and the Forest Industry in Japan* (Vancouver: University of British Columbia Press, 2002), pp. 145–147; Roy, "National Forest," pp. 60, 69; Totman, *History,* p. 499. Gaimushō, *Environment,* p. 46, points out that in 1991, 86 percent of Japan's planted forests were younger than thirty-five years old, not yet ready for harvest.

58. Totman, *History,* p. 500. See Yoshiya Iwai, "New Relationship between Forests and City Dwellers in Japan," in Yoshiya Iwai, ed., *Forestry and the Forest Industry in Japan* (Vancouver: University of British Columbia Press, 2002), p. 279; Iwai, "Introduction," p. xvii. In 2000 plantation forests, mainly pine and eucalyptus, covered 1.9 million square kilometers worldwide, up from 1.2 million in 1995. China and India accounted for 42 percent of the total in 2000. Stephen Hesse, "Industrial Forestry: Too Much of a Good Thing," *Japan Times* online, November 26, 2005. See *Mainichi shinbun* online, April 20, 2009; *Japan Today* online, April 24, 2009; *Daily Yomiuri,* May 13, 2009, p. 4.

59. Iwai, "New Relationship," p. 278; Iwai, "Introduction," pp. xvi–xvii.

60. Summarized in Ishimure Michiko, *Tenko* (Tokyo: Asahi Shinbunsha, 1997). The Nature Conservation Society of Japan is Nihon Shizen Hogo Kyōkai. Global warming is thought to bring deer to Oze, destroying wetlands and grasses. *Mainichi shinbun* online, November 23, 2009.

61. *Japan Times* online, September 11, 2008; Martin Fackler, "Grass-Roots Uprising Against River Dam Challenges Tokyo," *New York Times* online, March 3, 2009; Nihon Shizen Hogo Kyōkai, *Yutaka,* pp. 16–17; *Kyōdō News on the Web,* June 26, 2008; Bruce Allen, "Introduction," in Ishimure Michiko, "*Lake of Heaven,* Dams, and Japan's Transformation," trans. Bruce Allen, *Japan Focus* online, February 27, 2006, pp. 1–2; Hoyano Hatsuko, "Struggle over the Arase Dam: Japan's First Dam Removal Begins," trans. Adam Lebowitz, *Japan Focus* online, July 30, 2004, pp. 1–2. The Arase Dam in Kumamoto, erected in 1955, was ordered removed in 2004. Governors of four prefectures demanded in late 2008 that the government abandon plans to dam the Daido River in Shiga Prefecture.

62. Alex Kerr, *Dogs and Demons: The Fall of Modern Japan* (London: Penguin, 2001), pp. 15–18; Robert Stolz, "Remake Politics, Not Nature: Tanaka Shōzō's Philosophies of 'Poison' and 'Flow' and Japan's Environment," *Japan Focus* online, January 23, 2007; *Daily Yomiuri* online, March 13, 2009. In March 2009, 63 percent of Japan's governors and big-city mayors called for abolishing unfunded mandates. Concrete embankments were first used in Japan in 1903 on the Tone River. Because of artificial banks and jetties, only 7 percent of Japan's sandy beaches were still considered "natural" in a 2008 study. *Daily Yomiuri* online, November 30, 2008.

63. See Karen L. Thornber, "Myopic Hyperopia and Environmental Crises in East Asian Literatures," paper, New England Association for Asian Studies, Boston, October 18, 2008. Once dams are built, removing them creates another set of environmental problems.

64. Nihon Shizen Hogo Kyōkai, *Yutaka*, p. 1; Oyadomari, "Politics," pp. 346–347; *Daily Yomiuri* online, January 10, 2009. The shrine at Nikkō is noted for the 12,500 cryptomeria lining its thirty-seven-kilometer-long approach road built in the seventeenth century.

65. Roy, "National Forest," pp. 74–76; Takayanagi, "Treatment," p. 302; Martin Fackler, "Flush with Cash, More Asian Tourists Flock to Japan," *New York Times* online, July 26, 2008.

66. André Sorensen, "Changing Governance of Shared Spaces: Machizukuri as Institutional Innovation," in André Sorensen and Carolin Funck, eds., *Living Cities in Japan: Citizens' Movements, Machizukuri and Local Environments* (London: Routledge, 2007), pp. 73–74.

67. Patricia G. Steinhoff, "Protest and Democracy," in Takeshi Ishida and Ellis Krauss, eds., *Democracy in Japan* (Pittsburgh: University of Pittsburgh Press, 1989), pp. 178–180. See William Marotti, "Japan 1968: The Performance of Violence and the Theater of Protest," *The American Historical Review* 114, no. 1 (2009): pp. 97–135.

68. See Robert A. Scalapino, *The Japanese Communist Movement, 1920–1966* (Berkeley: University of California Press, 1967), pp. 132–134; Margaret A. McKean, *Environmental Protest and Citizen Politics in Japan* (Berkeley: University of California Press, 1981); Frank K. Upham, "Unplaced Persons and Movements for Place," in Andrew Gordon, ed., *Postwar Japan as History* (Berkeley: University of California Press, 1993), pp. 342–344; James W. White, "The Dynamics of Political Opposition," in Andrew Gordon, ed., *Postwar Japan as History* (Berkeley: University of California Press, 1993), pp. 437–438.

69. Tokyo Metropolitan Government, *City Planning*, p. 46.

70. Satō and Shimoyama, *Landscape Planning*, p. 8. Line drawing is *senbiki*. In 1968 Japan had 647 cities, 1,984 towns, and 625 villages.

71. Sakamoto, *Nihon*, p. 25.

72. Hanayama, *Land*, pp. 30, 35; Ueda, *Midori*, p. 166.

73. André Sorensen, "Centralization, Urban Planning Governance, and Citizen Participation in Japan," in Carola Hein and Philippe Pelletier, eds., *Cities, Autonomy, and Decentralization in Japan* (London: Routledge, 2006), p. 108; Tokyo Metropolitan Government, *City Planning*, pp. 90, 97. Under the Urban Green Space Protection Law of 1973, Tokyo protected 67 hectares within the ward area and 370 hectares elsewhere as working farmland. *Japan Today* online, December 30, 2009.

74. Ueda, *Midori*, pp. 166–168, 177.

75. See Ishida, "Local," pp. 39–40.

76. Shin, *Toshi kōen*, pp. 202–203.

77. Kōen Ryokuchi Iji, *Kōen ryokuchi*, p. 29; Shin, *Toshi kōen*, pp. 165, 200. Tokyo's goal was 3,780 hectares of green space by 1985.

78. Osakafu Dobokubu Kōenka, ed., *Osakafu toshi kōen ichiranhyō* (Osaka: Osakafu, 1985), pp. 24–25. As of 1985 Osaka had 3,053 hectares of green space.

79. Shin, *Toshi kōen*, p. 154. See Ueda, *Midori*, pp. 19–20, 140–142; Ishikawa, *Toshi*, p. 266.

80. Nihon Toshi Sentā, *Toshi*, pp. 92, 105; Shin, *Toshi kōen*, p. 159. See Sorensen, *Making of Urban Japan*, pp. 225, 230.

81. Suematsu, *Tokyo*, 2:58.

82. Tanaka Kakuei, *Nihon rettō kaizōron* (Tokyo: Nikkan Kōgyō Shinbunsha, 1972).

83. Toshi Kōentō Seibi Kinkyū Sochihō, 1972, quoted in Shin, *Toshi kōen*, p. 158.

84. Shiojima, *Midori*, pp. 31–32; Ueda, *Midori*, pp. 255–256; Shin, *Toshi kōen*, p. 155.

85. *National Report*, p. 33.

86. Ueda, *Midori*, p. 257.

87. Shinji, *"Nō,"* p. 125; Shiojima, *Midori*, pp. 38, 163, 167; Ueda, *Midori*, p. 257; Nihon Kōen Ryokuchi Kyōkai, *Kōen ryokuchi manyuaru*, p. 256. The first five-year plan was replaced after three years, during which time the central government spent ¥560 billion of the budgeted ¥900 billion. See Shiojima, *Midori*, p. 44.

88. See ibid., pp. 38–39.

89. Nihon Kōen Ryokuchi Kyōkai, *Kōen ryokuchi manyuaru*, pp. 292–293; Hanayama, *Land*, pp. xiii–xiv.

90. Nihon Kōen Ryokuchi Kyōkai, *Kōen ryokuchi manyuaru*, pp. 292–293, 306. See also pp. 298–305.

91. Zenkoku Shizen Hogo Rengō, ed., *Shizen hogo no tebiki* (Tokyo: Shōheisha, 1974), pp. 96–97.

92. Sōrifu, *Kankō*, p. 87; Oyadomari, "Politics," pp. 352–353; Kankyōchō, *Shizen*, p. 10. The Japan Union for Nature Conservation is Zenkoku Shizen Hogo Rengō.

93. Kankyōchō, *Shizen*, p. 10; Oyadomari, "Politics," pp. 355–356; Sōrifu, *Kankō*, p. 87.

94. Nihon Shizen Hogo Kyōkai, *Shizen hogo o ika ni susumeru ka* (Tokyo: Nihon Shizen Hogo Kyōkai, 1975), pp. 57–58.

95. Yanagida Yukio, *Kankyōhō nyūmon* (Tokyo: Saimaru Shuppankai, 1972), p. 82.

96. Oyadomari, "Politics," p. 383; Zenkoku, *Shizen*, 1:301–305.

97. Ueda, *Midori*, p. 143; Kokuritsu, *Nihon no shizen kōen*, p. 10.

98. Nihon Shizen Hogo Kyōkai, *Yutaka*, pp. 3–4; Nihon Shizen Hogo Kyōkai, *Shizen hogo*, preface; Sōrifu, *Kankō*, p. 88.

99. Seta, *Saiseisuru kokuritsu kōen*, p. 168.

100. Yanagida, *Kankyōhō*, p. 82.

101. Oyadomari, "Politics," p. 374.

102. Sakamoto, *Nihon*, p. 117. The parks cover twenty-three square kilometers. See Shin, *Toshi kōen*, pp. 169–170; Kōen Ryokuchi Kanri Zaidan, *Ryokka bunka no chishiki nintei shiken kōshiki zenmondaishū* (Tokyo: Tokyo Shoseki, 2004), p. 14; Sōrifu, *Kankō*,

p. 94; Nihon Kōen Ryokuchi Kyōkai, *Kokuei kōen* (Tokyo: Nihon Kōen Ryokuchi Kyōkai, 1990), p. 3. Japanese government parks are *kokuei kōen*.

103. Kōen Ryokuchi Kanri Zaidan, ed., *Kōen Ryokuchi Kanri Zaidan 30nenshi* (Tokyo: Kōen Ryokuchi Kanri Zaidan, 2004), preface, p. 1; Satō and Shimoyama, *Landscape Planning,* pp. 9–10, 63, 66–67; Kōen Ryokuchi Iji Kanri Kenkyūkai, ed., *Kōen ryokuchi,* p. 22. Central government contributions to construction and land purchases totaled ¥47.5 billion through 1982. The central government also paid half the annual operating costs of Japanese government parks, about ¥13 billion in 2004.

104. Shinrin Kōen, *Shinrin Kōen gaido bukku* (Saitama: Shinrin Kōen, 2005), p. 2. Musashi Hills Woodland Park is Musashi Kyūryō Shinrin Kōen.

105. Yabe, *Tokyo kōen sanpo,* p. 7.

106. "Green Culture," http://www.green-culture.com/portal/index.html (accessed December 2, 2005).

107. Sōrifu, *Kankō,* p. 197. Attendance statistics were notoriously inexact, especially since most Japanese natural parks lacked admission fees. See also Kankyōchō, *Quality,* pp. 301–302; Brendan F. D. Barrett and Riki Therivel, *Environmental Policy and Impact Assessment in Japan* (New York: Routledge, 1991), p. 142. Sōmushō Gyōsei Hyōkakyoku, *Shizen kankyō hozen ni kansuru gyōsei hyōka* (Tokyo: Sōmushō, 2002), p. 7, estimates that as of 2000 national parks drew 382 million visitors, quasi-national parks 296 million, and prefectural natural parks 274 million. The peak year was 1992, with a combined total of just over 1 billion. See Kankyōshō, *Kankyō tōkeishū,* p. 193. The estimated attendance at national parks for the year ended March 2007 was 352 million. See Seta, *Saiseisuru kokuritsu kōen,* p. 8.

108. See Oyadomari, "Politics," pp. 402–407.

109. Kankyōchō, *Nature Conservation Administration in Japan* (Tokyo: Kankyōchō, 1985), p. 17.

110. Brian Woodall, "The Politics of Land in Japan's Dual Political Economy," in John O. Haley and Kozo Yamamura, eds., *Land Issues in Japan: A Policy Failure?* (Seattle: Society for Japanese Studies, 1992), pp. 136–137; Seta, *Saisei kokuritsu kōen,* p. 169. The resort law is *Sōgō Hoyō Chiiki Seibihō.*

111. Yamaichi Shōken Keizai Kenkyūjo, *Sangyō no subete, 1990* (Tokyo: Yamaichi Shōken Keizai Kenkyūjo, 1990), p. 245; Yamane Ichigen, "Gekitotsu! Tsutsumi Seiji vs. Yoshiaki no rettō rizōto daisensō," *Gendai,* December 1988, p. 109; Honma Yoshito, "Dangers of the Resort-Building Drive," *Japan Echo* 17, no. 3 (1990): p. 72; Havens, *Architects of Affluence,* pp. 210–213; Barrett and Therivel, *Environmental Policy,* p. 81; Ueda, *Midori,* p. 325.

112. Tawara, *Hokkaido,* p. 48. See Shiojima, *Midori,* pp. 42, 45.

113. Kensetsushō, *Nihon no toshi seisaku,* p. 310.

114. Nihon Kōen Ryokuchi Kyōkai, *Kōen ryokuchi manyuaru,* p. 287; Kensetsushō data, reprinted in Shin, *Toshi kōen,* p. 158.

115. See Shinji, "Kōen no rekishi," p. 97.

116. Shinji, *"Nō,"* p. 126; Sorensen, *Making of Urban Japan,* pp. 277–279.

117. Kensetsushō, *Nihon no toshi*, p. 407. See Nihon Toshi Sentā, *Toshi*, p. 7.

118. Shin, *Toshi kōen*, p. 200. Tokyo city parks covered 1,780 hectares in 1971 and 5,480 in 1993.

119. Ibid., pp. 431–433.

120. Tokyo Metropolitan Government, *City Planning*, pp. 41–42; Sorensen, *Making of Urban Japan*, pp. 243–245; Hanayama, *Land*, pp. 36–37.

121. Shin, *Toshi kōen*, p. 244; Sōrifu, *Kankō*, p. 93.

122. Shiojima, *Midori*, p. 105. See Ueda, *Midori*, p. 221.

123. Sōrifu, *Kankō*, p. 199; Nihon Kōen Ryokuchi Kyōkai, *Kōen ryokuchi manyuaru*, p. 17; Suzuki and Sawada, *Kōen no hanashi*, p. 43; Sakamoto, *Nihon*, pp. 38–39; Shiojima, *Midori*, pp. 88, 91, 93–96; Satō and Shimoyama, *Landscape Planning*, p. 13; Shin, *Toshi kōen*, p. 175; Katō Akira and Takeuchi Denshi, *Shin toshi keikaku gairon* (Tokyo: Kyōritsu Shuppan, 2004), p. 179.

124. Construction Ministry statistics, reproduced in Shiojima, *Midori*, p. 33.

125. Shinji Isoya, *Midori no machizukurigaku* (Kyoto: Gakugei Shuppansha, 1987), p. 178; Tokyoto Seikatsu Bunkakyoku Kokusai Kōryūbu Gaijika, *2nd Long-Term Plan for the Tokyo Metropolis* (Tokyo: Tokyo Metropolitan Government, 1987), p. 244.

126. Ueda, *Midori*, p. 253.

127. Aoki Kōichirō, *Machigai darake no kōen zukuri: Sore de mo kōen o tsukuru riyū* (Tokyo: Toshi Bunkasha, 1998), p. 55; Maruta Yorikazu, *Toshi ryokuka keikakuron* (Tokyo: Maruzen, 1994), p. 33; Ishikawa, *Toshi*, pp. 296–297; Shin, *Toshi kōen*, p. 285; Ueda, *Midori*, pp. 249–251.

128. Ueda, *Midori*, p. 252; *Ryokuka kenchiku nenkan 2005* (Tokyo: Sōjusha, 2005), p. 52. See Asaba Yoshikazu, *Satoyama kōen to "Shimin no Mori" zukuri no monogatari* (Tokyo: Haru Shobō, 2003), pp. 125–136.

Chapter 5: Parks and New Eco-Regimes

1. Kōen Ryokuchi Iji, *Kōen ryokuchi*, pp. 28–29; Suzuki and Sawada, *Kōen no hanashi*, p. 6; Ueda, *Midori*, p. 258. City parks in 1991 numbered 59,324 covering 673 square kilometers. In 2003 there were 84,994 city parks on 1,010 square kilometers.

2. Kōen Ryokuchi Iji, *Kōen ryokuchi*, pp. 28–30; Suzuki and Sawada, *Kōen no hanashi*, p. 6. As of 2006 Kobe had 16.5 square meters of park space per resident, Sendai 12.4, and Sapporo 10.8, the three leading cities in Japan. Tokyo's ward area had 4.5 square meters per capita and the metropolis as a whole had 5.5. Japanese government data for major world cities published in 2009 showed New York with 29.1, Berlin with 27.4, London with 25.3, and Paris with 11.8. Tokyoto Kensetsukyoku Kōen Ryokuchibu, ed., *Tokyoto no kōen ryokuchi mappu 2009*.

3. Kankyōshō, *Kankyō tōkeishū* (2005), p. 190. About 19 percent of the country's land area is uncultivated; the rest is planted or otherwise cultivated. Natural parks exist

in all classifications of green areas. Basic green space plans are *midori sansan*. Civic reconstruction is *machizukuri*.

4. Kankyōshō, *Kankyō tōkeishū* (2005), p. 200; Sōmushō, *Shizen,* pp. 13–14. Figures are as of 2005.

5. Sōmushō, *Shizen,* p. 4.

6. Kankyōshō, *Kankyō tōkeishū* (2008), pp. 258–259. Figures are for the year ending March 2006.

7. Sōmushō, *Shizen,* p. 11; *Toshi kōen* 169 (July 2005), p. 10; Seta, *Saiseisuru kokuritsu kōen,* p. 292.

8. Kankyōshō, *Kankyō tōkeishū* (2008), p. 260; Sōmushō, *Shizen,* p. 4.

9. Gaimushō, *Environment,* p. 139.

10. Kankyōchō, *Nature,* pp. 19–20. In 1988 the Environment Agency listed 188 plant species as endangered.

11. See Takayanagi, "Treatment," p. 303; Miyaoka Isao, *Legitimacy in International Society: Japan's Reaction to Global Wildlife Preservation* (New York: Palgrave Macmillan, 2004), p. 44.

12. Kankyōchō, *Nature,* p. 6; Environmental Information Center, *Aspects of Nature: National Survey on the Natural Environment, Japan* (Tokyo: Kankyōchō, 1989), p. 7.

13. Kankyōchō, *Nihon no shizen kankyō* (Tokyo: Kankyōchō, 1982), pp. 49, 58; Kankyōshō, *Kankyō hakusho,* p. 136. In 2004 the plant species included 16,500 fungi, 7,000 vascular plants, and 5,500 seaweeds and algae.

14. Gaimushō, *Environment,* p. 45; Kankyōshō, *Kankyō hakusho,* p. 142.

15. Robert A. Askins, "Conservation of Japanese Birds" (unpublished manuscript, Connecticut College, 2003), p. 26; Fisher, Simon, and Vincent, *Wildlife,* pp. 222–223; *Japan Journal* 2, no. 9 (2006): p. 5; *Japan Times,* June 5, 2007, p. 2; *Japan Today* online, October 7, 2007; *New York Times,* November 7, 2007, p. A4; *Daily Yomiuri* online, January 12, 2008; *Kyōdō News* online, February 13, 2009. The red-crested crane is *tanchō.*

16. Askins, "Conservation," pp. 5, 7.

17. *Daily Yomiuri,* July 3, 2007, p. 20.

18. *Japan Today* online, March 1, 2007.

19. Conservation International report, 2005, quoted in *Japan Today* online, February 3, 2005. The Okinawa woodpecker is *noguchigera* and the Japanese macaque is *Nihonzaru.*

20. Miyaoka, *Legitimacy,* pp. 47, 124–125.

21. Ron Carle, "Democracy in Action: Heritage Preservation as a Social Movement," *Asian Cultural Studies* 32 (2006): pp. 141–146.

22. Angela S. Ildos and Giorgio G. Bardelli, *The Great National Parks of the World* (Heathrow, Fla.: AAA Publishing, 2001), p. 12; *Daily Yomiuri* online, July 15, 2005; *Japan Today* online, July 7, 2008; "Japan's UNESCO World Heritage Sites," http://www.japan-guide.com/e/e2251.html (accessed July 5, 2009); *Mainichi shinbun* online, January 24, 2009.

23. Mitsuda Hisayoshi and Charles Geisler, "Imperiled Parks and Imperiled People: Lessons from Japan's Shiretoko National Park," *Environmental History Review* 16, no. 2 (1992): pp. 26–27; *New York Times,* November 7, 2007, p. A4.

24. *Daily Yomiuri,* June 3, 2004; *Japan Times* online, May 8, 2004, December 30, 2004; *Daily Yomiuri* online, October 20, 2004, July 15, 2005.

25. *Mainichi shinbun* online, August 24, 2009.

26. Kankyōchō, *Nature,* p. 23; Jeffrey Kingston, *Japan's Quiet Transformation: Social Change and Civil Society in the Twenty-first Century* (London: RoutledgeCurzon, 2004), pp. 147–148; *Japan Times* online, November 9, 2005; *Daily Yomiuri* online, October 4, 2008; "The Annotated Ramsar List: Japan," http://ramsar.org/profile/profiles_japan.htm (accessed July 5, 2009). There were 1,814 Ramsar sites worldwide in November 2008.

27. Nihon Shizen Hogo Kyōkai, *Yutaka,* p. 23; Kokuritsu Kōen Kyōkai, *National Parks,* p. 49; Oyadomari, "Politics," p. 291; Kankyōshō, *Kankyō tōkeishū* (2008), p. 313; *Daily Yomiuri,* May 16, 2005, p. 3.

28. *Daily Yomiuri,* June 20, 2007, p. 2. The imperial grant was 570 hectares.

29. Sawaji Osamu, "Back to the Roots," *Japan Journal* 2, no. 5 (2005): pp. 6–7.

30. *Daily Yomiuri,* May 7, 2005, p. 12; *Japan Times* online, March 14, 2006.

31. Itō Taiichi and Tanaka Nobuhiko, eds., *Social Roles of Forests for Urban Population: Forest Recreation, Landscape, Nature Conservation, Economic Evaluation and Urban Forestry* (Tokyo: Japan Society of Forest Planning Press, 2004), p. i; Inose Naoki, *Nihonkoku no kenkyū tsuzuku* (Tokyo: Bungei Shunjū, 2002), pp. 26–44; Roy, "National Forest," p. 77.

32. Mitsui, "National," p. 148; Roy, "National Forest," p. 87. See Kerr, *Dogs and Demons,* p. 54; Kunimatsu Yoshitsugu, "Felling Forestry Firms' Towering Debt: Who Will Save the Forests?" *Japan Focus* online, October 6, 2005.

33. Nōrin Chūkin Sōgō Kenkyūjo, *Satochi shizen chiikitō shizen kankyō hozen chōsa hōkokusho, Heisei kyūnendo* (Tokyo: Nōrin Chūkin Sōgō Kenkyūjo, 1998), p. 59; Tō Kimiharu, personal communication, October 1, 2003. See Catherine Knight, "Natural Environments, Wildlife, and Conservation in Japan," *Japan Focus* online, January 25, 2010.

34. Kankyōshō, *Kankyō tōkeishū* (2005), pp. 191–192; Kankyōshō, *Kankyō hakusho,* p. 143; Matsushita, "National," pp. 87–91.

35. Noguchi Hiroyuki, "Out of the Woods," *Japan Journal* 3, no. 4 (2006): pp. 8–9; Stolz, "Remake Politics."

36. Kingston, *Japan's Quiet Transformation,* pp. 141–143; Inoue Yūichi, "Dam Shame: Tokyo and Kansai Flush with Water," *Japan Focus* online, March 23, 2006; *Japan Times* online, September 4, 2005; *Daily Yomiuri* online, July 30, 2008; Chris Betros, "Tokyo Won't Be Able to Cope with Katrina-like Flooding," *Japan Today* online, August 1, 2008.

37. John Knight, *Waiting for Wolves in Japan: An Anthropological Study of People-Wildlife Relations* (Oxford, Eng.: Oxford University Press, 2003), p. 193; *Japan Times*

online, October 17, 2004, December 9, 2005; *Japan Today* online, October 12, 2004, April 6, 2008.

38. Kankyōshō, *Quality of the Environment in Japan 2002* (Tokyo: Kankyōshō, 2002), p. 207; Kankyōchō, *Nature,* pp. 22–23; Takayanagi, "Treatment," pp. 298–301; Knight, *Waiting for Wolves,* pp. 45–46, 89, 124–126, 152–157; *Japan Today* online, October 12, 2004. See Brett L. Walker, *The Lost Wolves of Japan* (Seattle: University of Washington Press, 2005). The Japanese serow is a kind of goat antelope.

39. Takayanagi, "Treatment," p. 304. See *Japan Today* online, January 4, 2008.

40. Wilhelm Vosse, "Need for a New Movement? A Fragmented Environmental Movement in Times of Global Environmental Problems," in Klaus Vollmer, ed., *Environmental Policies and Ecological Issues in Japan and Eastern Asia: Transnational Perspectives* (Munich: Iudicium, 2006), p. 111. As of late 2008, the prime minister's office calculated that 10,102 of Japan's 35,659 nonprofits (including many NGOs not meeting official criteria as NPOs) were active in environmental preservation. Simon A. Avenell, "Civil Society and the New Civic Movements in Japan," *Journal of Japanese Studies* 35, no. 2 (2009): p. 282.

41. Hasegawa Kōichi, Shinohara Chika, and Jeffrey Broadbent, "Volunteerism and the State in Japan," *Japan Focus* online, December 26, 2007; Suda Yuka, "Nonprofit Organizations Undergo Profound Change in the U.S. and Japan," *Center for Global Partnership* online, http://www.cgp.org/index.php?option=article&task=default&articleid=325 (accessed July 5, 2009).

42. Nihon Shizen Hogo Kyōkai, *Yutaka,* p. 5; Kankyōchō, *Nature,* pp. 18, 27.

43. Katō Mineo, *Mokutekichi wa kokuritsu kōen* (Morioka: Shinzansha, 2001), p. 206.

44. Kokuritsu Kōen Kyōkai, *Kokuritsu kōentō minkan katsuyō tokutei shizen kankyō hozen katsudō (gurīn wākā) jigyō suishin chōsa hōkokusho, Heisei 13nendo* (Tokyo: Kokuritsu Kōen Kyōkai, 2002), preface, p. 8; Shizen Kōen Zaidan, *Kokuritsu kōen no shizen kankyō no hogo kanri jigyō hōkokusho, Heisei 14nendo* (Tokyo: Shizen Kōen Zaidan, 2003), preface, pp. 1, 107.

45. Tanaka Atsuo, *Nihon no mori wa naze kiki na no ka* (Tokyo: Heibonsha, 2002), pp. 70–71. See Iwai, "New Relationship," pp. 286–297; Mariko Yasumoto, "Calls for Change as WHS Status Threatens One of Japan's Gems," *Japan Times* online, February 6, 2005; *Japan Times* online, November 26, 2005.

46. Vosse, "Need," p. 120. In 2003 there were 1,165 volunteer groups serving in Japan's forests. Avenell, "Civil Society," notes that many civic movements cooperate closely with government.

47. Nōrin Chūkin, *Satochi,* pp. 1, 7; Takeuchi Kazuhiko, Washitani Izumi, and Tsunekawa Atsushi, eds., *Satoyama no kankyōgaku* (Tokyo: Tokyo Daigaku Shuppankai, 2001), preface, pp. 1–2; Knight, *Waiting for Wolves,* p. 30.

48. Tsunekawa Atsushi, "Strategic Management of Satoyama Landscapes," in Takeuchi Kazuhiko, Robert D. Brown, Washitani Izumi, Tsunekawa Atsushi, and Yokohari Makoto, eds., *Satoyama: The Traditional Rural Landscape of Japan* (Tokyo: Springer-Verlag, 2003), pp. 184–185; Kuramoto Noboru, "Citizen Conservation of Satoyama

Landscapes," in Takeuchi Kazuhiko, Robert D. Brown, Washitani Izumi, Tsunekawa Atsushi, and Yokohari Makoto, eds., *Satoyama: The Traditional Rural Landscape of Japan* (Tokyo: Springer-Verlag, 2003), p. 24; Robert D. Brown and Yokohari Makoto, "Ideological Contribution of Satoyamas," in Takeuchi Kazuhiko, Robert D. Brown, Washitani Izumi, Tsunekawa Atsushi, and Yokohari Makoto, eds., *Satoyama: The Traditional Rural Landscape of Japan* (Tokyo: Springer-Verlag, 2003), pp. 1–2.

49. Inamori Mitsuhiko, *Satoyama monogatari* (Tokyo: Shinchōsha, 1995). See Iizawa Kōtarō, "Man and Nature in Harmony," *Japan Journal* 3, no. 11 (2007): p. 20; Takeuchi et al., *Satoyama no kankyōgaku*, preface; Nōrin Chūkin, *Satochi*, pp. 10, 20. The Environment Ministry's Third National Biodiversity Strategy of November 2007 called for further rural restoration to protect threatened species.

50. Shishitsuka no Shizen to Rekishi no Kai, *Shishitsuka no satoyama* (Tsuchiurashi: Shishitsuka no Shizen to Rekishi no Kai, 2003).

51. See Brown and Yokohari, "Ideological Contribution," p. 3; *Japan Journal* online, January 2010.

52. Kankyōshō, *Kankyō hakusho*, p. 153; *Japan Journal* online 4, no. 12 (2008). Beginning in 1995 the former head of the Environment Agency, Seta Nobuya, led four to five ecotours per year for groups of twenty to thirty persons via the Asahi Cultural Center. Seta was appointed chair of the National Parks Association of Japan in 2006. Seta, *Saiseisuru kokuritsu kōen*, p. 313.

53. Muneta Yoshifumi, a professor of tourism at Kyoto Prefectural University, quoted in *Japan Times* online, February 14, 2009.

54. *Japan Today* online, November 12, 2008; *Japan Times* online, October 7, 2007. *Mainichi shinbun* online reported on December 29, 2008, that more companies favored a green tax than opposed it. The Democratic Party of Japan proposed a possible green tax to begin in 2011. *Japan Times* online, December 15, 2009.

55. *Kyōdō News on the Web*, January 3, 2009.

56. Itō Taiichi, "Shizen chiiki rekuriēshon keikaku ni okeru yūryōka no tenkai," *Shinrin Keikaku Gakkaishi* 39, no. 2 (2005): p. 183.

57. Nihon Shizen Hogo Kyōkai, *Yutaka*, p. 4.

58. Nihon Shizen Hogo Kyōkai, *21seiki no shizen o kangaeru—kokuritsu kōen no risōzō o motomete* (Tokyo: Nihon Shizen Hogo Kyōkai, 2001), pp. 6–7.

59. "Tokyo's Big Change: The 10-Year Plan," http://www.metro.tokyo.jp/ENGLISH/PROFILE/policy03.htm (accessed July 6, 2009).

60. Tokyo Toshi Keikakukyoku Sōmubu, *Planning of Tokyo*, p. 13.

61. "The 3-Year Plan," http://www.metro.tokyo.jp/ENGLISH/PROFILE/policy04.htm (accessed July 6, 2009). The plan covers 334 projects from 2008 to 2010. The sea forest will cover eighty-eight hectares.

62. Shinji, "*Nō*," p. 126.

63. Ibid., p. 127; Kōen Ryokuchi Gyōsei Kenkyūkai, ed., *Kaisei toshi kōen seido Q & A* (Tokyo: Gyōsei, 1993), p. 3; Ueda, *Midori*, p. 329; Shin, *Toshi kōen*, p. 170.

64. Ishikawa, *Toshi,* p. 276; Ichikawa, *Bunka,* p. 130; Ueda, *Midori,* pp. 186–187, 285, 313; Kōen Ryokuchi Gyōsei Kenkyūkai, ed., *Gaisetsu atarashii Toshi Ryokuchihō Toshi Kōenhō* (Tokyo: Gyōsei, 2005), pp. 20–21.
65. Nihon Kōen Ryokuchi Kyōkai, *Kōen ryokuchi manyuaru,* p. 3.
66. Thomas Feldhoff, "Japan's Construction Lobby and the Privatization of Highway-related Public Corporations," in André Sorensen and Carolin Funck, eds., *Living Cities in Japan: Citizens' Movements, Machizukuri and Local Environments* (London: Routledge, 2007), pp. 97, 100; Woodall, "Politics of Land," pp. 136–137; Brian Woodall, *Japan Under Construction: Corruption, Politics, and Public Works* (Berkeley: University of California Press, 1996), p. 61; Brian Woodall, personal communication, June 23, 2009. See Richard Katz, *Japan: The System that Soured—The Rise and Fall of the Japanese Economic Miracle* (Armonk, N.Y.: M. E. Sharpe, 1998), pp. 34–35, 181–182.
67. Ishikawa, *Toshi,* pp. 304–305; Tokyoto Toshi Keikakukyoku Sōmubu, *Planning of Tokyo,* pp. 5–7; Ishida, "Local," pp. 45–47; Sorensen, "Centralization," pp. 104–105.
68. Kōen Ryokuchi, *Gaisetsu,* pp. 4–6, 19–22; Sanada, *Toshi,* p. 2; *Ryokuka kenchiku nenkan 2005,* pp. 43–45.
69. *Japan Times* online, April 9, 2006.
70. Nihon Kōen Ryokuchi Kyōkai, *Kōen ryokuchi manyuaru,* p. 3.
71. Ibid., pp. 3–6; Kondō, *Toshi,* pp. 43–45; Tsurumaki Yasuo, *Okujō kara no kankyō kakumei* (Tokyo: IN Tsūshinsha, 2002), p. 50.
72. *Toshi kōen* 169 (2005): pp. 46, 51; Tokyoto Toshi Seibikyoku Toshi Kibanbu Shisetsu Keikakuka, ed., *Toshi keikaku kōen ryokuchi no seibi hōshin* (Tokyo: Tokyoto, 2006), p. 5; Tokyoto, *3rd,* pp. 93, 109.
73. *Tokyoto Kōen Shingikai, 2003* (Tokyo: Tokyoto, 2003), p. 10, cited in Shin, *Toshi kōen,* p. 184; Tokyoto Zōen Ryokukagyō Kyōkai, ed., *Tokyoto ryokuka hakusho 22* (Tokyo: Tokyoto Zōen Ryokukagyō Kyōkai, 2003), p. 6. Operating costs of Tokyo city parks, exclusive of capital improvements, were ¥42 billion for the fiscal year ending in March 2004 and budgeted at ¥37 billion in the year ending in March 2006. *Toshi kōen* 169 (2005), 46, 51.
74. Kōen Ryokuchi Iji, *Kōen ryokuchi,* p. 29; Shin, *Toshi kōen,* p. 200; Toshi Bōsai, *Tokyoto,* p. 31; Suematsu, *Tokyo,* 1:1. In 1993 Tokyo had 8,034 city parks covering fifty-five square kilometers.
75. Shin, *Toshi kōen,* p. 192.
76. Aoki, *Machigai,* p. 14.
77. *Daily Yomiuri,* May 10, 2005, p. 3. Within two years 331 benches were in place.
78. Tokyoto Toshi Seibikyoku, *Midori,* pp. 31–32; Aoki Kōichirō, *Kōen no riyō* (Tokyo: Chikyūsha, 1984), pp. 6, 208–209; Tokyoto Kensetsukyoku, *Mappu 2009.*
79. Tokyoto Kōen Kyōkai, http://www.tokyo-park.or.jp (accessed July 6, 2009).
80. Shin, *Toshi kōen,* pp. 241–242; *Boston Globe,* February 12, 2007, p. A2. Many parks in Boston, New York, Atlanta, St. Louis, and the Presidio National Park in San Francisco are managed by nonprofit trusts or private foundations.

81. Tokyoto Toshi Seibikyoku, *Toshi keikaku*, p. 45; Tokyoto Toshi Seibikyoku, *Midori*, preface, pp. 1, 22–29, 39–40. Private-sector parks are *minsetsu kōen*.

82. Tokyoto Toshi Seibikyoku, *Midori*, p. 51; Katō Akinori, *Nihonteki hiroba no aru machi: Midori mizu tsuchi* (Tokyo: Purosesu Ākitekuchua, 1993), pp. 16–17, 84; Toshi Ryokuka Gijutsu Kaihatsu Kikō, ed., *Shinryoku kūkan dezain fukyū manyuaru* (Tokyo: Seibundō Shinkōsha, 1995), p. 14; Nikkei Ākitekuchua, ed., *Jitsurei ni manabu okujō ryokuka* (Tokyo: Nikkei BPsha, 2003), pp. 14–15. See Ueda, *Midori*, p. 41; Sanada, *Toshi*, p. 2. Some Tokyo wards set stiffer regulations for greenery on buildings. Hyōgo Prefecture adopted the 2001 Tokyo metropolitan requirements in 2002.

83. Funase Shunsuke, *"Okujō ryokuka" kanzen gaido* (Tokyo: Tsukiji Shokan, 2003), pp. i, 40; Kondō, *Toshi*, p. 43; *Japan Today* online, August 12, 2005, November 27, 2009.

84. Hardy, "People of the Garden," pp. 163–165; *Japan Times* online, August 29, 2007.

85. Kondō, *Toshi*, pp. 200–203, 245; *Ryokuka kenchiku nenkan 2005*, pp. 14–17; *Kyōdō News on the Web*, August 30, 2006; *Daily Yomiuri* online, August 14, 2008.

86. *GMA News* online, February 17, 2009; Abby R. Margolis, "Samurai Beneath Blue Tarps: Doing Homelessness, Rejecting Marginality and Preserving Nation in Ueno Park" (PhD dissertation, University of Pittsburgh, 2002); *Japan Today* online, September 1, 2008. Hundreds or perhaps thousands of young homeless persons stay overnight in Internet cafes.

87. Shin, *Toshi kōen*, pp. 269–270; Itō, *Ima*, p. 41; Melanie Burton, "Hurting Japan's Homeless," *Japan Times* online, January 18, 2005; Karen A. Foster, "Time Well Spent," *Japan Times* online, September 27, 2005. In 2009 the Welfare Ministry classified 16,000 people as homeless; the actual number may be three times this figure. A sizable minority lived on and off in parks.

88. Yoshihara Satoshi, "Kōen no hōmuresu," in Itō Yukio, ed., *Ima, kōen de nani ga okite iru ka* (Tokyo: Gyōsei, 2002), pp. 44–48. See Overmyer-Velázquez, "Visions of the Emerald City," pp. 13, 189; Hardy, "People of the Garden," pp. 142, 207, 224.

89. Burton, "Hurting"; Fisher, "Time"; *Tokyo Weekender* online, May 6, 2004; *Metropolis* online, March 9, 2007; News from A.P., *New York Times* online, Dec. 29, 2007; *Japan Today* online, January 15, 2010.

90. *Kansai Window Kippo News*, April 5, 2006; *Japan Times* online, January 31, 2006, February 3, 2007, October 4, 2008, November 23, 2009.

91. *Japan Times* online, January 30, 2007.

92. See Masami Iwata and Akihiko Nishizawa, eds., *Poverty and Social Welfare in Japan* (Melbourne: Trans Pacific Press, 2008).

93. *Japan Today* online, January 6, 2009, January 28, 2009; *Mainichi shinbun* online, January 18, 2009.

94. http://www.mottainai.info (accessed June 17, 2009); *Mainichi shinbun* online, June 23, 2009. World food aid for 2009–2010 was $20 billion. *Kyodo News on the Web*, July 11, 2009; *Mainichi shinbun* online, October 21, 2009; *Japan Times* online, January 5, 2010. The national poverty figure of 15.7 percent was for the year ending March 2008.

95. Theodore C. Bestor, *Neighborhood Tokyo* (Stanford, Calif.: Stanford University Press, 1989), p. 113. Civic reconstruction is *machizukuri*.

96. Ishida Yorifusa, *Nihon kingendai toshi keikaku no tenkai 1868–2003* (Tokyo: Jichitai Kenkyūsha, 2004), p. 263; Watanabe, "State"; Watanabe Shun'ichi, "Participatory Machizukuri (Community Building) in Japan," paper, Ninth International Planning History Conference, Helsinki, August 20–23, 2000; Sorensen, *Making of Urban Japan*, pp. 269–272, 309–314; Watanabe Shun'ichi, "Machizukuri in Japan," in Carola Hein and Philippe Pelletier, eds., *Cities, Autonomy, and Decentralization in Japan* (London: Routledge, 2006), pp. 133–134.

97. Kimura Shōzaburō, ed., *Machizukuri no kokoro: Miryoku aru chiiki bunka no sōzō* (Tokyo: Gyōsei, 1990), p. 177.

98. Esashi Yōji, *Toshi ryokuka shinseiki* (Tokyo: Heibonsha, 2000), pp. 1, 7.

99. Shinji Isoya, *Boranteia jidai no midori no machizukuri* (Tokyo: Tokyo Nōdai Shuppankai, 2008), p. 91.

100. André Sorensen and Carolin Funck, "Conclusions: A Diversity of Machizukuri Processes and Outcomes," in André Sorensen and Carolin Funck, eds., *Living Cities in Japan: Citizens' Movements, Machizukuri and Local Environments* (London: Routledge, 2007), p. 271.

101. Carolin Funck, "Machizukuri, Civil Society, and the Transformation of Japanese City Planning," in André Sorensen and Carolin Funck, eds., *Living Cities in Japan: Citizens' Movements, Machizukuri and Local Environments* (London: Routledge, 2007), p. 154.

102. *Japan Today* online, January 18, 2005. In the first six years under the new law, only 23 of 16,000 groups seeking nonprofit status from the government were approved. See also Shin, *Toshi kōen*, p. 277.

103. Nihon Toshi Keikaku Gakkai, ed., *Toshi keikaku no chihō bunken: Machizukuri no jissen* (Tokyo: Gakugei Shuppansha, 1999), pp. 3, 234, 237; Shin, *Toshi kōen*, pp. 234, 276–277; Kanai Toshiyuki, "Vectors of Change in Japan's Political and Fiscal Decentralization," *Social Science Japan* 37 (2007): p. 3; "Our Town," *Japan Journal* online, May 2008; Ono Sawako, ed., *Konna kōen ga hoshii* (Tokyo: Tsukiji Shokan, 1997), pp. 17–18.

104. Ishida, *Nihon kingendai*, p. 301; Miyanishi Yūji, "Cheer for Kobe-Style Machizukuri Organizations" (2002), http://www.gakugei-pub.jp/kobe/key_e/en2002.htm, (accessed July 6, 2009); Shin, *Toshi kōen*, p. 233.

105. Ueda, *Midori*, preface; Shinji, *Boranteia*, pp. 11–12, 115–121.

106. Shinji, "Nō," p. 133; *Daily Yomiuri*, May 19, 2007, p. 3. "Involving society in management" is *kanri noshakaika*; "social management" is *kanri shakai*.

107. Kameyama Hajime and Matsuzaki Yuriko, *Yasashii hito o tsukuru kōen e—yunibāsaru dezain no tenkai* (Tokyo: Shinjusha, 2004), pp. 24, 32–33; Tokyo Nōgyō Daigaku Tanki Daigakubu Kankyō Ryokuchi Gakka, ed., *Minna no kōenzukuri* (Tokyo: Tokyo Nōgyō Daigaku Shuppankai, 2002), p. 7. In 2009 the Ministry of Health, Labor, and Welfare estimated that 3.6 million Japanese had physical disabilities. See

Fujimoto Tarō, "Building a Barrier-Free Society," *Japan Today* online, January 29, 2009.

108. *Japan Today* online, September 11, 2008.

109. Chihō Bunken Ikkatsuhō (1999), quoted in Shin, *Toshi kōen,* p. 249.

110. Ueda, *Midori,* pp. 261–263; Ishida, *Nihon kingendai,* p. 314; Kohara Takaharu, "The Great Heisei Consolidation: A Critical Review," *Social Science Japan* 37 (2007): pp. 7–10.

111. Ueda, *Midori,* preface; Shin, *Toshi kōen,* pp. 251–252, 278–279.

112. *Japan Journal* online, May 2008; Kanai, "Vectors," pp. 3–6.

113. *Daily Yomiuri,* May 19, 2007, p. 3; Kankyōshō, *Kankyō hakusho* (2004), p. 145; Watanabe, "State."

Afterword

1. *Mainichi Daily News* online, August 29, 2008.

2. *Ryokuka kenchiku nenkan 2005,* pp. 42–43.

3. Toshihisa Asano, "Citizens' Movements to Protect the Water Environment: Changes and Problems," in André Sorensen and Carolin Funck, eds., *Living Cities in Japan: Citizens' Movements, Machizukuri and Local Environments* (London: Routledge, 2007), p. 203. The Third Scenic Green Space Law is Keikanryoku Sanpō.

4. *Japan Today* online, October 30, 2008; *Japan Today* online, March 6, 2009. Japan in 2009 ranked highest among 133 countries in health and hygiene but third from lowest in receptiveness to tourism.

5. See Kankyōshō, *Kankyō hakusho* (2009), pp. 2–3; Jared Diamond, *Collapse: How Societies Choose to Fail or Succeed* (New York: Viking, 2005), p. 469.

6. *Japan Today* online, December 13, 2008.

7. Stephen Hesse, "Asia's First Lady of the Environment," *Japan Times* online, November 30, 2008.

8. Stephen Hesse, "'Sustainability' in a Japanese Way," *Japan Times* online, February 22, 2009.

Sources Cited

Abe Isoo. *Ōyō shiseiron*. Tokyo: Nikkō Yūrindō, 1908.

———. "Teito no kensetsu to sōzōteki seishin." *Kaizō* 5, no. 11 (1923): pp. 49–71.

———. *Toshi mondai: Abe Isoo kōjutsu*. Tokyo: Waseda Daigaku Shuppankai, ca. 1910.

Adachi Kenzō. "Kokuritsu Kōen Hōan teian no riyū." *Kokuritsu kōen* 3, no. 3 (1931): pp. 2–3.

———. "Kokuritsu kōen mondai ni tsuite." *Kokuritsu kōen* 3, no. 1 (1931): pp. 1–2.

Adams, Alexander B., ed. *First World Conference on National Parks: Proceedings*. Washington, D.C.: National Park Service, U.S. Department of the Interior, 1962.

Aikawa Sadaharu and Fuse Rokurō. *Yoyogi Kōen*. Tokyo: Kyōgakusha, 1981.

Akao, Ken-ichi. "Private Forestry." In Yoshiya Iwai, ed., *Forestry and the Forest Industry in Japan*, pp. 24–40. Vancouver: University of British Columbia Press, 2002.

Allen, Bruce. "Introduction." In Ishimure Michiko, "*Lake of Heaven*, Dams, and Japan's Transformation," pp. 1–2. Translated by Bruce Allen. *Japan Focus* online, February 27, 2006.

Allen, Joseph R. "Taipei Park: Signs of Occupation." *The Journal of Asian Studies* 66, no. 1 (2007): pp. 159–199.

Amino Yoshihiko. *Muen, kugai, raku: Nihon chūsei no jiyū to heiwa*, expanded ed. Tokyo: Heibonsha, 1987.

"The Annotated Ramsar List: Japan." http://ramsar.org/profile/profiles_japan.htm. Accessed July 5, 2009.

Aoi Akihito. *Shokuminchi jinja to teikoku Nihon*. Tokyo: Yoshikawa Kōbunkan, 2005.

Aoki Kōichirō. *Kōen no riyō*. Tokyo: Chikyūsha, 1984.

———. *Machigai darake no kōen zukuri: Sore de mo kōen o tsukuru riyū*. Tokyo: Toshi Bunkasha, 1998.

Arriola, Andreu, et al. *Modern Park Design: Recent Trends*. Amsterdam: Thoth, 1993.

Asaba Yoshikazu. *Satoyama kōen to "Shimin no Mori" zukuri no monogatari*. Tokyo: Haru Shobō, 2003.

Asano, Toshihisa. "Citizens' Movements to Protect the Water Environment: Changes and Problems." In André Sorensen and Carolin Funck, eds., *Living Cities in Japan:*

Citizens' Movements, Machizukuri and Local Environments, pp. 189–205. London: Routledge, 2007.

Askins, Robert A. "Conservation of Japanese Birds." Unpublished manuscript, Connecticut College. New London, 2003.

———. Personal communication. April 6, 2004.

Avenell, Simon A. "Civil Society and the New Civic Movements in Japan." *Journal of Japanese Studies* 35, no. 2 (2009): pp. 247–283.

Azuma Ryōzō. *Amerika kokuritsu kōen kō.* Tokyo: Awaji Shobō, 1948.

Balmori, Diana. "Park Redefinitions." In Herbert Muschamp et al., *The Once and Future Park,* pp. 39–45. New York: Princeton Architectural Press, 1993.

Barrett, Brendan F. D., and Riki Therivel. *Environmental Policy and Impact Assessment in Japan.* New York: Routledge, 1991.

Barshay, Andrew. *State and Intellectual in Imperial Japan: The Public Man in Crisis.* Berkeley: University of California Press, 1988.

Baudrillard, Jean. *The Mirror of Production.* Translated by Mark Poster. St. Louis, Mo.: Telos Press, 1975.

Beard, Charles A. *The Administration and Politics of Tokyo: A Survey and Opinions.* New York: Macmillan, 1923.

Bernstein, Andrew. *Modern Passings: Death Rites, Politics, and Social Change in Imperial Japan.* Honolulu: University of Hawai'i Press, 2006.

Bestor, Theodore C. *Neighborhood Tokyo.* Stanford, Calif.: Stanford University Press, 1989.

Betros, Chris. "Tokyo Won't Be Able to Cope with Katrina-like Flooding." *Japan Today* online, August 1, 2008.

Blaxell, Vivian. "Designs of Power." *The Asia-Pacific Journal* online 35, no. 2 (August 31, 2009): pp. 1–18.

Bourdieu, Pierre. *Distinction: A Social Critique of the Judgment of Taste.* Translated by Richard Nice. Cambridge, Mass.: Harvard University Press, 1984.

Brombert, Victor. *In Praise of Antiheroes.* Chicago: University of Chicago Press, 1999.

Brown, Robert D., and Yokohari Makoto. "Ideological Contribution of Satoyamas." In Takeuchi Kazuhiko, Robert D. Brown, Washitani Izumi, Tsunekawa Atsushi, and Yokohari Makoto, eds., *Satoyama: The Traditional Rural Landscape of Japan,* pp. 1–7. Tokyo: Springer-Verlag, 2003.

Brulle, Robert J. *Agency, Democracy, and Nature: The U.S. Environmental Movement from a Critical Theory Perspective.* Cambridge, Mass.: MIT Press, 2000.

Bunkachō Bunkazai Hogobu, ed. *Tennen kinenbutsu jiten.* Tokyo: Daiichi Hōki Shuppan, 1971.

Burchell, Graham, Colin Gordon, and Peter Miller, eds. *The Foucault Effect: Studies in Governmentality with Two Lectures by and an Interview with Michel Foucault.* London: Harvester Wheatsheaf, 1991.

Burton, Melanie. "Hurting Japan's Homeless." *Japan Times* online, January 18, 2005.

Caracas, Cary. "Remembering and Memorializing the Tokyo Air Raids." Unpublished manuscript, University of California, Berkeley, 2003.

Carle, Ron. "Democracy in Action: Heritage Preservation as a Social Movement." *Asian Cultural Studies* 32 (2006): pp. 141–155.

Carter, Paul. *The Road to Botany Bay: An Essay in Spatial History.* Boston: Faber and Faber, 1987.

Chadwick, George F. *The Park and the Town: Public Landscape in the 19th and 20th Centuries.* New York: Praeger, 1966.

Chamberlain, Basil H., and W. B. Mason. *Handbook for Travellers in Japan,* 3rd ed. Yokohama: Kelly & Walsh, 1891.

Chen Yuanyang. *Taiwan no genjūmin to kokka kōen.* Fukuoka: Kyushu Daigaku Shuppankai, 1999.

Choi, Ellie Y. "Laying Claim to the Diamond Mountains: Travel and the Historical Imagination." Paper, Association for Asian Studies Annual Meeting. Atlanta, Ga., April 3–6, 2008.

———. "Space and National Identity: Yi Kwangsu's Vision of Korea during the Japanese Empire." PhD Dissertation, Harvard University, 2009.

Club Smart Life, ed. *Tokyo yasuragi kūkan mappu.* Tokyo: Tokyo Shoseki, 2004.

Collins, Sandra. *The 1940 Tokyo Games: The Missing Olympics.* London: Routledge, 2007.

Cranz, Galen. *The Politics of Park Design: A History of Urban Parks in America.* Cambridge, Mass.: MIT Press, 1982.

Cronon, William. *Changes in the Land: Indians, Colonists, and the Ecology of New England.* New York: Hill and Wang, 1985.

———. "The Trouble with Wilderness; or, Getting Back to the Wrong Nature." In William Cronon, ed., *Uncommon Ground: Rethinking the Human Place in Nature,* pp. 69–90. New York: W. W. Norton, 1995.

Cybriwsky, Roman. *Tokyo: The Shogun's City at the Twenty-First Century.* New York: John Wiley & Sons, 1998.

Dan Inō. *The Reconstruction of Tokyo and Aesthetic Problems of Architecture.* Tokyo: Japan Council of the Institute of Pacific Relations, 1931.

Daston, Lorraine, and Fernando Vidal., eds. *The Moral Authority of Nature.* Chicago: University of Chicago Press, 2004.

Davis, Ann Marie L. "Exporting (Double) Standards and Western Morality: Compulsory Venereal Disease Testing in the Japanese Treaty Ports, 1860–1890." Lecture, Modern Japanese History Workshop, Waseda University, May 12, 2006.

Diamond, Jared. *Collapse: How Societies Choose to Fail or Succeed.* New York: Viking, 2005.

DiSilvestro, Roger L. *Reclaiming the Last Wild Places: A New Agenda for Biodiversity.* New York: John Wiley & Sons, 1993.

Doell, Charles E., and Gerald B. Fitzgerald. *A Brief History of Parks and Recreation in the United States.* Chicago: Athletic Institute, 1954.

Dower, John W. *Embracing Defeat: Japan in the Wake of World War II*. New York: W. W. Norton, 1999.

Elliott, Hugh, ed. *Second World Conference on National Parks*. Morges, Switz.: International Union for Conservation of Nature and Natural Resources, 1974.

Enbutsu, Sumiko. "Drenched in History: Scenic Senzoku Pond." *Japan Times* online, October 3, 2003.

———. "It's a Stroll in the Park to Find the Old Yoyogi." *Japan Times* online, December 3, 2004.

Environmental Information Center. *Aspects of Nature: National Survey on the Natural Environment, Japan*. Tokyo: Kankyōchō, 1989.

Ericson, Steven J. *The Sound of the Whistle: Railroads and the State in Meiji Japan*. Cambridge, Mass.: Harvard University Council on East Asian Studies, 1996.

Esashi Yōji. *Toshi ryokuka shinseiki*. Tokyo: Heibonsha, 2000.

Fackler, Martin. "Flush with Cash, More Asian Tourists Flock to Japan." *New York Times* online, July 26, 2008.

———. "Grass-Roots Uprising Against River Dam Challenges Tokyo." *New York Times* online, March 3, 2009.

Feldhoff, Thomas. "Japan's Construction Lobby and the Privatization of Highway-related Public Corporations." In André Sorensen and Carolin Funck, eds., *Living Cities in Japan: Citizens' Movements, Machizukuri and Local Environments*, pp. 91–112. London: Routledge, 2007.

Fisher, James, Noel Simon, and Jack Vincent. *Wildlife in Danger*. New York: Viking, 1969.

Foster, Karen A. "Time Well Spent." *Japan Times* online, September 27, 2005.

Foucault, Michel. *The Foucault Reader*. Edited by Paul Rabinow. New York: Pantheon, 1984.

Frome, Michael. *Regreening the National Parks*. Tucson: University of Arizona Press, 1992.

Fujii, James A. "Introduction." In Maeda Ai, *Text and the City: Essays on Japanese Modernity*, ed. James A. Fujii, pp. 1–17. Durham, N.C.: Duke University Press, 2004.

Fujimori Terunobu. *Meiji no Tokyo keikaku*, 3rd ed. Tokyo: Iwanami, 2004.

Fujimoto Tarō. "Building a Barrier-Free Society." *Japan Today* online, January 29, 2009.

Fujitani, Takashi. *Splendid Monarchy: Power and Pageantry in Modern Japan*. Berkeley: University of California Press, 1996.

Fukada Takahiro. "New Tourism Agency to Act as Policy 'Control Tower.'" *Japan Times* online, October 1, 2008.

Fukukawa Shinji and Ichikawa Hiroo, eds. *Gurōbaru furonto Tokyo*. Tokyo: Toshi Shuppan, 2008.

Fukutomi Hisao and Ishii Hiroshi, eds. *Midori no keikaku: toshi kōen to shizen kōen*. Tokyo: Chikyūsha, 1985.

Funase Shunsuke. *"Okujō ryokuka" kanzen gaido*. Tokyo: Tsukiji Shokan, 2003.

Funck, Carolin. "Machizukuri, Civil Society, and the Transformation of Japanese City Planning." In André Sorensen and Carolin Funck, eds., *Living Cities in Japan: Citizens' Movements, Machizukuri and Local Environments*, pp. 137–156. London: Routledge, 2007.

Gaimushō. *Environment and Development: Japan's Experience and Achievement—Japan's National Report to UNCED 1992.* Tokyo: Gaimushō, 1991.

Garon, Sheldon. *Molding Japanese Minds: The State in Everyday Life.* Princeton, N.J.: Princeton University Press, 1997.

Garvin, Alexander. *The American City: What Works, What Doesn't,* 2nd ed. New York: McGraw-Hill, 2002.

Gavin, Masako. *Shiga Shigetaka, 1863–1827: The Forgotten Enlightener.* Richmond, Surrey, Eng.: Curzon, 2001.

Golany, Gideon S., Keisuke Hanaki, and Osamu Koide, eds. *Japanese Urban Environment.* Oxford, Eng.: Pergamon, 1998.

Gordon, Andrew. *Labor and Imperial Democracy in Prewar Japan.* Berkeley: University of California Press, 1991.

———, ed. *Postwar Japan as History.* Berkeley: University of California Press, 1993.

Gordon, Colin. "Governmental Rationality: An Introduction." In Graham Burchell, Colin Gordon, and Peter Miller, eds., *The Foucault Effect: Studies in Governmentality with Two Lectures by and an Interview with Michel Foucault,* pp. 1–51. London: Harvester Wheatsheaf, 1991.

"Green Culture." http://www.green-culture.com/portal/index.html. Accessed December 2, 2005.

Habermas, Jürgen. *The Structural Transformation of the Public Sphere.* Translated by Thomas Burger. Cambridge, Mass.: MIT Press, 1989.

Haley, John O., and Kozo Yamamura, eds. *Land Issues in Japan: A Policy Failure?* Seattle: Society for Japanese Studies, 1992.

Hanayama Yuzuru. *Land Markets and Land Policy in a Metropolitan Area: A Case Study of Tokyo.* Boston: Oelgeschlager, Gunn & Hain, 1986.

Hanes, Jeffrey E. *The City as Subject: Seki Hajime and the Reinvention of Modern Osaka.* Berkeley: University of California Press, 2002.

Hardacre, Helen, and Adam L. Kern, eds. *New Directions in the Study of Meiji Japan.* Leiden: Brill, 1997.

Hardy, Thomas S. "People of the Garden: Aesthetics in Everyday Life in a Tokyo Neighborhood." PhD Dissertation, New School for Social Research, 1986.

Harigaya Shōkichi. *Bunmei kaika to kōen.* Tokyo: Tokyo Nōgyō Daigaku Shuppankai, 1990.

Harvey, David. *Justice, Nature, and the Geography of Difference.* Cambridge, Mass.: Blackwell, 1996.

Hasegawa Kōichi, Shinohara Chika, and Jeffrey Broadbent. "Volunteerism and the State in Japan." *Japan Focus* online, December 26, 2007.

Hastings, Sally Ann. *Neighborhood and Nation in Tokyo, 1905–1937.* Pittsburgh: University of Pittsburgh Press, 1995.

Havens, Thomas R. H. *Architects of Affluence: The Tsutsumi Family and the Seibu- Saison Enterprises in Twentieth-Century Japan.* Cambridge, Mass.: Harvard University Council on East Asian Studies, 1994.

———. *Artist and Patron in Postwar Japan: Dance, Music, Theater, and the Visual Arts, 1955–1980.* Princeton, N.J.: Princeton University Press, 1982.

———. *Valley of Darkness: The Japanese People and World War Two.* Lanham, Md.: University Press of America, 1986.

Hayasaka Ichirō. "Taiwan no kokuritsu kōen." *Taiwan Hakubutsu Gakkai kaihō* 151 (1936): pp. 182–189.

———. "Taiwan no kokuritsu kōen jigyō ni taisuru kibō." *Taiwan no sanrin* 123 (1936): pp. 238–241.

Hecht, Susanna, and Alexander Cockburn. *Fate of the Forest: Developers, Destroyers and Defenders of the Amazon.* London: Verso, 1989.

Hein, Carola. "Visionary Plans and Planners: Japanese Traditions and Western Influences." In Nicholas Fiévé and Paul Waley, eds., *Japanese Capitals in Historical Perspective: Place, Power and Memory in Kyoto, Edo and Tokyo,* pp. 309–346. London: RoutledgeCurzon, 2003.

Hein, Carola, and Philippe Pelletier, eds. *Cities, Autonomy, and Decentralization in Japan.* London: Routledge, 2006.

Hein, Laura E. "Growth Versus Success: Japan's Economic Policy in Historical Perspective." In Andrew Gordon, ed., *Postwar Japan as History,* pp. 99–122. Berkeley: University of California Press, 1993.

Henry, Todd A. "Respatializing Chosŏn's Royal Capital: The Politics of Japanese Urban Reforms in Early Colonial Seoul, 1905–1919." In Timothy Tangherlini and Sallie Yea, eds., *Sitings: Critical Approaches to Korean Geography,* pp. 15–38. Honolulu: University of Hawai'i Press and Center for Korean Studies, University of Hawai'i, 2008.

Hesse, Stephen. "Asia's First Lady of the Environment." *Japan Times* online, November 30, 2008.

———. "Industrial Forestry: Too Much of a Good Thing." *Japan Times* online, November 26, 2005.

———. "'Sustainability' in a Japanese Way." *Japan Times* online, February 22, 2009.

Hibiya 100. Tokyo: Ueda Shoten, 1984.

Hirano Kanzō. "Kitamura Tokutarō: Nihon no ryokuchi keikaku no paionia." *Randosukēpu kenkyū* 58, no. 1 (1994): pp. 1–4.

Hokkaido University. *The Botanic Garden Field Science Center for Northern Biosphere.* Sapporo: Hokkaido University, 2005.

Honda Seiroku. "Fūkei no riyō to tennen kinenbutsu ni taisuru yo no konponteki shuchō." *Shiseki meishō tennen kinenbutsu* 4, no. 8 (1921): p. 91.

———. *Honda Seiroku taiken 85nen.* Tokyo: Kōdansha, 1952.

———. "Kokuritsu kōen." In Teien Kyōkai, ed., *Toshi to kōen,* pp. 1–11. Tokyo: Seibidō, 1924.

Honma Yoshito. "Dangers of the Resort-Building Drive." *Japan Echo* 17, no. 3 (1990): pp. 72–76.

Horkheimer, Max, and Theodor W. Adorno. *Dialectic of Enlightenment.* Translated by John Cumming. New York: Herder and Herder, 1972.

Howell, David L. *Geographies of Identity in Nineteenth-century Japan.* Berkeley: University of California Press, 2005.

Hoyano Hatsuko. "Struggle over the Arase Dam: Japan's First Dam Removal Begins." Translated by Adam Lebowitz. *Japan Focus* online, July 30, 2004, pp. 1–2.

Hu Wenqing. *Taiwan de kungyuan.* Taibei: Yuanzu Wenhua, 2007.

Hur, Nam-lin. *Prayer and Play in Late Tokugawa Japan: Asakusa Sensōji and Edo Society.* Cambridge, Mass.: Harvard University Asia Center, 2000.

Hyōgoken Engei Kōen Kyōkai, ed. *Hyōgo Kenritsu Maiko Kōen hyakunenshi.* Akashi: Hyōgoken Engei Kōen Kyōkai, 2001.

Ibarakiken Kankō Kyōkai, ed. *Kōdōkan to Kairakuen.* Mito: Ibarakiken Kankō Kyōkai, 1962.

Ichikawa Hiroo. *Bunka to shite no toshi kūkan.* Tokyo: Chikura Shobō, 2007.

Ide Hisato, ed. *Ryokuchi kankyō kagaku.* Tokyo: Asanuma Shoten, 1997.

Iizawa Kōtarō. "Man and Nature in Harmony." *Japan Journal* 3, no. 11 (2007): pp. 20–21.

Ildos, Angela S., and Giorgio G. Bardelli. *The Great National Parks of the World.* Heathrow, Fla.: AAA Publishing, 2001.

"Illustration of Industrial World Exposition Site in Austria." http://jpimg.digital.archives. go.jp/kokuseisai/category/drawing/austria_e.html. Accessed June 30, 2009.

Inagaki Ryūichi. "Taiwan ni okeru kokuritsu kōen mondai." *Kokuritsu kōen* 8, no. 1 (1936): pp. 6–9.

Inamori Mitsuhiko. *Satoyama monogatari.* Tokyo: Shinchōsha, 1995.

Inose Naoki. *Nihonkoku no kenkyū tsuzuku.* Tokyo: Bungei Shunjū, 2002.

Inoshita Kiyoshi. *Inoshita Kiyoshi chosakushū toshi to midori.* Tokyo: Tokyoto Kōen Kyōkai, 1973.

Inoue Enryō. *Tetsugakudō annai,* rev. ed. Tokyo: Tetsugakudō, 1924.

Inoue Tomoichi. *Jichi yōgi.* Tokyo: Hakubunkan, 1909.

Inoue Yūichi. "Dam Shame: Tokyo and Kansai Flush with Water." *Japan Focus* online, March 23, 2006.

Ishida, Takeshi, and Ellis S. Krauss, eds. *Democracy in Japan.* Pittsburgh: University of Pittsburgh Press, 1989.

Ishida Yorifusa. "Local Initiatives and the Decentralization of Planning Power in Japan." In Carola Hein and Philippe Pelletier, eds., *Cities, Autonomy, and Decentralization in Japan,* pp. 25–54. London: Routledge, 2006.

———. *Mori Ōgai no toshiron to sono jidai.* Tokyo: Nihon Keizai Hyōronsha, 1999.

———. *Nihon kindai toshi keikaku no hyakunen.* Tokyo: Jichitai Kenkyūsha, 1987.

———. *Nihon kindai toshi keikakushi kenkyū.* Tokyo: Kashiwa Shobō, 1987.

———. *Nihon kingendai toshi keikaku no tenkai 1868–2003*. Tokyo: Jichitai Kenkyūsha, 2004.

Ishii Hiroshi and Woo Hyung Taek. "Kankoku no kokuritsu kōen (1)." *Kokuritsu kōen* 380 (1981): pp. 6–12.

Ishikawa Mikiko. *Toshi to ryokuchi*. Tokyo: Iwanami, 2001.

Ishikawa Sadatoshi. "Taiwan ni okeru kokuritsu kōen no enkaku." *Kokuritsu kōen* 10, no. 1 (1938): pp. 6–7.

Ishimure Michiko. *Tenko*. Tokyo: Asahi Shinbunsha, 1997.

Ishiuchi Nobuyuki. *Kinuta Ryokuchi (Kinuta Fuamirī Pāku)*. Tokyo: Kyōgakusha, 1981.

Isoda Kōichi. *Shisō to shite no Tokyo: Rokumeikan no keifu*. Tokyo: Ozawa Shoten, 1991.

Itō Kunie. *Kōen no yō to bi*. Kyoto: Dōhōsha, 1988.

Itō Taiichi. "The Influence of the American Concept of a National Park on Japan's National Park Movement." In *National Park Ideas, Part 4*, pp. 195–205. Yellowstone National Park, Wyo.: National Park Service, 2004.

———. "Influence of Forestry on the Formation of National Park Policy in Japan." *Journal of Forest Planning* 2 (1996): pp. 85–95.

———. Personal communication. May 17, 2006.

———. "Shizen chiiki rekuriēshon keikaku ni okeru yūryōka no tenkai." *Shinrin Keikaku Gakkaishi*, 39, no. 2 (2005): pp. 183–196.

Itō Taiichi and Tanaka Nobuhiko, eds. *Social Roles of Forests for Urban Population: Forest Recreation, Landscape, Nature Conservation, Economic Evaluation and Urban Forestry*. Tokyo: Japan Society of Forest Planning Press, 2004.

Itō Takehiko. *Kokuritsu Kōenhō kaisetsu*. Tokyo: Kokuritsu Kōen Kyōkai, 1931.

Itō Yukio, ed. *Ima, kōen de nani ga okite iru ka*. Tokyo: Gyōsei, 2002.

Itoh, Takashi. "Design and Layout Plan of Bridges and Parks in Reconstruction Project after the Great Kanto Earthquake." In Tokyo Metropolitan University, ed., *Tokyo: Urban Growth and Planning*, pp. 96–101. Tokyo: Tokyo Metropolitan University, 1998.

Iwai, Yoshiya. "Introduction." In Yoshiya Iwai, ed., *Forestry and the Forest Industry in Japan*, pp. xii–xx. Vancouver: University of British Columbia Press, 2002.

———. "New Relationship between Forests and City Dwellers in Japan." In Yoshiya Iwai, ed., *Forestry and the Forest Industry in Japan*, pp. 278–291. Vancouver: University of British Columbia Press, 2002.

———, ed. *Forestry and the Forest Industry in Japan*. Vancouver: University of British Columbia Press, 2002.

Iwamoto, Jun'ichi. "The Development of Japanese Forestry." In Yoshiya Iwai, ed., *Forestry and the Forest Industry in Japan*, pp. 3–9. Vancouver: University of British Columbia Press, 2002.

Iwata, Masami, and Akihiko Nishizawa, eds. *Poverty and Social Welfare in Japan*. Melbourne: Trans Pacific Press, 2008.

Iwata Shūkō. *Taiwan kokuritsu kōen gashū*. Taihoku: Taiwan Kokuritsu Kōen Kyōkai, 1940.

Jacobs, Jane. *The Death and Life of Great American Cities.* New York: Random House, 1961.

"Japan's First Ambassadors to the U.S." http://jasgp.org/content/view/431/179/. Accessed June 30, 2009.

"Japan's UNESCO World Heritage Sites." http://www.japan-guide.com/e/e2251.html. Accessed July 5, 2009.

Jinnai, Hidenobu. *Tokyo: A Spatial Anthropology.* Translated by Kimiko Nishimura. Berkeley: University of California Press, 1995.

Jones, Karen R., and John Wills. *The Invention of the Park from the Garden of Eden to Disney's Magic Kingdom.* Cambridge, Eng.: Polity Press, 2005.

Jordan, David P. *Transforming Paris: The Life and Labors of Baron Haussmann.* New York: Free Press, 1995.

Kamahori Miki. "Japan's Cultural Heritage Preservation Policy." *Japan Journal* online 4, no. 10 (2007).

Kameyama Hajime and Matsuzaki Yuriko. *Yasashii hito o tsukuru kōen e—yunibasāru dezain no tenkai.* Tokyo: Shinjusha, 2004.

Kanai Toshihiko. *Shinjuku Gyoen,* rev. ed. Tokyo: Tokyoto Kōen Kyōkai, 1993.

Kanai Toshiyuki. "Vectors of Change in Japan's Political and Fiscal Decentralization." *Social Science Japan* 37 (2007): pp. 3–6.

Kanda, Kōji. "Landscapes of National Parks in Taiwan During the Japanese Colonial Period." In Mizuuchi Toshio, ed., *Representing Local Places and Raising Voices from Below,* pp. 112–119. Osaka: Osaka City University, Department of Geography and Urban Culture Research Center, 2003.

Kankyōchō. *Nature Conservation Administration in Japan.* Tokyo: Kankyōchō, 1985.

———. *Nihon no shizen kankyō.* Tokyo: Kankyōchō, 1982.

———. *Quality of the Environment in Japan 1980.* Tokyo: Ōkurashō Insatsukyoku, 1981.

Kankyōchō Shizen Hogokyoku. *Shizen hogo gyōsei no ayumi.* Tokyo: Daiichi Hōki Shuppan, 1981.

Kankyōshō. *Kankyō hakusho.* Tokyo: Gyōsei, 2004.

———. *Kankyō tōkeishū.* Tokyo: Kankyōshō, 2005, 2008.

———. *Quality of the Environment in Japan 2002.* Tokyo: Kankyōshō, 2002.

Karan, Pradyumna P. *Japan in the 21st Century: Environment, Economy, and Society.* Lexington: University Press of Kentucky, 2005.

Kashima Shigeru. "Hibiya Kōen o tsukutta Honda Seiroku to iu hito." *Tokyojin* 18, no. 11 (2003): pp. 108–113.

Katayama Sen. *Toshi shakaigaku.* Tokyo: Shakaishugi Toshokan, 1903.

Katō Akinori. *Nihonteki hiroba no aru machi: Midori mizu tsuchi.* Tokyo: Purosesu Ākitekuchua, 1993.

Katō Akira and Takeuchi Denshi. *Shin toshi keikaku gairon.* Tokyo: Kyōritsu Shuppan, 2004.

Katō Mineo. *Mokutekichi wa kokuritsu kōen.* Morioka: Shinzansha, 2001.

Katō Sadamichi. "The Three Ecologies in Minakata Kumagusu's Environmental Movement." *Organization & Environment* 12 (1999): pp. 85–98.

Katō Yūzō, ed. *Yokohama Past and Present.* Yokohama: Yokohama City University, 1990.

Katz, Richard. *Japan: The System that Soured—The Rise and Fall of the Japanese Economic Miracle.* Armonk, N.Y.: M. E. Sharpe, 1998.

Kawakami Sachio. *Koishikawa Shokubutsuen.* Tokyo: Kyōgakusha, 1981.

Kawamoto Akio. *Sumida Kōen.* Tokyo: Kyōgakusha, 1981.

Kensetsushō, ed. *Nihon no toshi.* Tokyo: Daiichi Hōki Shuppan, 1990.

———, ed. *Nihon no toshi seisaku.* Tokyo: Gyōsei, 1984.

Kerr, Alex. *Dogs and Demons: The Fall of Modern Japan.* London: Penguin, 2001.

Kimura Hideo. *Toshi bōkū to ryokuchi kūchi.* Tokyo: Nihon Kōen Ryokuchi Kyōkai, 1990.

Kimura Shōzaburō, ed. *Machizukuri no kokoro: Miryoku aru chiiki bunka no sōzō.* Tokyo: Gyōsei, 1990.

Kingston, Jeffrey. *Japan's Quiet Transformation: Social Change and Civil Society in the Twenty-first Century.* London: RoutledgeCurzon, 2004.

Knight, Catherine. "Natural Environments, Wildlife, and Conservation in Japan." *Japan Focus* online, January 25, 2010.

Knight, John. *Waiting for Wolves in Japan: An Anthropological Study of People-Wildlife Relations.* Oxford, Eng.: Oxford University Press, 2003.

Kobayashi Yasushige. *Ueno Kōen,* rev. ed. Tokyo: Tokyoto Kōen Kyōkai, 1994.

Kōda Rohan. *Ikkoku no shuto: Hoka ippen.* Tokyo: Iwanami, 1993 (1899).

Kodansha Encyclopedia of Japan, 9 vols. Tokyo: Kōdansha, 1983.

Kōdansha Sōgō Hensankyoku, ed. *Nihon no tennen kinenbutsu.* Tokyo: Kōdansha, 2003.

Kōen Ryokuchi Gyōsei Kenkyūkai, ed. *Gaisetsu atarashii Toshi Ryokuchihō Toshi Kōenhō.* Tokyo: Gyōsei, 2005.

———, ed. *Kaisei toshi kōen seido Q & A.* Tokyo: Gyōsei, 1993.

Kōen Ryokuchi Iji Kanri Kenkyūkai, ed. *Kōen ryokuchi no iji kanri to sekisan,* 4th rev. ed. Tokyo: Keizai Chōsakai, 2005.

Kōen Ryokuchi Kanri Zaidan. *Ryokka bunka no chishiki nintei shiken kōshiki zenmondaishū.* Tokyo: Tokyo Shoseki, 2004.

———, ed. *Kōen Ryokuchi Kanri Zaidan 30nenshi.* Tokyo: Kōen Ryokuchi Kanri Zaidan, 2004.

Kohama Seikō. "Kokuritsu kōen no shimei." *Taiwan no sanrin* 123 (1936): pp. 2–5.

Kohara Takaharu. "The Great Heisei Consolidation: A Critical Review." *Social Science Japan* 37 (2007): pp. 7–11.

Koishikawa Kōrakuen. Wooden plaque outside main entrance to the park.

Kojima Usui. *Nihon Arupusu,* 4 vols. Tokyo: Maekawa Bun'eikaku, 1910–1915.

Kokuritsu Kōen Kyōkai. *Kokuritsu kōen annai.* Tokyo: Kokuritsu Kōen Kyōkai, 1933.

———. *Kokuritsu kōentō minkan katsuyō tokutei shizen kankyō hozen katsudō (gurīn wākā) jigyō suishin chōsa hōkokusho, Heisei 13nendo.* Tokyo: Kokuritsu Kōen Kyōkai, 2002.

Kokuritsu Kōen Kyōkai, comp. *National Parks of Japan.* Tokyo: Tokyo News Service, 1957.

Kokuritsu Kōen Kyōkai and Nihon Shizen Hogo Kyōkai, eds. *Nihon no shizen kōen.* Tokyo: Kōdansha, 1989.

Kondō Mitsuo. *Toshi ryokuka tokuhon.* Tokyo: Enu Teī Esu, 2007.

Kōseishō Kokuritsu Kōenkyoku and Kokuritsu Kōen Kyōkai. *Nihon no kokuritsu kōen.* Osaka: Sanwa Ginkō, 1964.

Koshizawa Akira. *Fukkō keikaku: Bakumatsu no taika kara Hanshin Awaji daishinsai made.* Tokyo: Chūō Kōronsha, 2005.

Kostof, Spiro. *America by Design.* New York: Oxford University Press, 1987.

Kosugi Takemi. *Hama Rikyū Teien,* rev. ed. Tokyo: Tokyoto Kōen Kyōkai, 1994.

Kubo Mikio. "Taiwan no kokuritsu kōen." *Kokuritsu kōen* 386 (1982): pp. 16–19.

Kuck, Loraine E. *World of the Japanese Garden: From Chinese Origins to Modern Landscape Art.* New York: Weatherhill, 1966.

Kume Kunitake. *Tokumei zenken taishi: Beiō kairan jikki,* vol. 1. Tokyo: Hakubunsha, 1878.

Kunikida Doppo. "Musashino" (1898). In Kunikida Doppo, *Musashino.* Tokyo: Min'yūsha, 1901.

Kunimatsu Yoshitsugu. "Felling Forestry Firms' Towering Debt: Who Will Save the Forests?" *Japan Focus* online, October 6, 2005.

Kuramoto Noboru. "Citizen Conservation of Satoyama Landscapes." In Takeuchi Kazuhiko, Robert D. Brown, Washitani Izumi, Tsunekawa Atsushi, and Yokohari Makoto, eds., *Satoyama: The Traditional Rural Landscape of Japan,* pp. 23–35. Tokyo: Springer-Verlag, 2003.

Kushner, Barak. *The Thought War: Japanese Imperial Propaganda.* Honolulu: University of Hawai'i Press, 2006.

Kyū Furukawa Teien. Tokyo: Tokyoto Kōen Kyōkai, 2004.

Larsson, Gerhard. *Land Readjustment: A Modern Approach to Urbanization.* Brookfield, Vt.: Avebury, 1993.

Lefebvre, Henri. *The Production of Space.* Translated by Donald Nicholson-Smith. Cambridge, Mass.: Blackwell, 1991.

Leheny, David R. *The Rules of Play: National Identity and the Shaping of Japanese Leisure.* Ithaca, N.Y.: Cornell University Press, 2003.

Long, Hoyt J. "On Uneven Ground: Provincializing Cultural Production in Interwar Japan." PhD Dissertation, University of Michigan, 2007.

Louwerse, David. "Why Talk About Park Design." In Andreu Arriola et al., *Modern Park Design: Recent Trends,* pp. 9–16. Amsterdam: Thoth, 1993.

Maeda Ai. *Genkei no Meiji.* Tokyo: Asahi Shinbunsha, 1978.

———. *Text and the City: Essays on Japanese Modernity.* Edited by James A. Fujii. Durham, N.C.: Duke University Press, 2004.

Maejima Yasuhiko. *Hibiya Kōen,* rev. ed. Tokyo: Tokyoto Kōen Kyōkai, 1994.

———. *Inokashira Kōen,* rev. ed. Tokyo: Tokyoto Kōen Kyōkai, 1995.

———. *Tokyo kōenshi banashi.* Tokyo: Tokyoto Kōen Kyōkai, 1989.

Maki Fumihiko. *Miegakuresuru toshi: Edo kara Tokyo e.* Tokyo: Kajima Shuppankai, 1980.

Makiguchi Tsunesaburō. *Jinsei chirigaku.* Tokyo: Bunkaidō, 1903.

Margolis, Abby R. "Samurai Beneath Blue Tarps: Doing Homelessness, Rejecting Marginality and Preserving Nation in Ueno Park." PhD Dissertation, University of Pittsburgh, 2002.

Marotti, William. "Japan 1968: The Performance of Violence and the Theater of Protest." *The American Historical Review* 114, no. 1 (2009): pp. 97–135.

Marra, Michele [Michael F. Marra], trans. and ed. *A History of Modern Japanese Aesthetics.* Honolulu: University of Hawai'i Press, 2001.

Maruta Yorikazu. *Toshi ryokuka keikakuron.* Tokyo: Maruzen, 1994.

Maruyama, Masao. *Studies in the Intellectual History of Tokugawa Japan.* Translated by Mikiso Hane. Tokyo: University of Tokyo Press, 1974.

Maruyama Hiroshi. *Kindai Nihon kōenshi no kenkyū.* Kyoto: Shibunkan Shuppan, 1994.

Marx, Leo. *The Machine in the Garden: Technology and the Pastoral Ideal in America.* New York: Oxford University Press, 1964.

Masai, Yasuo. "The Human Environment of Tokyo." In Gideon S. Golany, Keisuke Hanaki, and Osamu Koide, eds., *Japanese Urban Environment,* pp. 57–74. Oxford, Eng.: Pergamon, 1998.

Matsushita, Koji. "National Forest Management." In Yoshiya Iwai, ed., *Forestry and the Forest Industry in Japan,* pp. 84–117. Vancouver: University of British Columbia Press, 2002.

Matsushita, Koji, and Kunihiro Hirata. "Forestry Owners' Associations." In Yoshiya Iwai, ed., *Forestry and the Forest Industry in Japan,* pp. 41–66. Vancouver: University of British Columbia Press, 2002.

Maxey, Trent E. "Defining the 'Greatest Problem': Religion and State Formation in Meiji Japan." Lecture, Harvard University, October 17, 2008.

McClelland, Linda Flint. *Building the National Parks: Historic Landscape Design and Construction.* Baltimore: The Johns Hopkins University Press, 1998.

McKean, Margaret A. *Environmental Protest and Citizen Politics in Japan.* Berkeley: University of California Press, 1981.

McNeely, Jeffrey A., Jeremy Harrison, and Paul R. Dingwell, eds. *Protecting Nature: Regional Reviews of Protected Areas.* Gland, Switz.: International Union for Conservation of Nature and Natural Resources, 1994.

Miller, Ian J. "Didactic Nature: Exhibiting Nation and Empire at the Ueno Zoological Gardens." In Gregory M. Pflugfelder and Brett L. Walker, eds., *JAPANimals: History and Culture in Japan's Animal Life,* pp. 273–313. Ann Arbor: University of Michigan Center for Japanese Studies, 2005.

Mitchell, John Hanson. *The Wildest Place on Earth: Italian Gardens and the Invention of Wilderness.* Washington, D.C.: Counterpoint, 2001.

Mitchell, Timothy. *Colonising Egypt.* Berkeley: University of California Press, 1991.

Mitrašinović, Miodrag. *Total Landscape, Theme Parks, Public Space.* Aldershot, Eng.: Ashgate, 2006.

Mitsuda Hisayoshi and Charles Geisler. "Imperiled Parks and Imperiled People: Lessons from Japan's Shiretoko National Park." *Environmental History Review* 16, no. 2 (1992): pp. 23–39.

Mitsui, Shoji. "National and Regional Forest Policies." In Yoshiya Iwai, ed., *Forestry and the Forest Industry in Japan,* pp. 145–158. Vancouver: University of British Columbia Press, 2002.

Miyanishi Yūji. "Cheer for Kobe-Style Machizukuri Organizations" (2002). http://www.gakugei-pub.jp/kobe/key_e/en2002.htm. Accessed July 6, 2009.

Miyaoka Isao. *Legitimacy in International Society: Japan's Reaction to Global Wildlife Preservation.* New York: Palgrave Macmillan, 2004.

Miyoshi Manabu. *Shokubutsu seitai bikan.* Tokyo: Fuzanbō, 1902.

Mizuuchi Toshio, ed. *Representing Local Places and Raising Voices from Below.* Osaka: Osaka City University, Department of Geography and Urban Culture Research Center, 2003.

Mori Mamoru. *Rikugien,* 3rd ed. Tokyo: Tokyoto Kōen Kyōkai, 2001.

Mori Midori and Hibi Sadao. *Tokyo midori sansaku.* Osaka: Hoikusha, 1988.

Mori Ōgai and Koike Masanao. *Eisei shinpen.* Tokyo: Nankōdō, 1897.

Morohashi Tetsuji. *Dai Kanwa jiten,* 13 vols. Tokyo: Taishūkan Shoten, 1955–1960.

Morton, Timothy. *Ecology without Nature: Rethinking Environmental Aesthetics.* Cambridge, Mass.: Harvard University Press, 2007.

Munroe, Alexandra, ed. *New Public Architecture: Recent Projects by Fumihiko Maki and Arata Isozaki.* New York: Japan Society, 1985.

Murakushi Nisaburō. *Kokuritsu kōen seiritsushi no kenkyū: Kaihatsu to shizen hogo no kakushitsu o chūshin ni.* Tokyo: Hōsei Daigaku Shuppankyoku, 2005.

Murasaki Nagaaki. *Taihoku shashinchō.* Taihoku: Shinkōdō Shoten, 1913.

Muschamp, Herbert. "Looking Beyond Vision." In Herbert Muschamp et al., *The Once and Future Park,* pp. 11–14. New York: Princeton Architectural Press, 1993.

———, et al. *The Once and Future Park.* New York: Princeton Architectural Press, 1993.

Nagamine, Haruo, ed. *Urban Development Policies and Programmes.* Nagoya: United Nations Centre for Regional Development, 1986.

Naikaku Sōridaijin Kanbō Kōhōshitsu. *Toshi kōen ni kansuru seron chōsa.* Tokyo: Naikaku, 1967.

Naimushō. *Preservation of Natural Monuments in Japan.* Tokyo: Department of Home Affairs, 1926.

Nakabayashi Itsuki. "Concentration and Deconcentration in the Context of the Tokyo Capital Region Plan and Recent Cross-Border Networking Concepts." In Carola Hein and Philippe Pelletier, eds., *Cities, Autonomy, and Decentralization in Japan,* pp. 55–80. London: Routledge, 2006.

Nakayama Tōru. *Osaka no midori o kangaeru.* Osaka: Tōhō Shuppan, 1994.

Narumi Masayasu. *Yokohama Yamate Kōen monogatari.* Yokohama: Yūrindō, 2004.

Nash, Roderick F., ed. *American Environmentalism*. New York: McGraw-Hill, 1990.

———. "The Roots of American Environmentalism." In John R. Stilgoe, Roderick F. Nash, and Alfred Runte, *Perceptions of the Landscape and Its Preservation*, pp. 29–50. Indianapolis: Indiana Historical Society, 1984.

———. *Wilderness and the American Mind*, 4th ed. New Haven, Conn.: Yale University Press, 2001.

National Report of Japan Prepared for Habitat: United Nations Conference on Human Settlements. Tokyo: Government of Japan, 1976.

National Science Museum, Tokyo. *The Institute for Nature Study*. Tokyo: National Science Museum, 1992.

Nelson, John K. *Enduring Identities: The Guise of Shinto in Contemporary Japan*. Honolulu: University of Hawai'i Press, 2000.

Nelson, Michael P., and J. Baird Callicott, eds. *The Wilderness Debate Rages On*. Athens: University of Georgia Press, 2008.

Neumann, Mark. *On the Rim: Looking for the Grand Canyon*. Minneapolis: University of Minnesota Press, 1999.

Neumann, Roderick P. *Imposing Wilderness: Struggles over Livelihood and Nature Preservation in Africa*. Berkeley: University of California Press, 1998.

Newton, Norman T. *Design on the Land: The Development of Landscape Architecture*. Cambridge, Mass.: Harvard University Press, 1971.

Nihon Kōen Ryokuchi Kyōkai. *Kokuei kōen*. Tokyo: Nihon Kōen Ryokuchi Kyōkai, 1990.

———, ed. *Kōen ryokuchi manyuaru*. Tokyo: Nihon Kōen Ryokuchi Kyōkai, 2004.

———, ed. *Nihon no toshi kōen*. Tokyo: Nihon Kōen Ryokuchi Kyōkai, 1978.

Nihon Kōtsū Kōsha. *Kokuritsu kōen to kokutei kōen*. Tokyo: Nihon Kōtsū Kōsha, 1970.

Nihon Shizen Hogo Kyōkai. *21seiki no shizen o kangaeru—kokuritsu kōen no risōzō o motomete*. Tokyo: Nihon Shizen Hogo Kyōkai, 2001.

———. *Shizen hogo o ika ni susumeru ka*. Tokyo: Nihon Shizen Hogo Kyōkai, 1975.

———. *Yutaka na shizen, fukai fureai, pātonāshippu: 21seiki no kokuritsu kōen no arikata o kangaeru*. Tokyo: Nihon Shizen Hogo Kyōkai, 2000.

Nihon Toshi Keikaku Gakkai, ed. *Toshi keikaku no chihō bunken: Machizukuri no jissen*. Tokyo: Gakugei Shuppansha, 1999.

Nihon Toshi Sentā. *Toshi to kōen ryokuchi: Ningensei kaifuku e no michi*. Tokyo: Nihon Toshi Sentā, 1974.

Nikkei Ākitekuchua, ed. *Jitsurei ni manabu okujō ryokuka*. Tokyo: Nikkei BPsha, 2003.

Nish, Ian, ed. *The Iwakura Mission in America and Europe: A New Assessment*. Richmond, Surrey, Eng.: Japan Library, 1998.

Nishimura Yukio. *Toshi hozen keikaku*. Tokyo: Tokyo Daigaku Shuppankai, 2004.

Nishiyama Yasuo. "Western Influence on Urban Planning Administration in Japan: Focus on Land Management." In Haruo Nagamine, ed., *Urban Development Policies and Programmes*, pp. 315–355. Nagoya: United Nations Centre for Regional Development, 1986.

Noguchi Hiroyuki. "Out of the Woods." *Japan Journal* 3, no. 4 (2006): pp. 6–10.

Nomoto Kyōhachirō. *Meiji kinen Nihon daikōen sōsetsugi.* Tokyo: Nomoto Kyōhachirō, 1908.

Nōrin Chūkin Sōgō Kenkyūjo. *Satochi shizen chiikitō shizen kankyō hozen chōsa hōkokusho, Heisei kyūnendo.* Tokyo: Nōrin Chūkin Sōgō Kenkyūjo, 1998.

Numata Makoto. *Seitaigaku hōhōron.* Tokyo: Kokon Shoin, 1967.

Ōbayashi Munetsugu. *Toshi shakai seisaku to shite no kōen mondai.* Tokyo: Ōhara Shakai Mondai Kenkyūjo, 1923.

Oelschlaeger, Max. *The Idea of Wilderness: From Prehistory to the Age of Ecology.* New Haven, Conn.: Yale University Press, 1991.

Ōi Michio. *Fūkei e no banka: Watakushi no shizen hogoron.* Tokyo: Anvieru, 1978.

——. "The Role of National Parks in Social and Economic Development Process." In Hugh Elliott, ed., *Second World Conference on National Parks,* pp. 1–10. Morges, Switz.: International Union for Conservation of Nature and Natural Resources, 1974.

Okada, Richard. "'Landscape' and the Nation-State: A Reading of *Nihon fūkeiron.*" In Helen Hardacre and Adam L. Kern, eds., *New Directions in the Study of Meiji Japan,* pp. 90–107. Leiden: Brill, 1997.

Okada Kōyō. *Taiwan kokuritsu kōen shashinshū.* Taihoku: Taiwan Kokuritsu Kōen Kyōkai, 1939.

Okada Masahiko. "Taking a Walk around the Hall of Philosophy: Science, Philosophy, and Religion in Modern Japan." Lecture, University of Chicago, May 1, 2005.

Okamoto, Shumpei. *The Japanese Oligarchy and the Russo-Japanese War.* New York: Columbia University Press, 1970.

Ono Ryōhei. *Kōen no tanjō.* Tokyo: Yoshikawa Kōbunkan, 2003.

Ono Sawako, ed. *Konna kōen ga hoshii.* Tokyo: Tsukiji Shokan, 1997.

Osaka Shiyakusho. *An Outline of Municipal Administration of the City of Osaka, 1930.* Osaka: Osaka Shiyakusho, 1930.

Osakafu Doboku Kōenka, ed. *Osakafu toshi kōen ichiranhyō.* Osaka: Osakafu, 1985.

"Our Town." *Japan Journal* online, May 2008.

Overmyer-Velázquez, Mark. "Visions of the Emerald City: Politics, Culture, and Alternative Modernities in Oaxaca City, Mexico, 1877–1920." PhD Dissertation, Yale University, 2002.

Ōya Reijō. *Kōen oyobi undōjō: Keikaku sekkei sekō.* Tokyo: Shōkabō, 1930.

Oyadomari, Motoko. "The Politics of National Parks in Japan." PhD Dissertation, University of Wisconsin, Madison, 1985.

Peattie, Mark R. "Japanese Treaty Port Settlements in China, 1895–1937." In Peter Duus, Ramon H. Myers, and Mark R. Peattie, eds., *The Japanese Informal Empire in China, 1895–1937,* pp. 166–209. Princeton, N.J.: Princeton University Press, 1989.

Pflugfelder, Gregory M., and Brett L. Walker, eds. *JAPANimals: History and Culture in Japan's Animal Life.* Ann Arbor: University of Michigan Center for Japanese Studies, 2005.

Preisser, Evan. Personal communication. March 9, 2005.

Pulvers, Roger. "Japan's Wild Scientific Genius: Minakata Kumagusu." *Japan Focus* on-line, January 20, 2008.

Pyle, Kenneth B. *The New Generation in Meiji Japan: Problems of Cultural Identity, 1885–1895.* Stanford, Calif.: Stanford University Press, 1969.

Richey, Charles A. *A Study of the Japanese National Parks April–August 1948.* Tokyo: General Headquarters, Supreme Commander for the Allied Powers, Civil Information and Education Section, 1948.

Robertson, Jennifer. *Native and Newcomer: Making and Remaking a Japanese City.* Berkeley: University of California Press, 1991.

Rogaski, Ruth. *Hygienic Modernity: Meanings of Health and Disease in Treaty-Port China.* Berkeley: University of California Press, 2004.

Roy, Michael Jay. "National Forest Management in Hokkaido, Japan: Biodiversity Conservation Considerations." PhD Dissertation, University of Montana, 1998.

Runte, Alfred. *National Parks: The American Experience,* 3rd ed. Lincoln: University of Nebraska Press, 1997.

——. "Preservation Heritage: The Origin of the Park Idea in the United States." In John R. Stilgoe, Roderick F. Nash, and Alfred Runte, *Perceptions of the Landscape and Its Preservation,* pp. 53–75. Indianapolis: Indiana Historical Society, 1984.

Ryokuka kenchiku nenkan 2005. Tokyo: Sōjusha, 2005.

Sakamoto Shintarō. *Nihon no toshi kōen: Sono seibi no rekishi.* Tokyo: Intarakushon, 2005.

Sanada Junko. *Toshi no midori wa dō arubeki ka.* Tokyo: Gihōdō, 2007.

Sand, Jordan. *House and Home in Modern Japan: Architecture, Domestic Space, and Bourgeois Culture, 1880–1930.* Cambridge, Mass.: Harvard University Asia Center, 2003.

Sassen, Saskia, ed. *Deciphering the Global: Its Scales, Spaces and Subjects.* New York: Routledge, 2007.

Satō Akira and Shimoyama Shigemaru. *Landscape Planning and Recreation in Japan.* Tokyo: Nihon Kōen Ryokuchi Kyōkai, 1985.

Sawaji Osamu. "Back to the Roots." *Japan Journal* 2, no. 5 (2005): pp. 6–11.

Scalapino, Robert A. *The Japanese Communist Movement, 1920–1966.* Berkeley: University of California Press, 1966.

Schencking, J. Charles. "The Great Kanto Earthquake and the Culture of Catastrophe and Reconstruction in 1920s Japan." *Journal of Japanese Studies* 34, no. 2 (2008): pp. 295–331.

Schuyler, David. *The New Urban Landscape.* Baltimore: The Johns Hopkins University Press, 1986.

Scott, James C. *Seeing Like a State: How Certain Schemes to Improve the Human Condition Have Failed.* New Haven, Conn.: Yale University Press, 1998.

Seidensticker, Edward. *Low City, High City: Tokyo from Edo to the Earthquake.* New York: Knopf, 1983.

Senge Tetsumaro. "The Educational Contributions of National Parks in Japan." In Alexander B. Adams, ed., *First World Conference on National Parks: Proceedings,* pp.

239–246. Washington, D.C.: National Park Service, U.S. Department of the Interior, 1962.

———. "Kokuritsu Kōen Kyōkai 50nen o kaerimite." *Kokuritsu kōen* 355 (1979): pp. 10–17.

Seta Nobuya. *Saiseisuru kokuritsu kōen: Nihon no shizen to fūkei o mamori, sasaeru hitotachi.* Tokyo: Asahi Bīru, 2009.

Seymour, Whitney North, Jr., ed. *Small Urban Spaces: The Philosophy, Design, Sociology, and Politics of Vest-pocket Parks and Other Small Urban Spaces.* New York: New York University Press, 1969.

Shibano Kōichirō. *Kankyōchō.* Tokyo: Kyōikusha, 1975.

Shibata Tokue. *Nihon no toshi seisaku: Sono seiji keizaigakuteki kōsatsu.* Tokyo: Yūhikaku, 1978.

Shiga Shigetaka. *Nihon fūkeiron.* Tokyo: Iwanami, 1937.

Shimazu, Naoko. *Japanese Society at War: Death, Memory and the Russo-Japanese War.* Cambridge, Eng.: Cambridge University Press, 2009.

Shin Yongcheol. *Toshi kōen seisaku keiseishi: Kyōdōkei shakai ni okeru midori to ōpun supēsu no genten.* Tokyo: Hōsei Daigaku Shuppankyoku, 2004.

Shinji Isoya. *Boranteia jidai no midori no machizukuri.* Tokyo: Tokyo Nōdai Shuppankai, 2008.

———. "Kōen no rekishi." In Suzuki Tetsu, Higuchi Tadahiko, Shinji Isoya, Kobayashi Haruto, and Takano Fumiaki, *Kōenzukuri o kangaeru,* pp. 44–104. Tokyo: Gihōdō, 1993.

———. *Midori no machizukurigaku.* Kyoto: Gakugei Shuppansha, 1987.

———. *"Nō" no jidai—surō na machizukuri.* Kyoto: Gakugei Shuppansha, 2003.

Shinrin Kōen. *Shinrin Kōen gaido bukku.* Saitama: Shinrin Kōen, 2005.

Shiojima Dai. *Midori no chōsen.* Tokyo: Kajima Shuppankai, 1982.

Shirahata Yōzaburō. *Kindai toshi kōenshi no kenkyū: Ōka no keifu.* Kyoto: Shibunkan Shuppan, 1995.

———. "Kōen nante mō iranai." *Chūō kōron* 1272 (1991): pp. 184–197.

Shishitsuka no Shizen to Rekishi no Kai. *Shishitsuka no satoyama.* Tsuchiurashi: Shishitsuka no Shizen to Rekishi no Kai, 2003.

Shizen Kōen Zaidan. *Kokuritsu kōen no shizen kankyō no hogo kanri jigyō hōkokusho, Heisei 14nendo.* Tokyo: Shizen Kōen Zaidan, 2003.

Short, Kevin. *Nature in Tokyo: A Guide to Plants and Animals in and around Tokyo.* Tokyo: Kodansha International, 2000.

Simmons, Ian G. *Earth, Air and Water: Resources and Environment in the Late 20th Century.* London: Edward Arnold, 1991.

———. *Environmental History: A Concise Introduction.* Oxford, Eng.: Blackwell, 1993.

Smith, Neil. *Uneven Development: Nature, Capital and the Production of Space.* New York: Blackwell, 1984.

Sollers, Werner. *Neither Black nor White yet Both: Thematic Explorations of Interracial Literature.* Cambridge, Mass.: Harvard University Press, 1997.

Solnit, Rebecca. *Savage Dreams: A Journey into the Hidden Wars of the American West.* San Francisco: Sierra Club, 1994.

Sōmushō Gyōsei Hyōkakyoku. *Shizen kankyō hozen ni kansuru gyōsei hyōka.* Tokyo: Sōmushō, 2002.

Son Chŏng-mok [Sohn Jung Mok]. *Nihon tōchika Chōsen toshi keikakushi kenkyū.* Translated by Nishigaki Yasuhiko, Ichioka Miyuki, and Lee Jong Hee [Yi Chong-hŭi]. Tokyo: Kashiwa Shobō, 2004.

Sorensen, André. "Centralization, Urban Planning Governance, and Citizen Participation in Japan." In Carola Hein and Philippe Pelletier, eds., *Cities, Autonomy, and Decentralization in Japan,* pp. 101–127. London: Routledge, 2006.

———. "Changing Governance of Shared Spaces: Machizukuri as Institutional Innovation." In André Sorensen and Carolin Funck, eds., *Living Cities in Japan: Citizens' Movements, Machizukuri and Local Environments,* pp. 56–90. London: Routledge, 2007.

———. *Land Readjustment and Metropolitan Growth: An Examination of Suburban Land Development and Urban Sprawl in the Tokyo Metropolitan Area.* Oxford, Eng.: Elsevier Science, 2000.

———. *The Making of Urban Japan: Cities and Planning from Edo to the Twenty-first Century.* London: Routledge, 2002.

Sorensen, André, and Carolin Funck. "Conclusions: A Diversity of Machizukuri Processes and Outcomes." In André Sorensen and Carolin Funck, eds., *Living Cities in Japan: Citizens' Movements, Machizukuri and Local Environments,* pp. 269–279. London: Routledge, 2007.

———, eds. *Living Cities in Japan: Citizens' Movements, Machizukuri and Local Environments.* London: Routledge, 2007.

Sōrifu Shingishitsu, ed. *Kankō gyōsei hyakunen to Kanko Seisaku Shingikai sanjūnen no ayumi.* Tokyo: Gyōsei, 1980.

Steinhoff, Patricia G. "Protest and Democracy." In Takeshi Ishida and Ellis S. Krauss, eds., *Democracy in Japan,* pp. 171–198. Pittsburgh: University of Pittsburgh Press, 1989.

Stolz, Robert. "Remake Politics, Not Nature: Tanaka Shōzō's Philosophies of 'Poison' and 'Flow' and Japan's Environment." *Japan Focus* online, January 23, 2007.

Suda Yuka. "Nonprofit Organizations Undergo Profound Change in the U.S. and Japan." *Center for Global Partnership* online. http://www.cgp.org/index.php?option=article &task=default&articleid=325. Accessed July 5, 2009.

Suematsu Shirō. *Tokyo no kōen tsūshi,* expanded ed., 2 vols. Tokyo: Tokyoto Kōen Kyōkai, 1996.

Sutherland, Mary, and Dorothy Britton. *National Parks of Japan.* Tokyo: Kodansha, 1980.

Suzuki Satoshi and Sawada Seiichirō. *Kōen no hanashi.* Tokyo: Gihōdō, 1993.

Suzuki Tetsu, Higuchi Tadahiko, Shinji Isoya, Kobayashi Haruto, and Takano Fumiaki. *Kōenzukuri o kangaeru.* Tokyo: Gihōdō, 1993.

Szonyi, Michael. *Cold War Island: Quemoy on the Front Line.* New York: Cambridge University Press, 2008.

Taiwan Kokuritsu Kōen Kyōkai. "Jo." In Okada Kōyō, *Taiwan kokuritsu kōen shashinshū,* p. 1. Taihoku: Taiwan Kokuritsu Kōen Kyōkai, 1939.

Takao Shinrin Sentā. *Mori e yōkoso.* Hachiōji: Rin'yachō Kanto Shinrin Kanrikyoku, 2005.

"Takaosan ni Tonneru o Horasenai" Hyakumannin Shomei Jikkō Iinkai. *Kokutei kōen Takaosan no shizen o Ken'ōdō kara mamorō!!* Pamphlet, May 8, 2005.

Takatō Shoku. *Nihon sangakushi.* Tokyo: Hakubunkan, 1906.

Takayanagi, Atsushi. "Treatment of Forests and Wildlife in Modern Society." In Yoshiya Iwai, ed., *Forestry and the Forest Industry in Japan,* pp. 292–306. Vancouver: University of British Columbia Press, 2002.

Takeuchi Kazuhiko, Robert D. Brown, Washitani Izumi, Tsunekawa Atsushi, and Yokohari Makoto, eds. *Satoyama: The Traditional Rural Landscape of Japan.* Tokyo: Springer-Verlag, 2003.

Takeuchi Kazuhiko, Washitani Izumi, and Tsunekawa Atsushi, eds. *Satoyama no kankyōgaku.* Tokyo: Tokyo Daigaku Shuppankai, 2001.

Takeuchi Keiichi. "Landscape, Language and Nationalism in Meiji Japan." *Hitotsubashi Journal of Social Studies* 20 (1988): pp. 35–40.

———. "The Significance of Makiguchi Tsunesaburō's *Jinsei chirigaku* (Geography of Human Life) in the Intellectual History of Geography in Japan." *Journal of Oriental Studies* 14 (2004): *Special Series: The Spirit of India,* pp. 112–132.

Taki Kōji. *Tennō no shōzō.* Tokyo: Iwanami, 1988.

Tamura Tsuyoshi. "Introduction." In Kokuritsu Kōen Kyōkai, comp., *National Parks of Japan,* pp. 1–5. Tokyo: Tokyo News Service, 1957.

———. *Kokuritsu kōen kōwa.* Tokyo: Meiji Shoin, 1948.

———. *Nihon no kokuritsu kōen.* Tokyo: Kokuritsu Kōen Kyōkai, 1951.

———. "Taiwan kokuritsu kōen no shimei." *Taiwan no sanrin* 123 (1936): pp. 6–8.

———. *Zōen gairon.* Tokyo: Seibidō Shoten, 1918.

———. *Zōengaku gairon.* Tokyo: Seibidō Shoten, 1925.

Tanaka Atsuo. *Nihon no mori wa naze kiki na no ka.* Tokyo: Heibonsha, 2002.

Tanaka Kakuei. *Nihon rettō kaizōron.* Tokyo: Nikkan Kōgyō Shinbunsha, 1972.

Tanaka Kōtarō, ed. *Ueno Kōen to sono shūhen me de miru hyakunen no ayumi.* Tokyo: Ueno Kankō Renmei, 1973.

Tanaka Masahiro. *Nihon no shizen kōen: Shizen hogo to fūkei hogo.* Tokyo: Sagami Shobō, 1981.

———. *Tokyo no kōen to genchikei.* Tokyo: Keyaki Shuppan, 2005.

Tanaka Yoshio. *Yokohama kōen monogatari.* Tokyo: Chūō Kōronsha, 2000.

Tangherlini, Timothy, and Sallie Yea. "Introduction." In Timothy Tangherlini and Sallie Yea, eds., *Sitings: Critical Approaches to Korean Geography,* pp. 1–11. Honolulu: University of Hawai'i Press and Center for Korean Studies, University of Hawai'i, 2008.

Tate, Alan. *Great City Parks.* London: Spon Press, 2001.

Tatsumi Shin'ya. *Kōbe kara no kōen bunka: Hyōgo no kōen 1868–2000.* Osaka: Burēn Sentā, 2000.

Tawara Hiromi. *Hokkaido no shizen hogo: Sono rekishi to shisō,* expanded ed. Sapporo: Hokkaido Daigaku Tosho Kankōkai, 1987.

———. *Midori no bunkashi: Shizen to ningen no kakawari o kangaeru.* Sapporo: Hokkaido Daigaku Tosho Kankōkai, 1991.

———. "Shizen kōen no rekishi." In Fukutomi Hisao and Ishii Hiroshi, eds., *Midori no keikaku: Toshi kōen to shizen kōen,* pp. 113–133. Tokyo: Chikyūsha, 1985.

Teien Kyōkai, ed. *Toshi to kōen.* Tokyo: Seibidō, 1924.

"The 3-Year Plan." http://www.metro.tokyo.jp/ENGLISH/PROFILE/policy04.htm. Accessed July 6, 2009.

Thomas, Julia Adeney. *Reconfiguring Modernity: Concepts of Nature in Japanese Political Ideology.* Berkeley: University of California Press, 2001.

———. "'To Become as One Dead': Nature and the Political Subject in Modern Japan." In Lorraine Daston and Fernando Vidal, eds., *The Moral Authority of Nature,* pp. 308–330. Chicago: University of Chicago Press, 2004.

Thornber, Carol. Personal communication. November 18, 2005.

Thornber, Karen Laura. *Empire of Texts in Motion: Chinese, Korean, and Taiwanese Transculturations of Japanese Literature.* Cambridge, Mass.: Harvard University Asia Center and Harvard-Yenching Institute, 2009.

———. "Myopic Hyperopia and Environmental Crises in East Asian Literatures." Paper, New England Association for Asian Studies Annual Meeting. Boston, October 18, 2008.

Thünen, Johann Heinrich von. *Der Isolierte Staat.* Hamburg: F. Perthes, 1826.

Tō Kimiharu. Personal communication. October 1, 2003.

Tokyo Daigaku Daigakuin Rigakukei Kenkyūka Fuzoku Shokubutsuen, ed. *Koishikawa Shokubutsuen to Nikkō Shokubutsuen.* Tokyo: Koishikawa Shokubutsuen Kōenkai, 2004.

Tokyo Metropolitan Government. *A Hundred Years of Tokyo City Planning.* Tokyo: Tokyo Metropolitan Government, 1994.

———. *Tokyo: The Making of a Metropolis.* Tokyo: Tokyo Metropolitan Government, 1993.

———. *Twenty-Five Tales in Memory of Tokyo's Foreigners.* Tokyo: Tokyo Metropolitan Government, 1989.

Tokyo Metropolitan Park Association. *Kiyosumi Teien.* Tokyo: Tokyo Metropolitan Park Association, 2006.

———. *Koishikawa Kōrakuen Gardens.* Tokyo: Tokyo Metropolitan Park Association, 2005.

———. *Mukōjima Hyakkaen.* Tokyo: Tokyo Metropolitan Park Association, 2006.

———. *Rikugien.* Tokyo: Tokyo Metropolitan Park Association, 2006.

Tokyo Metropolitan University, ed. *Tokyo, Urban Growth and Planning 1868–1968.* Tokyo: Tokyo Metropolitan University, 1988.

Tokyo Municipal Office. *The Reconstruction of Tokyo.* Tokyo: Tokyo Municipal Office, 1933.

Tokyo Nōgyō Daigaku Daigakubu Kankyō Ryokuchi Gakka, ed. *Minna no kōenzukuri.* Tokyo: Tokyo Nōgyō Daigaku Shuppankai, 2002.

Tokyo Ryokuchi Keikaku Kyōgikai. *Jiko shūroku.* Tokyo: Tokyo Ryokuchi Keikaku Kyōgikai, 1939.

Tokyo Shiyakusho Kōenka, ed. *Tokyoshi kōen gaikan.* Tokyo: Tokyo Shiyakusho, 1923.

"Tokyo's Big Change: The 10-Year Plan." http://www.metro.tokyo.jp/ENGLISH/PROFILE/ policy03.htm. Accessed July 6, 2009.

Tokyoto Irei Kyōkai, ed. *Sensai ōshita kaisō jigyō shimatsuki.* Tokyo: Tokyoto Irei Kyōkai, 1985.

Tokyoto Kensetsukyoku Kōen Ryokuchibu. *Tokyoto no shizen kōen: Sono genjō to shōrai.* Tokyo: Tokyoto Kensetsukyoku Kōen Ryokuchibu, 1966.

———, ed. *Tokyoto no kōen ryokuchi mappu 2009.* Tokyo: Tokyoto, 2009.

Tokyoto Kōen Kyōkai. *Ueno Kōen monogatari: Kaien shikiten kara 120shūnen.* Tokyo: Tokyoto Kōen Kyōkai, 1996.

———, ed. *Tokyo no kōen 120nen.* Tokyo: Tokyoto Kensetsukyoku Kōen Ryokuchibu, 1995.

Tokyoto Kōen Shingikai, 2003. Tokyo: Tokyoto, 2003.

Tokyoto Seikatsu Bunkakyoku Kokusai Kōryūbu Gaijika. *2nd Long-Term Plan for the Tokyo Metropolis.* Tokyo: Tokyo Metropolitan Government, 1987.

———. *3rd Long-Term Plan for the Tokyo Metropolis.* Tokyo: Tokyo Metropolitan Government, 1991.

Tokyoto Toshi Keikakukyoku Sōmubu, ed. *Planning of Tokyo.* Tokyo: Tokyoto, 2002.

Tokyoto Toshi Seibikyoku Toshi Kibanbu Shisetsu Keikakuka, ed. *Toshi keikaku kōen ryokuchi no seibi hōshin.* Tokyo: Tokyoto, 2006.

Tokyoto Toshi Seibikyoku Toshi Kibanbu Shisetsu Keikakuka Kōen Ryokuchi Tantō, ed. *Midori no shinsenryaku gaidorain.* Tokyo: Tokyoto, 2006.

Tokyoto Zōen Kensetsu Jigyō Kyōdō Kumiai, ed. *Midori no Tokyoshi.* Tokyo: Shikōsha, 1979.

Tokyoto Zōen Ryokukagyō Kyōkai, ed. *Tokyoto ryokuka hakusho 22.* Tokyo: Tokyoto Zōen Ryokukagyō Kyōkai, 2003.

Toshi Bōsai Bika Kyōkai. *Tokyoto ni okeru sengo 50nen no kōen ryokuchi no hensen ni kansuru chōsa.* Tokyo: Toshi Bōsai Bika Kyōkai, 1997.

Toshi Ryokuka Gijutsu Kaihatsu Kikō, ed. *Shinryoku kūkan dezain fukyū manyuaru.* Tokyo: Seibundō Shinkōsha, 1995.

Toshima Hiroaki. *Ueno Kōen to sono fukin.* Tokyo: Hōshū Shoin, 1962.

Totman, Conrad D. *The Green Archipelago: Forestry in Preindustrial Japan.* Berkeley: University of California Press, 1989.

———. *A History of Japan.* Malden, Mass.: Blackwell, 2000.

———. *Japan's Imperial Forest Goryōrin, 1889–1946.* Folkestone, Kent, Eng.: Global Oriental, 2007.

————. "Unifying the Realm, Distressing the People: The Land-Tax Reform of 1871–1881." Unpublished manuscript, Yale University, 2001.

Tsai, Huiyu Caroline. *Taiwan in Japan's Empire Building: An Institutional Approach to Colonial Engineering.* London: Routledge, 2009.

Tseng, Alice Y. *The Imperial Museums of Meiji Japan: Architecture and the Art of the Nation.* Seattle: University of Washington Press, 2008.

Tsunashima Teiji, ed. *Nihon no kokuritsu kōen.* Tokyo: Nihon Kokuritsu Kōen Tosho Kankōkai, 1933.

Tsunekawa Atsushi. "Strategic Management of Satoyama Landscapes." In Takeuchi Kazuhiko, Robert D. Brown, Washitani Izumi, Tsunekawa Atsushi, and Yokohari Makoto, eds., *Satoyama: The Traditional Rural Landscape of Japan,* pp. 179–191. Tokyo: Springer-Verlag, 2003.

Tsurumaki Yasuo. *Okujō kara no kankyō kakumei.* Tokyo: IN Tsūshinsha, 2002.

Turner, James Morton. "From Woodcraft to 'Leave no Trace': Wilderness, Consumerism, and Environmentalism in Twentieth-Century America." *Environmental History* 7, no. 3 (2002): pp. 462–484.

Uchimura Kanzō. *Chirigakukō.* Tokyo: Keiseisha Shoten, 1894. Reprinted in 1897 by Keiseisha Shoten as *Chijinron.*

Uchiyama Masao, ed. *Toshi ryokuchi no keikaku to sekkei.* Tokyo: Shōkokusha, 1987.

Uchiyama Masao and Minomo Toshitarō. *Tokyo no yūenchi.* Tokyo: Kyōgakusha, 1981.

————. *Yoyogi no mori.* Tokyo: Kyōgakusha, 1981.

Ueda Yasuyuki. *Midori no toshi keikaku.* Tokyo: Gyōsei, 2004.

Uehara Keiji. *Kokuritsu kōen no hanashi.* Tokyo: Shinkōsha, 1924.

————. *Zōen taikei,* 8 vols. Tokyo: Kashima Shoten, 1974–1975.

Uno Tasuku. "Kaihatsu to hogo no chōwa wa dono yō ni shite torarete kita ka." *Kankō* 7, no. 5 (1972): pp. 3–7.

————. "Kokuritsu daikōen setchi ni kansuru kengi." *Kokuritsu kōen* 243 (1970): pp. 4–7.

Upham, Frank K. "Unplaced Persons and Movements for Place." In Andrew Gordon, ed., *Postwar Japan as History,* pp. 325–346. Berkeley: University of California Press, 1993.

Vollmer, Klaus, ed. *Environmental Policies and Ecological Issues in Japan and Eastern Asia: Transnational Perspectives.* Munich: Iudicium, 2006.

Vosse, Wilhelm. "Need for a New Movement? A Fragmented Environmental Movement in Times of Global Environmental Problems." In Klaus Vollmer, ed., *Environmental Policies and Ecological Issues in Japan and Eastern Asia: Transnational Perspectives,* pp. 107–122. Munich: Iudicium, 2006.

Walker, Brett L. *The Lost Wolves of Japan.* Seattle: University of Washington Press, 2005.

Wang Xianpu. "East Asia." In Jeffrey A. McNeely, Jeremy Harrison, and Paul R. Dingwell, eds., *Protecting Nature: Regional Reviews of Protected Areas,* pp. 161–175. Gland, Switz.: International Union for Conservation of Nature and Natural Resources, 1994.

Warner, Sam Bass, Jr. "Public Park Inventions: Past and Future." In Herbert Muschamp et al., *The Once and Future Park*, pp. 17–21. New York: Princeton Architectural Press, 1993.

Waseda Daigaku Kankō Gakkai. *Kokuritsu kōen.* Tokyo: Waseda Daigaku Kankō Gakkai, 1966.

Watanabe Shun'ichi. "Machizukuri in Japan." In Carola Hein and Philippe Pelletier, eds., *Cities, Autonomy, and Decentralization in Japan,* pp. 128–138. London: Routledge, 2006.

———. "Participatory *Machizukuri* (Community Building) in Japan." Paper, Ninth International Planning History Conference. Helsinki, August 20–23, 2000.

———. "Planning History of the Capital Tokyo." Unpublished manuscript, Tokyo University of Science. Tokyo, 2005.

———. "The State of the Art of Machizukuri." Lecture, Harvard University, February 27, 2004.

Wei Hongjin, ed. *Taiwan de guojia kungyuan.* Taibei: Yuanzu Wenhua, 2002.

West, Patrick C., and Steven R. Brechin, eds. *Resident Peoples and National Parks.* Tucson: University of Arizona Press, 1991.

Weston, Walter. *Mountaineering and Exploration in the Japanese Alps.* London: J. Murray, 1896.

White, James W. "The Dynamics of Political Opposition." In Andrew Gordon, ed., *Postwar Japan as History*, pp. 424–447. Berkeley: University of California Press, 1993.

Wigen, Kären. "Discovering the Japanese Alps: Meiji Mountaineering and the Quest for Geographical Enlightenment." *Journal of Japanese Studies* 31, no. 1 (2005): pp. 1–26.

Wilson, Roderick. "From *Sakariba* to City Parks: Public Space in Meiji-Period Tokyo." Unpublished paper, Stanford University, 2003.

Woo Hyung Taek. "The Social Impacts of Land Use Planning in the National Parks of South Korea." In Patrick C. West and Steven R. Brechin, eds., *Resident Peoples and National Parks,* pp. 263–274. Tucson: University of Arizona Press, 1991.

Woodall, Brian. *Japan Under Construction: Corruption, Politics, and Public Works.* Berkeley: University of California Press, 1996.

———. "The Politics of Land in Japan's Dual Economy." In John O. Haley and Kozo Yamamura, eds., *Land Issues in Japan: A Policy Failure?* pp. 113–148. Seattle: Society for Japanese Studies, 1992.

Yabe Tomoko, ed. *Tokyo kōen sanpo.* Tokyo: Burūsu Intāakushonzu, 2009.

Yamagata Saburō. "Taiwan kokuritsu kōen no shitei ni atarite." *Kokuritsu kōen* 10, no. 1 (1938): pp. 3–5.

Yamaichi Shōken Keizai Kenkyūjo. *Sangyō no subete, 1990.* Tokyo: Yamaichi Shōken Keizai Kenkyūjo, 1990.

Yamakawa Kikue. *Women of the Mito Domain: Recollections of Samurai Family Life.* Translated by Kate Wildman Nakai. Tokyo: University of Tokyo Press, 1992.

Yamamoto Tatsuo. "Jo." In Kokuritsu Kōen Kyōkai, *Kokuritsu kōen annai.* Tokyo: Kokuritsu Kōen Kyōkai, 1933.

Yamane Ichigen. "Gekitotsu! Tsutsumi Seiji vs. Yoshiaki no rettō rizōto daisensō." *Gendai,* December 1988, pp. 108–124.

Yanagida Yukio. *Kankyōhō nyūmon.* Tokyo: Saimaru Shuppankai, 1972.

Yasumoto Mariko. "Calls for Change as WHS Status Threatens One of Japan's Gems." *Japan Times* online, February 6, 2005.

Yokohama Gaikokujin Bochi. *Kōkai junro annaizu.* Yokohama: Yokohama Gaikokujin Bochi, n.d. [2007].

Yoshihara Satoshi. "Kōen no homuresu." In Itō Yukio, ed., *Ima, kōen de nani ga okite iru ka,* pp. 44–48. Tokyo: Gyōsei, 2002.

Yoshikawa Matsu and Takahashi Yasuo. *Koishikawa Kōrakuen,* 3rd ed. Tokyo: Tokyoto Kōen Kyōkai, 2001.

Yoshimi Shun'ya. *Hakurankai no seijigaku.* Tokyo: Chūō Kōronsha, 1992.

Zaslowsky, Dyan, and T. H. Watkins. *These American Lands: Parks, Wilderness, and the Public Lands.* Washington, D.C.: Island Press, 1994.

Zenkoku Shizen Hogo Rengō, ed. *Shizen hogo jiten,* expanded ed. Tokyo: Ryokufū Shuppan, 1996.

———, ed. *Shizen hogo no tebiki.* Tokyo: Shōheisha, 1974.

Index

About the Author

Thomas R. H. Havens is a professor of history at Northeastern University. In 1960 he first visited Tokyo's Shinjuku district, home of the Shinjuku Imperial Garden in the capital's busiest commercial, government, and transportation complex. Shinjuku and its public areas are key sites discussed in *Parkscapes* as well as in his *Radicals and Realists in the Japanese Nonverbal Arts: The Avant-Garde Rejection of Modernism* (University of Hawai'i Press, 2006), *Artist and Patron in Postwar Japan: Dance, Music, Theater, and the Visual Arts, 1955–1980* (1982), and *Architects of Affluence: The Tsutsumi Family and the Seibu-Saison Enterprises in Twentieth-Century Japan* (1994). His other book-length writings include *Nishi Amane and Modern Japanese Thought* (1970), *Farm and Nation in Modern Japan: Agrarian Nationalism, 1870–1940* (1974), *Valley of Darkness: The Japanese People and World War Two* (1978, 1986), *The Historical Encyclopedia of World War II* (coauthor) (1980), *Fire Across the Sea: The Vietnam War and Japan, 1965–1975* (1987), and *The Ambivalence of Nationalism: Modern Japan between East and West* (coeditor) (1990).

Production Notes for Havens | *Parkscapes*

Cover design by Julie Matsuo-Chun

Text design and composition by Publishers' Design and Production Services, Inc.
 with display type in Linotype Didot and text type in Minion Pro

Printing and binding by Edwards Brothers, Inc.

Printed on 60 lb. EB Opaque, 500 ppi